The National Underw

The Advisor's Guide to Annuities, 3rd Edition

By John L. Olsen, CLU, ChFC, AEP
and Michael E. Kitces, MSFS, MTAX, CFP®, CLU, ChFC, RHU, REBC, CASL, CWPP™

While there are many books purporting to tell you how to sell annuities, this is the only one giving you complete and current guidance on *whether* and *when* to sell them. It tells you how to avoid tax traps and serious legal complications and how to comply with the law, including the changing "standard of care," when you do sell or advise on annuities.

In short, this is the one book that serves as your objective, impartial guide through what annuities *can* and *cannot* do, their costs, and what risk-management features annuities offer—all delivered in easy-to-read language, fully sourced and cited throughout.

The Advisor's Guide to Annuities—now in its third, fully revised and completely updated edition—is the foundational reference on the topics of:

- When annuities are appropriate
- When they're not appropriate
- New, vital information on the 12 suitability factors
- The current marketplace for various types of annuities and annuity riders
- Taxation of annuities during the owner's lifetime and after death
- Important annuities features, with a cost-benefit discussion of each
- Index annuities
- Longevity annuities
- Using trusts with annuities
- The use of annuities in estate planning
- Tax traps that can get you into trouble
- The effect of section 989J of the Dodd-Frank law and its relation to the Suitability in Annuity Transactions Model Reg. of 2010
- And key arguments for and against using annuities

The day when advisors could rely on the old, tried-and-true rules is long gone. This book covers key developments in the field and keeps you current with all the changing requirements and proven practices.

The authors, Michael E. Kitces and John L. Olsen, are widely respected experts in the annuities field and financial advisors with decades of experience successfully guiding their clients. They have created a reader-friendly, go-to resource that is as valuable to veteran advisors as it is to those just starting out advising on annuities.

To place additional orders for *The Advisor's Guide to Annuities, 3rd Edition* or any of our products, or for additional information, contact Customer Service at **1-800-543-0874**.

The Advisor's Guide to Annuities

John Olsen, CLU, ChFC, AEP
Michael E. Kitces, MSFS, MTAX, CFP®, CLU

ISBN 978-1-936362-85-1

This publication is designed to provide accurate and authoritative information in regard to the subject matter covered. It is sold with the understanding that the publisher is not engaged in rendering legal, accounting or other professional service. If legal advice or other expert assistance is required, the services of a competent professional person should be sought. – From a Declaration of Principles jointly adapted by a Committee of The American Bar Association and a Committee of Publishers and Associations.

THE NATIONAL UNDERWRITER COMPANY

Copyright © 2005, 2009, 2012

Third Edition

The National Underwriter Company
5081 Olympic Blvd.
Erlanger, KY 41018

Printed in the United States of America

About Summit Business Media

Summit Business Media is the leading B2B media and information company serving the insurance, financial, legal and investment advisory markets. Summit strives to be "The Next Generation of Business Information" for executives and practitioners by providing breaking news and analysis, in-depth practice management strategies, business-building techniques and actionable data. Summit services the information needs of its customers through numerous channels, including digital, print, and live events. Summit publishes 16 magazines and 150 reference titles, operates 20 websites and hosts a dozen conferences, including the world's largest mining investment conference held each year in South Africa. Summit's Marketing Data division provides detailed information on millions of benefits plans, agents and advisors in the U.S.

Summit employs more than 300 employees in ten offices across the United States. For more information, please visit www.summitbusinessmedia.com.

About The National Underwriter Company

For over 110 years, The National Underwriter Company has been the first in line with the targeted tax, insurance, and financial planning information you need to make critical business decisions. Boasting nearly a century of expert experience, our reputable Editors are dedicated to putting accurate and relevant information right at your fingertips. With Tax Facts, Tools & Techniques, National Underwriter Advanced markets, Field Guide, FC&S®, and other resources available in print, on CD, and online, you can be assured that as the industry evolves National Underwriter will be at the forefront with the thorough and easy-to-use resources you rely on for success.

The National Underwriter Company
Update Service Notification

This National Underwriter Company publication is regularly updated to include coverage of developments and changes that affect the content. If you did not purchase this publication directly from The National Underwriter Company and you want to receive these important updates sent on a 30-day review basis and billed separately, please contact us at (800) 543-0874. Or you can mail your request with your name, company, address, and the title of the book to:

> The National Underwriter Company
> 5081 Olympic Boulevard
> Erlanger, KY 41018

If you purchased this publication from The National Underwriter Company directly, you have already been registered for the update service.

National Underwriter Company Contact Information

To order any National Underwriter Company title, please

- call 1-800-543-0874, 8-6 ET Monday – Thursday and 8 to 5 ET Friday

- online bookstore at www.nationalunderwriter.com, or

- mail to The National Underwriter Company, Orders Department, 5081 Olympic Blvd, Erlanger, KY 41018

Dedications

John L. Olsen

To Katherine, who continues, even after 38 years, to put up with more than she should.

Michael E. Kitces

To my friends and family, and especially my wife Ellie, for their understanding, patience, and support while I pursue my passion for financial planning.

Acknowledgments

Any book, even one by a single author, is invariably the product of many minds. The authors have been blessed by the willingness of friends and colleagues to share their insights with us and our readers. We wish to thank Jack Marrion, Bruce Tannahill, Jack Underwood, Garth Bernard, Stephanie Curry, Terry Altman, Moshe Milevsky, Peng Chen, Curtis Cloke, Kyle Bossard, Jay Adkisson, Mary Ann Mancini, Mel Warshaw, Steve Leimberg, April Caudill, Tom Hegna, Mike McGlothlin, Dick Weber, and Ben Baldwin. We'd also like to thank Kelly Maheu of National Underwriter Company for her willingness to support another edition of this book.

John L. Olsen, CLU, ChFC, AEP

Michael J. Kitces, MSFS, MTAX, CFP®, CLU, ChFC, RHU, REBC, CASL

Preface to the Third Edition

This book is the child of frustration. The authors have both been dealing with annuities for many years, and we had each been despairing over the lack of understanding of these instruments and of the absurdly partisan way in which annuities are regarded by many who write about them. Most articles we read about annuities were either "for" or "against" them, as if an annuity could be inherently either "good" or 'bad". Articles appearing in insurance industry magazines routinely touted annuities as the greatest thing since sliced bread, while many financial journalists appeared to regard them as little better than satanic devices. Sadly, both conditions persist, with no sign of change, as we write this.

As practicing advisors working with annuities on a regular basis and frequent speakers at industry events, we were painfully aware that even those involved in recommending or evaluating annuities–professional financial advisors–often demonstrate little understanding of how these tools work (and when they do not).

Something, we both felt, ought to be done. What was needed, we thought, was a source of information about annuities that would be both accurate and *balanced*. So, when we were approached by The National Underwriter Company for suggestions about potential book topics, the need for a book about annuities seemed clear, and we decided that we would take a stab at it.

The result is the book you are about to read. It was written, not for the consumer, but for the professional advisor–and that does not mean just those who sell annuities. Attorneys, accountants, financial planners, trust officers, and compliance officers. Anyone who may be called upon to render professional advice regarding an annuity–will, we hope- find this book worth reading.

The authors have tried to present the facts and to be as objective as possible in our conclusions. We have included a large amount of material about the taxation of annuities (including content we have never seen available in a product of this kind) and much about suitability and appropriateness. There is not a single sentence in here about how to sell annuities. There are many other books out there on that topic.

This book is entitled "The Advisor's Guide To Annuities, 3rd edition" because it is a revision and update of our previous book, *The Annuity Advisor*, 1st and 2nd editions. The title change reflects the fact that this book is part of a new series of Advisor's Guides, offered by Summit Business Media/The National Underwriter Co. We have updated the chapters on taxation of annuities to reflect new rules and rulings, expanded our treatment of the annuity as a planning tool, and included an entirely new chapter entitled "Suitability: The Changing Nature of the Standard", in which we discuss new developments in NAIC regulation, Section 989J of the Dodd-Frank financial reform act, and their possible impact on advisors selling annuities or other insurance products in the future.

We hope that you will find this book, not only instructive, but also genuinely useful.

John L. Olsen, CLU, ChFC, AEP

Michael J. Kitces, MSFS, MTAX, CFP®, CLU, ChFC, RHU, REBC, CASL

April 1, 2012

About the Authors

John L. Olsen, CLU, ChFC, AEP is a financial and estate planner practicing in St. Louis County, MO. John has been involved in the financial services industry since 1973. In addition to providing insurance, financial and estate planning services to his own clients, John works with other advisors on advanced cases and product selection and offers expert witness services in litigation involving annuities, insurance, and securities.

John is a past president of the St. Louis chapter of the National Association of Insurance and Financial Advisors, a former Board member of the St. Louis chapter of the Society of Financial Services Professionals, a current Board member of the St. Louis Estate Planning Council, and a member of the Editorial Advisory Board of *Tax Facts*. He is a highly sought-after speaker, having given presentations on financial, insurance, retirement, and estate planning and other topics to many industry groups. John can be reached at:

Olsen Financial Group
131 Hollywood Lane
Kirkwood, MO 63122
(314) 909-8818 (voice), (314) 909-7912 (fax), jolsen02@earthlink.net

Michael E. Kitces, MSFS, MTAX, CFP®, CLU, ChFC, RHU, REBC, CASL, is Director of Research for Pinnacle Advisory Group, a private wealth management firm located in Columbia, Maryland. In addition he is the publisher of the e-newsletter *The Kitces Report* and the blog *Nerd's Eye View* through his website Kitces.com, dedicated to advancing knowledge in financial planning.

Michael is extremely active at both the local and national level in the financial planning profession, serving on numerous boards and task forces. He is also a member of the Editorial Review Board for the Journal of Financial Planning, a commentator on retirement distribution and retirement planning issues for Leimberg Information Services Inc., and a co-founder of NexGen, a community of the next generation of financial planners that aims to ensure the transference of wisdom, tradition, and integrity, from the pioneers of financial planning to the next generation of the profession. For his active work in the profession, Michael was one of the 2010 recipients of the Financial Planning Association's "Heart of Financial Planning" awards for his dedication to advancing the financial planning profession. In addition, he has variously been recognized as financial planning's "Deep Thinker," a "Legacy Builder," an "Influencer," a "Mover & Shaker," and a "Rising Star in Wealth Management" by industry publications.

Michael welcomes your questions, comments, or inquiries at:

Pinnacle Advisory Group, Attn: Michael Kitces
6345 Woodside Court, Suite 100
Columbia, Maryland 21046
(410) 995-6630, michael@kitces.com

About the Developmental Editor

Rebecca von Gillern is a senior developmental editor with the Professional Publishing Division of the National Underwriter Company, Summit Business Media. She manages the editorial development of the Advisor's Guide and the Tools & Techniques series of investment and planning products. She also develops other financial services content for the company. Rebecca has been developing content for the higher education and business-to-business markets for the past sixteen years.

As the owner and principle editor for Bookworm Editorial Services, Rebecca was responsible for ensuring client satisfaction by collaborating with publishing company project teams and authors in the creation of publication strategies. Her work was focused on adding value through enhanced clarity, accuracy, and marketability of print and digital product.

She began her career with Thomson Learning, where she developed and revised federal and state taxation publications. At Thomson she also developed product in the disciplines of accounting, business communication, communication, introduction to business, management, marketing, and the sciences. She is a graduate of the University of Southern Mississippi.

About the Editorial Director

Diana B. Reitz, **CPCU, AAI**, is the editorial director of the Professional Publishing Division of The National Underwriter Company. As such she is responsible for the overall integrity of all division publications. She previously was the Director of the Property & Casualty Publishing Department of the Professional Publishing Division.

Ms. Reitz has been with The National Underwriter Company since 1998, when she was named editor of the Risk Financing and Self-Insurance manuals and associate editor of the *FC&S Bulletins*®. She also is coauthor of the National Underwriter publication, *Workers Compensation Coverage Guide,* and has edited and contributed to numerous other books and publications, including *The Tools & Techniques of Risk Management and Insurance, Claims* magazine, and *National Underwriter Property & Casualty* newsweekly.

Prior to joining The National Underwriter she was with a regional insurance broker, concentrating on commercial insurance. She is a graduate of the University of Maryland and St. Francis College.

About the Director of Product Development

Kelly B. Maheu, J.D., is the director of product development and content acquisition for the Professional Publishing Division of Summit Business Media. She is responsible for acquiring expert authored content and working closely with Summit's editorial, sales, marketing, and technology teams to develop professional online and print reference libraries.

Kelly began work at Summit in 2006 as an editor for Fire, Casualty and Surety Service (FC&S®). A graduate of the University Of Cincinnati College Of Law, Kelly worked in the legal and insurance fields for LexisNexis®, Progressive Insurance, and a Cincinnati insurance defense litigation firm prior to joining Summit. Kelly holds a BA from Miami University, with a double major in English/Journalism and Psychology.

Kelly has edited and contributed to numerous books and publications including the Personal Auto Insurance Policy Coverage Guide, Cyberliability and Insurance, The Tools and Techniques of Risk Management for Financial Planners, Claims Magazine, and ProducersWEB.

Table of Contents

Appendices and Index

Chapter 1

Basics of Annuities

What is an Annuity?

The term annuity simply means a series of regular payments over time. In popular usage, however, annuity generally refers to a contract or policy, issued by an insurance company, providing for payment of a regular income by the annuity issuer to the owner, over a specified period or for the life of an annuitant (see the section entitled "Parties to the Annuity Contract"). These contracts, called commercial annuities, are what we will be talking about throughout this book.

Types of Annuities

There are different types of annuities, which are generally classified according to three different parameters:

1. how the annuity is purchased;

2. when annuity payments are to begin; and

3. how the cash value in the annuity is invested.

How the Annuity is Purchased

There are generally two different ways an annuity is purchased. A **Single Premium** annuity is a contract purchased with a single payment, or premium. No further premiums are required, or even allowable. A **Flexible Premium** annuity is purchased with an initial payment (to establish the contract) and typically contains a series of premiums that may be paid whenever, and in whatever amount, the purchaser wishes, subject to policy minimums and maximums.

There is very little difference, if any, in the important policy provisions, guarantees, and payout options of the two types, and their tax treatment is identical. The significant distinction is simply that in some instances, contracts offered as single premium cannot receive additional subsequent payments, and therefore do not allow additional contributions under the original contract's terms—instead, additional money must be deposited to a new annuity contract.

When Annuity Payments Are to Begin

An **immediate annuity** is one in which regular income— or annuity—payments begin to be made to the owner[1] within one year of purchase. Another label sometimes used to describe an immediate annuity is **payout annuity**.

A **deferred annuity** is one in which annuity payments are deferred until later than one year after purchase—perhaps much later. The life of a deferred annuity is divided into two phases:

1.   The **accumulation phase**. This is the period from purchase of the contract until annuitization. Annuitization is the exercise, by the owner, of a contractual option to begin receiving regular annuity payments, in accordance with an annuity payout option (see the section entitled "Types of Annuity Payouts"). Deferred annuity contracts typically require annuitization by some specified date or age by specifying a maximum annuity starting date or maturity date (e.g., policy anniversary following annuitant's age 85, or annuitant's age 85). Newer contracts may permit further deferral of annuitization provided the request is received within a specified period of time prior to the maturity date.[2]

2.   The **distribution phase**. This is the period from annuitization until the annuity payments cease which may be at the end of the annuitant's life or after a specified number of years (see the section entitled "Types of Annuity Payouts").

Note: It is essential that the advisor understand the difference between an annuity contract's required annuity starting date (i.e., the date by which annuity payments must commence, absent an election to defer annuitization) and when annuitization is permitted under that contract. In January, 2005, a class-action lawsuit was filed alleging unsuitability, asserting that the deferred annuity purchased by a senior citizen allegedly did not permit annuity payments to begin until the annuitant's age was 115. However, it appears that age 115 was the contract maturity date, and annuity payments under the contract could start at any time the owner wished to annuitize. In fact, in some contracts a late maturity date is a benefit, allowing an owner to keep the contract in the accumulation phase as long as possible, if that is his/her wish.

There is no accumulation phase in the life of an immediate annuity, as annuity payments typically commence shortly after purchase, and must, by definition, commence within one year. Annuities that are in distribution phase (i.e., deferred annuities that have been annuitized and all immediate annuities) are said to be in payout status.

A third type of annuity, often called a **longevity annuity,** first appeared in the marketplace in 2007. It is similar to an immediate annuity in that it provides only for income (usually for life); there is no accumulation period. Unlike an immediate annuity, the longevity annuity income does not commence within one year of purchase; rather, it is deferred on until a future date, which is typically an advanced age such as age 85. See Chapter 13 for a detailed discussion of longevity annuities.

How the Cash Value in the Annuity is Invested

A fixed annuity is an annuity in which the contract value is measured in dollars. A variable annuity is one in which the contract value is measured in terms of units—either accumulation units or annuity units, depending upon whether the contract is in the accumulation phase or the distribution phase. In both cases, the value of each unit can—and probably will—vary each business day, according to the investment performance of the separate accounts[3] chosen by the contract owner. We will look at how accumulation units and annuity units work shortly. First, however, let's understand the basic investment difference between fixed and variable annuities.

Fixed Annuities

In a fixed annuity the contract values are guaranteed by the issuing insurance company. These values (discussed below) are all measured, as we've noted, in dollars. There is a common misconception that fixed, in the term fixed annuity, refers to the rate of interest credited to the contract. This is not correct. While some fixed deferred annuities provide guarantees as to the period during which the current interest rate will be credited, and all deferred annuities provide a guaranteed minimum interest rate that will be credited during the entire accumulation period, the term fixed, when used in reference to fixed annuities, properly refers, not to the interest rate, but to the fact that the contract values are measured in fixed units—namely, dollars.

What are these contract values? In a fixed immediate annuity, or a fixed deferred annuity that has been annuitized, the contract value guaranteed by the issuing insurer is the dollar amount of the periodic annuity payment (which may be payable monthly, quarterly, semi-annually, or annually). In a fixed deferred annuity, there are several contract values:

1.   **Cash Value**. The cash value, or accumulation value, of a fixed deferred annuity is the value on which interest is computed and to which interest is credited. It is generally the sum of all premium payments received, plus all prior interest credited, less any withdrawals (and, in the case of certain qualified annuities, unpaid loan interest). The

cash value of fixed deferred annuities is always guaranteed. The cash value of variable annuities is not, except for monies deposited into the fixed account option of such contracts.

2.   **Annuity Value**. The annuity value is the value to which an annuity payout factor will be applied if—and only if—the contract owner annuitizes the contract. In some deferred annuities, this value is identical to the cash value. In so-called tiered annuities (of the type where a higher interest rate is credited to the annuity value than is credited to the cash value) and in contracts providing for an annuitization bonus, the annuity value is higher than the cash value.

3.   **Surrender Value**. The surrender value of a deferred annuity is the cash value, less any applicable surrender charge and market value adjustment (see Chapter 5: Basic Costs of Annuities), that will be paid to the contract owner upon surrender of the contract.

The basic investment difference between fixed and variable annuities is that in a fixed annuity, either immediate or deferred, the contract owner is offered no investment choices within the contract and assumes no investment risk. In a fixed deferred annuity, the cash value, which includes all premium payments and prior interest credited, is guaranteed against loss, as is a minimum interest rate. All fixed deferred annuities also offer a current—nonguaranteed—interest rate. Some, but not all, contracts guarantee the current declared rate for a certain period of time.

It is essential for the advisor to understand that the guarantees in fixed annuities are only as good as the ability of the issuing insurer to pay them.

Variable Annuities

Variable annuities work very differently from fixed annuities, in both the accumulation phase and in the distribution phase.

The Accumulation Phase

In the accumulation phase of a variable deferred annuity,[4] each premium payment purchases, after applicable contract charges are deducted, a number of accumulation units for each investment subaccount chosen by the contract holder.

Example: Mr. Jones has chosen five investment subaccounts from among those available in his variable deferred annuity. He has directed that each premium payment[5] be allocated to these accounts as follows:

- Large Cap Growth Account A   20%

- Midcap Value Account M   20%

- Small Cap Value Account S   20%

- International Stock Acct I   15%

- Bond Account B   25%

The accumulation unit values of these accounts on the day his premium is received are as follows:

- Large Cap Growth Account A $21,435

- Midcap Value Account M $16,567

- Small Cap Value Account S $34,123

- International Stock Acct I $9,567

- Bond Account B $15,003

If Mr. Jones makes a premium payment of $1,000, and the contract charges applicable are $14, the net premium ($986) will purchase:

- Large Cap Growth Account A   9.1999 units

- Midcap Value Account M   11.9032 units

- Small Cap Value Account S   5.7791 units

- International Stock Acct I   15.4594 units

- Bond Account B   16.4300 units[6]

Accumulation unit values can, and often will, change each day according to the investment performance of the subaccounts, just as the net asset value of a mutual fund share does. However, there is a significant difference between the pricing of annuity accumulation units and that of mutual fund shares. When a mutual fund declares a dividend or capital gains distribution—through the realization of dividends or capital gains income by the fund—and the shareholder has elected to reinvest such distributions, additional shares are purchased for his account, and the price of all shares of the fund is reduced to reflect the distribution. If the shareholder has elected not to reinvest such distributions, he receives cash, and the share price is reduced. When a dividend or capital gain is realized by a variable annuity subaccount, the value of the accumulation unit is increased reflecting the dividend or gain received, but the number of units remains the same.

Investment Subaccounts

One of the main advantages of investing in a variable annuity is the access it provides to diversified investment types. The first variable annuities offered relatively few investment choices, and, often, the choices were limited to proprietary accounts; that is, accounts managed by the insurance company that issued the annuity, or a subsidiary. Many newer contracts offer subaccounts representing a wide variety of asset classes,[7] managed by a variety of money management firms. Typically, the contract owner is permitted to choose several subaccounts,[8] and to make exchanges among them—re-allocating existing contract values—and to reallocate ongoing contributions without charge.[9] Moreover, exchanges among subaccounts in a single contract are not taxable events for income tax purposes. These investment management features, together with features such as automatic portfolio rebalancing and dollar cost averaging from the annuity contract's fixed account[10] to the variable subaccounts, make the modern variable annuity a robust and powerful investment management tool.

The Distribution Phase

In the distribution phase, fixed annuities—either immediate contracts or deferred contracts that have been annuitized—provide a regular income by application of a chosen annuity payout factor to the amount that is converted to an income stream. For example, if Mr. Smith purchases a fixed immediate annuity for $100,000 or annuitizes a fixed deferred annuity having an annuity value of that same amount, and if he elects a Life and 10 Year Certain payout arrangement, and if the annual annuity payout factor for that option, for his age and sex, is 5.67, his annuity payments will be $5,670 per year from that point until the later of his death or the expiration of 10 years. Similarly, if he elects to annuitize a variable deferred annuity on a fixed annuity payout arrangement, and if the total value of the accumulation units in his contract, at the time of annuitization, is $100,000, he will receive that same income, assuming the same annuity payout factor.

If the annuity payout is to be on a variable basis, however, the amount annuitized (either a lump sum, in the case of an immediate variable annuity, or, in a deferred variable annuity, the current value of the accumulation units the owner wishes to annuitize[11]) is not converted to a fixed income stream by applying an annuity payout factor. Instead, the purchase payment or amount annuitized is used to buy a certain number of annuity units.[12] The process works as follows:

- First, the payment, or annuitization amount, is reduced by any contract fee applicable and by any state premium tax due, and allocated to the investment subaccounts chosen by the contract owner.

- Next, the insurance company computes an initial income payment amount for that portion of the purchase payment or annuitization amount allocated to each subaccount, using (a) the age and sex[13] of the annuitant and (b) an assumed investment rate (AIR). Many variable annuity contracts allow the purchaser to choose among several AIRs (e.g., 3%, 4%, 5%, and 6%). The higher the initial AIR chosen, the higher the initial variable income payment will be.

- Finally, the initial income payment is divided by the value of the annuity unit for each subaccount chosen. The result is the number of annuity units of that subaccount which will be purchased by that payment. Subsequent annuity payments will increase or decrease in proportion to the extent to which the net investment performance, after application of the separate account charges, of the chosen variable sub-accounts exceeds or lags the AIR.

Parties to the Annuity Contract

There are four parties to a commercial annuity contract.

1. The **annuity company** is the party that issues the policy, and is obligated to keep all the promises made in it.

2. The **annuitant** is the individual—and it must be an individual, a human being—who may or may not also be the owner of the policy. The age and sex of the annuitant determine—for life annuities—the amount of each annuity payment. The annuitant is merely the measuring life for purposes of annuity payment calculations. He or she has NO rights in the annuity contract as annuitant.

3. The **beneficiary** is the party who will receive any death benefit payable under the annuity, whether as a lump sum or a continuation of annuity payments. However, not all annuities will have a beneficiary because if payments cease at the annuitant's death, there is nothing for a beneficiary to receive. In most cases the beneficiary has no other rights, except if the beneficiary is named irrevocably.

4. The **owner** is the individual or entity—it need not be a human—that has all ownership rights in the contract, including the right to name the annuitant and beneficiary, to elect commencement of annuity payments, and to surrender the contract. Occasionally, advisors will suggest that a nonqualified annuity[14] be owned jointly; usually when the owners are a married couple. As will be discussed in Chapter 3, this arrangement can produce unexpected problems, and should be avoided unless the client and advisors are aware of the implications of such ownership.

Types of Annuity Payouts

An immediate annuity, or a deferred annuity that has been annuitized—where the contract owner has elected to begin receiving annuity payments—produces an income stream. The nature of this income stream can vary, according to the type of payout arrangement chosen.

The first arrangement, and the simplest, is **Life Only, No Refund**. When the contract owner elects this option, he or she will, upon annuitization, receive an income guaranteed to last for the annuitant's entire lifetime—no matter how long that annuitant lives. At the annuitant's death, no further payments will be due. Life Only, No Refund provides the highest payout of any of the annuity arrangements because if the annuitant dies prematurely—even if after receiving only one payment—the insurance company's obligation ceases. The insurance company, in making a Life Only, No Refund annuity payment guarantee, incurs no cost for guaranteeing a survivor benefit or, in the jargon of the insurance industry, a refund feature. It is the cost of these refund features which necessitates that annuity payments calculated using such a benefit be lower than the amount of a Life Only, No Refund annuity.

A second payout type is **Life Annuity, With Refund**. As with all life payout options, the main guarantee is that payments will continue for the annuitant's lifetime. But should the annuitant die during the refund period, the insurance company must pay the refund amount to the designated beneficiary.

Refund arrangements come in various flavors. The **Period Certain** refund type says that if the annuitant dies before the end of a certain period of time, payments will continue to the beneficiary for the remainder of that period. For example, the most common payout arrangement is **Life and 10-Year Certain**. This arrangement provides for payments that are guaranteed to continue for the annuitant's life, however long. If that annuitant should not live to receive 10 years' payments—if payments are monthly, that is 120 monthly payments—the remaining payments will continue to the beneficiary named in the policy until the 10-year term is complete.

The **Cash Refund** or **Installment Refund** payout option says that if the annuitant dies before receiving a specified amount—which may or may not be less than the amount originally annuitized—the balance will be paid to the beneficiary, either in a lump sum or in installments.

Not all annuities are payable for life. A third payout type, the so-called **Period Certain** option, pays an income for a certain period. A 20-year period certain payout option will pay for exactly 20 years and no more or fewer. If the annuitant dies during that period, payments continue to the beneficiary (or to a contingent annuitant if one is named). If the annuitant is still living at the end of 20 years, payments cease.

The terminology almost begs for misunderstanding. Life and 10-Year Certain sounds a lot like 10-Year Certain. But they are very different payout options. The first one will pay for the longer of 10 years or the annuitant's lifetime. The second will pay, in any and all events, for exactly and only 10 years. No more, no less. Many prospective annuity buyers will miss this distinction. No matter how careful the advisor is in explaining how that arrangement works, some people hear just the 10 Years part and focus on it. Many years ago, in talking with an elderly prospective client, one of the authors thought he had explained the Life and 10 Year Certain annuity he was recommending adequately. But, after he had finished, she expressed concern. "I like having that amount every month," she said, "and I especially like knowing that amount won't change, but I'm a bit worried. You see, I may live longer than 10 years, and then what?"

One way of avoiding this confusion, when structuring life annuities, is to consider using either Cash Refund or Installment Refund arrangements to address the risk of the annuitant's dying prematurely. It is far more easily explained and understood, and does not let the duration of the certain element distract attention from the lifetime guarantee,which is, the main purpose of the arrangement.

The fourth type of payout includes arrangements that cover more than one annuitant. The most common type is that of the various **Joint and Survivor** payout options and normally allows only two annuitants. These are life annuity payouts—they persist until both annuitants have died. The amount of the annuity payment may remain unchanged at the first death (this is called Joint and 100% Survivor) or may be reduced by some percentage or fraction. For example, Joint and ⅔ means that the surviving annuitant will receive, commencing at the death of the first annuitant, an income equal to ⅔ of the original annuity amount. Some contracts allow Joint and Survivor payouts with a refund feature. A much less common option than the Joint and Survivor arrangement is called **Joint Life**. It, too, covers two annuitants, but pays a benefit only until the first annuitant dies.

Now that we have the basics and terminology of annuities out of the way—and the authors thank you, dear reader, for your patience—let's get to what annuities are used for.

The Annuity as a Tool

Annuities are tools. They are acquired because the purchaser has a particular job to be done and is willing to exchange his money for a tool to do that job. In many ways, this exchange transaction is like the purchase of a hammer. The hammer has certain specifications—type and strength of the metal, length of the handle, size of the hammer head—and when purchased from a quality company, often comes with a guarantee that the product will perform as specified.

The important key to understand about this metaphor is that we generally do not buy a hammer simply because it happens to be cheaper, or lighter, or shinier than any other hand tool in the hardware store. We purchase it because we have a need, for example, to pound a nail into a piece of wood, or anticipate having a need in the future that we want to be prepared for, and we believe that a hammer is the best tool to fulfill that need.

In addition, there are many different situations where we might need a hammer, and each of those situations may call for a different one. Clearly, using a sledgehammer to drive a small nail into your drywall to hang a picture is the wrong tool for the job. Thus, the key in purchasing the right hammer is understanding the need and the job you're hoping to accomplish with it. Only once you understand the right situation for any particular hammer can you determine whether a hammer is the right tool for the job, and which type you need.

To complete the analogy, the key to decision-making when it comes to annuities is to first understand the problems for which the annuity can represent a solution. Only then can one actually determine whether an annuity is the right tool to solve the problem, and which sort of annuity will best accomplish the task.

Overview: The Annuity as a Problem-Solving Tool

We are all familiar with the kinds of problems that hammers solve, such as driving a small nail, pounding a large nail, or forcing a wedge between two pieces of wood to separate them. The problems that the annuity-as-a-tool are meant to solve are quite varied because of the broad number and types of annuity-tools available. That said, the problems that annuities solve—the needs that they meet—can be identified and separated into several general categories:

1. **The need for a known income stream**. This is what annuities do best, because annuities—whether deferred or immediate—are really designed to generate income. The known part may be the amount of the income stream, the duration, or both. The amount might be fixed or determined by a formula. The duration might be for a specified period, for the lifetime of the annuitant, or the longer of the two. The amount of each annuity payment may be greater than one could obtain, with absolute certainty, from other savings or investment vehicles. However, it must be noted that annuity income (meaning regular annuity payments, not partial withdrawals) are part principal. An annuitant is not living on her income, but on income and principal.

2. **The need for a guaranteed rate of return**. As we've noted, the current interest crediting rate in most deferred annuities may potentially be changed every quarter, year, or at the discretion of the insurance company. A notable exception is the so-called CD annuity—a fixed deferred annuity with multi-year current rate guarantees. Often, the rate guarantee extends to the end of the surrender charge period, which is usually six years or less. Depending upon contractual provisions, especially the surrender charge schedule, and whether interest rates are rising or falling, longer rate guarantee periods may offer lower or higher rates than shorter periods. In any event, the rate of return is contractually guaranteed.

3. **The need for a better nonguaranteed rate of return**. Although their current crediting rate is usually not guaranteed beyond an initial period, deferred annuities have, historically, paid somewhat higher current returns as a class, than some other fixed-dollar investments, such as passbook savings and certificates of deposit.

4. **The need or desire for tax advantages**. One of the main appeals of a deferred annuity is tax-deferred growth. Although the gain will ultimately be taxed (tax-deferred does not mean tax-free), tax deferral maximizes the benefit of compounding. Moreover, annual growth not distributed is not recognized as income for any tax purpose, including the taxability of Social Security benefits. Immediate annuities, too, receive

favorable income tax treatment. A portion of each annuity payment is considered return of principal and is not taxable.

5. **A guaranteed payment in the event of death**. Although annuities are not life insurance policies, and are not taxed as such, they can provide guaranteed death benefits. A fixed deferred annuity offers a guarantee of principal and previously credited interest, and most such contracts waive surrender charges upon death. Variable deferred annuities typically offer a guaranteed minimum death benefit. Immediate annuities, while designed to amortize both principal and earnings over the annuity payout period, may be structured with a refund feature to guarantee a minimum payout, whether to the living annuitant or her beneficiary, if the annuitant should die early. That said, annuities are designed primarily to provide living benefits. If a guaranteed death benefit is a client's main concern, life insurance is often a better tool, provided the client is insurable. Just as a hammer can be used to pry apart two-by-fours, a pry bar is probably a better choice, so long as the job does not involve driving nails.

Is an Annuity the Right Tool, and, If So, Which Kind Will Do the Best Job?

Now that we've defined some of the needs that annuities can solve, we will begin to focus on how to match particular kinds of annuities to manage the risks inherent in those needs, and understand the annuity as a **risk management** tool.

When the Client Needs a Known Income Stream

For the client who requires a certain income stream commencing within one year, an immediate annuity is an almost intuitive choice. Providing income— certain as to amount, duration, or both—is what an immediate annuity does. But first we need to ask a key question: For how long will the income stream be required?

If the need is for an income for life, an immediate life annuity makes good sense. It is the only financial instrument that can guarantee a specific amount of income for as long as the recipient lives. It allows the purchaser to manage the risk that the asset base that is used to create the payments may not earn an adequate rate of return, or may not be large enough to provide enough payments for life (i.e., the risk of outliving one's assets). Some immediate annuities can be structured so that annuity payments will increase each year by a specified percentage. This is sometimes known as the COLA (cost-of-living-adjustment) option. Unfortunately, many insurance companies do not offer such an option in their immediate annuity portfolios.

Similarly, if the need is for an income specified for a period of years, an immediate period certain annuity may be an appropriate choice. It, too, manages the risk of an unknown future rate of return over the time period, and the risk that the asset base, or the dollars used to create the income stream, may not be sufficient to produce the income required.

One risk often cited by critics of immediate annuities is that the buyer has locked in current interest rates. This criticism is generally voiced during periods when prevailing interest rates are unusually low. How valid is this criticism? In the authors' opinion, it has merit, from an investment perspective. The interest rate used in the calculation of the annuity payout factor—the number of dollars, per thousand dollars of purchase payment that the annuitant will receive each period—is, indeed, locked in. Should prevailing interest rates rise over the period of time during which annuity payments are made, those annuity payments will not reflect that rise. However, the authors feel that from a risk management perspective, this criticism is misdirected. If the goal is to ensure an income level, the relevant risk is whether the dollars invested to produce that income can do so with certainty. A rise in prevailing rates would not present that risk, but a decline would. To transfer that risk from the annuity buyer to the insurance company, the buyer must incur a cost. Locking in the annuity interest rate is part of that cost.

It should be noted, though, that the changes in interest rates used in immediate annuity calculations over the past two decades have been far less dramatic than the changes in interest rates for short-term instruments such as savings accounts and certificates of deposit. While it is true that the purchaser of an immediate annuity in January, 2009 is locking in an interest rate lower than would have been used for someone the same age and sex in, say, January, 1982, the difference is not nearly as great as one might think. By the same token, if interest rates should trend sharply upward in the next 10 years, the locked in rates 10 years hence will probably not be substantially greater than the current ones.

When the Client Needs a Guaranteed Rate of Return

When a specific minimum return on investment and preservation of principal is required to accomplish a particular goal, an immediate annuity makes no sense because it does not preserve principal. The income payments from an immediate annuity, while they may be larger than might be achievable from alternatives, are not just a return on investment, but a combination of return on and return of investment. However, a deferred annuity offering a multi-year interest rate guarantee may well provide a solution. The risk of getting an inadequate rate of return is managed by transferring it to the insurance company issuing the annuity. This provides a total or minimum rate of return guaranteed to equal or exceed the return required. However, it is important to note that there is a lack of liquidity cost associated with these annuities. This is because the insurance company makes its guarantees assuming it will have use of the money used to purchase the annuity. Typically, a deferred annuity contract does not become profitable for an insurer until after it has been in force for several years due to commissions, other issuing charges, administrative costs, deferred acquisition costs, taxes, and reserve requirements. If the annuity owner elects to surrender or take withdrawals from the annuity in the early contract years, he will usually be required to pay a surrender charge. The amount and terms of this vary considerably from contract to contract.

Recently, many variable deferred annuities have been marketed with guaranteed living benefits. The structure and provisions of these policies vary greatly, but it should be noted that the guarantees provided are typically not equivalent to the guaranteed minimum rate of return of fixed annuities, and usually require annuitization, minimum holding periods, or other conditions for the guarantees to be effective. For an extensive discussion of the various living benefits available with variable annuities, see Chapter 6.

When the Client Needs a Better Nonguaranteed Rate of Return

With the exception of fixed annuities with multi-year current rate guarantees, or so-called CD annuities, no deferred annuity guarantees the current rate of return for more than a year at most. Although, all fixed annuities offer a guaranteed minimum rate of return. Variable deferred annuities generally do not offer any guarantees of return or of principal, except where the fixed investment account is used or as provided by optional riders. That said, we should bear in mind that most other long-term investments do not offer such guarantees either. For clients who require a guarantee of principal and are willing to accept a current rate that may change, deferred fixed annuities may offer better returns than certificates of deposit or individual bonds. The interest rate history of many fixed annuities has exceeded that of CDs, although there can be no assurance that this will hold true in the future.

When comparing the interest crediting rate of a deferred annuity with that of an alternative, the diligent advisor will point out not only any applicable surrender charges, but also the early distribution penalty which applies to withdrawals taken prior to age 59½, unless an exception is available. See Chapter 2 for an in-depth discussion of the income taxation of annuities. Those are essential elements in any sound risk management decision. So, too, is the fact that earnings in deferred annuities are not taxed until distributed.

When the Client Wants and Needs Income Tax Deferral

Tax deferral is perhaps the most advertised and promoted advantage of deferred annuities. Earnings are not taxed until distributed, either to living contract owners or beneficiaries. The advantages of such deferral are well-recognized. However, the cost of such tax deferral, granted by Section 72 of the Internal Revenue Code, is a requirement in the same section that all distributions from annuities be taxed at ordinary income rates. No capital gains treatment is ever available under current law. Whether this trade-off is favorable, or appropriate, is a matter of considerable controversy. In the authors' view, it is always a matter of individual facts and circumstances, for reasons that will be discussed in later chapters.

When the Client Needs a Guaranteed Payment in the Event of Death

An often overlooked feature of deferred annuities is the right of the beneficiary to receive a guaranteed payment, or a payment determined by a guaranteed formula, in the event of death. This payment may not occur until the distant future, but upon purchase of the contract the owner knows exactly what the payment will be or how it will be determined.

When is this important? When the client requires that a certain amount be available upon death, regardless of investment performance in the meantime. This guarantee allows an annuity owner to manage the risk that inadequate investment performance will cause a smaller amount to pass to her beneficiaries than desired, regardless of actual investment performance over the time period until death. The authors strongly believe, however, that, when the need for such guaranteed death benefit is a primary concern, life insurance generally represents a far more efficient solution, if available.

Summary: The Annuity as a Tool

The guarantees that the annuity-tool provides allow clients and their advisors to solve certain problems and to meet certain needs. Specifically, it allows us to meet those needs despite risks that might cause us to fail. Thus, at its most fundamental level, annuities serve as tools that allow us to manage risks—specifically, the risks that:

- **distributions** from an investment will be inadequate to meet specified goals;

- **earnings** on an investment will be inadequate to meet specified goals; and

- the **amount available to heirs**, from the investment, will be inadequate to meet specified goals.

Our discussion of annuities, and potential applications for them, throughout the remainder of this book will proceed with the understanding that annuities are nothing more than risk management tools which allow us to accomplish certain needs and goals with certainty— or at least increased likelihood— because of the underlying guarantees that they hold.

Determining When a Risk Management Tool (Annuity) is Appropriate

In all cases, the annuity tool solution will have a cost associated with it—the cost of the annuity and the guarantees that it provides. Because of these costs, the solution provided often will not be the solution with the highest expected value or projected return on investment. However, the decision to accept a lower expected value, or net of costs, in exchange for a higher, or entirely guaranteed, probability of success is a risk-return tradeoff that can, and should, be examined and made on a case-by-case basis. In many instances, when presented with both options, the client will choose the option most likely to succeed, not the one with the highest expected return.

It is also important to remember that, in the search to maximize the probability of success, it is entirely possible that the client will not actually need to utilize the guarantees provided by an annuity. Annuities manage risks of loss; there is no guarantee that such losses will occur in the first place. Annuities offer purchasers options to utilize certain guarantees; they do not require the exercise of those options. Thus, it may be that a guarantee within a client's annuity is never actually put to use. Nonetheless, owning the annuity may very well have still been the right choice.

That the guarantees may never be put to use does not mean the cost of those guarantees was a waste. Your house may never burn down, but it is still prudent to maintain your homeowner's insurance and pay premiums for years. Doing so buys you a guarantee that you will not lose the entire value of your house, and may produce ancillary benefits such as allowing you to obtain a mortgage. In any event, it can provide you with invaluable peace of mind, and the ability to better enjoy your life knowing that a particular risk had been transferred—insured—away.

Endnotes

1. Some insurance companies will issue annuity checks to a nonowner annuitant if requested to do so by the owner.

2. Such deferral may require the insurance company's approval.

3. These are also referred to as investment subaccounts.

4. As we have noted, there is no accumulation phase in a variable immediate annuity.

5. After deduction for contract charges.

6. We have illustrated four decimal places precision for units purchased and three decimal places for unit values in this example. Some insurers use greater precision and some use less.

7. Asset classes are investment types having distinct risk/return characteristics, such as U.S. Large Cap Growth Stocks, Foreign Stocks, U.S. Real Estate, U.S. Long Term Gov't Bonds, etc.

8. Some contracts require a minimum initial and/or ongoing contribution per subaccount.

9. Most contracts impose a maximum on the number of exchanges permitted per month and may levy a charge for additional excess exchanges. These restrictions are generally in place to prevent active trading using the investment subaccounts, but are not intended to restrict normal occasional trading and re-balancing.

10. The fixed account in a deferred variable annuity typically guarantees a minimum interest rate and may offer a guaranteed duration for the current declared interest rate. In addition, the principal—including all prior credited interest—is typically guaranteed against loss.

11. Some variable deferred annuities permit partial annuitization. Others require that the entire value of the contractholder's accumulation units be annuitized.

12. Some variable annuity literature describes this process as a conversion of the existing accumulation units to annuity units.

13. If the annuity uses unisex annuity factors, the sex of the annuitant is not considered. Most commercial annuities use sex-distinct factors. Unisex factors are most often seen in contracts used to fund qualified retirement plans, where sex-distinct factors in such an employment context are considered to impose potentially unlawful discrimination.

14. An annuity purchased with after-tax dollars that will not fund an IRA or tax-qualified plan.

Chapter 2

Taxation of Annuity Benefits During Owner's Lifetime

The rules regarding taxation of annuities are complicated and, in many instances, not entirely clear. Unfortunately, it is very easy for an advisor to make mistakes in advising clients as to ownership, beneficiary designations, or distribution requirements. It is even easier to misinterpret or misapply the many complex rules governing lifetime withdrawals from annuities. Mistakes in these areas can have serious consequences both for the client and the advisor. For these reasons, we will devote considerable attention in this chapter not only to the rules themselves—including some that may be unfamiliar to the reader—but also to the practical, every day applications and implications of those rules.

The rules governing taxation of annuities are contained in Internal Revenue Code Section 72 (the Code) and the applicable Treasury regulations. However, it is extremely important for the reader to understand that most of Section 72 deals only with so-called nonqualified annuities, or annuities purchased with after-tax dollars, and not to fund tax-qualified individual retirement accounts (IRAs) or tax-qualified retirement plans. The tax rules regarding the deferral of tax on annual earnings within annuities and the methods for determining how much of each annuity payment is taxable refer only to nonqualified annuity contracts. On the other hand, qualified annuities[1] are governed by parts of the Code dealing with the specific type of plan the annuity is funding (e.g., Section 408 for traditional IRAs, Section 408A for Roth IRAs, and Section 401 for pension plans). The rules that govern an annuity that is not purchased to fund an IRA or qualified plan (i.e., the rules for nonqualified annuities) are totally inapplicable to an annuity that is purchased to fund such a plan (a qualified annuity). This distinction is often not understood, and one of the most common mistakes made by advisors in the area of retirement planning is an attempt to apply regular annuity rules to a qualified annuity. The rules discussed in this chapter apply only to nonqualified annuities, except where indicated.

While Section 72 also deals with policy dividends and forms of premium returns, we will focus solely in our discussion on just two types of payments:

1. amounts received as an annuity (i.e., annuity payments); and

2. amounts not received as an annuity (i.e., withdrawals, surrenders, and other non-annuity payouts).

All distributions from an annuity, whether made to a living owner or to a beneficiary, are either one or the other of these two types.

Before we examine these two types of distributions, however, one very important point bears repeating: distributions made from an annuity while the owner of the annuity contract is living are taxable to that owner—even if made to an annuitant who is a different individual. For example, if A owns an annuity of which B is the annuitant, payments are generally made to A. Some annuity issuers will issue checks directly to a nonowner annuitant if the owner directs, but, even so, the tax liability is that of the owner.

Amounts Received as an Annuity

"The term *annuity* includes all periodic payments resulting from the systematic liquidation of a principal sum."[2] It "refers not only [to] payments made for the life or lives, but also to installment payments that do not involve a life contingency; for example, payments under a fixed period or fixed amount settlement option."[3] Amounts received as an annuity are taxed under Section 72 (discussed below), which considers each payment to be part principal and part gain. The part representing principal is excluded from tax (as a return of principal); the part representing gain is taxable as ordinary income.[4] The formula for allocating the amount of principal and gain of each payment for fixed annuities is different from that used with variable annuities.

In the case of a fixed annuity, this calculation is done by applying an exclusion ratio which is the total investment in the contract—adjusted for the value of any refund feature elected—divided by the expected return, which, for life annuities, takes into account life expectancies.

$$\text{Exclusion Ratio} = \frac{\text{Total Investment Contract}}{\text{Expected Return}}$$

In the case of a variable annuity, the expected return is unknown and is considered, for purposes of the exclusion calculation, to be equal to the investment in the contract. The ratio used to determine the portion of each variable annuity payment includible in income is the investment in the contract, adjusted for the value of any refund feature elected, divided by the number of years over which it is anticipated that the annuity will be paid.[5] For a detailed description of each method, see Appendix C. Once all principal has been received tax-free, the entire annuity payment is taxable as ordinary income.[6] It is important to note that, where the annuity starting date was prior to January 1, 1987, the exclusion ratio continues to apply, even after all the principal has been recovered. Consequently, when addressing the taxation of an existing annuity payment stream, it is absolutely critical to know when payments began.

Annuity payments, or amounts received as an annuity, include payments from an immediate annuity, or from a deferred annuity that has been annuitized, where the owner of a deferred annuity has elected to commence regular annuity payments under an annuity option offered by that contract.

Amounts Not Received as an Annuity

The tax treatment of annuity distributions other than regular annuity payments, including partial withdrawals, surrenders, and other nonannuitized payouts, depends upon when the annuity contract was issued.

Contracts Entered Into After August 13, 1982

For contracts entered into after August 13, 1982, non-annuity distributions are taxed according to the interest first rule, sometimes referred to as Last In, First Out (LIFO). All distributions that are amounts not received as an annuity are considered income until all gain in the contract has been received.

Amounts not received as an annuity are any amounts received from an annuity that do not qualify as amounts received as an annuity. This distinction may appear obvious, but it is not quite that straightforward because of how Section 72 treats the word received. Amounts not received as an annuity include not only outright distributions such as partial withdrawals and death benefits not taken under an annuity option, but also policy dividends unless retained by the insurer as premiums or other consideration[7], amounts received as loans, "the value of any part of an annuity contract pledged or assigned,"[8] and amounts received on partial surrender. Such amounts "are taxable as income to the extent that the cash value of the contract immediately before the payment exceeds the investment in the contract."[9]

The preceding two sentences merit closer attention, however, because many advisors are unaware of these provisions. First, amounts taken from annuity contracts as loans are taxable,[10] although nonqualified annuity contracts generally do not contain loan provisions. Second, merely pledging an annuity as collateral for a loan causes recognition of income to the extent of the lesser of any gain or the portion of the annuity thus pledged.

Multiple Deferred Annuities: The Anti-Abuse Rule

One method of reducing the impact of the LIFO treatment of deferred annuities, for purchasers who contemplate using partial withdrawals, is to use multiple contracts.

> *Example*: Individual A purchases a single deferred annuity for $100,000. Five years later, it is worth $120,000. If A then withdraws $15,000, the entire $15,000 is taxable as ordinary income. Moreover, if A is under age 59½, he must pay the 10% penalty tax for premature distributions unless an exception to the penalty applies. If, however, A purchases 10 annuities for $10,000 each, and each annuity is worth $12,000 five years later, a surrender of one contract (for $12,000) and a withdrawal from a second, for $3,000, would produce a taxable amount of only $4,000 (the gain in the two annuities) for the same $15,000 withdrawal. Moreover, the penalty tax would be $400, instead of $1,500, as the penalty applies only to the taxable portion of early distributions.

Congress recognized this technique as abusive and enacted a provision that treats all annuities issued during a single calendar year and issued by the same insurance company as one annuity, for purposes of taxing withdrawals.[11] This provision does not apply to partial withdrawals or surrenders of deferred annuity contracts issued in the same calendar year by different insurance companies, or to deferred annuity contracts issued by the same insurance company in different calendar years.

Contracts Entered Into Before August 14, 1982

Amounts not received as an annuity from contracts entered into before August 14, 1982 and allocated to investments made before August 14, 1982 are taxed under the cost recovery rule, a treatment sometimes referred to as First In, First Out (FIFO). Under this rule, "the taxpayer may receive all such amounts tax-free until he has received tax-free amounts equal to his [total] pre-August 14, 1982 investment in the contract; [subsequent withdrawal] amounts are taxable only after such basis has been fully recovered."[12] It should be noted that this does not mean that all amounts not received as an annuity from an annuity contract entered into before August 14, 1982 are treated thus. Only amounts allocable to investments made before August 14, 1982 receive this treatment.

> *Example*: If a taxpayer had an annuity purchased in 1981 (thus, before August 14, 1982) for $25,000, and currently worth $125,000, the first $25,000 of withdrawals are received tax-free, and subsequent withdrawals are taxable as gain. If the taxpayer had made a total of $50,000 of deposits by adding another $25,000 in 1984, the taxpayer would still only be able to receive the first $25,000 tax-free because the second deposit—although attributable to a pre-August 14, 1982 annuity—would not be allocable to a pre-August 14, 1982 investment in the contract. Note that if the taxpayer's two deposits had occurred in 1983 and 1984 thus, after August 14, 1982, the post-August 14, 1982 rules would apply and the contract with a $50,000 investment and a $125,000 current value would be taxed as gains first, to the extent

of the $75,000 of gain inherent in the contract., Only then would withdrawals be a tax-free recovery of basis. Alternatively, if the $125,000 contract were annuitized, a portion of each payment would be a tax-free recovery of basis. This illustrates the three different ways that basis may be allocated to withdrawals from a contract: (1) all basis first and then gains for pre-August 14, 1982 contracts; (2) all gains first and then basis for post-August 14, 1982 contracts; and (3) pro-rata basis and gains on each payment for annuitized contracts.

Partial Versus Full Surrenders

Amounts withdrawn from an annuity, not allocable to pre-August 14, 1982 contributions, are treated as being taxable to the extent of gain in the contract. However, the method used to determine the amount of gain will vary depending on whether the withdrawal represents a partial or full surrender.

In the event of a partial surrender (i.e., a withdrawal for any amount less than the full value of the contract), the amount of gain is determined as the excess of the contract value over the investment in the contract (cost basis), without regard to any surrender charges. As a result, the amount of gain is calculated based on the gross cash value of the annuity to determine whether any of a withdrawal will be attributable to gain and subject to income taxation.[13]

On the other hand, if the withdrawal represents a full surrender of the contract, the preceding normal rule for withdrawals does not apply.[14] Instead, in the case of a full surrender, the tax code explicitly indicates that the amount of gain shall simply be the excess of the amount received (i.e., the actual net surrender value received) over the investment in the contract (cost basis).[15]

> *Example*: Taxpayer holds an annuity that was purchased for $100,000, the investment in the contract. The current cash value of the annuity is $105,000, and the annuity has a $10,000 surrender charge. Thus, the net surrender value of the annuity would be $95,000. If the taxpayer takes a partial withdrawal, the amount of gain in the contract would be $5,000, based on the current cash value of $105,000, without regard to any surrender charges. Thus, any partial withdrawal will be taxable up to the first $5,000 of gain, and only the remainder will be treated as a return of principal. However, if the entire annuity is surrendered, the total amount received will be $95,000, with an original investment in the contract of $100,000; consequently, in the case of a full surrender, the taxpayer will report no gain, and will be eligible for a $5,000 loss. See below for further discussion of the tax treatment of annuity losses.

In the second edition of this book, it was noted that, "in conversations with the authors, representatives of two major insurers said that their company's policy is to apply Section 72(e) (3)(A) both to partial withdrawals and total surrenders and, where the cash value of the contract before a total surrender, reckoned without regard to surrender charges, exceeds the holder's investment in the contract, they will issue a 1099 reporting such excess as gain—even if the net amount (after surrender charges) received by the holder on such surrender does not exceed the investment in the contract. The policies of those companies, in this regard, may have changed. When we attempted to learn the current policy of the two companies referred to, we were unsuccessful. One company simply did not respond to our inquiry; a representative of the other company told one of the authors that it was against their policy to make a public statement of their policy on this issue. To say the least, this highlights the tax uncertainty in the area, at least with respect to how it will be reported on a Form 1099-R to the IRS.

Nonetheless, the authors do not believe there should be any ambiguity, and that the rules are clear in stating that a partial surrender should ignore surrender charges when calculating gain under 72(e)(3)(A), while a total surrender under 72(e)(5)(E) should simply measure gains by comparing final net proceeds to investment in the contract/cost basis, which implicitly adjusts for surrender charges paid. Evidently, the IRS author of Private Letter Ruling 200030013 agrees with the latter statement, as the PLR includes the following text:

> "Section 72(e)(5)(E) provides a statutory exception to section 72(e)(2)(A). The rule of section 72(e)(2)(A) is not applicable if the amount received is "under a contract on its complete surrender, redemption, or maturity." Section 72(e)(5)(A) provides that in situations in which paragraph (e)(5) applies, then paragraphs (2)(B) and (4)(A) shall not apply and if paragraph (2)(A) does not apply, then the amount distributed shall be included in gross income, but only to the extent that it exceeds the investment in the contract (basis-first rule). The basis-first rule provides that the taxpayer does not have to include any amounts into income to the extent that it does not exceed the taxpayer's investment in the contract."

Thus, readers considering a deferred annuity contract should be aware of how the insurance company issuing the policy intends to interpret this issue.

Deferral of Tax on Undistributed Gain

One of the most often-cited advantages of deferred annuities is that the annual increase in the cash value of these contracts is not subject to tax until the gain is withdrawn. Indeed, this tax-deferred growth is often touted as the most important benefit offered by deferred annuities.[16] The authors believe that this is both an oversimplification and a mischaracterization. A deferred annuity is not merely a tax-management instrument. It is also a platform for various investment strategies, and a mechanism for ensuring a known or determinable stream of income for a definite period or for the whole of one or two lifetimes. But above all, in the authors' judgment, a deferred annuity—or an immediate annuity, for that matter—is a potent risk management tool. We will explore this last functionality in detail in Chapter 12. For the moment, however, it should be recognized that there is much more to a deferred annuity than tax deferral!

Advisors sometimes ask what specific section in the Internal Revenue Code states that growth in the cash value of a deferred annuity is not taxable until distributed. As we have noted, the tax treatment of nonqualified annuities is governed by Section 72, but there is no specific line or paragraph in that section granting such tax deferral. Rather, the various subsections of Section 72(e) define what distributions, including imputed distributions, such as policy gain in an annuity pledged as collateral for a loan, will be taxed as amounts not received as an annuity. Growth in the cash value, or annuity value or surrender value, is not among the items defined as such. It is, therefore, not taxable, currently, by implication.

When Does a Deferred Annuity NOT Enjoy Tax-Deferred Treatment?

Not all deferred annuities enjoy the benefit of tax-deferred growth. As IRC Section 72(u) states, contributions made after February 28, 1986, to annuity contracts held by a corporation or other entity that is not a natural person will not be treated as an annuity contract for tax purposes[17] and will not enjoy tax deferral. "Income on the contract"[18] will be treated, each year, "as ordinary income received or accrued by the owner during such taxable year."[19]

There are five exceptions to this rule (IRC Section 72(u)(3)).[20] It does not apply to a contract that:

(A) is acquired by the estate of a decedent by reason of the death of the decedent;

(B) is held under a qualified pension, profit sharing, or stock bonus plan, as an IRC Section 403(b) tax sheltered annuity, or under an individual retirement plan;

(C) is a qualified funding asset,[21] as defined in IRC Section 130(d) but without regard to whether there is a qualified assignment;

(D) is purchased by an employer upon the termination of a qualified pension, profit sharing, or stock bonus plan or tax sheltered annuity program and held by the employer until all amounts under the contract are distributed to the employee for whom the contract was purchased or to his beneficiary; or

(E) is an immediate annuity (i.e., an annuity that is purchased with a single premium or annuity consideration, the annuity starting date of which is no later than one year from the date of purchase, and which provides for a series of substantially equal periodic payments to be made no less frequently than annually during the annuity period).

Another very important exception to this general rule is granted by a sentence at the end of Section 72(u)(1), which states that "for purposes of this paragraph, holding by a trust or other entity as an agent for a natural person shall not be taken into account." In other words, if the nominal owner of the annuity is not a natural person but the beneficial owner is, the annuity will be treated as held by a natural person and treated as an annuity for tax purposes.

In what circumstances does this exception to an exception apply? In other words, when may a deferred annuity, held by a nonnatural person entity, be treated as an annuity and enjoy tax deferral? See Appendix C for a discussion of various letter rulings in which a trust has been held to be such an agent of a natural person. However, we would like to draw attention to one specific observation from that discussion, that we believe is worthy of the reader's attention:

> "It is clear that if all contributions to the contract are made after February 28, 1986 the requirements apply to the contract. It seems clear enough that if no contributions are made after February 28, 1986 to an annuity contract, a contract held by a nonnatural person is treated for tax purposes as an annuity contract and is taxed under the annuity rules... However, if contributions have been made both before March 1, 1986 and after February 28, 1986 to contracts held by nonnatural persons, it is not clear whether the income on the contract is allocated to different portions of the contract and whether the portion of the contract allocable to contributions before March 1, 1986 may continue to be treated as an annuity contract for income tax purposes. The Code makes no specific provision for separate treatment of contributions to the same contract made before March 1, 1986 and those made after February 28, 1986."[22]

What about a deferred annuity owned by a family limited partnership? Here, the applicability of the agent of a natural person exception is particularly unclear. The authors have not been able to locate any private letter rulings in which the IRS has held that such a partnership would qualify as such an agent, but Private Letter Ruling 199944020 is worthy of note. In this ruling, the IRS provides notice of a taxpayer withdrawal of a letter ruling request:

> "Two rulings were requested on the transaction described below. The first was whether the transfer of annuity contracts to a partnership in exchange for limited partnership interests qualified for nonrecognition under Section 72 (nonrecognition of gain or loss on contribution). The second is whether the annuity contracts after the transfer to the partnership will be considered as held by a natural person under Section 72(u)."[23]

Although the taxpayer requesting the letter ruling withdrew the request, Private Letter Ruling 199944020 states that:

> "We reached a tentatively adverse conclusion only with regard to the second requested ruling dealing with Section 72(u) (treatment of annuity contracts not held by natural persons)...
>
> Under the present facts, Partnership is not a mere agent holding the deferred annuities for natural persons, rather it is proposed that Partnership actually receive and possess the deferred annuities as property of Partnership, thus, subjecting this property to any possible claims of creditors against Partnership. By way of contrast, the example set forth in the drafting history of Section 72(u) clearly demonstrates that the agency exception was limited to a situation where a pure agency was created as the nonnatural person holding the property had no interest other than as agent. S. Rept. No. 99-313, 99th Cong., 2d Sess. 567

(Group annuity held by a corporation as agent for natural persons who are the beneficial owners, the contract is treated as an annuity). See also Joint Committee on Taxation Staff, *General Explanation of the Tax Reform Act of 1986*, 99th Cong., 2d Sess. 658 (1987) (If an employer holds a group policy to satisfy state group policy requirements, but has no right to any amounts contributed to the contract and all amounts are employee contributions, the employer is merely the nominal holder of the contract and the contract is not treated as held by a nonnatural person)."[24]

What is the significance of this letter ruling? First, it is only a private letter ruling. Moreover, its tentatively adverse conclusion was reached based on specific facts and circumstances. However, the authors believe that the conclusion reached was both logical and valid, and that the mere agency required for an entity to qualify as the "agent of a natural person" under Section 72(u)(1) is fundamentally incompatible with the nature of a valid business partnership in general, and, specifically, with the business purpose requirement the Service has applied to family limited partnerships in an estate planning context. Thus, in practice, the more successfully the taxpayer argues that the family limited partnership is a separate entity with a discrete business purpose to validate its discounts for estate planning purposes, the more it undermines the argument that the annuity should be tax-deferred under Section 72(u)(1). At the very least, a private letter ruling approving the claiming of the Section 72(u)(1) exception should be obtained before recommending that an annuity be owned by a family limited partnership.

Penalty for Early Distributions from a Deferred Annuity

In granting the benefit of tax-deferral to deferred annuities, Congress intended that they should be retirement plans. To discourage the use of annuities as short-term financial instruments by young people, it enacted Section 72(q), which imposes a 10% penalty tax on certain premature payments or distributions from annuity contracts. The penalty applies only to payments to the extent that they are includible in taxable income. There are certain distributions to which the penalty does not apply,[25] including those (IRC Section 72(q)(2)):

(A) made on or after the date on which the taxpayer attains age 59½;[26]

(B) made on or after the death of the holder or, where the holder is not an individual, the death of the primary annuitant;

(C) attributable to the taxpayer becoming disabled;[27]

(D) which are a part of a series of substantially equal periodic payments, not less frequently than annually, made for the life (or life expectancy) of the taxpayer or the joint lives (or joint life expectancies) of the taxpayer and his designated beneficiary;[28]

(E) from a qualified pension, profit sharing, or stock bonus plan, Section 403(b) annuity plan, or IRA;

(F)   allocable to investment in the contract before August 14, 1982;[29]

(G)   under a qualified funding asset;

(H)   subject to the 10% penalty for withdrawals from a qualified retirement plan;[30]

(I)   under an immediate annuity contract;

(J)   which are purchased by an employer upon the termination of a qualified plan and which is held by the employer until such time as the employee separates from service.

It is important to note that, under the exemption for an immediate annuity, Revenue Ruling 92-95 states that "where a deferred annuity contract was exchanged for an immediate annuity contract, the purchase date of the new contract for purposes of the 10% penalty tax was considered to be the date upon which the deferred annuity was purchased. Thus, payments from the replacement contract did not fall within the immediate annuity exception to the penalty tax."[31] This illustrates a significant common pitfall: where an immediate annuity is purchased directly, its payments will always be penalty-free; however, where an immediate annuity is acquired as part of an exchange from a deferred annuity contract, annuitization is not penalty-free unless the payments happen to meet another exception.

> *Example.* Assume individual A (under age 59½) purchases an immediate annuity for a 5-year period certain payout, and individual B (also under age 59½) acquires an immediate annuity via an exchange from an existing deferred annuity for a 5-year period certain payout. Individual A's payments will be penalty-free. Individual B's payments, however, will not, because a contract that was initially a deferred annuity and is converted to an immediate annuity later does not meet the immediate annuity requirements.[32]

> On the other hand, let's assume that both individuals A and B selected lifetime annuitization options. In this case, individual A's payments will again be penalty free. Individual B's payments will also be tax-free in this case, but not because the exchanged-for contract was an immediate annuity. Instead, individual B's payments should be tax-free, because they will also satisfy the requirements of subparagraph D, substantially equal periodic payments.

Where an annuity is held by a grantor trust, the application of the exceptions for the 10% premature withdrawal penalty appear to be more ambiguous. With respect to the age 59½ exception, the IRS has confirmed that the grantor's life will be the measuring life to determine whether the age 59½ exception has been met.[33] However, the guidance from the IRS on this issue addresses only the opportunity for a grantor trust-owned annuity to be eligible for the age 59½ based on the age of the grantor. It is not clear whether such an annuity ownership structure would also be eligible for exceptions based on the disability of the grantor, or to be made based on substantially equal periodic payments over the life of the grantor. Alternatively, it is notable that based on a clear application of the tax code itself, the opportunity to receive penalty-free distributions in the event of death will be triggered based on the life and death of the primary annuitant, not the grantor of the trust.[34]

In the case of an annuity held by a nongrantor trust, where the trust taxpayer has no age or life expectancy, it does not appear that the trust would be eligible for a premature withdrawal exception on account on age 59½, disability, or for substantially equal periodic payments. Instead, the annuity proceeds could only be accessed penalty tax-free as a withdrawal due to the death of the primary annuitant, or by distributing the annuity itself to a trust beneficiary for subsequent withdrawal.[35] However, some commentators have suggested that if the trust is simply the beneficial holder of the annuity on behalf of a trust beneficiary, then the benenficiary's age should be available for at least the age 59½ exception, especially in the case of a simple trust.[36] Other commentators have suggested that, per the rules under IRC Section 72(s)(6), the company might look to the primary annuitant to evaluate whether early withdrawal penalty exceptions may apply where the holder of the annuity is not a natural person. Although technically, 72(s)(6) explicitly states its annuitant-in-lieu-of-holder rule applies only for the purposes of subsection (s). Suffice it to say, in the case of a nongrantor trust, the determination of whose age/health is used to determine the exceptions to the early withdrawal penalty remains uncertain, and reporting in certain situations may vary from one insurer to another.

On the other hand, in the case where the nongrantor trust is also not eligible to be treated as an agent for a natural person, the contract itself will not be treated as an annuity for tax purposes; although this makes all gains in the contract taxable annually, it would also mean indirectly that the annuity would not be subject to the 10% early withdrawal penalty.[37]

Tax Deduction for Annuity Losses

An income tax deduction for a loss may be taken by a taxpayer only when the loss is incurred in connection with the taxpayer's trade or business or in a transaction entered into for profit.[38]

> "Generally, the purchase of a personal annuity contract is considered a transaction entered into for profit. Consequently, if a taxpayer sustains a loss upon surrender of a refund annuity contract, he may claim a deduction for the loss, regardless of whether he purchased the contract in connection with his trade or business or as a personal investment. The amount of the loss is determined by subtracting the cash surrender value from the taxpayer's basis for the contract. His basis is gross premium cost less all amounts previously received tax-free under the contract (e.g., any excludable dividends and the excludable portion of any prior annuity payments). The loss is ordinary loss, not capital loss. Rev. Rul. 61- 201, 1961-2 CB 46; *Cohan v. Comm.*, 39 F.2d 540 (2nd Cir. 1930), *aff'g*, 11 BTA 743. But if the taxpayer purchased the contract for purely personal reasons, and not for profit, no loss deduction will be allowed. For example, in one case, the taxpayer purchased annuities on the lives of relatives, giving the relatives ownership of the contracts. Later he acquired the contracts by gift and surrendered them at a loss. The court disallowed a loss deduction on the ground that the contracts were not bought for profit but to provide financial security for the relatives. *Early v. Atkinson*, 175 F.2d 118 (4th Cir. 1949)."[39]

How is this loss claimed on taxpayer's income tax return? There is some dispute as to the correct method for claiming the loss. "Some say that the loss should be treated as a miscellaneous itemized deduction that is not subject to the 2% floor on miscellaneous itemized deductions. Others, including some at the Internal Revenue Service in unofficial comments, say it is a miscellaneous itemized deduction subject to the 2% floor. And finally, others take a more aggressive approach and say that the loss can be taken on the front of the Form 1040 on the line labeled 'other gains or (losses)'."[40]

The authors believe that the proper place to take this deduction is as a miscellaneous itemized deduction subject to the 2% floor in light of Section 67(b), which states that all deductions are miscellaneous itemized deductions unless specifically listed in Sections 67(b)(1) through Sections 67(b)(12)—and deferred annuities surrendered at a loss are not so enumerated. Section 67(b) was designed as a catch-all category for, quite literally, any miscellaneous itemized deductions not specified by the tax code to be taken elsewhere, and accordingly it appears appropriate to claim annuity losses there. Notably, as of 2011, the IRS updated Publication 575 to indicate that nonqualified annuity losses should be taken in this manner; regrettably, though, the IRS has not yet provided any binding guidance on the issue.

Unfortunately, this is clearly not the most favorable treatment, due to the application of the 2% of AGI floor on itemized deductions, the requirement for itemized deductions to exceed the threshold of the standard deduction, the phaseout of itemized deductions for high-income taxpayers—currently repealed but scheduled to return in 2013—and, most significantly, the adjustment (loss) of miscellaneous itemized deductions for the purposes of Alternative Minimum Tax under Section 55(b)(1)(A)(i). Nonetheless, at this point a more favorable treatment of annuity losses would require an Act of Congress to change or adopt a more favorable provision in the tax code.

Tax Treatment of Hybrid Annuity/Long-Term Care Policies

Under the Pension Protection Act of 2006, Congress established provisions for the favorable tax treatment of a hybrid annuity/long-term care insurance policy (and also hybrid life insurance/long-term care policies).[41]

Effective on January 1, 2010, the new rules stipulated that when an annuity policy also provides long-term care insurance benefits, the long-term care policy will be treated as a separate contract for tax purposes; accordingly, any benefits payments from the long-term care portion of the policy will be received tax-free, not as taxable distribution from the annuity.[42] In addition, any premiums extracted from the annuity policy for long-term care coverage will not be treated as a taxable distribution from the annuity; instead, the cost basis of the annuity will be adjusted downwards (but not below $0) for any long-term care premiums.[43] However, no medical expense deduction will be allowed for long-term care premiums extracted directly from the cash value of the hybrid annuity. Notably, this treatment—which effectively treats all long-term care insurance premiums as being paid with after-tax dollars (the cost basis of the annuity)—can actually be less favorable on an ongoing basis than simply paying premiums with outside dollars and claiming any available Federal or state long-term care insurance premium deductions or credits. Although, for some taxpayers ineligible for such deductions or credits due to income, this aspect of tax treatment is a moot point. On the other hand, hybrid annuity/long-term care policies may still be preferred for their underwriting flexibility and partial-self-insurance benefits features, regardless of tax treatment.

The new rules apply only to nonqualified annuities[44] (i.e., not annuities held inside of a retirement account).

Exchanges of and for Annuities

Under IRC Section 1035, "no gain or loss shall be recognized on the exchange of" a life insurance policy for an annuity[45] or an annuity contract for another annuity contract,[46] under the so-called like-kind exchange rules. Instead, the acquired annuity receives a carryover basis from the surrendered insurance or annuity policy.[47] It is notable that an exchange of an annuity policy for a life insurance policy is not eligible for 1035 exchange treatment,[48] although the reverse transaction is.

Where a policy is exchanged not solely in kind, and is instead exchanged for another policy of lesser value, and the owner also receives cash or other property to boot, this causes recognition of taxable gain for the lesser of the amount of boot received or unrecognized gain.[49] However, if the owner has exchanged an annuity at a loss, the receipt of boot does not cause the loss to be recognized.[50] If an annuity meets the provisions of Section 1035, then no loss will be recognized, and the receipt of boot cannot change this. In addition, it is notable that application of Section 1035 is mandatory when its provisions are met—it is not an election, but is instead an automatic provision that applies when its stipulations are satisfied.

When a life insurance policy with a loan is exchanged for an annuity, the extinguishing of the loan with the proceeds of the insurance policy is considered to be the receipt of boot to the extent of the loan. Consequently, gain recognition will occur for the lesser of boot received (loan extinguished) or gain in the contract. Unfortunately, while transfer of the loan to an acquired life insurance contract will allow the insurance policy owner to avoid boot treatment,[51] this option is not available for an annuity, because a loan against an annuity is considered a withdrawal.[52]

Over the years, the IRS has clarified its views on what does and does not constitute a 1035 exchange through a series of revenue rulings, and to some extent through private letter rulings. Thus, the IRS has declared that a surrender and immediate subsequent purchase of an annuity does not qualify as a 1035 exchange if the taxpayer ever has control of the proceeds of the initial annuity.[53] However, a taxpayer can exchange an annuity into an existing annuity,[54] can combine multiple policies into a single annuity,[55] or can exchange a policy plus cash to a receiving annuity[56] The receipt of cash in an exchange can be taxable boot, but the addition of cash to the exchange is not boot.

Under the new rules for hybrid annuity/long-term care insurance policies, Congress expanded Section 1035 to explicitly allow the exchange of a traditional annuity for a hybrid annuity/long-term care policy on a tax-deferred basis.[57] In addition, the new rules also allow for the direct tax-free exchange of an annuity policy for a qualified long-term care insurance policy.[58]

For many years, there was question about whether a taxpayer could complete a partial 1035 exchange, where a partial surrender from an annuity is exchanged for a new annuity contract while the remaining cash value stays in the existing, original policy. The IRS fought transactions of this nature for fear that taxpayers would use it as a tax avoidance scheme, where a partial exchange is completed and the new annuity is subsequently surrendered for a smaller recognized taxable gain than would have occurred if the original annuity contract had been partially surrendered. However, after losing a partial 1035 exchange case in court,[59] the IRS finally acquiesced to allow partial 1035 exchanges.[60]

Under current final rules issued in 2008, as updated by Revenue Procedure 2011-38, partial 1035 exchanges are allowed as long as the taxpayer does not take any withdrawals from either contract (the old or the new one) within 180 days of the partial exchange.[61] When a partial 1035 exchange is completed, the basis is divided pro rata between the old contract and the new one based on the relative value of the contracts when the split occurred. If a withdrawal does occur from either contract within the 180-day period, it will be taxed "in a manner consistent with its substance, based on general tax principles and all the facts and circumstances," generally as either boot received (from the original contract) and/or as a distribution.[62] A partial exchange of an existing deferred annuity into an immediate annuity is guaranteed to be treated as a tax-deferred 1035 exchange, as long as the immediate annuity is payable for a period of at least 10 years or for the lifetime(s) of the annuitant.[63] Notably, a prior rule in the temporary guidance issued in 2003, requiring that the taxpayer should not have contemplated inappropriate withdrawals at the time of the partial exchange, is not present in the final rules, nor is the rule from the 2008 guidance that stipulated an early withdrawal, within the 180 day period, can be excused if made for certain specified reasons (e.g., due to death, disability, divorce, or loss of employment).

Annuity contributions generally retain their original character after a Section 1035 exchange. Consequently, a contract with pre-August 13, 1982 contributions will retain treatment of those contributions even if the contract is subsequently exchanged via Section 1035[64] (see prior discussion of contracts entered into before August 13, 1982). Note, however, that a contract with pre-October 21, 1979 contributions will not retain the step-up in basis treatment at the death of the owner.[65] However, this tracing of the original contract contributions has its drawbacks: when a deferred annuity is exchanged for an immediate annuity, the original contribution date holds as the purchase date for the immediate annuity, and if not within one year of original purchase, the immediate annuity will not qualify for Section 72(q)(2)(I) provisions for the avoidance of the early withdrawal penalty.

A planning technique sometimes recommended by aggressive planners involves the harvesting of an otherwise nondeductible loss in a life insurance policy by using a tax-free exchange of that policy, under IRC Section1035, for a deferred annuity having no surrender charges, and subsequent surrender of that annuity, which will have acquired the substituted cost basis of the exchanged life policy, for an allegedly deductible loss. In the authors' opinion, the success of this strategy is questionable if the annuity is surrendered shortly after the exchange. The IRS may well regard this as a step transaction and disallow the loss deduction, holding that the substance of the transaction—the surrender of the original life insurance policy—holds over the form of the transaction, the apparent surrender of an annuity policy. In addition, there is some risk that the IRS will adjust the cost basis of life insurance in such situations by reducing it for prior cost of insurance charges, dramatically diminishing or eliminating any losses, as applies when a life insurance policy is sold to an unrelated person or otherwise disposed of, especially for a loss.[66]

Gift or Sale of an Annuity

If the owner of an annuity transfers that annuity, by sale, to another taxpayer, there may be both gift tax and income tax consequences. Annuities may also be transferred by gift. Although gifts are not subject to income tax, they may be subject to federal and/or state gift tax.

Gift of a Deferred Annuity

An individual who transfers an annuity contract issued after April 22, 1987, for less than full and adequate consideration, is treated as having received as an amount not received as annuity an amount equal to the excess of the cash surrender value of the contract at the time of transfer over the investment in the contract at that time.[67] Thus, the transferor realizes, in the year of the transfer, any gain on the contract. The transferee's cost basis will be the donor's adjusted cost in light of the tax recognition event, plus the donee's cost (if any), adjusted for, or increased by any gift tax actually paid.

An exception regarding the timing of income recognition applies if the contract was entered into prior to April 23, 1987; in such cases, the gain is not recognized by the donor until it is surrendered by the donee, although it is still the donor that recognizes the gain.[68] In this case, the subsequent gain after the transfer date would be taxable to the donee; only the embedded gain as of the transfer date is taxable back to the original donor. If there is a partial surrender by the donee of a pre-April 23, 1987 contract, there is no current guidance about how to apportion the gain recognition between the pre-transfer amount allocable to the donor and the post-transfer amount allocable to the donee. Nonetheless, the normal rules to determine the taxable gain for amounts not received as an annuity still apply, including the gains-first standard rule, and also the opportunity to harvest pre-August 13, 1982, cost basis first.

If the receiving donee is a charity, then a charitable deduction will also be available. For a post-April 22, 1987 annuity, the full value of the contract will be eligible for a charitable deduction,[69] but only because the full amount of the gain is recognized on the transfer. Thus, the value of the charitable deduction has been effectively reduced by the amount of gain that was also recognized on the transfer. In the case of a pre-April 23, 1987 annuity, where the donation is for ordinary income property and there is no income recognition at the time of transfer—because the gain is delayed until the donee surrenders the contract—the charitable deduction allowed will be limited to the cost basis of the contract as a donation of ordinary income property.[70] Notably, if the charity surrenders the gifted contract in the year received, the net result is equivalent under either treatment. In addition, when property is donated with a fair market value which is less than the cost basis (i.e., property at a loss) the amount of the gift is restricted to the fair market value of the property.[71]

So the bottom line is that the taxation of any gain in an annuity contract cannot be avoided or shifted to another party via a gift. The gain will still be fully recognized by the donor. At best, the timing of that gain recognition may be delayed, depending on when the contract was issued, and when the donee ultimately surrenders the contract. Consequently, it will virtually always be best to surrender an annuity first and then donate it, allowing the donor to recognize the annuity loss, or recognize the gain but ensure that the charitable deduction will be for the fair market value of the contract. In most cases, though, this usually means that it's in the client's best interests to donate some other kind of appreciated property instead for various estate or charitable planning purposes in the first place!

There are some exceptions to the gratuitous transfer rules, though. This rule does not apply to transfers between spouses or between former spouses incident to a divorce and pursuant to an instrument executed or modified after July 18, 1984.[72] In addition, "the IRS has ruled privately that the distribution of an annuity contract by a trust to a trust beneficiary will not be treated as an assignment for less than full and adequate consideration (i.e., a gift) since, for purposes of this rule, the trust is not considered to be an individual."[73]

Sale of a Deferred Annuity

The naming of a new owner of an annuity in exchange for full and adequate consideration is a sale of the annuity. The seller must recognize any gain as ordinary income.[74] However, there is no clear case law, statute, or regulations regarding the tax treatment of an annuity sale where the sale price exceeds the surrender value of the contract.[75]

In the case of a deferred annuity, the best analogous treatment may be the taxation of life insurance to a third party, which is currently treated as ordinary income to the extent of existing gain in the contract, and capital gains for any excess amount realized above the cash surrender value of the annuity.[76]

The treatment of the sale of a deferred annuity for a loss remains unclear. Some have theorized that it is still subject to the existing treatment for a loss when an annuity is surrendered (i.e., miscellaneous itemized deduction subject to the 2%-of-AGI floor), while others suggest that perhaps ordinary loss or even capital loss treatment would be more appropriate; the IRS has thus far remained silent on the issue.

In the case of an immediate annuity (i.e., where the contract is sold after maturity), "the cost basis of the contract, for purposes of computing the seller's gain, must be reduced by the aggregate excludable portions of the annuity payments that have been received. But the adjusted cost basis cannot be reduced below zero, for example, where the annuitant has outlived his life expectancy and was able to exclude amounts in excess of his net premium cost on a contract that was annuitized prior to January 1, 1987.[77] The taxable gain can never be greater than the sale price. Where an [immediate] annuity contract is sold for less than its cost basis, apparently the seller realizes an ordinary loss."[78]

Transfers of Annuities to Trusts

Generally speaking, the transfer of ownership of an annuity is a taxable event for both income tax and gift tax purposes, as discussed above. When ownership of an annuity is transferred to a trust, though, the tax consequences depend upon the nature of the trust.

1. The transfer of an annuity from an owner to the owner's revocable trust is not a taxable event for income or gift tax purposes, assuming that the trust is fully revocable and, thus, does not represent a completed gift or a change in ownership.[79]

2. The transfer of an annuity from an owner to the owner's irrevocable grantor trust is a problematic situation under the existing guidance on annuities. Although some would assert that the transfer should not be a taxable event for income tax purposes, because the trust is a grantor trust, the contribution of an annuity may be a taxable gift, since the gift is irrevocably completed. To the extent that the recognition of gain for an annuity transfer occurs anytime there is a "transfer without full and adequate consideration,"[80] and a contribution to an irrevocable grantor trust as a taxable gift without consideration, it thus appears to constitute a transfer without consideration. The authors believe that there is a risk that a transfer to an irrevocable grantor trust may still result in the recognition of gain when the transfer occurs, notwithstanding the trust's grantor status. In addition, to the extent that gain is triggered by any annuity not for full and adequate consideration, even a partial transfer with retained rights that represents an incomplete gift may still trigger income tax recognition as a transfer. As of the publication of the third edition of this book, the IRS has still not issued definitive guidance on this issue. See treatment of this issue in Chapter 8, Annuities and Trusts.

3. The transfer of an annuity from an owner to the owner's irrevocable nongrantor trust will trigger recognition of policy gain, because the transfer is without adequate consideration and the owner of the trust for income tax purposes is unambiguously someone other than the grantor, by virtue of the trust not being a grantor trust.[81] In

addition, such transfers should be conducted cautiously, because if the transferee trust does not qualify as the agent of a natural person, the contract will no longer qualify as an annuity for income tax purposes,[82] and any income on the contract will be treated as taxable ordinary income to the trust owner,[83] in addition to the income tax gain recognition upon the transfer itself to the original owner. Moreover, the full value of the annuity will be considered a taxable gift for gift tax purposes, less the annual exclusion amount, if applicable.

Annuities Held within IRAs

An annuity held in an individual retirement account (IRA)—a so-called qualified annuity— is taxed first and foremost under the rules applicable to retirement accounts; the general rules applicable to annuities under Section 72 do not apply. In this context, the annuity held within an IRA is simply an asset the IRA owns in a manner not unlike the IRA's ownership of a stock or bond.

However, due to perceived abuses where annuities have been held inside of IRAs as a method to avoid income taxation, the IRS and Treasury have altered the method by which annuities are valued for certain IRA taxable events in an effort to crack down on inappropriate tax avoidance strategies. As a result, special rules apply to the valuation of annuities held inside of IRAs for the purpose of both the calculation of required minimum distributions from annuities, and also when an IRA Roth conversion includes an annuity.

Required Minimum Distributions for IRA Annuities

When an annuity is held by an IRA, the annuity continues to be taxed under the rules applicable to IRAs; as a result, the IRA annuity will be subject to required minimum distributions under the normally applicable rules for IRA owners.

In calculating a required minimum distribution, the general rule requires IRA owners to divide the value of the entire interest of the IRA by the applicable distribution period. However, in the case of an IRA owned annuity, the value of the entire interest must include both the actual dollar value of the contract, and the actuarial present value of any additional benefits, measured without regard to the individual's actual health.[84]

This requirement to include the actuarial present value of additional benefits is directed primarily towards the death and living benefit riders associated with today's variable annuity contracts. The concern of the Treasury was that in some situations, the fair market value of the annuity recognizing the value of additional benefits could be significantly higher than the actual dollar value of the annuity, producing a disparity that would result in an artificially reduced withdrawal for required minimum distribution purposes. For example, an annuity having a cash value of $300,000, but a current death benefit of $500,000, would arguably be worth something more than just $300,000 for an 88-year-old annuity owner. Under the new rules, the actuarial value of the excess $200,000 of pending death benefit would increase the total value of the account to something more than $300,000, and that higher value must be used to calculate the year's required minimum distribution.

To simplify the application of this rule slightly, the Treasury regulations do provide that if the value of any additional benefits are reduced on a pro-rata basis in the event of withdrawals, and the actuarial present value would add less than 20% to the value of the annuity, then the value of the additional benefits may be disregarded, and the entire interest will simply be treated as the actual dollar value of the contract.[85] In addition, if the only additional benefit is a return of premium death benefit guarantee, then the additional death benefit can be ignored for valuation purposes, regardless of the actuarial present value of that guarantee.[86]

Many contracts will be able to ignore the application of these new rules, because the value of additional benefits is not likely to add more than 20% to the value of the contract for relatively new contracts; but this exception still only applies to contracts where withdrawals will reduce the benefits on a pro-rata basis. Readers should be cautious on this issue, because many of today's additional benefit riders, particularly living benefit riders, do not exclusively offer pro-rata withdrawals. Many of these provide dollar-for-dollar withdrawals instead, or a hybrid treatment of partial dollar-for-dollar up to a specified amount followed by pro-rata withdrawals. In such cases, the entire amount of the actuarial present value must be included for required minimum distribution purposes. In most cases, annuity owners will need to contact the annuity company to obtain a valuation—incorporating the actuarial present value of rider benefits—for required minimum distribution purposes. On the other hand, it's important to note that the valuation of the annuity should only be its cash value plus the actuarial present value of its other benefits. Thus, an annuity with a cash value of $300,000 and a death benefit of $500,000 would have a value of $300,000 plus the cost of one-year term insurance for the remaining $200,000 death benefit based on the annuity owner's current age; it would not be appropriate to simply calculate the RMD based on the $500,000 gross death benefit amount.

In extreme cases, the requirement to incorporate the actuarial value of riders can actually cause a cash shortage for the annuity itself. In contracts where withdrawals reduce the death benefit on a dollar-for-dollar basis, some annuity owners have chosen to nearly exhaust the cash value of the contract, retaining only a death benefit. For example, if the owner of the aforementioned annuity with a $300,000 cash value and a $500,000 death benefit took a $299,000 withdrawal, the remaining annuity would have a $1,000 cash value and a $201,000 death benefit, anticipating that a required minimum distribution would only withdraw a fraction of the $1,000 death benefit. However, if the age of the annuity owner is high enough, such that the actuarial present value of the annuity increases significantly, it may even be possible that the required minimum distribution based on the actuarial value would be higher than the entire $1,000 cash value! In this case, the IRA owner may wish to take a withdrawal from another IRA to satisfy the required minimum distribution, since ultimately, all required minimum distributions and their tax consequences may be aggregated amongst IRAs.[87] However, if no other IRAs remain, the annuity owner may be forced to liquidate the entire annuity contract simply to extract the required minimum distribution, forfeiting the entire death benefit in the process.

Roth Conversions for IRA Annuities

Where an IRA annuity is converted to a Roth, the fair market value of the annuity must be included in income for the purposes of the Roth conversion.[88] In the case of a Roth conversion, similar rules to those applicable for determining required minimum distributions must be applied to ensure that the annuity contract is fairly valued.

In final Treasury regulations issued in the summer of 2008, the Treasury indicated three allowable methods to determine the fair market value of an IRA annuity for Roth conversion purposes. These methods are:

- *Comparable Contract.* Where the insurance company currently offers annuity contracts similar to the contract owned in the IRA, the fair market value of the annuity is the cost to acquire a comparable contract from the insurer at the annuity owner's current age under market conditions available at the time. If the conversion occurs soon after the annuity is sold, a comparable contract value may simply be the premiums paid for the existing annuity.[89]

- *Reserve Method.* Where there is no comparable contract currently available in the marketplace to provide a cost comparison for valuation purposes, the fair market value may be determined based on the interpolated terminal reserve held by the annuity company on the date of the conversion, plus the proportionate part of the gross premium last paid if that premium covers a period extending beyond the conversion date.[90]

- *Accumulation Method.* As an alternative to the aforementioned methods, the taxpayer may value the annuity using the same rules applicable for determining value under the required minimum distribution rules discussed earlier. In this case, the annuity's fair market value is equal to the actual dollar value of the contract, plus the actuarial present value of any additional benefits. However, in the case of a Roth conversion valuation, the actuarial present value of all additional benefits must be included, and even a de minimis value cannot be disregarded. Furthermore, no distributions can be assumed in the process of determining the actuarial present value of benefits. Finally, any front-end loads or other non-recurring charges assessed in the 12 months preceding the conversion must also be added back into the value.[91]

In practice, most taxpayers holding deferred annuities inside of an IRA will use the third method—the accumulation method—as it is the easiest match for today's IRA annuities, especially variable annuities with various living and death benefit riders. Notably, though, the Treasury Regulations state that "if, because of the unusual nature of the contract, the value determined under [one of these methods] does not reflect the full value of the contract, that method may not be used."[92]

If the annuity contract is surrendered pursuant to the Roth conversion rollover itself, the fair market value for tax purposes will be considered to be the cash surrender value of the annuity (i.e., the net amount actually transferred), assuming no rights of the annuity are retained.[93]

The purpose of these rules is to eliminate any possibility that an IRA annuity owner can attempt to evade income taxation by artificially reducing the value of an annuity at the time of Roth conversion given that subsequent qualified withdrawals from the Roth IRA would also be tax-free.

Endnotes

1. Technically, qualified annuity refers only to an annuity purchased to fund a qualified retirement plan offered by a participant's employer, such as a pension or profit sharing plan, 403(b) plan, SEPP, etc. An IRA (either traditional or Roth) is not a qualified plan, in the strict sense of that term. However, many, but not all, of the rules governing IRAs are similar to—and in some cases, identical to—those governing qualified plans, such as the required minimum distribution rules (RMD rules of Section 401(a)(9), and very different from the rules governing ordinary savings plans, so that the terms qualified annuity and qualified money (to describe money held in a qualified plan) are commonly used in reference to an annuity purchased to fund a qualified plan or an IRA.

2. *Tax Facts on Insurance & Employee Benefits* (The National Underwriter Company, 2012), Q 353.

3. *Ibid.*

4. IRC Sec. 72(b); Treas. Reg. §1.72-3.

5. Treas. Reg. §1.72-2(b)(3).

6. IRC Sec. 72(b)(2).

7. IRC Sec. 72(e)(1)(B); *Tax Facts on Insurance & Employee Benefits* (The National Underwriter Company, 2012), Q 355.

8. *Tax Facts on Insurance & Employee Benefits* (The National Underwriter Company, 2012), Q 355.

9. *Tax Facts on Insurance & Employee Benefits* (The National Underwriter Company, 2012), Q 355; IRC Sec. 72(e)(3).

10. IRC Sec. 72(e)(4)(A).

11. IRC Sec. 72(e)(11).

12. *Tax Facts on Insurance & Employee Benefits* (The National Underwriter Company, 2012), Q 355; IRC Sec. 72(e)(5).

13. IRC Secs. 72(e)(2)(B) and 72(e)(3)(A).

14. IRC Secs. 72(e)(5)(E) and 72(e)(5)(A).

15. IRC Sec. 72(e)(5)(A)(ii).

16. It is worth stating, again, that the word "deferred," in the term "deferred annuity" does not refer to the tax treatment just described, but to the fact that annuity income will not commence immediately upon purchase of the contract, but will instead be deferred until some point in the future. Some deferred annuities impose a limit upon deferral by mandating that annuity payments commence no later than at annuitant's attainment of a certain age.

17. IRC Sec. 72(u)(1)(A).

18. Income on the contract is the excess of (1) the sum of the net surrender value of the contract at the end of the taxable year and any amounts distributed under the contract during the taxable year and any prior taxable year over (2) the sum of the net premiums (amount of premiums paid under the contract reduced by any policyholder dividends) under the contract for the taxable year and prior taxable years and any amounts includable in gross income for prior taxable years under this requirement. IRC Sec. 72(u)(2)." *Tax Facts on Insurance & Employee Benefits* (The National Underwriter Company, 2012), Q 354.

19. IRC Sec. 72(u)(1)(B).

20. IRC Sec. 72(u)(3).

21. A qualified funding asset is any annuity contract issued by a licensed insurance company that is purchased and held to fund periodic payments for damages, by suit or agreement, on account of personal physical injury or sickness. IRC Sec. 130(d).

22. *Tax Facts on Insurance & Employee Benefits* (The National Underwriter Company, 2012), Q 354.

23. Let. Rul. 199944020.

24. *Ibid.*

25. The authors' descriptions of the Section 72(q)(2) exceptions have been abbreviated for clarity. For more detailed descriptions, see *Tax Facts on Insurance & Employee Benefits* (The National Underwriter Company, 2012), Q 356.

26. In the authors' opinion, "Taxpayer," here, refers to the taxpayer responsible for paying the tax on a distribution. If A, age 81, owns an annuity of which B, age 55, is annuitant, and requests a withdrawal, that withdrawal is not subject to the 10% penalty because A, as owner of the contract, is liable for tax on the distribution, even if the distribution is made directly to B, at A's direction.

27. "Disabled" is defined in Section 72(m)(7), which states: "[F]or purposes of this section, an individual shall be considered to be disabled if he is unable to engage in any substantial gainful activity by reason of any medically determinable physical or mental impairment which can be expected to result in death or to be of long-continued and indefinite duration. An individual shall not be considered to be disabled unless he furnishes proof of the existence thereof in such form and manner as the Secretary may require."

28. Under IRS Notice 2004-15, 2004-9 IRB 526, taxpayers seeking substantially equal periodic payments from annuities under Section 72(q)(2)(D), may rely on the guidance of IRS Notice 89-25 1989-1 CB 662, as modified by Revenue Ruling 2002-62, 2002-2 CB 710, which provides explanation and rules regarding substantially equal periodic payments from retirement accounts under Section 72(t).

29. This provision is actually somewhat redundant. Section 72(q)(1) already indicates that the penalty will apply only to amounts includable in gross income, and Section 72(e)(5) already indicates that withdrawals allocable to investment in the contract before August 14th, 1982 will not be included in income (and thus could not be subject to penalty).

30. This prevents the imposition of a Section 72(q)(1) early withdrawal penalty on a qualified annuity that is already subject to the early withdrawal penalty rules under Section 72(t).

31. Rev. Rul. 92-95, 1992-2 C.B. 43.

32. Section 72(u)(4)(B) requires the annuity starting date to be no later than 1 year from the date of purchase to qualify as an immediate annuity—when the purchase date of the original contract must be applied under Revenue Ruling 92-95, it will almost always be beyond the 1-year period.

33. Treasury General Information Letter, issued June 29, 2001.

34. IRC Secs. 72(q)(2)(B), 72(s)(6).

35. Let. Ruls. 9204010, 9204014, and 199905015.

36. Underwood, J. Gary, "Trust Ownership of Nonqualified Annuities: General Consideration for Trustees", *Journal of Financial Service Professionals*, May, 2010. See also Treasury Regulation 1.652(b)-1 and H R Report No 99-841 (TRA 1986).

37. IRC Sec. 72(u).

38. IRC Sec. 165.

39. *Tax Facts on Insurance & Employee Benefits* (The National Underwriter Company, 2012), Q 379.

40. *Ibid.*

41. Section 844 of Pension Protection Act of 2006.

42. IRC Section 7702B(e)(1),

43. IRC Section 72(e)(11).

44. IRC Section 7702B(e)(4).

45. IRC Sec. 1035(a)(1).

46. IRC Sec. 1035(a)(3).

47. IRC Secs. 1035(d)(2), 1031(d).

48. Treas. Reg. §1.1035-1(c).

49. IRC Secs. 1035(d)(1), 1031(b).

50. IRC Secs. 1035(d)(1), 1031(c).

51. Let. Ruls. 8604033, 9044022.

52. IRC Sec. 72(e)(4)(A).

53. Let. Ruls. 8515063, 8810010.

54. Rev. Rul. 2002-75, 2002-2 CB 812.

55. Let. Rul. 9708016.

56. Let. Rul. 9820018.

57. IRC Section 1035(b)(2).

58. IRC Section 1035(a)(3).

59. *Conway v. Comm.*, 111 TC 330 (1998).

60. See Rev. Rul. 2003-76, 2003-2 CB 355.

61. See Rev. Proc 2008-24, 2008-13 IRB 684, *superseding*, IRS Notice 2003-51, 2003-2 CB 362, Sec. 4.01.

62. Rev Proc 2011-38, Section 2.09 & 4.01.

63. Rev Proc 2011-38, Section 2.07, 2.09, and also Section 2113 of the Small Business jobs Act of 2010.

64. Rev. Rul. 85-159, 1985-2 CB 29.

65. See Rev. Rul. 79-335, 1979-2 CB 292, Let. Rul. 9245035, and TAM 9346002.

66. Revenue Ruling 2009-13; also, Keystone Consolidated Publishing Co (1932) 26 BTA 1210 and Century Wood Preserving Co v. Commission (1934, CA3) 13 AFTR 910.

67. IRC Sec. 72(e)(4)(C).

68. Revenue Ruling 69-102.

69. Treas. Reg. 1.170A-4(a).

70. IRC Section 170(e)(1)(A).

71. Treas. Reg. §1.170A-1(c)(1).

72. IRC Sec. 72(e)(4)(c)(ii).

73. PLRs 9204010, 9204014, 199905015, and 201124008.

74. *First Nat'l Bank of Kansas City v. Comm.*, 309 F.2d 587 (8th Cir. 1962) *aff'g*,*Katz v. Comm.*, TC Memo 1961-270; *Roff v. Comm.*, 304 F.2d 450 (3rd Cir. 1962) *aff'g*, 36 TC 818; *Arnfeld v. U.S.*, 163 F. Supp. 865 (Ct. Cl. 1958), *cert. denied*, 359 U.S. 943.

75. For example, assume an annuity with a $50,000 cost basis and a $75,000 surrender value were sold for $85,000. Perhaps this is because it provides a contractual interest rate guarantee that is more appealing than current market rates. Clearly the $25,000 gain from cost basis to surrender value must be taxed as ordinary income; however, it is not clear whether the additional $10,000 of gain would be taxed as though it were an amount not received as an annuity (i.e., ordinary income treatment), or the sale of the entire annuity contract as though it were a capital assets (i.e., capital gain treatment).

76. Revenue Ruling 2009-13.

77. Treas. Reg. §1.1021-1; *Tax Facts on Insurance & Employee Benefits* (The National Underwriter Company, 2012), Q 381.

78. IRC Secs. 671 - 677.

79. Treas. Reg. §25.2511-2(c).

80. IRC Sec. 72(e)(4)(C)

81. IRC Sec. 72(u)(1).

82. IRC Sec. 72(u)(1)(B).

83. IRC Sec. 2503(b).

84. Treas. Reg. §1.401(a)(9)-6, Q&A-12(a) & (b).

85. Treas. Reg. §1.401(a)(9)-6, Q&A-12(c)(1).

86. Treas. Reg. §1.401(a)(9)-6, Q&A-12(c)(2).

87. IRC Section 408(d)(2).

88. Treas. Reg. §1.408A-4, Q&A-14(a).

89. Treas. Reg. §1.408A-4, Q&A-14(b)(2)(i).

90. Treas. Reg. §1.408A-4, Q&A-14(b)(2)(ii).

91. Treas. Reg. §1.408A-4, Q&A-14(b)(2)(iii).

92. Treas. Reg. 1.408A-4, Q&A-14(b)(1).

93. Treas. Reg. §1.408A-4, Q&A-14(a)(2).

Chapter 3

Taxation of Annuity Death Benefits

The taxation of death benefits of nonqualified annuities is a particularly difficult subject for many advisors. Most of the difficulty lies not in whether or how such proceeds are taxable, but in when and how they must be paid out to beneficiaries. The rules governing required payouts upon death are complicated and sometimes unclear. In at least one important area, when and how a nonspousal beneficiary of a deferred annuity must take death proceeds, the rules in the Internal Revenue Code appear to be contradictory (see the section entitled "What About 72(h),"). Fortunately, not all of the rules are this difficult. We will begin our examination with the easier stuff—the relatively straightforward rules of how death proceeds of nonqualified annuities are treated for estate tax purposes.

Estate Taxation

If the value of an annuity contract does not terminate entirely upon the death of the contract owner, leaving nothing to pass to the owner's estate or beneficiaries, any remaining value is taxable in the owner's estate for estate tax purposes.[1] Whether any value remains depends upon whether the contract is, at the time of owner's death, in payout status or not, and, if so, the terms of the payout arrangement. An annuity is said to be in payout status on or after its annuity starting date[2] – i.e., if it is either an immediate annuity or a deferred annuity that has been annuitized.

Estate Taxation of Annuities in Payout Status

What is the estate tax value of an annuity in payout status? This depends upon the payout arrangement. Let's examine each of the five possibilities:

1. If the decedent was receiving a life only annuity,[3] payments ceased with her death; thus, no property interest remains to be included in her gross estate.[4]

2. If the decedent was receiving a life annuity with a refund feature that was still operative, the value of that refund feature is includible in the decedent's gross estate.

    Example A: Decedent elected to take a life annuity, payable monthly, with a 10-year (120 month) certain refund feature,[5] commencing on June 1, 2003. She died in May, 2012, after receiving 108 monthly payments. Twelve additional payments were due under the refund feature. The value of these payments, to be included in the decedent's estate, is what the insurance company issuing the annuity would charge for a contract paying a comparable annuity—12 payments of the specified monthly amount.[6] Value at date of death is used, even where the executor elects alternate valuation.[7]

    Example B: Decedent elected a life annuity with a cash refund feature. If annuity payments received by her, during her lifetime, were less than the value of the cash refund.[8] The value includible in the decedent's estate is presumably the amount received by the beneficiary.

3. If the decedent was receiving a life annuity with a refund feature that had expired, payments ceased with her death; thus, no property interest remains to be included in her gross estate.

    Example: Decedent elected to take a life annuity, payable monthly, with a 10-year certain refund feature,[9] commencing on June 1, 2002. She died in August, 2012, after receiving 123 monthly payments. As the number of payments guaranteed in the refund feature had been received by the decedent during her lifetime, the refund feature had been satisfied. No payments were due to any beneficiary, and no value remained to be includible in the decedent's estate.

4. If the decedent was receiving, and was the owner of, a Joint and Survivor Annuity, the value of the survivor's annuity is "the amount the same insurance company would charge the survivor for a single life annuity [for equivalent payments for life] as of the date of the first annuitant's death."[10] The amount includible in the decedent's estate depends on who paid for the annuity and whether the joint annuitants were husband and wife. If the deceased owner-annuitant, in a nonmarried situation, contributed the entire purchase price, the full value of the survivor's annuity is includible in the deceased's estate. If not, the annuity is includible in the decedent owner's estate only

to the extent of his or her contribution.[11] If the annuity was paid for entirely by the surviving annuitant, its value is not includible in the deceased annuitant's estate.[12] If the joint annuitants were husband and wife, 50% of the valuation amount is presumed to be contributed by the decedent and attributable to his/her estate, although it's not entirely clear whether the consideration furnished standard of Section 2039 may trump the presumed 50%/50% split of Section 2040.[13]

5. If the decedent was receiving a Period Certain Annuity, the value of the remaining payments includible in the decedent's estate is what the same insurance company would charge for a Period Certain Annuity for the number of payments remaining.[14]

It is worth noting that in some situations, interest rates or even mortality tables may have changed from original annuity issuance to the date of decedent's death. Consequently, the valuation of the survivor's portion of the annuity could be substantially more or less expensive than the pricing may have been at the original purchase date.

Estate Taxation of Annuities Not in Payout Status

A deferred annuity where the owner has not yet elected an annuity settlement option, or annuitization—where the owner dies before the annuity starting date—is not in payout status.[15] The death benefit of the annuity as of owner's death, including any death benefit enhancements that adjusted the value of the annuity due to the owner's death, is fully includible in the owner's estate, either under Section 2039 (which relates to the estate taxation of annuities) or under Section 2033, which relates to property which the decedent had an interest in, for estate tax purposes.

What if the owner is not the annuitant? The annuitant of a deferred annuity not in payout status generally has no property rights under the contract. The annuity is property, and both the income tax and estate tax liabilities are those of the owner. However, because the tax code, and many annuity contracts, may make reference to both the annuitant and the owner at various points, the tax rules can get very complicated, as we will see later on, where owner and annuitant are not the same individual.

Income Taxation of Death Benefits

Annuities in Payout Status: Immediate Annuities, and Deferred Annuities Where Holder Dies after Annuity Starting Date

Death proceeds of an immediate annuity or a deferred annuity that has been annuitized are governed by Section 72(s)(1)(A), which states that:

"[I]f any holder of such contract dies on or after the annuity starting date and before the entire interest in such contract has been distributed, the remaining portion of such interest will be distributed at least as rapidly as under the method of distributions being used as of the date of his death."

If the death proceeds—the remaining portion of such interest—are taken by the beneficiary either as a lump sum (e.g., by accelerating the remaining payments due at death) or in installments other than payments calculated by application of a new annuity option,[16] proceeds will be excludible from income until the total amount the beneficiary receives, when added to the amounts the annuitant received tax-free, is equal to the annuitant's investment in the contract, unadjusted for the value of the refund feature.[17] Amounts received by the beneficiary in excess of the investment in the contract are taxed as ordinary income. Note that this FIFO basis first treatment of beneficiary payments is different than the standard, income/gains first treatment of annuity withdrawals and different from the pro-rata exclusion ratio treatment of annuity payments made to the contract owner. This applies only when the annuitant of an annuitized deferred annuity died when a refund element provides for continuing annuity payments to a beneficiary and where that beneficiary elects to receive those continuing payments as the annuitant had been receiving them.

If the total payments thus made to beneficiary are less than the annuitant's investment in the contract and the annuitant's annuity starting date was after July 1, 1986, the beneficiary may take an income tax deduction for any such unrecovered investment once all payments have been received.[18]

Important Note: Whose Tax Is It, Anyway—Annuitant, Owner (Holder), Taxpayer?

Unfortunately, for those trying to make sense of annuity taxation, the relevant rules in the Internal Revenue Code and the Treasury regulations, as well as many reference sources that cite case law, often refer to annuitant when applying tax rules. The often confusing implication is that the owner and the annuitant are always the same individual and can be used interchangeably. This is generally a holdover from a time when all annuities were annuitant-driven—that is, an annuity paid a death benefit upon the death of the annuitant—and when tax law focused upon the annuitant, rather than the owner, which the Internal Revenue Code and Treasury regulations consistently refer to as the holder.

Where the annuitant and owner/holder are the same individual, there is no distinction to be made or inferred. However, where they are not, the rules—and the explanations of those rules in even the best reference sources—can be confusing. It is vital we remember that the tax liability for payments made from annuities, whether amounts received as an annuity or amounts not received as an annuity, are generally the tax responsibility of the contract owner if that owner is living—even if the payments are actually made to another individual such as a nonowner annuitant. However, if the payments are made to a beneficiary, by reason of the death of either the annuitant or owner, the tax liability is that of the beneficiary-payee.

Consider, for example, the following explanation from *Tax Facts on Insurance & Employee Benefits* (2012 edition), Q 370:

> "The beneficiary will have no taxable income unless the total amount the beneficiary receives when added to amounts that were received tax-free by the annuitant (the excludable portion of the annuity payments) exceeds the investment in the contract."

Strictly speaking, that ought to read "…that were received tax-free by the annuitant, or contract owner, if the owner was not the annuitant." Similarly, an observation that "proceeds will be excludible from income until the total amount beneficiary receives, when added to the amounts annuitant received tax-free, equal annuitant's 'investment in the contract', unadjusted for the value of the refund feature" would be more accurate if stated as "proceeds will be excludible from income until the total amount beneficiary receives, when added to the amounts annuitant received without tax to the equal owner's 'investment in the contract owner.'"

However, such precision would very likely be a cure worse than the disease—increasing, rather than reducing, reader confusion. The authors merely wish to make clear that references such as annuitant's investment in the contract should be understood to mean owner's investment in the case where the owner and the annuitant are two different individuals.

Annuities Not In Payout Status: Deferred Annuities, Where the Holder Dies before the Annuity Starting Date

The income tax rules regarding death benefits of deferred annuities not in payment status constitute one of the most difficult and confusing areas of annuity planning. Most of this confusion lies not in how taxable amounts are determined—the excess of value over investment in the contract/cost basis—but in how and when death proceeds must be received by the beneficiary under tax law. To understand these required minimum distributions from deferred annuities after death, we must first understand when death proceeds are payable—that is, whose death triggers the payment of the proceeds. In all cases, though, any amounts included in income will be taxed as ordinary income.

An annuity is said to be annuitant-driven when payment of the death benefit to the beneficiary will be made upon the death of the annuitant. When the death benefit is payable to the beneficiary upon death of the owner, the annuity is said to be owner-driven.

One might think that any annuity contract is either one or the other, but it is not quite that simple. All deferred annuity contracts issued since January 18, 1985, are owner-driven, because no annuity contract issued since that date will be treated as an annuity contract for tax purposes unless it contains language requiring the force out provisions of Section 72(s).[19] That Code provision mandates distributions from annuity contracts upon the death of the holder.[20]

Section 72(s) is entitled "Required Distributions Where Holder Dies Before Entire Interest Is Distributed." It is a very important section that should be well understood by anyone selling or offering advice on the subject of annuities. Failure to understand the rules set out in this section can be hazardous to your career! If the owner, annuitant, and beneficiary designations of an annuity are made without a clear understanding of the rules discussed below, the result could be a required distribution of that annuity at a time and in a manner never intended or desired by the client.

Before getting into a detailed examination of Section 72(s), the authors want to make three observations about it. First, it is not nearly as simple or straightforward as it may appear. Second, it applies only when the holder of an annuity contract dies. Third, holder is an exceedingly slippery term. Generally speaking, it means the owner (i.e., the individual named as owner of the annuity contract). However, when an annuity is owned by a nonnatural entity such as a trust or corporation, the Code will deem the annuitant to be the holder, even if that individual is not the owner named in the contract.[21]

With those observations in mind, let's look at what Section 72(s)(1) says:

"In General. A contract shall not be treated as an annuity contract for purposes of this title [i.e. for income tax purposes] unless it provides that:

"(A) if any holder of such contract dies on or after the annuity starting date and before the entire interest in such contract has been distributed, the remaining portion of such interest will be distributed at least as rapidly as under the method of distributions being used as of the date of his death; and

(B) if any holder of such contract dies before the annuity starting date, the entire interest in such contract will be distributed within 5 years after the death of such holder."

We have seen the first rule (Section 72(s)(1)(A)) before in our discussion of the income tax treatment of annuities in payout status. This refers to immediate annuities and deferred annuities that have been annuitized.

The second rule in Section 72(s)(1)(B) is the default rule for annuities not in payout status (i.e. deferred annuities that have not been annuitized). It says that, upon the death of the holder, the proceeds of the annuity must be paid out within five years of holder's death. This rule applies unless an exception is available. The subsections that follow, Sections 72(s)(2) and 72(s)(3), provide the two allowable exceptions. Neither exception is available unless the annuity is payable to a designated beneficiary, which is defined by Section 72(s)(4) as "any individual designated a beneficiary by the holder of the contract."

The key word here is individual. An individual must be a natural person—a human being. A trust, for example, cannot be a designated beneficiary, because it is not an individual. It is important to note that, unlike recent new regulations regarding distributions from IRAs payable to trusts, there are no look-through provisions for trust beneficiaries of annuities; since the trust itself is not a natural person, it cannot be a designated beneficiary, even if the beneficiaries of the trusts are natural persons! Any beneficiary that is not a designated beneficiary, or a natural person is not entitled to either of the two exceptions we are about to discuss.

The first exception to the default five-year rule allows the designated beneficiary to take the proceeds over a period longer than five years. Section 72(s)(2) permits proceeds to be distributed "over the life of such designated beneficiary or over a period not extending beyond the life expectancy of such beneficiary." Note that it does not require that the beneficiary take proceeds over his or her remaining lifetime, but merely states that the distribution period cannot be longer than that. For instance, a period certain annuity payout (e.g. 20-Year Certain) is acceptable, provided that beneficiary's life expectancy is at least 20 years.

If an annuity option (e.g. a life annuity with or without a refund feature or a period certain annuity) is elected by the beneficiary, the payments will be taxed according to the regular annuity rules of Section 72(b)(1). "The exclusion ratio for the payments would be based on the deceased annuitant's [remaining] investment in the contract and the beneficiary's expected return. If life contingency is involved in the settlement arrangement, the beneficiary's life expectancy as of his or her annuity starting date would be used in computing expected return."[22]

If the insurance company that issued the annuity permits it, the beneficiary may also elect to take death proceeds in an arrangement often referred to as a stretch annuity. This arrangement, first permitted in Private Letter Ruling 200151038, allows the beneficiary to take proceeds by using a fractional method, whereby the amount of each payment would be determined by applying divisors from the Unified Table used for Required Minimum Distributions from IRAs and qualified plans. For younger beneficiaries, the required minimum payments thus calculated are substantially smaller in the earlier years than those that would be required under any life annuity or period certain option, allowing these beneficiaries to defer receiving a greater amount of proceeds to later years. As the gain in proceeds not yet received, or constructively received, is not yet taxable, this represents an opportunity for greater tax deferral. But how should each income payment to the beneficiary be taxed? Private Letter Ruling 200151038 is silent on this point, stating:

> "Specifically, no opinion is expressed on whether payments made to the designated beneficiary under the procedures described in Requested Rulings 1, 2, and 3, above (the optional distribution procedures), are amounts received as an annuity, taxable under Section 72(a) and (b), or amounts not received as annuity taxable under Section 72(e)."

However, a subsequent Letter Ruling, Private Letter Ruling 200313016, held that such payments, made in accordance with the life expectancy fraction method, will, to the extent that they do not exceed the amounts required by such calculation, qualify as amounts received as an annuity. Under such treatment, a portion of each annuity payment is excluded from tax, as a return of principal (see Chapter 2), which is more favorable that the standard gains first, to the exent of any gain treatment for withdrawals from deferred annuities.

However, a caveat should be noted with regard to this conclusion. After having elected one of three payout arrangements, of which one was the fractional method, the beneficiaries of the annuity issued by the insurance company that requested the ruling were allowed two additional options. Option 1 permitted the beneficiary to take, at any time, the entire remaining balance in a lump sum. Option 2 permitted additional partial withdrawals over and above those distributions required by the payout method. The ruling specifically stated that the result previously mentioned—that payments made to beneficiaries would be treated as amounts received as an annuity—applied only to beneficiaries who elect Option 1. The remaining balance is to be taken in a lump sum. No opinion is expressed regarding those who elect Option 2.

What can we say about the options that these rulings allow a beneficiary of a nonqualified annuity? First, we are obliged to note that these are only private letter rulings; consequently, they may not be relied upon by anyone other than the taxpayer to whom they were issued. Second, whether the IRS will consider fractional method annuity payments made to beneficiaries as amounts received as an annuity is moot if the issuer of the annuity will not permit such a payout arrangement. Some issuers do not permit this, as they cannot be certain that the PLR guidance will be allowable for their annuities and contract holders. It is essential that the advisor discussing this option be aware of whether the issuer of the annuity in question will permit it in the first place.

When it is permitted, the fractional method—essentially, a form of stretch annuity planning—can be extremely attractive. Many beneficiaries also select this option because it allows payments to occur across the lifetime of the beneficiary without actually requiring annuitization of the proceeds, which provides additional liquidity for beneficiaries that do not require the guarantees of annuitization, without forfeiting the tax deferral of keeping most of the money in the annuity until a future date. Furthermore, some annuity companies will allow the annuity owner, while still alive, to select a particular beneficiary payout period that the beneficiary must follow as part of the contractual annuity agreement, thus preventing the beneficiary from having fully liquid access to the proceeds at the owner's death, without necessitating the use of a trust. This may be attractive for some contract owners, especially given the lack of a stretch option for trusts as beneficiaries.

The second exception to the five-year rule of Section 72(s)(1) is available only to a beneficiary who is the surviving spouse of the holder. This exception, allowed under Section 72(s)(3), permits that surviving spouse-beneficiary to treat the decedent's annuity as her own as if she were owner of the contract from inception. It is extremely important that the advisor understand that spousal continuation applies only in the situation just stated. For example, it is not available to a surviving spouse who is trustee of a trust named as beneficiary of decedent spouse's annuity.[23] It is also not available to a beneficiary who owned an annuitant-driven annuity of which his spouse was annuitant (e.g., where H is the owner and W is the annuitant of an annuitant-driven contract, and W dies, H receives the death proceeds of the annuity he owns and must recognize the income without the opportunity to elect spousal continuation).

The Section 72(s)(2) annuitization exception to the five-year rule requires that "such distributions begin not later than 1 year after the date of the holder's death or such later date as the Secretary may by regulations prescribe." Many advisors interpret these words to mean that the beneficiary has one year from the date of holder's death to elect this option. Indeed, some insurance companies may, by current practice, allow the beneficiary up to one year to make such an election. This interpretation could pose a serious problem for clients and advisors who rely upon it. Why? Because of a Code section that is often ignored: Section 72(h).

What About IRC Section 72(h)?

Section 72(h) is entitled "Option To Receive An Annuity In Lieu Of A Lump Sum." It states that, if:

(1) a contract provides for payment of a lump sum in full discharge of an obligation under the contract, subject to an option to receive an annuity in lieu of such lump sum;

(2) the option is exercised within 60 days after the day on which such lump sum first became payable; and

(3) part or all of such lump sum would (but for this subsection) be includible in gross income by reason of subsection (e) (1),

then, for purposes of this subtitle, no part of such lump sum shall be considered as includible in gross income at the time such lump sum first became payable.

What does this mean, in normal English? It means that: (1) if an annuity provides the beneficiary the option to take death proceeds as an annuity, in lieu of taking a lump sum settlement, and (2) if the beneficiary exercises, within sixty days of the owner's death,[24] the option to take an annuity, and (3) if part or all of the proceeds would be includible in the beneficiary's estate if taken in a lump sum (e.g., the contract was an annuity, not qualifying for the tax-free treatment of death benefits that life insurance contracts enjoy under Section 101(a)); then (4) the entire taxable portion of this death benefit will not be taxable to the beneficiary in the year of the owner's death. The beneficiary, by electing to take the proceeds as an annuity, will, instead, be taxed on those proceeds as received, under the regular annuity rules–provided that he or she exercises such an annuitization option within 60 days of the owner's death.

This 60-day requirement of Section 72(h)(2) appears to conflict with the one-year requirement of Section 72(s)(2)(C), even though they are not speaking of the same thing. The latter requirement concerns only when the first annuity payment must be made if regular annuity rule taxation is to be available; the former states when the exercise of the annuity option must be made to achieve that result. This suggests that the proper process is to elect to take death proceeds as an annuity within 60 days of the death of the annuitant or owner, with the first payment to commence within one year of that result, thus satisfying both rules—because the election of the annuity option is the exercise thereof. However, insurance companies typically offer beneficiaries annuity payment options only on an immediate annuity basis— where the first payment will commence one month or so from the date of election. Practically speaking, this means that the first annuity payment will probably be made much sooner than one year from death, but, in any event, the exercise of the option to receive payments must be made within 60 days.

Some commentators believe that Section 72(s) trumps Section 72(h), arguing that the former section is some 20 years newer than the latter. Moreover, it is argued, the legislative history of Section 72 shows a Congressional intent to bring parity to the rules governing required distributions from nonqualified annuities and those governing required distributions from IRAs and qualified plans. The default five-year rule—an exception for annuitization not extending life expectancy commencing within one year—and the spousal continuation provisions of Section 72(s) certainly resemble corresponding provisions in Section 401(a)(9). However, Section 72(h) was neither modified nor repealed by Congress, either when it enacted Section 72(s), or when it later amended it. Moreover, Section 72(s) says nothing about when or how distributions from an annuity must be recognized by the beneficiary as income for tax purposes; it merely mandates what distributions must occur from the contract for it to qualify as an annuity contract in the first place.

By contrast, Section 72(h) speaks directly to the taxability of death benefits, declaring basically that if a beneficiary of a contract which allows a lump sum payout as an alternative to an annuity does not exercise the option to take proceeds as an annuity within 60 days, that beneficiary will be in constructive receipt of the entire contract gain in the year of the owner's or annuitant's death. In other words, if the beneficiary has the option to take a lump sum, and does not elect an annuity payout within 60 days of the date of death, the beneficiary must recognize all of the gain, and must do so regardless of whether he actually withdraws all or any of the death benefit proceeds that year.

In the authors' opinion, a beneficiary's election to take the death proceeds of an annuity, as an annuity, must be made within 60 days of the date on which those proceeds first became available, if the contract otherwise provides for a lump sum payout. This applies both to deferred annuity and immediate annuity contracts. An insurance company may, by its current practice, permit a beneficiary to make such election as late as one year after the holder's death, and may issue tax reporting forms reflecting the availability of regular annuity rule tax treatment. But the IRS may not accept such a position, because Section 72(h) is still on the books. It may be that a late election by a beneficiary to take proceeds as an annuity will escape IRS notice, particularly if the insurance company issues Forms 1099 reflecting regular annuity rule taxation, but, to be sure of that treatment, the beneficiary should make this election within 60 days of the date of death of the original annuity owner.

It should be noted, at this point, that the apparent conflict between Sections 72(h) and 72(s) does not come into play when the annuity death benefit is paid by reason of the death of a non-owner annuitant, where the annuity contract was annuitant-driven and the nonowner annuitant died. Section 72(h) applies when the death benefit of any annuity contract is payable, as long as it provides for both lump sum and annuity payouts to the beneficiary. Section 72(s) applies only when the holder/owner of an annuity dies. But some annuities pay a death benefit upon the death of either the owner or the annuitant. What are the income tax rules in that situation?

When Section 72(s) Does Not Apply: Income Tax Treatment of Death Proceeds of an Annuity Not in Payment Status When NonOwner Annuitant Dies

Annuities that are not annuitant-driven (i.e., are owner-driven) pay a death benefit only upon the death of the owner, and the income tax rules governing those death benefits are those we have just reviewed. However, annuities that are annuitant-driven pay a death benefit upon the death of the annuitant or the owner—the annuitant under contractual annuitant-driven provisions, and the owner under required provisions as dictated by Section 72(s)(1). In the case of an annuitant-driven annuity where the annuitant and owner are different individuals and the annuitant has died but the owner has not, the rules are somewhat different.

In the situation just described, Section 72(h) applies. If the beneficiary does not elect, within 60 days of annuitant's death, to take proceeds as an annuity—if the contract even offers this option—the proceeds will be considered amounts not received as an annuity.[25] The proceeds in excess of the investment in the contract (i.e. the gain) will be taxable to the beneficiary in the year of the annuitant's death.[26] In this case, because there has been no death of a holder to which Section 72(s) might apply, there are no grounds to make an election under any time period except during the 60-day window of Section 72(h).

If the beneficiary is the surviving spouse of either the owner or annuitant, the spousal continuation option of Section 72(s)(3) is not available in this situation, because that option applies only when the beneficiary is the surviving spouse of a deceased holder/owner. If the beneficiary is under age 59½, the exemptions from the 10% penalty tax, under Section 72(q), that would apply had the owner died are similarly unavailable.

Due to all of these complications, including the time requirements of Section 72(h), loss of spousal continuation options of Section 72(s), and the potential premature distribution penalties of Section 72(q), the authors strongly caution against ever establishing an annuitant-driven contract where the owner and annuitant are different individuals.

Jointly Held Annuities

Nonqualified annuities sold to married individuals are often placed in joint ownership. Often, there are good reasons for this, but the advisor should be aware of potential problems with this arrangement. Ownership of assets held jointly, with rights of survivorship (JTWROS) ordinarily vests immediately, upon the death of one tenant, in the surviving tenant(s). This does not apply, however, to annuities owned in this manner. As we have seen, IRC Section 72(s) (1)(B) requires that when any owner of an annuity dies before the annuity starting date, the proceeds of that annuity must be distributed within five years, unless the exceptions of Sections 72(s)(2) or 72(s)(3) apply.

Section 72(s)(3) provides what is often termed the spousal continuation option, whereby the surviving spouse of the deceased owner may elect to treat the annuity as his or her own. In the authors' opinion, this applies only when the surviving spouse is the designated beneficiary of the deceased owner. If the annuity is owned jointly by a husband and wife, but the beneficiary is their daughter, and either of the couple dies, the distribution must be made to the daughter under the terms of Section 72(s). However, this view is not shared by some insurance companies. Both of the authors have been informed, in conversations with insurance company representatives, that the contracts of a particular insurance company provide that under the factual situation given above, that the surviving spouse-owner would be able to exercise the spousal continuation option of Section 72(s)(3). In one conversation, the insurance company representative stated that this would be so if the contract were not annuitant-driven, but that if it were, payment to the daughter as beneficiary would be required to be made, in accordance with the Section 72 rules.[27]

The authors know of no authority supporting this position, or, for that matter, the position that a surviving owner can ever elect spousal continuation if he or she is not the designated beneficiary of the deceased owner. On what basis might one assert the contrary? At least one insurance company's annuity provides that if the contract is owned jointly, the surviving owner will be deemed to be the primary beneficiary, regardless of any prior beneficiary designation. That is certainly an interesting approach, but it relies, not on any putative right of the surviving owner, but on the fact that he or she would be the primary beneficiary. The authors have heard of but have not been able to verify an annuity that defines the death benefit as payable, when the contract is owned jointly, only upon the death of the second joint owner, but would have serious concerns that this might contravene the death of any holder language of Section 72(s)(1).

The authors offer a strong suggestion to the reader to be very careful in dealing with joint ownership of annuities. If you believe that joint ownership is appropriate, and especially if a third party will be named as beneficiary, you should be certain of the insurer's policies with regard to payment of death benefits, and verify that the provisions of the annuity contract are consistent with the desired result. In addition, it is notable that in any situation where an annuity is jointly held between two individuals who are not husband-wife, the clear application of the 72(s) rules dictate that the contract must begin distributions after the death of the first owner, and no continuation will be available becaues the surviving owner—even if named as beneficiary—is not a surviving spouse eligible for 72(s)(3) spousal continuation.

When the Beneficiary is a Trust

Probably the most confusing area of annuity taxation is determining which distribution rules apply when (a) the annuity is not in payout status and (b) the owner and/or beneficiary is a trust and (c) either the annuitant or owner of the annuity dies. This is such a complicated area that the authors have devoted a separate chapter of this book to it. See Chapter 8, Annuities and Trusts.

Annuities and Step-up in Basis at Death

Variable annuity contracts issued before October 21, 1979 are potentially eligible for a step-up in basis at the death of the owner under Section 1014.[28] This step-up in basis applies to contributions made to these contracts, including any contributions applied to an annuity contract after that date that were pursuant to a binding commitment entered into before that date,[29] and their attributable earnings.

> "The basis of the contract in the hands of the beneficiary will be the value of the contract at the date of the decedent's death (or the alternate valuation date). If that basis equals the amount received by the beneficiary there will be no income taxable gain and the appreciation in the value of the contract while owned by the decedent will escape income tax entirely. But where a variable annuity contract purchased before October 21, 1979 had been exchanged for another variable annuity contract under IRC Section 1035 after October 20, 1979 and the annuity owner died prior to the annuity starting date, the beneficiary was not entitled to a step-up in basis."[30]

It is important to note that these rulings were written in the context of variable annuities. However, the authors have discovered no reason why fixed deferred annuities acquired prior to 1979 should not be eligible for comparable step-up in basis treatment under Section 1014, as the tax code does not otherwise make any distinctions between fixed and variable annuities for tax purposes.

Beneficiary's Income Tax Deduction for Federal Estate Tax Attributable to Annuity Gain—IRC Section 691(c)

As was noted earlier, the value of an annuity is includible in the estate of the owner for estate tax purposes, and the as-yet-untaxed gain is taxable to the beneficiary for income tax purposes. This double taxation is reduced, but not avoided entirely, by an income tax deduction available to the beneficiary under IRC section 691(c), under the so-called Income in Respect of a Decedent rules:

> "Income in respect of a decedent is subjected to the federal estate tax in the decedent's estate and to federal income tax in the hands of the person who receives it. Also, such income may be subject to the generation-skipping transfer tax. . . Section 691(c) alleviates the hardship of the double taxation somewhat by allowing the recipient an income tax deduction for that portion of these taxes attributable to the inclusion of the net value of the income right. Where the income would have been ordinary income in the hands of the decedent, the deduction is an itemized deduction.[31]

> The amount of the deduction is determined by computing the federal estate tax, or generation-skipping transfer tax, with the net income in respect of a decedent included and then recomputing the federal estate tax with the net income in respect of a decedent excluded. The difference in the two results is the amount of the income tax deduction. Thus, the amount deductible equals (a) the federal estate tax on the taxable estate, minus (b) the federal estate tax on the taxable estate less net IRD.

> If two or more persons will receive income in respect of the same decedent, each recipient is entitled to that share of the total deduction which is in the same proportion that his share of income in respect of a decedent bears to the total gross income in respect of a decedent that was included in the gross estate. For example, a recipient who is entitled to 1/4 of the income is also entitled to 1/4 of the deduction. This is so, even though none of the federal estate tax is attributable to the income received by that particular recipient—for example where his income was offset by an equivalent amount of deductions.[32]

> The deduction is taken only as the income is received, and in the same proportion. For example, say that the income in respect of a decedent will be received by only one person, and will be received in equal amounts over a 10-year period. The recipient may take 1/10 of the total deduction in each of the 10 taxable years."[33]

It should be emphasized that the deduction is only for the gain in the contract, and only to the extent of the federal estate tax. Any state estate or inheritance tax would not be considered for purposes of this deduction.

1035 Exchanges of Annuities after Death of the Holder

As discussed in Chapter 2, section 1035 of the tax code allows for the exchange of an annuity for another annuity contract in a like-kind exchange, without recognition of gain. These rules allow an annuity holder to exchange one annuity contract for another, perhaps to obtain different or more appealing investment options or guarantees, while deferring any income tax liability associated with a gain.

The question often arises about whether an annuity contract can be exchanged for another under a 1035 exchange by a beneficiary, after death of the original holder. Unforutnately, there is no directly on-point guidance from the IRS or Treasury regarding this issue, but in the authors' opinion such a strategy is probably a stretch under the existing tax code.

After all, the provisions that allow an annuity contract to be eligible for a 1035 exchange refer directly to a contract which depends in part on the life expectancy of the insured, and/or is payable for the life of the annuitant[34]—yet once the holder of the contract has passed away, the annuity is arguably no longer an ongoing contract of insurance, but is merely a prior contract of insurance in the process of paying out its benefits to the stated beneficiaries.

Some insurance companies have suggested that they would be willing to accept a 1035 exchange of an inherited annuity contract on behalf of a beneficiary, retaining the inherited annuity titling to signify the status of the contract, in a manner similar to how inherited IRAs are transferred from one trustee to another. Unfortunately, though, this may not be good enough to avoid IRS scrutiny; even if the company receiving the inherited annuity is willing to accept a 1035 exchange, if the distributing company does not interpret the rules in the same manner, they will likely still classify the transaction as a distribution, and issue a Form 1099-R accordingly, forcing the beneficiary to dispute the taxable amounts shown on the IRS reporting. In addition, a 1035 exchange is only allowed if the contract is assigned directly from one insurer to another, and an annuity company that doesn't acknowledge 1035 exchanges of inherited contracts may not even cooperate with the 1035 exchange requirements; unlike traditional IRA rollovers, the beneficiary cannot try to complete the exchange simply by receiving a distribution and rolling it over to another annuity.

Nonetheless, there is arguably little reason for the IRS to prohibit 1035 exchanges of annuities after the death of the holder, especially in the case of a deferred annuity. The existing difficulties in doing so are rooted in the apparent gaps in the tax code and regulations to allow such exchanges, not a deliberate act of tax policy to prohibit them. Accordingly, further clarity may be achieved in the future, and some taxpayer may at some point decide to attempt such an exchange and submit for a Private Letter Ruling to support it. In the meantime, though, annuity beneficiaries should proceed with extreme caution, as post-death 1035 exchanges are not clearly blessed by the tax code and regulations in current form, nor will many insurance companies cooperate with any attempt to complete such an exchange.

Endnotes

1. IRC Secs. 2039, 2033.
2. Also referred to as "Annuity Commencement Date."
3. Also called straight life annuity or life annuity with no refund.
4. *Tax Facts on Insurance & Employee* Benefits (The National Underwriter Company, 2012), Q 417.
5. This arrangement is variously called Life with 10-Year Certain, Life-10 Yr. Continuous and Certain, or the like. If annuity payments are to be made monthly, it may be called Life and 120 Months Certain.

6. Treas. Reg. §20.2031-8(a).

7. IRC Sec. 2032(a)(3).

8. The value of the cash refund guaranteed is typically less than the amount annuitized under this option.

9. This arrangement is variously called Life with 10-Year Certain, Life-10 Yr. Continuous and Certain, or the like. If annuity payments are to be made monthly, it may be called Life and 120 Months Certain.

10. *Tax Facts on Insurance & Employee Benefits* (The National Underwriter Company, 2012), q 421.

11. Treas. Reg. §20.2039-1(c), Ex. 1., and IRC Section 2039(b).

12. Treas. Reg. §20.2039-1(c).

13. IRC Section 2040(b).

14. Treas. Reg. §20.2031-8(a).

15. An immediate annuity is in payout status by definition.

16. If the beneficiary elects to change the amount or duration of annuity payments, this constitutes electing a new annuity option. This election would cause the payments to be taxed under the regular annuity rules. However, such a change will not be permitted if the payments would not distribute proceeds at least as rapidly as the annuitant had been receiving them. IRC Sec. 72(s)(1)(A).

17. Treas. Reg. §1.72-11(c).

18. IRC Sec. 72(b)(3)(A).

19. It is important to note, with regard to this owner-driven vs. annuitant-driven distinction, that certain riders and enhanced death benefits of deferred annuities may be 'annuitant-driven' and take effect only at the death of an annuitant, despite the fact that the annuity itself must be paid out to the beneficiary on the death of the owner, per Section 72(s)(1). For this reason, the advisor should be very cautious about annuitant-driven contracts where the owner and annuitant are different individuals.

20. Section 72(s)(1) was amended by the Tax Reform Act of 1986, changing the holder to read any holder. This change had serious implications for jointly held contracts (as discussed later in the text), and applies to contracts issued since April 22, 1987. Also added were Sections 72(s)(6) and 72(s)(7), which deal with annuities held by other than natural persons.

21. IRC Section 72(s)(6).

22. Treas. Reg. §1.72-11(e).

23. Let. Rul. 200323012, issued to the surviving spouse who was trustee of a joint revocable trust named as beneficiary of annuity contracts owned by that trust, of which the decedent husband was the annuitant, held that the surviving spouse/beneficiary could elect the Section 72(s)(3) spousal continuation option, but the facts of that case were unusual—the spouse had such liberal powers and access to the trust that it was as though she were the directly named beneficiary. Most commentators believe that the trustee of a trust named as beneficiary of an annuity will not be able to elect such treatment or the annuitization option of Section 72(s)(2) in all normal cases. Moreover, most insurance companies, in the authors' experience, will, at this time, not consent to such a result without, at the very least, a ruling from the IRS.

24. Presumably, the date of owner's death would be the date on which such lump sum first became payable.

25. In this instance, the 60 day vs. one year conflict discussed above is irrelevant. Section 72(s) does not apply, because the death benefit is paid by reason of the death of the annuitant, not the owner.

26. IRC Sec. 72(e)(2)(B).

27. In addition, it is important to note that in this situation, the surviving spouse would be the owner of an annuity that must be paid to the beneficiary (the daughter), and consequently could be deemed to make a gift to the daughter of the annuity death benefit upon the death of any holder. This is not unlike the similar consequences when a husband owns an insurance policy on his wife, with his daughter as the beneficiary, and the wife dies, causing the death benefit owned by the husband to be paid to the daughter.

28. In theory this step-up in basis for pre-1979 contracts may no longer apply if Section 1014 ceases to apply in the face of a repeal of estate taxes.

29. Rev. Rul. 79-335, 1979-2 C.B. 292.

30. *Tax Facts on Insurance & Employee Benefits* (The National Underwriter Company, 2012), Q 396. See also Rev. Rul. 70-143, 1970-1 C.B. 167, and TAM 9346002; Let. Rul. 9245035.

31. Rev. Rul. 78-203, 1978-1 CB 199.
32. IRC Sec. 691(c).
33. *Advanced Sales Reference Service*, The National Underwriter Company, Sec. 53, ¶20.15(d).
34. IRC Section 1035(b)(1); IRC Section 1035(b)(2).

Chapter 4

Basic Costs of Annuities

Thus far in this book, we have examined the basic structures of annuities and how distributions are taxed. Later, we will consider the benefits annuities can provide. In this chapter, we will focus on one of the most controversial—and often misunderstood—aspects of annuities: their costs. The controversy and misunderstanding is chiefly due to two conditions:

1. The cost factors are almost always very complicated, and sometimes, bewilderingly so.

2. These cost factors are often poorly communicated—both by the advisor to the purchaser to whom the annuity is being recommended, and to that advisor by the insurance company issuing the annuity contract.

The responsibility for this poor communication is a matter of considerable debate. Some consumerists hold the advisor chiefly, if not solely, responsible for a purchaser's lack of understanding. Class-action lawsuits have asserted that the onus lies, ultimately, with the insurance companies, citing confusing, even allegedly misleading, training and marketing materials. The authors believe that, where an annuity purchaser can legitimately state that he or she did not understand the costs of the annuity, there is plenty of blame to go around. The same holds true with respect to the benefits of that annuity.

That being said, the fact remains that the costs of nearly all annuity contracts offered today are often hard to understand and appreciate fully, especially when the benefits derived from those costs are also complicated. Complex cost and benefit structures, however fully disclosed, run the risk of being misunderstood, and even the best explanations can be recalled imperfectly. The annuity advisor must have a very clear understanding of the costs and benefits of those contracts he or she deals with and be willing to spend whatever time is required in perfecting a clear explanation of both.

Cost Factors in Immediate Annuities

The least complex cost structure is that of the fixed Single Premium Immediate Annuity (fixed SPIA). These contracts generally assess no front-end sales charge or annual contract charges. A few fixed SPIAs permit commutation[1] or partial withdrawals, and may assess a charge for these distributions. Most, however, do not permit these changes to the original payout structure, but instead require that once annuity payments have commenced, no withdrawals or lump sum surrender will be permitted. The only cost component in these contracts is reflected in the payout factors, both those guaranteed in the contract and those offered on a currently available basis.

Annuity Payout Factors

An annuity payout factor, or annuity factor, is a number usually expressed with two decimal precision. It represents the dollar amount of each annuity payment, per thousand dollars of proceeds placed under the annuity option.

> *Example:* The sample table below shows that the annual payment for a life only annuity,[2] for a male age 65 or a female age 59,[3] will be $6.38, for each thousand dollars of annuity purchase payment. Thus, a single premium of $125,500 will purchase an annual annuity payment of $800.69 (125.5 x 6.38). The same sum would purchase an annual annuity of $672.68 (125.5 x 5.36) if payments are to persist for the greater of the life of the annuitant or twenty years (Life & 20 Years Certain).

Male Age	Female Age	Life Only	L&10YC	L&20YC	L&Cash Ref
65	59	6.38	6.09	5.36	5.61
66	60	6.57	6.24	5.42	5.72

The amount of each payment is guaranteed never to change, unless the annuity provides for a cost of living adjustment (COLA). At the time of this writing, most annuities—both immediate and deferred—do not provide for any COLA adjustments. Some offer a single fixed COLA choice (e.g., payments to increase at 3% per year). Very few, however, offer a choice of different COLA percentages (e.g., 3% or 5%), or any kind of COLA that adjusts to a specified inflation factor (e.g., the Consumer Price Index (CPI)). Fortunately for consumers, there is a trend in newer annuity contracts toward offering COLA choices. In the authors' opinion, this is both necessary and long overdue. Annuity payout factors reflect an insurance company's estimate of life expectancy, or mortality, expenses, and interest rates. These estimates change over time. The annuity payout factors offered to current purchasers of immediate annuities and to owners of deferred annuities choosing to annuitize their contracts can change as frequently as weekly. Of course, once one purchases an immediate annuity or elects an annuitization option in one's deferred annuity, the payout factor used to calculate the initial payment is all that matters. All future payments will be based upon that same and sole factor, which never changes once payments begin.

Note to Third Edition: Sadly, the situation has not changed much in the years since the first edition. COLA riders are still rare, and typically offer only a few choices of various fixed percentages by which annuity payments will increase; COLA provisions that link annuity payment amounts directly to changes in an external inflation index (e.g,. CPI-U) are still very rare.

For purchasers of deferred annuities, there are two sets of annuity factors that may come into play. Every deferred annuity contract contains guaranteed minimum annuity payout factors. These are based on very conservative assumptions, and are generally considerably lower—that is, providing for lower annual payments per thousand dollars annuitized—than the current factors offered by the same insurer, for use with the same annuity. In fact, in the authors' experience, there has rarely been a time when the current factors were not significantly higher than the guaranteed ones.

Does this mean that the cost of these guaranteed annuity payout factors is wasted money? In the authors' view, the answer is no—even though these guaranteed factors have never yet been as attractive as the current ones. Americans are living longer with each passing decade. A breakthrough in gerontological medicine producing greatly increased average life expectancies, especially if accompanied by a prolonged period of low interest rates or, especially, a period of deflation, could produce future current annuity payout factors less attractive than those guaranteed in existing deferred annuity contracts. Is this likely? Perhaps not. But, as we have noted before, an annuity is primarily a risk management instrument. The presence of these guarantees allows the purchaser to manage the risk that future annuity payout rates (based on longer life expectancies or lower interest rates) will not produce sufficient income.

The other type of immediate annuity is the variable single premium immediate annuity (variable SPIA). Like its fixed cousin, the variable SPIA provides for an income commencing within one year of purchase; unlike the fixed variety, however, the amount of each annuity payment is not fixed,[4] because the annuity cash value is invested in variable subaccounts. A variable annuity, whether immediate or deferred, assesses expense charges at both the sub-account and contract, or wrapper levels. These charges, the form of which is generally the same for immediate annuities as for deferred ones, will be covered in the discussion on costs in variable deferred annuities.

Cost Factors in Deferred Annuities

The overhead costs of deferred annuities are considerably more complex than those of immediate contracts. Historically, fixed deferred annuities have contained fewer, and simpler, charges than variable deferred contracts, but, in recent years, the complexity of both types has increased substantially.

Note on Nomenclature: While immediate annuities are always purchased with a single premium, a deferred annuity, of either the fixed or variable type, may be purchased either with a single premium (Single Premium Deferred Annuity, or SPDA) or may permit, but not necessarily require, ongoing periodic premiums (Flexible Premium Deferred Annuity, or FPDA). As if this were not complicated enough, the labels SPDA and FPDA are typically used in connection only with fixed contracts, just as the term SPIA, for single premium immediate annuity is, in common practice, applied only to fixed contracts, even though it is properly applicable to variable contracts as well. To avoid adding to the confusion, the authors suggest using complete terminology (e.g., fixed SPIA, variable SPIA, flexible premium deferred variable annuity, etc.)

Fixed Deferred Annuities

Charges assessed in fixed annuities may include any or all of the following:

Front-End Sales Charge

Until fairly recently, an initial sales charge, or load—generally, a percentage of the initial premium—was a common contract expense. Very few fixed deferred annuities offered today assess such a charge, as it was notably unpopular with consumers.

Surrender Charges

A surrender charge, as its name implies, is assessed upon the surrender of an annuity contract, or upon withdrawal of more than the policy's free withdrawal amount. Typically, fixed annuities allow the contract owner to withdraw up to 10% of the account balance, per year, without penalty. There are numerous variations of this provision, such as permitting this penalty-free amount to be cumulative or allowing a penalty-free withdrawal of all previously credited interest, but 10% per year without penalty is fairly standard. Recently, some issuers of index annuities have pared back the free withdrawal provisions of new offerings to permit a smaller penalty-free withdrawal in the first year or so. According to one actuary, this allows the issuer to offer increased benefits such as a higher participation rate than would otherwise be possible.

Surrenders, or withdrawals in excess of this penalty-free amount, are generally subject to a surrender charge. While the mechanics of this charge vary widely from contract to contract, the usual format is a declining surrender charge schedule—such as 6% in the first contract year, 5% in the second, 4% in the third, and so on—until the surrender charge reaches zero. In flexible premium contracts, the surrender charge schedule may be fixed, terminating at the end of specified number of years from issue, or rolling, applying the schedule separately to each deposit. This is a moot point with single premium annuities, which, as we have noted, do not allow subsequent deposits.

Many deferred annuities, both fixed and variable, include provisions that waive the imposition of surrender charges in certain circumstances. Most contracts waive the charges upon the death of the owner, or annuitant, if the contract is annuitant-driven. Many also provide a waiver if the owner, or annuitant is confined to a nursing home, is disabled, or suffers one of several listed dread diseases.

Considering how much criticism is leveled at surrender charges by many financial journalists and those who simply don't like annuities on principle, a comment or two may be in order, at this point, on why surrender charges exist in the first place.

A schedule of surrender charges is an alternative to a front-end sales charge. Both exist to allow the issuing company to recover acquisition costs—the costs of putting the annuity policy in force. Even in today's high-tech world, this cannot be done for free. The most controversial—even notorious—acquisition cost is the selling commission paid to the agent who sells the annuity. Most annuities are sold by commissioned advisors, who are compensated in this fashion. Practically all fixed annuities are of this sort. However, not all variable annuities are commissionable. An increasing number of variable annuities are of the type usually called low load. They pay no sales commissions. Not coincidentally, they generally assess no surrender charges.

If, at this point, you are thinking that the purpose of surrender charges is to pay the sales commission, you are basically right. The insurance company pays that commission when it issues the annuity and it needs to recover that cost. But the surrender charge almost always declines over time—after a few years, to zero. Why is that? It is because the insurance company knows that if the annuity owner keeps the policy in force for long enough, it will recover its acquisition costs from other moving parts in the annuity contract. In the case of a fixed annuity, the interest rate spread (i.e., the difference between what the company earns on invested annuity premiums, and what it credits to those annuities) will, in time, not only make up the commission cost, but make the annuity contract profitable to its issuer. In the case of a variable annuity, there's no interest rate spread, and thus it is the insurance costs that bring about this same result. A front-end sales charge would do the job, too. But front-end sales charges are unattractive to buyers, which is why most annuities no longer impose them.

So, if the sales commission is an acquisition cost, surrender charges, in lieu of an initial sales charge, pay that cost, right? Basically, yes. It's not quite that simple, but that's the gist of it. So, if the annuity pays no sales commission, there's no need for surrender charges.

Seems simple enough. But sales commissions are not the only acquisition costs. Even when an insurance company markets a particular annuity contract through fee-only advisors as a commission-free product, it cannot produce that product for free. Not only are there development costs that any prudent company will expect to recover, but also costs of issue and administration. And then, there is the matter of profit. The insurance company expects to make money selling the annuity, and prices it with that expectation. In the case of a fixed annuity, profit—and cost recovery—come from the interest rate spread. In a variable annuity, which has no such spread, they come mainly from insurance charges. Thus, insurance companies attempt to make up for the fact that there are not any surrender charges on such low load or commission-free products through other costs, or by the attempt to generate additional sales with the marketability of a low load or commission-free label.

Market Value Adjustment

There may be a market value adjustment (MVA) upon surrender of the contract or upon a partial withdrawal. If so, then the surrender value or withdrawn amount is usually decreased if a benchmark interest rate—a specified, well-recognized external index—is higher, when the contract is surrendered, than it was at the time of issue. The surrender value will be increased if the reverse is true. The purpose of this adjustment is to compensate the insurance company for the risk that contract owners will withdraw money when the market value of the investments backing the annuity is low. In the case of fixed annuities, this generally means bonds. Since bond prices are inversely related to interest rates, the market value of the investments backing the annuity will generally be lowest when interest rates have risen. Generally, this is the exact time that investors may want to withdraw their money to re-invest in a new contract with higher than-current rates—thus the need for the insurance company to protect itself from this risk. However, MVAs are a risk-sharing feature, because, if the external index is lower at the time of withdrawal or surrender than it was at issue, and the value of the underlying bonds is correspondingly higher—again, because bond prices are inversely related to interest rates—the contract owner benefits from the adjustment. Generally, an MVA is assessed only on withdrawals in excess of the penalty-free withdrawal amount, and usually does not apply after the expiration of the surrender charge period.

Interest Rate Spread

In a fixed deferred annuity, the issuing company's profit derives chiefly from the interest rate spread, or the difference between what the company can earn on invested annuity premiums and what it will credit to the cash value of those contracts. In a sense, this spread is a cost of the contract, if one assumes that the annuity investor would otherwise be able to earn the same rate as the insurance company. However, this assumption may not be reasonable.

In nearly all fixed deferred annuities, this spread is not guaranteed, or even revealed directly to the contract holder. It may be calculated, of course, provided one knows both the rate credited to an annuity during a certain period and the rate the insurance company earned during that same period. However, not all insurers credit interest in the same manner, or even credit interest in the same manner to all fixed annuities they have issued. To understand how interest rate spread works as a contract cost, we must understand how interest is credited to fixed deferred annuities.

Guaranteed Interest Rate

All fixed deferred annuities guarantee a minimum interest crediting rate. Regardless of future conditions, interest will be credited each period to the annuity at a rate at least equal to this guaranteed rate.[5] In addition, every deferred annuity of which the authors are aware also provides for the crediting of current, nonguaranteed interest at a rate, which may be higher, but cannot be lower than the guaranteed rate.

Current Interest Rate Crediting Methods

There are four basic methods of crediting current interest to conventional nonindex fixed annuities.

1. *Portfolio Method.* For an annuity that uses this method, all contracts will be credited each period with the same current, non-guaranteed interest rate, regardless of when annuity contributions (premiums) were received, except for contracts that are still within an initial interest rate guarantee period.

2. *New Money or Pocket of Money Method.* For an annuity using this method, the rate of interest credited to all contracts will depend upon when the premiums were received. For flexible premium annuities, this can mean that a particular annuity contract might receive, on any given interest crediting date, several different rates, each applied to the pocket of money received during the time period specified for that pocket.

    Example: Mr. Jones' flexible premium annuity was issued June 30, 2009. Interest is credited each year, at a rate determined annually. On June 30, 2012, the contract is credited with the following:

    a.   4.00% for all premiums received in the period 1/1/2009 – 12/31/2009

    b.   3.89% for all premiums received in the period 1/1/2010 – 12/31/2010

    c.   3.80% for all premiums received in the period 1/1/2011 – 12/31/2011

    d.   3.56% for all premiums received in the period 1/1/2012 – 12/31/2012

3. *Tiered Interest Rate Method: Type One.* In this method, the interest rate credited to a contract depends upon the cash value of the annuity.

    Example: Ms. Smith's annuity credits interest according to the following current schedule:

    a.   4.00% for the first $50,000 of cash value

    b.   4.25% for the next $50,000 of cash value

    c.   4.5% for cash value in excess of $100,000

4. *Tiered Interest Rate Method: Type Two.* In this method, interest is credited at one rate if the owner annuitizes the contract and at a lower rate if the contract is surrendered. In these contracts, the value is generally reported as two separate items: (a) the annuity

value and (b) the cash value or contract value. The cash value will be reduced, on surrender of the contract, by any surrender charge applicable. The amount payable at the owner's or annuitant's death may be either the cash value or annuity value, depending upon contract terms, and a surrender charge may or may not apply.

Interest Rate Guarantee Period

Sometimes the current interest rate of a newly issued fixed deferred annuity may be guaranteed for a specific period. If so, then at the expiration of this period, renewal interest is credited according to the crediting method used for that particular contract—subject, of course, to the guaranteed minimum rate.

Interest Rate Renewal History

One item that every advisor who is considering recommending a fixed deferred annuity must consider is the history of the issuing insurance company with regard to renewal interest rates. Renewal rates, except for contracts in the interest rate guarantee period, are entirely at the discretion of the issuing insurer and subject, of course, to the minimum rate guaranteed in the contract. Some insurers have a distinguished history of declaring renewal interest at competitive levels. Others, unfortunately, do not. In the 1980s and 1990s, a few insurers offered fixed deferred annuities at initial rates well above the level offered by most competitors and, as soon as the interest rate guarantee period elapsed, renewed these contracts at, or barely above, the guaranteed rate. Fortunately for consumers, most insurance companies did not play this game. Nevertheless, the risk with this sort of bait and switching is one the prudent advisor must take into consideration. The authors strongly advise taking a close look at the published history of renewal crediting rate of any insurance company whose products you are considering.[6]

A final observation on the subject of interest rate crediting is in order. It may appear to the advisor inexperienced in fixed deferred annuities that renewal interest rates, while they may drop from the initial level to as low as the guaranteed rate, may also rise at that point—even beyond that initial level—if interest rates are increasing at that time. That may appear logical, but it is not likely to happen. In the authors' experience, insurance companies rarely declare renewal interest rates at a level higher than the initial rate. This may, of course, be due to the fact that, for the past thirty years and more, interest rates have, in general, been trending downward. Nevertheless, there have been short periods, during those decades, during which rates increased. In those periods, the initial rate offered by insurance companies, on their fixed deferred annuities, did increase—but the renewal rates for existing contracts did not.

Bail-Out Interest Rate

Some fixed deferred annuities provide that, if renewal interest is ever credited below a certain specified rate, or the bail-out rate, surrender charges will be waived for a certain time period, allowing the contract owner to bail out of the contract without charges. Of course, the premature withdrawal penalty of Section 72(q) will apply if the owner is under age 59½ and no other exception to the penalty is available. Bail-out rate annuities were very popular in the volatile interest environment of the 1980s and 1990s, but are much less common today.

Bonus Interest Rates

A policy feature that has become very popular in both fixed and variable deferred annuities is the crediting of so-called bonus interest. Typically, bonus interest is interest, over and above the current rate, that is applied to deposits in the first year or first few years,[7] and is immediately vested. That is, the contract owner is not required to keep the contract for a set period, or to annuitize, to earn it. However, it is important to note that generally the surrender charges may be slightly higher on such contracts, the interest guarantees may be lower, or the current crediting rate may be lower—in other words, the general paradigm that "there's no such thing as a free lunch" still holds true, and the insurance company likely will still find some way to make up the cost of the bonus payment.

A variation on this theme is the annuitization bonus, which provides that a certain interest rate (e.g., 5%) will be credited to the contract, in addition to the regular interest, upon annuitization.

Bonus annuities, deferred annuities offering the crediting of an up-front interest rate bonus, have come under considerable criticism in recent years from some financial journalists and from more than a few regulators. Interestingly, it is not the additional interest crediting that has drawn the criticism, but the additional costs of these contracts. This has been especially true of index annuities. Most of the condemnation has been directed at the steeper and longer surrender charge schedules of these contracts. The authors hold no brief either for or against bonus annuities, but we do believe that any assesment of their value or appropriateness ought to balance their negatives against their benefits they offer. Typically, a bonus annuity is very much like a nonbonus annuity offered by the same insuer, except for (a) the additional interest bonus and (b) increased cost factors.

The Interest Rate Bonus

The additional interest rate offered as a bonus is typically credited to contributions made to the contract in the first year or first few years. In some contracts, this additional interest is vested immediately—that is, it cannot be taken back, even if the buyer surrenders the contract. In others, it may vest over a period of years. In some contracts, the bonus is forfeitable if the contract owner does not annuitize the contract over at least a minimum number of years. Some contracts offer as much as a 10% bonus to all contributions made during the first several years.

The Costs of the Interest Rate Bonus

All bonus annuities offer the additional interest in exchange for costs higher than if no bonus were creditable. In variable annuities, this cost is typically a higher contract charge (Mortality and Expense Charge) and/or a steeper or longer surrender charge schedule—a schedule in which the surrender charge starts at a higher level and/or persists for a greater number of years. In nonvariable contracts, which typically assess no ongoing contract charges, the surrender charge schedule is steeper and/or longer than for a nonbonus contract.

Many critics of annuities have focused upon contracts with very steep and lengthy surrender charge schedules as though they are, ipso facto, bad, for any buyer—but, especially, for a senior citizen. Indeed, regulators in several states have banned the sale to a senior citizen of any deferred annuity with a surrender charge schedule exceeding ten years or with an initial surrender charge exceeding ten percent. Contracts allowable under this rule are known as ten-ten annuities. In a few states, ten-ten annuities are all that any purchaser, of any age, may buy. The rationale often given for such a rule is that no one, especially a senior citizen, ought to be subject to a loss of interest and, possibly, principal as well, for more than a decade.

This may appear entirely reasonable to many readers. Why, after all, should one have to pay a penalty for getting to one's own money, especially when that penalty endures for many years? The authors suggest that one answer to that question would be that the question itself begs another—whether the money in question is, in fact, the buyer's own. In the case of a nonforfeitable interest rate bonus, we believe that it is arguably not. The issuing insurer can afford to credit such additional interest—over and above the annual interest—only if it can be assured of having the full purchase payment of the annuity to invest, so that the excess of what it earns, above what it will pay to the contract owner each year—or what it will extract in expenses—will reimburse it for that initial bonus credited. This increased liquidity cost is, quite simply, what the buyer must accept if he or she wants that bonus interest.

Let us pose a hypothetical arbitration case, in which the plaintiff argues that the surrender charge schedule of the bonus annuity he bought was unconscionable and the sale clearly unsuitable. It is established that the surrender charge of that contract was both long and steep, declining from a first year charge of 19% to zero only after fifteen years. But it is also established that the bonus paid in the first year of that annuity was 10% of the purchase payment. The annual interest paid each year on that contract was credited to 110% of that buyer's actual investment.

Was this annuity unconscionable? Would it be arguably suitable for any buyer, especially a senior citizen? The authors believe that a proper answer to both questions must look at the facts and circumstances of the case. Had the advisor established the client's need for liquidity during that surrender charge period? If so, did the advisor confirm that the client had other liquid assets that could be tapped for reasonably foreseeable needs during that period and that the client fully understood and agreed to the constraints upon liquidity of his investment in that annuity? What was the purpose of the annuity—the job to be done? If the client intended to take distributions of interest only from the annuity each year, it is undeniable that interest computed on 110% of a given sum will always produce a greater cash flow distribution than that same rate of interest computed on 100% of that sum.

The authors are certainly not arguing that deferred annuities with steep and long surrender charge periods are necessarily good for a client; we argue only that for a particular client, in a particular situation, they ought not to be dismissed out of hand, without a consideration of whether they would meet that client's requirements, especially if a bonus is involved.

The authors sometimes hear the following complaint from critics of bonus annuities: "If you get the bonus, but the insurer recovers the whole bonus though increases costs anyway, why bother?" The answer is that, for a bonus annuity which differs from its nonbonus cousin only in (a) the bonus, and (b) steeper and longer surrender charges, but not actually higher ongoing costs or a reduced interest crediting rate, the owner of such a contract who does not surrender it early gets the benefit of the bonus without actually paying its cost, or the surrender charges. As noted in the hypothetical example above, for a buyer who intends to withdraw interest each year, the additional interest created by the bonus may well be worth the bother.

CD-Annuities

A relatively recent development in fixed deferred annuities is the so-called CD-annuity. This type of contract typically guarantees the initial interest crediting rate for the duration of the surrender charge period, which is typically six years or less. As its name suggests, this product was developed as an alternative to certificates of deposit. While the assurance of receiving a known interest rate for several years, with freedom from surrender charges at the end of that period, is certainly attractive, especially when the tax liability for all the interest is deferred, the existence of the Section 72(q) penalty makes this type of contract a questionable short-term savings vehicle for those who will be under age 59½ at its maturity.

Contract Charges

Some fixed deferred annuities assess an annual contract charge, though most do not. Some contracts that do assess an annual contract charge will waive that charge when the account balance exceeds a certain amount (e.g., no contract charges for annuities with a balance in excess of $50,000).

Let's look now at the costs of variable deferred annuities. As was noted, the number and complexity of charges in variable annuities is greater than those in fixed contracts, and it is the former that are usually being referred to in critics' attacks on annuity costs.

Variable Deferred Annuities

Front-End Sales Charges

Front-end sales charges are generally equally as unpopular with variable annuities as they are with fixed annuities. Interestingly, though, some issuers of variable deferred annuities are offering new contracts with a front-end sales load in lieu of surrender charges. These contracts, sometimes called A-share-type annuities, may owe their existence to the heightened regulatory scrutiny and frequent bad press aimed at B-share-type mutual funds and traditional variable annuity costs. In addition to imposing no surrender charges, they may offer smaller annual costs, including mortality and expense charges.

Surrender Charges

Surrender charges in variable annuities work just as they do in fixed annuities.

Insurance Charges

The insurance charges in variable annuities are just plain confusing to almost everyone. Part of this confusion stems from the practice of some commentators on annuities to refer to the total insurance costs of these policies as mortality and expense charges. However, mortality and expense, or M&E as it is usually called, is only one of the components of insurance expenses. In this discussion, we will use the classification employed by Morningstar, Inc., Total Insurance Expense, which works like this:

The category of Total Insurance Expense consists of three elements:

1.   Mortality and expense charges (M&E)

2.   Administrative charges

3.   Distribution charges

The mortality and expense charge is defined by Morningstar as "the percentage of the subaccount's assets that the insurance company deducts to cover costs associated with mortality and expense risk. Specifically, it can serve as a source of profit for the insurance company [if mortality is more favorable than expected] in addition to compensating the company for offering features such as the variable-annuity death benefit and for compensation."[8]

Administrative charges are defined by the same source as "the percentage of the subaccount's daily net assets deducted by the insurance company to cover the costs involved in offering and administering the variable annuity, such as the cost of distribution and printing of correspondence."[9]

Of distribution charges, Morningstar says, "When applicable, these fees compensate the agent, broker, or financial planner who sold the policy."[10]

What does all that mean in plain English? It means that these insurance charges are imposed:

•   first, to compensate the issuing company for risks it incurs related to mortality (basically, the risk that they have underestimated longevity) and expenses (underestimation of various operating expenses, including government-imposed premium taxes); and

- second, to pay selling and distribution expenses, including printing costs and agents' commissions.

As we have noted, these separate charges are not imposed by fixed annuities. But fixed annuities have the interest rate spread, from which the cost of these risks can be, and is, recovered.

We also need to note that M&E is but one component of total insurance expense. Some commentators, when they use the term M&E mean just that component, but others—probably most—use it to mean the total figure. It is important, when comparing different variable annuities, to be sure to compare apples with apples. One low-load annuity, for example, is reported as having an M&E charge of ten basis points, but a total insurance expense of 30 basis points. Advisors must not mix the two terms.

As if that were not confusing enough, we need, also, to be aware that the benefits paid for by the total insurance expense of one variable annuity contract may not be the same as those paid for by the total insurance expense of another contract. The minimum death benefit, for example, could be significantly different. Or there may be other optional benefits, the charges for which are included in total insurance expense.

We will look, in Chapter 5, at some of the optional benefits commonly offered in variable annuity contracts, as well as some of the enhancement features used. But, first, it is essential that we understand that, for variable annuities, the total annual overhead cost to the contract owner is not just the sum of the annual contract charge plus the total insurance expense. There is also the annual expense charge imposed at the separate account level. This charge, called fund expense, is analogous to the expense ratio of a mutual fund, and is defined in Morningstar's *Principia®* as "the percentage of assets deducted each year for underlying fund operating expenses, management fees, and all other asset-based costs incurred by the fund, excluding brokerage fees."[11]

Fund expenses vary considerably, both from contract to contract and, especially, according to the type of account. Money market and index accounts typically have the lowest fund expense, with bond accounts somewhat higher, general equity accounts even higher, and specialty accounts (e.g., natural resources, real estate) with the highest fund expense.

The sum of (a) fund expense and (b) total insurance expense equals the total annual overhead cost to the annuity contract owner. Well, almost. There may also be an annual contract charge, but that is usually about $30 per year, and is often waived for contracts with balances exceeding specified levels, not a percentage of the annuity balance.

What do these various charges and expenses amount to, in percentage terms? The average M&E expense for variable annuities, according to Morningstar (2012) is 1.25%.[12] The average fund expense was 0.97%, and the average total expense (total insurance expenses plus fund expenses) was 2.35%. This does not count the contract charge, which is measured in dollars, or the surrender charge, as the surrender charge is payable only on surrenders or withdrawals in excess of the penalty-free amount.

L Share Annuities

Recently, annuity companies have begun to offer an L Share contract providing the same features and benefits as their standard variable annuity contract, but with a shortened surrender charge schedule. Typically, the initial surrender charge is the same as the standard share class, but it declines to zero more rapidly. The trade-off for this benefit is typically a higher annual M&E charge.

> *Example*: One insurer's standard share class variable annuities imposes the following surrender charge schedule—7%, 6%, 6%, 5%, 4%, 3%, 2%, 0%. Surrender charges cease in year 8. The M&E charge for that contract, assuming a standard death benefit, is 1.25%. The L share variant of that contract imposes surrender charges of 7%, 6%, 5%, 0%. Surrender charges cease in year 4. The M&E charge, for the same standard death benefit is 1.50%.

Is the shortened surrender charge period worth an additional annual cost of 0.25%? For some clients, it may be worth it. For others, it may not.

P Share Annuities

Some clients may be willing to bear longer surrender charge schedules in return for lower annual costs. The so-called P share variant offers this trade-off. The insurer cited in the above example issues a P share contract with surrender charges of 8%, 8%, 8%, 7%, 6%, 5%, 4%, 3%, 2%, 0%. Surrender charges cease in year 10. The M&E charge, for the same standard death benefit, is 1.15%.

Is the longer and heftier surrender charge schedule worth the lower annual cost? Again, some clients will prefer this option; others will not. The relative importance of surrender charges, in the overall value proposition represented by a deferred annuity, whether fixed or variable is almost always a matter of client perception. For an investor who does not intend to take distributions from her annuity until many years after buying it, surrender charges may be of little importance. She may be happy to bear higher and longer charges, and assume a greater liquidity risk in exchange for lower annual costs. For another investor, however, being able to get at his money whenever he wants, without charges, may be a prerequisite. The L Share contract and free withdrawal provisions were devised to be more attractive to him—as were no-commission zero surrender charge contracts. In any case, the prudent advisor should consider that a deferred annuity is, generally speaking, a long term investment and that regulators and broker-dealer compliance officers certainly consider it as such.

Endnotes

1. Commutation is the right of an annuity contract holder to surrender a policy in payout status for a lump sum, in lieu of the remaining annuity payments. This is generally determined as the present value of remaining payments, with some minor adjustments to compensate the insurance company for the change.

2. A life only annuity pays for the life of the annuitant. Payments cease at the annuitant's death, regardless of when death occurs.

3. Most annuity contracts are issued on a sex-distinct basis, recognizing that females live longer, on average, than males. A few contracts use unisex rates—where the payout factor for a male is always the same as for a female of the same age. These are usually employed in group retirement plans where sex-distinct annuity factors have been judged to be discriminatory.

4. Variable SPIAs typically offer a fixed account option, which does provide for fixed amounts. The present discussion refers, however, to amounts placed under the variable payout option.

5. Conventional fixed deferred annuities typically credit interest annually. Some index annuities do as well. However, some index annuities may credit interest every two or three years or, in the case of term end point contracts, only at the end of the initial term period (see Chapter 7).

6. This applies, not just to annuities, but also to other products—notably, universal life policies. Many insurance companies publish their interest rate crediting history. In addition, an excellent, and unbiased, source for such information is A.M. Best (www.ambest.com).

7. Some contracts provide for the payment of bonus interest at certain policy anniversaries (e.g., at the end of the 5th and 10th year).

8. Morningstar® *Principia*® software, Variable Annuity/Life module. Quoted from the online help section.

9. *Ibid.*

10. *Ibid.*

11. *Ibid.*

12. http://awgmain.morningstar.com/webhelp/glossary_definitions/va_vl/pol_M_E_Risk.html.

Chapter 5

Optional Benefits
in Variable Annuities

The total insurance expenses described in Chapter 4 are the standard costs for the standard features of a typical variable deferred annuity. The principal benefits typically purchased by these expenses are:

1.   The guaranteed death benefit provided by the contract, without election of optional, extra-cost riders. An interesting development in the annuity marketplace has been the decision by a few annuity providers to offer variable contracts with no death benefit guarantee whatsoever—not even a return of premium provision. Most variable annuities, however, offer at least that level of death benefit guarantee.

2.   The guaranteed annuity payout factors, providing a minimum annuity payment if the contract is annuitized under one of the annuity payment options, regardless of future changes in longevity or interest rates.

Most deferred variable annuities marketed today offer additional, optional benefits at additional cost. New policy enhancements are introduced by one company or another nearly every month, and the variety—and complexity—of options available is downright staggering. Some relate to the guaranteed value at the death of the annuitant or owner, and are generally termed death benefit enhancements, discussed at the end of this chapter. Others—indeed, most of the recently-introduced options—fall into the category of living benefits.

Living Benefits

The living benefit riders offered in deferred variable annuity contracts refer to benefits that a contract holder can exercise while still alive. They are not triggered only by the death of either the annuitant or owner). Strictly speaking, the term should include benefits such as the guaranteed annuity payout factors, the availability of the various investment sub-accounts and cost-free transfers among those sub-accounts, dollar cost averaging, and automatic rebalancing. However, in practice, living benefits[1]—especially when the reference is to enhanced living benefits—generally means any of these four enhancement features:

1. Guaranteed Minimum Income Benefit (GMIB)

2. Guaranteed Minimum Accumulation Benefit (GMAB)

3. Guaranteed Minimum Withdrawal Benefit (GMWB)

4. Guaranteed Lifetime Withdrawal Benefit (GLWB). This is similar but not an identical alternative to the GMWB.

Availability of Enhanced Living Benefits

Some variable annuity contracts permit these enhanced living benefit options to be elected only at the time of contract issue. Others permit them to be added later. Some contracts permit election of only one of these benefits. After electing one of these benefits, the contract owner may or may not be permitted to discontinue it and cease paying its cost.

Guaranteed living benefit riders are also available in many index annuities. The costs and benefit levels are different, from the costs and benefits of these riders when applied to a variable annuity, A discussion of these differences, and possible differences in efficacy, appears at the end of this chapter.

Guaranteed Minimum Income Benefit

The Guaranteed Minimum Income Benefit (GMIB) guarantees a minimum income to the annuitant, regardless of adverse investment performance of the variable annuity contract. The amount of the guaranteed income is typically calculated by applying a guaranteed interest rate (usually 5%-7%) to the initial payment to produce a benefit base[2] from which the GMIB payments are calculated. It is extremely important that the advisor understand that this rate does not guarantee a future account balance that may be withdrawn as a lump sum! The only thing guaranteed by a GMIB benefit is that the benefit base can be annuitized at certain guaranteed payout factors, ultimately providing a certain level of income the annuitant is guaranteed to receive in the future. Advisors must understand that this guarantee comes only with certain conditions.

Annuitization Generally Required

Variable annuity contracts offering a GMIB benefit generally require that the benefit base, and thus the entire contract, be annuitized for the GMIB to be applicable. Usually, the annuitization must be for the life of the annuitant, and, in some cases, must be elected within a 30- or 60-day window each year (typically, immediately following a contract anniversary), following the expiration of a waiting period, which is usually 7-10 years. Annuitization that uses the GMIB benefit base is not available during the waiting period. Often, the GMIB provision will also require an annuitization age setback—typically, from three to seven years—where the actual age of the annuitant will be reduced, by the number of years specified in the setback requirement, and the special GMIB annuity factor for that adjusted age is used to determine the annuity amount. It is important to note that the downward adjustment of the annuitization age will spread payments over a longer period of time, resulting in a lower payment amount. This represents an indirect cost of utilizing the GMIB rider.

Calculation of the GMIB

The GMIB is calculated by using special annuity payout factors that are generally significantly lower[3]—that is, they produce lower annuity payments per dollar of principal applied—than the factors the insurer offers to owners of deferred annuity contracts wishing to annuitize on a regular basis, using the cash value or annuity value of their contracts.[4] The special GMIB payout factor for the payout option chosen (e.g., Life & 10-Year Certain) and the annuitant's age—or adjusted age, if applicable—is applied to the benefit base, rather than the cash value or annuity value of the contract, to determine the guaranteed income under the GMIB provision.

Obviously, electing the GMIB payout with its reduced annuity factors would not be advisable if the contract annuitization value exceeds the benefit base, or , if the investment performance has produced a cash value available for annuitization than is greater than the initial premium, compounded at the GMIB guarantee rate.[5] However, if the benefit base exceeds the actual account balance (the cash value or annuity value), that greater amount is used to produce the GMIB annuity amount. In Figure 5.1, the account balance at the end of 15 years is $198,196, and the benefit base is $226,090. This represents the primary potential benefit of the GMIB rider: the ability to elect to annuitize a lifetime stream of payments based on a higher benefit base if contract performance turns out to be unfavorable, thereby guaranteeing a certain income stream in the future regardless of market performance, while still providing the investor with the opportunity to participate in the investment potential of the variable subaccounts selected.

What is not so obvious is that the election to annuitize using the GMIB may not be advantageous for the contract owner even if the benefit base is higher than the account balance. This is because the lower payout factors used in the GMIB, and the age setback, if applicable, may produce a lower annuity amount than the higher regular payout factors applied using the annuitant's actual age to the annuitization value. In this situation, regular annuitization would be more profitable. To avoid unintentionally annuitizing for a lower payment under the

Figure 5.1

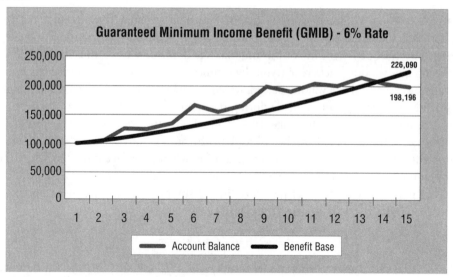

GMIB, some contracts will always pay, upon the owner's election to annuitize under the GMIB, the higher of (1) the regular annuity payout factor chosen, applied to the regular annuitization value, or (2) the GMIB payout factor, applied to the GMIB benefit base. However, from a practical perspective, if the annuitization payment available under the GMIB is inferior, the client will simply make a decision to utilize the existing annuity cash value in whatever manner desired (e.g., systematic withdrawals, cash value annuitization regardless of the GMIB, or simply continued accumulation/deferral).

The income guaranteed under a GMIB annuitization is an option. The contract owner may always elect not to exercise that option, for reasons such as the income amount is unattractive, or the GMIB annuitization, like regular annuitization, is generally irrevocable. In that scenario, some might argue that the cost of the GMIB was wasted money. However, the authors disagree. The GMIB option, like an option traded on the stock market, is not worthless simply because the purchaser never exercises it.

The GMIB typically requires annuitization on a fixed basis. That is, the special annuity factor used creates an income stream that is not only guaranteed, but also fixed in amount. Some annuity contracts however, also offer the GMIB with variable annuitization, using variable annuity units. In the authors' opinion, the choice is a valuable one, particularly for those who are especially worried about future inflation rates, who anticipate a lengthy retirement income period, or both.

Because of the complexity in how the benefit base is determined, and the even greater complexity in how the GMIB annuity payments are calculated, due to the application of different annuity factors and potentially an age setback, it is often advisable to focus on the actual dollar amount of the guaranteed annuity payment at a particular point in the future. By comparing actual guaranteed dollar payments at a particular point in the future, it becomes easier to compare the GMIB benefit to other income options in the contract or to GMIB riders of other variable annuity contracts. Some companies may offer a lower interest rate applied to the benefit base but higher annuity factors, or apply an unusually high interest rate to the benefit base but include a substantial age setback. By viewing the GMIB benefit in terms of the actual dollar payments that will be received, evaluation may be easier, and clearer, despite all of the moving parts. But the prudent advisor should be careful to consider the inherent time value of money when evaluating guaranteed payments in the future based on a lump sum deposited today.

Withdrawals and the GMIB

GMIB options often permit the contact owner to make withdrawals before, or even after, exercise of the GMIB option. Such withdrawals reduce the benefit base from which the guaranteed minimum income is calculated. Two methods of reduction are used:

1. Dollar-for-dollar reductions adjust the benefit base downward by one dollar for each dollar withdrawn. Usually, this dollar for dollar treatment, if offered, is available only for withdrawals up to a specified percentage of the prior year's account balance or benefit base.[6] Withdrawals in excess of this percentage then reduce the benefit base proportionally. However, for older GMIB contracts (e.g., prior to 2002), dollar for dollar treatment often applied up to the entire value of the annuity contract.

2. Proportional reductions, also called pro rata reductions, adjust the benefit base downwards by the proportion that the withdrawal represents of the current account value.

Where the benefit base exceeds the account value, the proportional method will produce a greater reduction in the benefit base than a dollar-for-dollar method, which is less favorable for the annuity holder. Conversely, where the benefit base is less than the account value, the proportional method will produce a smaller reduction in the benefit base than the dollar-for-dollar method.

These same two methods are used in the guaranteed minimum death benefit discussed below. See that discussion for an example.

Step-Up and the GMIB

Often, the GMIB rider includes a step-up option. This allows the contract owner to step-up, or increase, the benefit base if the account balance has grown to exceed it. Typically the comparison between the account balance and the benefit base is applied on the contract anniversary. In the chart in Figure 5.2, the GMIB benefit base is stepped up to the greater account balance in year six. This option is typically subject to restrictions as to the number and timing of step-ups.

Figure 5.2

Some GMIB provisions require the contract owner to elect to step-up the benefit base; others will step-up that value automatically, at specified intervals, if the contract value at those times exceeds the previously established benefit base. Typically, a step-up in the benefit base—particularly if it is optional and requires a voluntary election—imposes a new waiting period before that new benefit base may be applied under the GMIB payout option.

The interaction between riders for a contract that includes both a step-up feature and a growth rate on the benefit base will depend on the contract. For some contracts, the growth rate will only apply to the original contributions. In other cases, it will apply to whatever the current benefit base is, thereby accruing the growth rate on top of any recent step-up adjustments. This difference can be significant and reminds us that it is critical to read the details of the provisions regarding death benefit options as they appear in the prospectus. Reading the brochure designed for the client or even the agent's guide is simply not enough.

Withdrawals under the GMIB

Most GMIB riders permit the contract owner to make contract withdrawals up to a specified percentage of the account balance or benefit base on a dollar-for-dollar basis. Thus, any withdrawals will reduce both the contract cash value and the GMIB benefit base by the amount withdrawn, thus reducing both the lump sum surrender value and the amount that can be annuitized under the GMIB guarantee. It is very important that the advisor understand the impact of withdrawals in excess of the specified percentage, which is often, 6%. Some contracts provide that, while withdrawals up to that percentage will reduce the GMIB benefit base on a dollar-for-dollar basis, any excess withdrawal will reduce that benefit base proportionally. For a contract that has been significantly depleted—where the annuity owner is relying on the guarantee—a pro-rata excess withdrawal from a contract with little remaining cash value can catastrophically reduce the benefit base.

In other contracts, typically older ones, an excess withdrawal will reset the benefit base to the then-current contract cash value—perhaps even if a withdrawal exceeds the specified percentage by only a dollar! Excess withdrawals have a similar effect on the guaranteed death benefit in most variable annuities (see "Impact of Withdrawals on Death Benefit," later in this chapter). In short, the authors recommend that advisors be very cautious in considering any withdrawal from a GMIB rider in excess of the annual specified percentage, particularly in situations where the annuity's cash value is significantly below the benefit base.

Cost of the GMIB

The current cost of a GMIB rider varies from contract to contract, but is generally about 100 basis points per year.[7] In some contracts, this cost is assessed against the account value; in others, it is assessed against the benefit base. In some contracts, the GMIB charge, as a percentage of the benefit base or account balance, is fixed; in others, the charge may be increased. It is often difficult to tell. For example, one major insurer's prospectus says, "currently, we deduct a charge equal to 0.50% per year of the average Protected Income Value for the period the charge applies." The word "currently" at the beginning of the statement suggests, to the authors, at least, that the percentage charged is not guaranteed. However, representatives of that insurer assured one of the authors that it has never been, and will not be, changed. We suggest that advisors make sure that such assurances are in writing.

Guaranteed Minimum Accumulation Benefit

The guaranteed minimum accumulation benefit (GMAB) is the second of the four basic types of optional living benefits offered in variable deferred annuity contracts. As with the other three enhanced living benefits, the GMAB consists of several moving parts.

Guarantee Period

Unlike the GMIB, which promises a future minimum income value, the GMAB guarantees a future account value. It does not do this by guaranteeing a minimum growth per year, but by promising that the account balance will be equal, at a minimum, to the GMAB guarantee amount at the end of the guarantee period,[8] which is typically 7 to 10 years. Thus, if the account value is less than the GMAB guarantee amount at the end of the guarantee period, the account value will be adjusted upwards to equal the GMAB guarantee amount.

The guarantee amount is generally the initial investment, in the case of single premium contracts, or all contributions made during the guarantee period, in flexible premium contracts. This guarantee of principal is sometimes referred to as the base guarantee of the GMAB provision. The base guarantee may also incorporate an interest bonus by guaranteeing a percentage greater than 100 of such amounts (e.g.: 120% of premiums, or 120% or premiums paid within the first 120 days of the contract).

Step-Up Provision

The step-up provision in a GMAB rider operates to provide additional downside guarantees in the event that the cash value of the annuity rises above the initial principal amount. Note that this is different from how step-up provisions work with GMIB riders. The opportunity to step-up the GMAB guarantee amount to the current cash value may be available every certain number of years, every year, or at any policy anniversary where the current value exceeds the prior anniversary's value by a certain percentage. When a step-up option is exercised, a new guarantee period begins, and the new, stepped-up value guarantee is not applied to the contract to adjust the account value until the end of this new period (see Figure 5.3). However, the original benefit amount, or the contract owner's contributions, is in many contracts, guaranteed indefinitely from the end of the original guarantee period.

Figure 5.3 illustrates a GMAB where the policy owner elected to step up the GMAB benefit base to the cash value at the end of the fifth year. The GMAB had a 7 year guarantee period, meaning that the greater of the original contribution or this stepped-up amount was available at the end of the twelfth policy year. Typically, GMAB riders do not require annuitization.

Figure 5.3

Asset Allocation May Be Required

Most insurers manage the risk inherent in the GMAB by imposing restrictions upon the asset allocation permitted to contract holders who purchase the GMAB rider. Often, funds with high volatility are not available, and many contracts require that the contract owner choose one of several defined model portfolios. Alternatively, the insurer may reserve the right to move funds from the variable subaccounts chosen to the fixed account or more conservative separate accounts. The conditions under which this may occur are not always clear from a reading of the prospectus, and point of sale marketing materials often ignore this issue entirely.

Withdrawals

Withdrawals may be, but are not always, permitted from contracts in which the GMAB rider has been purchased. If so, they may reduce the guarantee amount on a dollar-for-dollar basis, a proportional basis, or a combination of the two (e.g., dollar-for-dollar for withdrawals not exceeding 5% of the guarantee amount; proportional, for any excess).

Annuitization Generally Not Required

Unlike the GMIB, the GMAB generally does not require annuitization. If the GMAB guarantee amount is greater than the contract's cash value at the end of the GMAV waiting period, the difference will be added, by the insurer, to the cash value, in the form of additional accumulation units of the subaccounts chosen, and the GMAB rider, and charges to same, will cease. The increased cash value may then be re-allocated to any of the contracts' available subaccounts, as the GMAB asset allocation restriction will no longer apply. It is worth noting that if the GMAB rider is applied at the end of the guarantee period, the account value itself is typically adjusted upwards as appropriate immediately, providing additional amounts invested for future growth in the contract from that point forward.

Cost of the GMAB

The cost of the GMAB, like the cost of some other enhanced living benefits discussed, varies considerably. Some contracts charge about 25 basic points per year, but others charge as much as 100. This cost is typically assessed against the annuity account value. Some insurers offer an enhanced GMIB that includes a principal guarantee similar to a GMAB. While many variable annuity contracts offered a GMAB only a few years ago, few do so, as of December, 2011. No index annuities of which the authors are aware offer it, which simply makes sense, given that the principal of an index annuity is guaranteed anyway.

Guaranteed Minimum Withdrawal Benefit

The third of the basic enhanced living benefits is the guaranteed minimum withdrawal benefit. This can be a confusing benefit for at least two reasons. First, the structure of this benefit is, in almost every contract, exceedingly complicated. Second, there are two variations of this benefit: (1) what the authors call the True Guaranteed Minimum Withdrawal Benefit (GMWB) and (2) The Guaranteed Lifetime Withdrawal Benefit (GLWB). Regrettably, the first label is sometimes used, usually by academics and journalists, to describe either type.[9] The GMWB and GLWB are, in fact, different provisions. To avoid this confusion, the authors suggest that the GLWB be considered as a fourth type of living benefit; the first three being the GMIB, GMAB, and GMWB.

The True GMWB

Strictly speaking, the term Guaranteed Minimum Withdrawal Benefit (GMWB) describes a contract provision that guarantees only the return of principal, or of a protected withdrawal value, (or benefit base) over time, through systematic withdrawals. It does NOT guarantee an income for life. That is how we will use the term in this book. The amount guaranteed to be available via withdrawals may be the owner's total contributions to the annuity (the principal) or a greater protected withdrawal value, such as the annuity cash value at the time of the first withdrawal.

The GMWB specifies a maximum percentage, typically, 5%, 6%, or 7%, of the protected withdrawal amount that may be withdrawn without resetting, or adjusting downward, that protected withdrawal amount. The benefit of the GMWB to the contract owner—and the risk to the issuing insurance company—is that the insurer must permit withdrawals, not exceeding the specified percentage, of the remaining principal or the protected withdrawal amount, even if the annuity cash value has fallen to zero due to adverse investment performance. This means that the annuity holder may be able to deposit an amount to the annuity contract and withdraw that entire principal amount at a specified percentage annually until all principal has been recovered, regardless of investment performance, as can be seen in Figure 5.4.

Figure 5.4

It is vitally important that the advisor know the impact upon the GWMB guarantee if the contract owner makes withdrawals exceeding the specified percentage. Some contracts will, in this circumstance, reset the protected withdrawal amount to the then-current cash value, which in a declining market—while withdrawals are also occurring—could be substantially lower. In some contracts, this reset can occur if any excess withdrawals occur, even if that excess is only a dollar.

When does the presence of a GMWB add value? Some commentators suggest that the GMWB rider provides value only if the investor's account balance falls to zero before the expiry of the GMWB period. As shown in Figure 5.5, the rider guarantees the contract owner the right to take withdrawals up to 7% per year until the guarantee amount is exhausted. In this case, that is approximately 14.3 years (100/7). If actual contract performance results in cash value remaining at the end of that period, the GMWB could be said to have been worthless. However, in the authors' view, that is rather like saying an insurance policy has been worthless to any insured who has not submitted a claim. The assurance of a benefit if certain bad things happen must surely have value even if those bad things don't happen.

Moreover, most GMWB riders issued today guarantee a benefit base greater than the investor's total contributions, either by an interest bonus applied to each contribution or by compounding contributions by a specified rate of interest until the earlier of the first withdrawal or a specified year, which is often year 10.

Figure 5.5

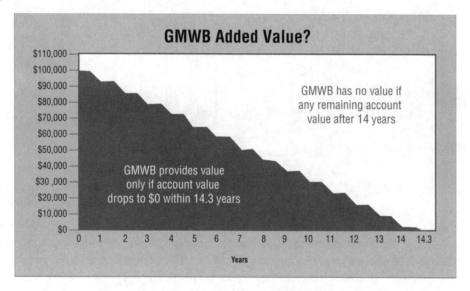

GMWB May Require No Waiting Period

Typically, GMWB provisions do not require a waiting period before withdrawals can begin under the guarantee, although some contracts impose such a requirement.

Asset Allocation May Be Required

Some GMWB provisions, like most GMAB provisions, impose restrictions on the investment choices available to the contract owner. Certain variable subaccounts—typically, those having high price volatility—may be unavailable, or election of a diversified model portfolio may be required.

Reset Option

Most GMWB provisions allow the contract owner an option, similar to the step-up option often permitted by GMIB provisions, to reset the protected withdrawal amount to the annuity cash value if that value has risen due to investment gains. The owner may, thus, lock in these gains and is entitled to take the stepped-up benefit base by withdrawals not exceeding the specified percentage (in this example, 7% per year) until that benefit base is exhausted, regardless of how long that takes (see Figure 5.6). In some contracts, a step-up option is available only at certain contract anniversaries. In others, it is available each year until a certain age. In this example, only three step-up elections are shown, for clarity.

Figure 5.6

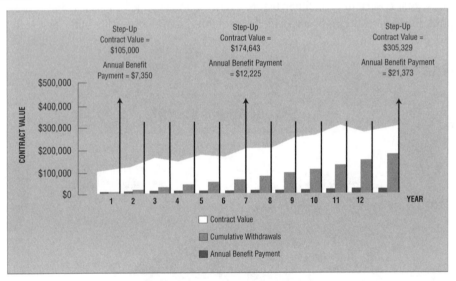

GMWB with Step-Up Provision

In so doing, the contract owner who has elected the GMWB option ensures a greater guaranteed withdrawal amount, because the GMWB withdrawal percentage will apply to this greater protected withdrawal amount. Reset may be permitted only at certain option dates, such as every five years, on each contract anniversary, or at any anniversary where the annuity cash value has increased by at least a certain percentage over the previous year's value. Recently, the frequency of step-up option dates has increased significantly. Some contracts permit step-ups annually, or even more frequently, but only if the account balance exceeds the previously established benefit base amount.

Cost of GMWB

The current cost for the GMWB option is typically in the range of 60-90 basis points per year; the maximum cost is in the range of 120-150 basis points per year. Some contracts waive this cost if no GMWB withdrawals are made within a specified period (e.g., 7 years) following election of the option, but will continue the GMWB provision in force. Most insurers reserve the right to increase the rider cost to a specified maximum or to the then-current cost if the benefit base is stepped-up. The true GMWB, with no guarantee that income payments will persist for life, is far less popular today than when it was introduced.

Guaranteed Lifetime Withdrawal Benefit (GLWB)

The other type of withdrawal benefit that is sometimes referred to, misleadingly, as a GMWB or lifetime GMWB is the Guaranteed Lifetime Withdrawal Benefit. The GLWB is by far the most popular living benefit; 95% of variable annuity contracts now offer this rider and nearly 70% of buyers opted to purchase it in 2010.[10] It is similar to the GMWB, but with one very significant difference. Here, the operative term is lifetime. The contract owner is guaranteed the right to withdraw up to the specified percentage of the benefit base each year for life, even if the account balance falls to zero, and even if cumulative withdrawals exceed the original benefit base, or protected value. By contrast, the GMWB guarantees such payments, even if the annuity account value falls to zero, but only to the point where cumulative withdrawals equal, or have exhausted, the benefit base.

Like the GMWB, the GLWB typically does not impose a waiting period before withdrawals can be made. However, the guaranteed compounding component of the benefit base generally ceases upon the later of the first withdrawal or the expiration of a specified period, which is often 10 years.

In some contracts, the GLWB is an option within the GMWB rider. In those riders, if withdrawals commence prior to a specified age, the contract owner is guaranteed the right to withdraw up to the specified percentage of the benefit base, which may be stepped-up if that option was elected or is automatic, until that benefit base is exhausted. At that point, the guarantee ceases. If withdrawals commence after a specified age, withdrawals up to a specified percentage, which may be different from the percentage permitted for earlier withdrawals, are guaranteed for life, or for the joint life of policy owner and spouse.

The utility of a step-up option in a GLWB, once withdrawals have begun, is rarely made clear from either prospectus language or point of sale marketing materials. It is true that, in many contracts, if the account balance exceeds the remaining benefit base, at a step-up option date, that benefit base may be increased to the level of the account balance. However, the likelihood of such a scenario is questionable. Typically, withdrawals reduce the benefit base. For a step-up to be profitable, or even available, to the contract owner, the account balance must have increased by more than the sum of the annual withdrawals taken and the GLWB rider cost since the last step-up option date. For example, if the GLWB withdrawal percentage is 5% and the total annual costs of the VA total 3% (e.g.: an M&E charge of 1.4%, subaccount fees of 0.6% and a GLWB rider cost of 1%), the contract must grow by at least 8%.[11] This is certainly possible, even with the asset allocation restrictions typically imposed when the GLWB is chosen. If it occurs even once, the contract owner will benefit from the resulting step-up every year from that point on, for life.

But the step-up election may increase the GMWB rider cost, making the hurdle the account balance growth must overcome even higher for future step-ups.

The authors are not suggesting that the step-up provision in the GLWB is not worth it. To a particular client, who has been informed as to how it works and what is required for it to be available, it may well be worth it. But the key word here is informed. In the authors'experience, variable annuity marketing materials generally do not address the issue just described. For the contract owner to know, the advisor must know, and be willing to educate her client. It may be best—for both client and advisor—to think of the GLWB income, once it has commenced, as being a flat amount since the risk in an adverse market is that the market will decline and, thus, no future step-up may ever apply.

GLBs Expire at Annuization

It is vitally important that the advisor understand that all of the living benefit guarantees described above (GMIB, GMAB, GMWB, and GLWB) operate only in the accumulation phase of the annuity—that is, prior to annuitization. When the contract owner elects an annuity payout option, whether fixed or variable, all of these guarantees expire. Of course, in the case of the GMAB and the GMIB, it may be more appropriate to say that the benefits mature. If the GMAB value exceeds the cash value of the contract and the waiting period has passed, the annuitization value of the contract will be the GMAB value because the cash value will have been stepped-up to the GMAB value at the end of this waiting period. If the GMIB value exceeds the cash value, the higher (former) value may be used as the annuitization value, but this will require use of the special GMIB payout factors. As noted above, these factors are usually significantly less than the regular payout factors available to contract holders wishing to annuitize the cash value. This could result in a lower annuity payment than would be payable by annuitizing the lower cash value, using the regular payout factors, except in contracts guaranteeing the higher of the two income amounts.

Recent Industry Trends in Guaranteed Living Benefits

In the past 3 years, there have been many changes in insurers' marketing of guaranteed living benefits. Several major insurers have discontinued offering guaranteed living benefits and some have discontinued issuing variable annuity contracts altogether. Those insurers remaining in the living benefit market have all raised the current cost of riders, decreased the benefit levels, or both. This trend is due to several factors—chiefly, the significant decline in interest rates coupled with the dramatic increase in the volatility of equity markets. In some cases, it may also be the result of underpricing; some insurers were probably not charging enough for these benefits originally, but have now increased their pricing to reflect the increased cost, especially hedging costs. It is worth noting that if recent price increases mean that prior contracts were underpriced, the obvious implication is that earlier versions of living benefit riders may have been especially good values.

In addition to price changes, current offerings generally impose increased restrictions upon the asset allocation of contract cash values. As hedging strategies continue to evolve, further restrictions and, perhaps, more sophisticated asset allocation requirements may be expected.

Assessing the Value of a Guaranteed Living Benefit

In 2008, the TIAA-CREF Research Institute published a paper that sought to determine the value of a guaranteed lifetime withdrawal benefit.[12] It concluded that there is little, if any value, to this rider in nearly all situations.[13] The paper asserts that:

> "This product only has value if the performance of the underlying funds is extremely poor. For example, if the S&P index has a 0% return for 20 years, and the policyholder is still alive, then the $5,000 income guarantee has value; at that point the account balance is zero but annual payments of $5,000 will continue for life. But the vast majority of the time, the investor is only receiving his or her own money back, along with its investment earnings. And for this he or she is paying as much as 75 or even 100 basis points per year. In addition, as we will demonstrate later, annuitization is a better way to guarantee lifetime income. We think this point is important enough that it bears repeating. If market performance is similar to the past few decades, the buyer is paying for an insurance feature that has little value."

We believe that this reveals a fundamental misunderstanding of the subject. The first two sentences state that the only way this contractual provision can have value is if it pays off. That's investment logic, and it's quite correct—when applied to an investment problem.

However, the GLWB is not an investment feature. It's a risk management feature. It's insurance. The investor is paying to transfer to the insurance company the risk that the annuity investment performance will not produce at least a certain level of income.

The TIAA-CREF authors say that this is a bad deal because the probability that the GLWB will produce more income than the annuity without such a benefit, where both are invested identically, is so small that it's not worth the cost. But can the economic value of an insurance guarantee be reckoned purely by examining the probability that the event insured against will occur? We do not believe that is an appropriate way to analyze the value of a GLWB, or, indeed, any insurance feature. The benefit to the buyer of insurance isn't a probability, but a certainty. For someone who ran out of money yesterday, because she bought a variable annuity without a GLWB and investment losses caused her account balance to fall below the level needed to support the distributions from that contract that she required, it doesn't matter what percentile of the whole population she ended up in, or that the statistics predicted that she probably would not have run out of money. Nor does it matter that most people in her age cohort haven't (yet). What really matters is that she's now 100% broke!

Other studies of GLWBs have addressed this issue in a way that recognizes that an insurance feature cannot be analyzed merely by assessing its profitability to the buyer.

In October, 2007, Ibbotson released a study entitled *Retirement Portfolio And Variable Annuity With Guaranteed Minimum Withdrawal Benefit (VA+GMWB)*, comparing four traditional portfolios (Conservative, Moderately Conservative, Moderate, and Aggressive) with a variable annuity having a GMWB component, invested in a Moderate Aggressive model. The *VA+GMWB* allocation had a higher equity exposure than the average of the portfolios on the other side of the comparison, but that higher allocation did not, in the authors' opinion, translate into a higher risk to income level because the GMWB hedged that risk. It should be noted that this study ignored the risk that the insurer might not be able to pay the income guaranteed by the GMWB.

More recently, Garth Bernard and David Blanchett have published analyses of the value of the GLWB that are well worth reading. Blanchett's article,[14] published in the July, 2011 issue of the *Journal of Financial Planning*, compares the probability of a retiree's actually needing income from a lifetime withdrawal rider with the net cost of that rider, which Blanchett, like TIAA-CREF refers to as a GMWB. He finds that that probability of needing income is approximately 3.4% for males, 5.4% for females, and 7.1% for a couple, given current prevailing lifetime distribution factors, or guaranteed withdrawal rates. The rider will pay off, he notes, only if both of two conditions are true: (a) that the portfolio can no longer sustain the guaranteed withdrawal rate, and (b) the annuitant is still alive. The net cost of the rider, from the perspective of the annuitant as a percentage of annuity total value, is approximately 6.5% for males, 6.1% for females, and 7.4% for couples. Thus, he concludes, "the guaranteed income in [an annuity containing a GLWB rider] may be a relatively inexpensive form of 'longevity insurance'. Just because the overall expected net value of a longevity protection strategy is negative, does not mean that it does not offer a valuable benefit to a retiree. This is a fundamental truth that is either overlooked or ignored by many critics of annuity protection features, who often fail to recognize that, in Blanchett's words, "the cost of any insurance product should be expected to be negative."

Garth Bernard's article,[15] in the March, 2010 issue of the *Journal of Financial Service Professionals*, makes this same point—that any insurance product will not pay off, on average. That is, that the buyer cannot expect to profit from purchasing insurance protection, because if the average insured experiences a profit, the insurer issuing the coverage will go broke.

Bernard concludes that:

- the younger the purchase age, the more valuable the [GLWB] rider;

- the sooner withdrawals begin, the less valuable the rider;

- the rider may never produce the insurance company's own money; that is, that the rider is in the money, on average, only after several decades;

- a SPIA may produce better results if withdrawals are to begin immediately; and

- a longevity annuity may produce better results if income is to commence after many years.

Bernard's first two conclusions are self-explanatory. The fourth and fifth conclusion illustrate that either an immediate or future annuitized stream of income, providing the contract owner with no right to discontinue payments and take the annuity cash value in a lump sum, will generally provide a higher rate of income than a GLWB which does provide such a right. But what does that third point mean?

When is the GLWB in the Money?

Bernard calculates that for a GLWB with a roll up rate of 7% (i.e.: that the benefit base is guaranteed to increase by 7% per year), guaranteeing a lifetime withdrawal rate of 5% of the benefit base at the time withdrawals commence, and where underlying investments earn 7% per year, the annuity account value will fall to zero after 30 years. Of course, the rider provides that income payments will continue for the lifetime of the annuitant, even if that makes payments persist beyond 30 years. Nonetheless, payments under the GLWB return only the contract owner's own money for the first 30 years[16] until his/her own cash value is depleted, and only then is the contract in the money by actually paying the insurance company's money out to the annuitant. Other studies have calculated a different in the money point, which is to be expected, as that result will vary, depending upon the assumptions made as to roll up rate, guaranteed withdrawal rate, and return on investments.

The Guaranteed Lifetime Withdrawal Benefit in Index Annuities

While guaranteed living benefit riders have been offered in variable annuities for about 15 years, they have only recently been available in indexed annuities. By far the most popular guaranteed living benefit in index annuities is the lifetime withdrawal rider (GLWB). A few contracts offer a Guaranteed Minimum Accumulation Benefit (GMAB) rider; to the authors' knowledge, no index annuity offers a GMWB or GMIB rider.

Garth Bernard observes[17] that GLWBs in index annuities work in identical fashion to GLWBs in variable contracts. He argues that they both exhibit the same potential benefits and shortcomings, but that the key distinguishing characteristic is the level of fees. Fees for the GLWB rider on an index annuity are typically substantially less than those for the same rider on a variable annuity. Bernard argues that there are two key implications to the principal protection and fee differences between the two types of contracts:

1. That "when the total fees in a VA with a GLWB are taken into account, the reduction in the expected performance of the VA may bring it closer to what would be expected of a fixed annuity. It becomes more bond than equity.

2.   A GLWB with a given feature-set (i.e.: annual increase on the income base and guaranteed withdrawal factor), costs substantially less to deliver on an FIA platform than a VA platform."

While the first point is arguable, the second is certainly true. The issuer of a GLWB rider on an index annuity does not face the same hedging costs as the issuer of a VA with that same rider, as the value of an index annuity cannot decline due to market losses. These lower costs are reflected in the lower charge for the rider in index annuity contracts.

Which is better—a GLWB in a VA or one in an index annuity? Bernard's answer is "it depends." "Clearly", he writes, "one cannot make a valid comparison simply by looking at the design features of the GLWBs and the underlying products to be compared—there are just too many moving parts." The authors agree. Indeed, the question of whether a variable annuity with a GLWB rider is better or worse than an index annuity, with or without that rider, is a difficult one. Perhaps more importantly, it seeks to compare two very different instruments. A variable annuity, particularly one in which the cash value is invested in equities subaccounts, as a distinctly different risk/reward potential than an annuity in which there is no risk of loss of principal.

The authors are often asked by advisors why a guaranteed living benefit rider would make any sense in a deferred annuity which guarantees both principal and a minimum rate of return, such as an index annuity. In the case of either a GMIB or GMWB, the answer is "it would make no sense, which is why no index annuity offers such a benefit". However, GLWB riders are available in many index annuities. They will provide a benefit if the net return on the annuity is less than the roll up rate guaranteed by the rider.

Death Benefit Enhancements

The industry standard death benefit in variable annuities was, for many years, the greater of: (1) the amount originally invested—less any withdrawals, or (2) the account balance at death. Often, surrender charges were waived upon death, and most contracts offered today contain this waiver.

Most variable deferred annuity contracts available today offer much more liberal death benefit guarantees, though these enhanced death benefits are generally available only at extra cost, either by additional cost for the rider, or by incorporating the guarantee into the base contract for a higher M&E cost. Some contracts offer a choice of several death benefit provisions.

The typical enhanced death benefit of a modern variable deferred annuity is a guarantee to pay the highest value of:

1.   total contributions made, or less withdrawals;

2.   the cash value at the time of death, usually without regard for any surrender charges;

3.   the highest cash value as of certain prior dates, such as as of any prior policy anniversary or as of the 5th, 10th, 15th, or 20th policy anniversaries. This is often referred to as a ratcheted death benefit, and is typically restricted to policy anniversaries prior to a certain maximum age (e.g., age 85).

4.   total contributions made, or less withdrawals, accumulated at a specified rate of interest (e.g., 5%). This option typically provides that accrual ceases at a certain maximum age (e.g., age 85).

The cost of such an enhanced death benefit is typically 35 basis points or less per year. As with some living benefits, the cost may be calculated based on the annuity account value, or the guaranteed death benefit amount. Typically, this cost is the same for all contract owners, regardless of sex, health status, or age up to the allowable maximum. This makes the benefit a significantly better deal for some than for others.

Impact of Withdrawals on Death Benefit

An extremely important provision in any variable deferred annuity contract is the one specifying what adjustments will be made to the death benefit as a result of any partial withdrawals. Some contracts reduce the death benefit by withdrawals made, on a dollar-for-dollar basis. Others reduce it proportionally, by the percentage that the withdrawal represents of the cash value.

If the death benefit equals the current cash value, these two formulas will produce the same result. However, if the death benefit does not exceed the current cash value, the proportional method produces a higher remaining death benefit after withdrawal. The death benefit may be less than the current cash value if:

1.   the death benefit is a basic return-of-premium death benefit and the contract has appreciated since inception;

2.   the death benefit is a guaranteed return on contributions structure where the subaccounts have outperformed the guaranteed interest rate; or

3.   the death benefit is an annual step-up option, and the contract value has increased since the last anniversary step-up occurred, but the increase will not be credited until the next anniversary.

Example: Where Death Benefit Does Not Exceed Current Cash Value

Total Contributions to Annuity	$100,000
Current Cash Value	$150,000
Death Benefit Guarantee	$125,000
Withdrawal	$ 10,000

Dollar-for-Dollar Reduction in Death Benefit
    $125,000 - $10,000 = $115,000 (Death Benefit following withdrawal)
Proportional Reduction In Death Benefit
    $10,000 / $150,000 = 6.66667%
    $125,000 x 6.66667% = $8,333
    $125,000 – $8,333 = $116,667 (Death Benefit following withdrawal)

Example: Where Death Benefit Exceeds Current Cash Value

However, when the death benefit exceeds the current cash value, the dollar-for-dollar method results in a higher after-withdrawal death benefit than the proportional method. In the following example, the annuity owner invested $100,000. At one point, a later policy anniversary, the cash value had grown to $150,000. Subsequently, the cash value dropped to $75,000 due to poor investment results. The annuity offers an annual ratchet death benefit guarantee, whereby that earlier high water mark of $150,000 was locked in as the guaranteed death benefit.

Total Contributions to Annuity	$100,000
Current Cash Value	$ 75,000
Death Benefit Guarantee	$150,000
Withdrawal	$ 10,000

Dollar-for-Dollar Reduction in Death Benefit
    $150,000 - $10,000 = $140,000 (Death Benefit following withdrawal)
Proportional Reduction in Death Benefit
    $10,000 / $75,000 = 13.33333%
    $150,000 x 13.33333% = $20,000
    $150,000 – $20,000 = $130,000 (Death Benefit following withdrawal)

This distinction can be very important if the client is concerned with the amount to be left to heirs. It is particularly significant when a client is considering making a partial tax-free exchange of an existing annuity to a new annuity under Section 1035. If the existing contract uses a dollar-for-dollar method for reducing the death benefit, and the account value is less than the death benefit, then a partial withdrawal of all but the minimum amount necessary to maintain the existing contract can leave much of that contract's death benefit intact while allowing the client to invest most of its former cash value in a new, and better, annuity. It is presumed that the client, and his advisor, would not consider making the exchange unless the new annuity is significantly better, for the client's purposes, than the existing one.

Whose Death Triggers the Death Benefit Guarantee?

As was discussed in Chapter 3, all annuities issued since January 18, 1985 must provide that the contract value will be paid to the beneficiary upon the death of the contract owner/holder, in accordance with rules specified in Code Section 72(s). This rule of tax law mandates only that the contract value be paid upon the death of the contract owner. However, it does not necessarily mean that the guaranteed minimum death benefit of the contract will be payable. Whether that is the case is not a matter of tax law, but, rather, depends upon the terms of the annuity contract. Some, but not all, contracts are annuitant-driven; that is, they state that the contractual death benefit, including any optional, or enhanced death benefit guarantees, will be payable only upon the death of the annuitant. In such contracts, if the annuitant and the owner are different individuals, the owner's death will trigger payouts of the contract value, under Section 72(s), but will not trigger payment of the guaranteed minimum death benefit, which is payable, in annuitant-driven contracts, only upon death of the annuitant. Of course, where annuitant and owner are the same individual, this point is moot. But where they are not, it is extremely important that the advisor and the client know whose death will trigger the death benefit minimum guarantee—and who will receive that benefit. As noted in an earlier chapter, one annuity contract provides that, upon the death of an annuitant, the death benefit will be paid to the beneficiary named in the contract. But upon the death of a nonannuitant owner, the contract value will be distributed to: (a) the contingent owner, if named; or (b) to the surviving joint owner, if named, otherwise; (c) to the estate of the owner! The authors doubt that any prospective purchaser of that annuity—or most advisors—would expect such a result.

Death Benefit Guarantee is Not Applicable after Annuitization

A point that may be overlooked in many sales presentations is the fact that the guaranteed minimum death benefit—a point often emphasized in these presentations—is operative only when the annuity contract is in the accumulation phase; that is, before the owner has exercised an option to annuitize the contract. Upon annuitization, the death benefit guarantees described above cease to exist. If the advisor is emphasizing the advantages to the client, and the client's family, of the death benefit guarantees in a deferred annuity, it is essential that he or she make clear when those guarantees are no longer operative. This is of particular importance if the client has chosen a GMIB rider because electing to annuitize the benefit base will terminate any guaranteed death benefit.

IRD Tax Offset Benefit

As the Guaranteed Minimum Accumulation Benefit can be said to preserve principal against market loss, a rider in some variable annuities is designed to preserve earnings against loss wrought by annuity taxation. As discussed in Chapter 3, the undistributed and untaxed earnings, or gain in a deferred annuity is subject to tax, both if distributed to a living contract holder and to a beneficiary, following holder's death. Sometimes called an Earnings Preservation Benefit, this rider adds to the death benefit otherwise payable an additional amount to offset the reduction in the death benefit represented by income—and perhaps estate—tax due from the beneficiar(ies). Typically, this amount is a percentage of the contract earnings. For example, if Dave buys an annuity for $100,000 that has a death benefit of $200,000 at his death and the contract contains a 40% Earnings Preservation Rider, the total death benefit would be $240,000 ($200,000 death benefit + ($100,000 earnings times 40%).

Endnotes

1. While the guaranteed living benefits in annuity contracts are, strictly speaking, living benefit riders—because they're optional provisions that ride on the basic contract—the term living benefits is almost universally used to describe these riders, and the authors use that term to avoid confusion.

2. This value is also known as the Income Base or Protected Value.

3. The interest rate used in calculating these special payout factors is less than the rate used to calculate the regular payout factors. Often, this special interest rate is 2.0% or 2.5%, although it may be as high as 3.5% in some older GMIB riders.

4. See "Annuity Payout Factors" in Chapter 4.

5. In many contracts, the annuitization value is equal to the cash value. However, in some, a separate, and higher, account balance is available upon annuitization. This may result from the annuitization value's being computed using an interest rate higher than that used for the cash value or from the insurer's including an initial bonus interest in the annuitization value, but not the cash value available on a lump sum surrender. Some deferred annuities do not offer a lump sum surrender option. These contracts may never be cashed in, but must be placed under an annuity payout option. This is rare in variable contracts, but less so in either conventional or indexed fixed annuities.

6. However, in the older first generation of GMIB riders, unlimited dollar-for-dollar treatment was more common.

7. A basis point is 1/100th of a percent. Therefore, 30 bps = 0.30%. Basis points are useful terms for describing the magnitude of difference between two values, each of which is expressed in percentage terms. For example, if A = 6% and B = 4%, B is 200 basis points less than A. To say that "B is 2% less than A" would be incorrect, literally speaking. (100% - 2% = 98%, and 98% of 6% is 5.88%).

8. Also called the waiting period or vesting period.

9. For example, in October, 2007, Ibbotson released a paper entitled *Retirement Portfolio and Variable Annuity with Guaranteed Minimum Withdrawal Benefit (VA+GMWB)*. The GMWB provision studied was a lifetime income benefit, in which income payments would not cease if the protected amount (benefit base) fell to zero.

10. Milliman study (2011), cited in "BenefitsPro" website (http://www.benefitspro.com/2011/06/13/study-15-of-vas-with-glwb-started-withdrawals-in-f).

11. The growth rate required for a step up to be triggered may be even greater than that described if the rider cost is based on the benefit base rather than upon the account value. In that situation, the cost of the rider, relative to the annuity cash value, could be greater than its nominal cost, which is stated as a percentage of account balance.

12. TIAA/CREF Research Institute, "The 5% Guaranteed Minimum Withdrawal Benefit: Paying Something For Nothing?", April, 2008.

13. Many studies of the guaranteed lifetime withdrawal rider refer to it as a GMWB, which may confuse readers who are aware that GMWB is, in most industry marketing material, used to describe the Guaranteed Minimum Withdrawal Benefit, a minimum withdrawal benefit guaranteed only to return the benefit base through a series of withdrawals; Strictly speaking, a GMWB does not guarantee that those payments will persist for the life of the recipient. By contrast, the term GLWB, or Guaranteed Lifetime Withdrawal Benefit describes a minimum withdrawal benefit where payments *are* guaranteed for the lifetime of the recipient (or, if a joint rider is elected, for the lifetime of the recipient and his/her spouse). It is that benefit which the TIAA-CREF paper describes.

14. Blanchett, David, "The Expected Value of a Guaranteed Minimum Withdrawal (GMWB) Rider", *Journal of Financial Planning,* July, 2011

15. Bernard, Garth, "Measuring the Value of a Guaranteed Lifetime Withdrawal Benefit", *Journal of Financial Service Professionals,* March, 2010

16. Bernard, *Ibid,* p. 39

17. Bernard, Garth, "The GLWB Conundrum" (unpublished white paper).

Chapter 6

The Variable Annuity
as an Investment

In earlier chapters, the authors have made the point that an annuity is primarily a risk management tool and only secondarily an investment. Arguably, there are exceptions. A short-term CD annuity and, perhaps, an index annuity, might properly be viewed as primarily a savings instrument. On the whole, however, many—if not most—deferred annuities are purchased and sold as investments, and this is particularly true of variable deferred annuities.

Because the variable deferred annuity is typically sold as an investment, in this chapter we will examine it as an investment, using as our framework a model that one of the authors uses to describe the process of financial and estate planning. Then we will relate various characteristics of the variable annuity to three key aspects of the overall planning process, focusing on the extent to which these characteristics provide solutions to the needs that cause consumers to purchase financial instruments—investments—in the first place.

The Model

The process of financial and estate planning may be described as a 3-legged stool. The three legs are:

1. Accumulation

2. Conservation

3. Distribution

From the standpoint of the planning process, each leg, or aspect, represents a need, or combination of needs, that must be satisfied if the plan is to be successful. From the standpoint of a deferred variable annuity, each aspect is reflected in one or more characteristics of the annuity that are designed to satisfy the need in question. We will examine each leg, first as a component of the planning process and, then, as a need for which certain features of the variable annuity were designed to provide a solution.

Leg One: Accumulation

The accumulation goal, as many investors perceive it, is to amass as much capital as possible, by achieving the highest investment returns possible, consistent with acceptable risk. The authors believe that, while this maybe a valid investment objective, it is not a good planning objective. Rather, we think, one should aim for maximizing the probability of achieving one's goals. Often, goals are expressed in the form of income. To satisfy these income goals, a tool designed specifically to create income may be more efficient than one designed to create a future lump sum that can then be tapped to create income. There is good evidence that a combination of (1) instruments designed for pure wealth accumulation and (2) purely income instruments can produce higher probabilities of overall plan success than pure accumulation instruments by themselves.[1] In so doing, a combination is actually addressing both the client's accumulation goal and his or her conservation goal.

That said, let's stay focused on the accumulation goal, and ask, "how can a variable annuity help the investor to achieve this goal?"

The Variable Deferred Annuity as an Accumulation Instrument

The efficient accumulation of wealth is the object of all investment methodologies, including the widely used and popular Modern Portfolio Theory (MPT). This theory holds that, to achieve the highest returns possible, with the least amount of investment risk—or, viewed another way, to minimize the investment risk necessary to achieve a given portfolio rate of return—one should construct a diversified portfolio, composed of asset classes, that:

1. offers the opportunity, through a broadly diversified portfolio, to achieve the return necessary to achieve planning goals with the least amount of risk where risk is traditionally defined as volatility—usually measured by standard deviation.

2. reduces risk by constructing the portfolio efficiently from components that represent asset classes that are, to the extent possible, as weakly correlated—or even negatively correlated—as possible. This requires that the investment vehicle provide a sufficient variety of asset classes to allow construction of such a portfolio.

3. can be adjusted periodically. Many theorists believe that periodic rebalancing of the portfolio is essential, by selling those components that have outperformed expectations

and buying those that have underperformed, so as to bring the proportions of the components back to the original optimum mix. How often such rebalancing should occur is a matter of considerable debate.

4.   can be adjusted with as little expense (e.g., transaction costs, taxes, etc.) as possible.

How Does a Variable Annuity Allow the Investor to Build Such a Portfolio?

1. A Broadly Diversified Portfolio.

Early variable annuities offered only limited investment choices, often managed by the issuing insurance company. Today's contracts typically provide the policy owner access to a wide variety of investment subaccounts,[2] managed by several different independent money management firms, in addition to a fixed subaccount, which acts much like a fixed annuity, and for which separate management charges are not assessed. Some variable annuities offer 30 or more variable subaccounts from dozens of money managers. Generally, these subaccounts are actively managed and are sometimes said to be clones of mutual funds offered outside the annuity by the money manager.

However, it is very important that the advisor understand that the term clone, in this context, is misleading. For example, an annuity may contain a subaccount called Atropos Growth Opportunities, managed by, say, Olympia Capital Investments. Olympia may offer, outside the annuity, a mutual fund with the exact same name. But this does not mean that they are managed by the same individuals or that they have precisely the same investment objectives or investment policies. Nor does it mean that the fees and expenses are the same. Even when the same individual manages both, and when the investment policies of both are essentially the same, that manager may employ different strategies in the annuity than for the mutual fund. Tax considerations alone might suggest the use of different strategies. Realized gains in a mutual fund must, by law, be distributed to shareholders of a mutual fund and are currently taxable even if reinvested.

Consequently, advisors should avoid referring to these subaccounts as clones and, most certainly, should never use the performance history of one when discussing the other. Moreover, as noted in Chapter 1, the pricing of a variable annuity subaccount is different from the pricing of a mutual fund. Reinvested gains in a mutual fund purchase additional shares having, at the time of distribution, the same value as the original shares. By contrast, gains in a variable annuity subaccount do not purchase additional shares; instead, the value of the shares is adjusted to reflect those reinvested gains.

Similarly, though, most variable subaccounts are actively managed, as are most mutual funds. Recently, more and more variable annuities have added passively managed subaccounts designed to match the performance of an external index such as the S&P 500.

2. An Efficient Portfolio.

The availability of a wide variety of investment subaccounts, representing many asset classes, may allow the owner of today's variable annuity to construct a portfolio that is not only diversified but theoretically efficient. It is comprised of asset class components that are weakly, or even negatively, correlated, such that they do not perform in lockstep with one another. We say "may allow" because few, if any, variable annuity issuers provide the annuity owner, or his or her advisor, for that matter, with a tool to construct such an efficient portfolio. This construction is usually done by means of a technique known as Mean-Variance Optimization, and the software tool used to employ it is usually known as an optimizer. As of this writing, the authors know of no variable annuity issuer that provides either the client or the client's advisor with an optimizer, either on a website or in illustration software.

Of course, the client's advisor may have access to such an optimizer, either incorporated in a financial planning software package or a stand alone software package. However, even access to this tool will not suffice unless the advisor also knows some vitally important data about the subaccounts to be used to create the optimum portfolio. The required data includes:

- the expected mean return of the asset class;[3]

- the expected volatility of the asset class, as measured by its Standard Deviation (SD);

- the coefficient of correlation of the performance of every subaccount to be considered to the performance of every other subaccount to be considered;

- the historical time period to which these data refer.

Few, if any, variable annuity issuers provide all of this information. All provide historical return data, however, and an advisor who has access to an analysis tool such as Microsoft Excel®, expertise in using its statistical functions, and historical return data for all sub-accounts to be considered for a common time period of significant duration (we suggest at least ten years) can derive the remaining data, which can then be plugged into an optimizer.[4]

Realistically, though, few advisors will do this. First, because it requires statistical expertise that many advisors do not possess, and, second, because there is a much easier way to do the optimization—or, at least, there appears to be.

Some advisors will choose specific investment sub-accounts within the annuity to represent asset classes (e.g., Olympia Giant Growth to represent large cap growth stocks) and create an optimized portfolio from those accounts, using optimizer software and the statistical data, such as Mean, SD, and coefficient of correlation, supplied with the software, representing the asset classes themselves. The subaccounts will, in this procedure, be acting as proxies for the asset classes.

Use of an optimizer program in this way is fairly common among advisors seeking to build optimized portfolios from actively managed mutual funds. Applying it to actively managed variable annuity subaccounts is not much different, and the results should be no less credible. The problem is the results will not be credible—whether it is mutual funds or variable annuity sub-accounts that are being optimized—if they are actively managed.

The manager of an actively managed fund or variable annuity subaccount seeks to distinguish the performance of the account from its peers, hopefully, by outperforming them. That is what sells the fund and that is what produces the manager's bonus. If the benchmark for a fund is a particular index, the fund manager will seek to outperform that index. But the whole idea of using a proxy for something is to obtain results as close as possible to the values that would be produced if that something were the thing used. The very idea of a proxy, a substitute—deliberately managed to produce results different from the object for which it is substituted—is self-contradictory.

In the authors' opinions, use of Mean-Variance Optimization (MVO) has its uses, but it is not nearly the ideal tool that many advisors suppose it to be when it's used as just described. By definition, any fund or subaccount with a low R-Squared value,[5] in relation to the asset class for which it is standing proxy, will not perform in accordance with the expectations for that asset class. The lower the R-Squared value, the greater the dissonance. The authors believe that MVO is a much more reliable and credible tool when the correlation between the asset classes chosen—to which the return, SD, and coefficients of correlation apply directly—and the proxies chosen to represent those asset classes is as close as possible. There is a fairly simple way to accomplish this objective: the proxies should be designed to mirror the asset classes they represent. If the asset class is, say, U.S. Small Cap Growth, as measured by the Russell 2000 Growth Index, then an excellent proxy would be an index fund or subaccount deliberately constructed to perform like that index.

Until a few years ago, index subaccounts were rarely offered in variable annuities. Recently, however, many contracts have added them, though usually only one or two broad, well-followed indices, such as the S&P 500. A few contracts also offer Exchange-Traded Fund (ETF) accounts, which are also designed to mirror various indices. The expense ratio of both types of accounts is generally much lower than that of their actively managed cousins, and one might wonder why, in light of the frequent criticism of variable annuities as being too expensive, we do not see more of them in the variable annuity marketplace. It's possible that they are less profitable to the annuity issuer than actively managed accounts. It may also be that passively-managed accounts are incompatible with the culture of many insurers, whose marketing usually highlights the investment managers available for their products. Whatever the reason, the debate between actively managed and passively managed still rages. Many commentators and a few scholars argue that active management can provide additional value, over and above the value expected from the asset class to which a fund is most closely related. For those who agree with this argument, a variable annuity offers a significant benefit that is often under-appreciated.

As noted earlier, many variable annuities offer dozens of separate subaccounts managed by perhaps a dozen or more money management firms. Often, these managers are chosen by the insurance company because they represent a specific style expertise. Olympia Capital Investments, for example, may be a highly respected growth manager that is particularly adept and successful at managing client money using that style. By contrast, Asgard Asset Management may be well known and respected as a value manager. Another management firm may be highly successful at bond investing. By including all three firms in its stable of managers, an annuity offers the policyholder the opportunity to choose, not only those asset classes that comprise the most appropriate portfolio for his or her goals, but to select managers for each class that are unusually good at managing that particular kind of investment.

3. Periodic Adjustment.

Nearly all variable annuities allow the switching of money among the various subaccounts without cost.[6] Moreover, such a transfer is not a taxable event for income tax purposes. This allows the annuity owner to adjust her portfolio to reflect changed objectives or time horizons, because a manager has consistently underperformed, or to rebalance the portfolio, to return the investment mix to original, or revised, percentage allocations. Most variable annuities offer the policy owner the opportunity to elect such re-balancing automatically, at various intervals; typically, annually, semi-annually, quarterly, or monthly, or when the existing percentage allocation of a holding varies from its target by at least a certain amount or percentage. Typically, there is no charge for this feature.

A related benefit allowed by many variable annuities is sometimes referred to as dollar cost averaging. This feature allows the contract owner with a lump sum to invest, who may be concerned about the risk of investing in the market at the wrong time (i.e., when share prices may be ready to fall), to deposit the lump sum into the fixed account of the annuity in an arrangement where a portion of this lump sum will be automatically transferred, each month, to variable subaccounts that she has selected, so that the entire sum will be transferred evenly across a certain time period, which is typically, six months or one year. Often, an annuity issuer will offer contract holders who elect this feature a higher-than-market interest rate on the funds remaining in the fixed account, which will, by operation of the feature, be entirely invested in the separate accounts at the end of the period.

4. Low Annual Cost.

The owner of a modern variable annuity can construct a portfolio of many individual subaccounts, representing a wide variety of investment types and managed by a diverse stable of professional money managers with different styles and expertise. She can adjust this portfolio periodically—in some contracts, as often as desired—at no cost and with no tax consequence, and may elect to have adjustments made automatically, at no cost. These are powerful and attractive portfolio management benefits, rarely available to regular taxable accounts, which are all too often ignored when the variable annuity is considered as a wealth accumulation tool.

Leg Two: Conservation

The second leg of our 3-legged stool model is wealth conservation. Here, the investor's goal is to keep his accumulated assets as safe as possible from loss, including loss due to:

- poor investment performance;

- taxes;

- bankruptcy or other failure by the institution holding the investment; or

- attacks by creditors.

How can a variable annuity help the investor achieve this goal?

1. Loss from Poor Investment Performance.

Loss due to poor investment performance can adversely affect both the annuity owner during his or her life and the owner's beneficiary, if the owner dies before the contract is surrendered or annuitized. Today's variable annuities contain several risk management features that can help the annuity owner manage the risk of such losses.

As described in Chapter 5, the living benefits in modern variable annuity contracts provide the contract owner with four basic assurances:

1. a guarantee of a minimum future accumulation value, through the guaranteed minimum accumulation benefit;

2. a guarantee of a minimum income, through the guaranteed minimum income benefit;

3. a guarantee of no loss of principal through a guaranteed minimum withdrawal benefit;

4. a guarantee of a minimum income for life through a guaranteed lifetime withdrawal benefit.

Newer combination riders, incorporating elements of all three benefits, provide these same assurances while offering greater flexibility.

As discussed in Chapter 5, the guaranteed death benefit in today's variable annuity contracts assures the owner that her beneficiary will receive at least the amount originally invested, plus depending upon policy terms, a minimum rate of return on that investment or all or part of previously credited gains.

Both the living and death benefits are, of course, insurance features. They are, however, arguably relevant to a proper evaluation of the variable annuity-as-investment, for anyone whose overall financial planning goals include a desire for conserving his invested wealth.

2. Loss Due to Taxes.

One of the most-cited benefits of any deferred annuity, including a deferred variable annuity, is that undistributed gain is not subject to current income taxes. Indeed, tax deferral is often said to be the main attraction of deferred annuities. This, in the authors' opinion, is unfortunate for two reasons.

First, this narrow focus ignores the many benefits offered by deferred annuities that have nothing to do with taxation. The investment aspects of a variable annuity just described may be sufficiently attractive to an investor to justify the annuity costs, irrespective of tax deferral. Moreover, an annuity is the only financial instrument that can guarantee its owner an income that he or she cannot outlive.

Second, the argument that tax deferral is the main benefit to be gained from owning a deferred annuity necessarily implies that anyone purchasing a deferred annuity inside an IRA or qualified plan foregoes that main benefit. It is certainly true that the holder of an IRA annuity does not get tax deferral, by reason of owning the annuity, because the IRA itself provides such deferral. However, there are other reasons why one might wish to fund an IRA, or qualified plan, with a deferred annuity.

All that being said, however, the tax deferral enjoyed by annuities is clearly a benefit. Dollars that would otherwise be lost to annual income tax are, in a deferred annuity, able to earn further gain. The miracle of compound interest, in which gain on an investment can, itself, earn yet more gain, is enhanced by yet another layer, producing what is sometimes called triple compounding. This is when: (1) the principal earns gain; (2) the after-tax gain earns gain; and (3) the gain that would otherwise be surrendered to pay tax can also earn further gain.

Of course, tax deferred does not mean tax-free! The untaxed gain will eventually be taxed, either to the living annuity holder or to the beneficiary. It will also be taxed as ordinary income. Whether the trade-off of tax deferral now, or a benefit, for ordinary income treatment later, which might be considered a cost of that benefit, is attractive or problematic depends upon a number of variables. This includes assumptions as to tax rate, for both the annuity and the alternative, investment return rate, and, most importantly, how the money will eventually be distributed. A comparison of a hypothetical variable annuity with a hypothetical mutual fund portfolio, taking into account all of these factors and some others, appears at the end of Chapter 12.

Many annuity versus investment alternative comparisons are pure accumulation scenarios. They reckon the worth of each side of the comparison in terms of an after-tax future lump sum.

In the authors' opinion, such an analysis is inherently faulty. The benefits of a deferred annuity include guaranteed annuity payout factors—assuranced that, regardless of future investment conditions or life expectancies, the annuity owner is assured of receiving at least a specified income, every year—or more frequent payment interval—for each dollar that is annuitized. This benefit does come at a cost, which is part of the M&E charges of a variable annuity. Moreover, the annuity owner may elect to annuitize, using the greater of the current, nonguaranteed payout factors or the payout factors guaranteed in the contract. While the latter have, historically, been less attractive and thus, rarely if ever used, they do represent minimum guarantees that might be of value in the future.

In summary, the question of whether the benefit of guaranteed annuitization rates is worth its cost is certainly arguable. To the authors' knowledge, there has rarely been a time when the guaranteed payout rates contained in an existing deferred annuity contract have been as attractive as payout rates available in single premium immediate annuity (SPIA) contracts. The holder of any nonannuity investment wishing to convert his accumulated wealth to a guaranteed income stream could elect to purchase a SPIA. However, the success of this scenario, as compared to investing in a deferred annuity at the outset, depends upon two assumptions:

1.   that the payout rates in SPIA contracts will always be more attractive than those guaranteed in today's deferred contracts;

2.   that the after-tax value of the accumulated wealth—invested in the alternative being considered—will, when invested in the SPIA, produce a greater income than the annuitized deferred annuity. If the alternative investment contains any as-yet-untaxed capital gains, the tax on that gain must be paid on the surrender of the investment. By contrast, the entire future value of the deferred annuity, including all untaxed gain, could be available to purchase the same SPIA, if the deferred annuity is exchanged for the SPIA in a tax-free exchange under Code section 1035.[7] Or the deferred annuity could be annuitized using the then-current payout factors available for holders of that contract, if they are more attractive than those of every SPIA the investor might consider. While that situation has not, to the authors' knowledge, occurred in the past, it might well occur in the future, if average longevity to increase.

A comparison of a variable annuity versus an investment alternative that addresses which alternative is better, purely in terms of an after-tax future lump-sum, does not consider the potential advantages of an exchange of such annuities. Moreover, it does not allow for even the possibility that the guaranteed payout factors in the deferred annuity might be more attractive than future SPIA rates. Whatever one believes, as to the latter possibility, it should be taken into account. Any comparison that ignores a benefit that is contractually guaranteed by one alternative but is absent in the other is hopelessly flawed, unless one is prepared to decree that benefit to be utterly worthless—now, and at every time in the future.

3. Loss Due to Bankruptcy or Other Failure of the Institution Holding the Investment.

All investors are, or should be, concerned with the extent to which they may lose money as a result of the bankruptcy, or other failure, of the institution holding that money. Investors in annuities should be aware that the cash value in their contracts is not insured by the FDIC. Fixed annuities are backed by the general assets of the issuing insurer and are subject to the creditors of that insurer. The situation with variable annuities is somewhat different. The investments in the variable subaccounts are not held by the insurer, are not protected from loss other than by operation of any living benefits elected by the annuity owner, and are not subject to the insurer's general creditors. However, the contractual guarantees—including annuity payout factors, guaranteed minimum death benefits and guaranteed living benefits—are, like the cash value of a fixed annuity, backed only by the financial resources of the issuing insurer. The advisor recommending—or even discussing—an annuity with a client should exercise special care to ensure that the client understands these limitations. That said, most alternative investments are not guaranteed against loss due to bankruptcy or insolvency, as many holders of stock and bond issues can attest. We mention the issue only because annuities are sometimes marketed by depository institutions whose regular accounts are insured, and because of frequently-cited regulatory concerns that the inapplicability of such insurance to annuities sold by those institutions—or by advisors not connected with such institutions—is not well understood by consumers.

That said, in all 50 states, as well as Puerto Rico and the District of Columbia, there are guarantee funds to reimburse owners of annuity and life insurance contracts from losses resulting from insurer insolvency. The coverage provisions and limits of these funds vary by state. Information on this topic is available at: www.annuityadvantage.com/stateguarantee.htm.

4. Loss to Judgment Creditors.

A serious concern for many investors is the extent to which their assets may be attached by judgment creditors. Many advisors are unaware of the special protections afforded annuities by the laws of many states. Unfortunately, the extent to which annuity cash values receive creditor protection and the limitations on such protection vary widely, and simple answers are—in this context—more than usually dangerous. Two sources of insightful information on this subject are the websites of the law firm of Donlevy-Rosen and Rosen (www.protectyou. com; see especially, www.protectyou.com/apn13-2-fr.html) and a marvelously informative and surprisingly humorous website devoted to estate planning and tax protestor and creditor protection scams (www.quatloos.com).

Leg Three: Distribution

The third leg of the planning stool is distribution. Here, there are typically two goals involved:

1.   during the investor's lifetime, to create income—in the amounts required—from accumulated capital;

2. at the investor's death, to ensure that the wealth passes, as efficiently as possible, to those intended.

How can a variable annuity help our investor to realize these goals?

Income

Annuities are particularly useful in meeting a goal of required income because income is what annuities are all about. Their effectiveness as accumulation instruments notwithstanding, annuities were originally developed for one purpose—to produce income. When the desire is for an income that will, in any and all events, last as long as the life of the recipient—however long that might be—an annuity is arguably the perfect instrument because it is the only instrument that is guaranteed to do so. Furthermore, all annuities can do so.

What a variable annuity can do in this regard, that no other financial instrument can, is produce an income stream that: (1) is guaranteed to last for the lifetime of the annuitant, assuming a life annuity payout option is elected; and (2) will fluctuate in amount—that is, the amount of each payment will vary—reflecting the performance of the underlying investments. This is the so-called variable annuity payout option in a variable deferred annuity contract and the basic structure of a variable immediate annuity.

Why is such a variable payout desirable? Well, initially it should be admitted that for some investors, it is not. Some investors will desire a guarantee—that annuity payments will never change. For those individuals, a fixed annuity payout is indeed more appropriate. This option is available in variable deferred annuity contracts, just as it is in their fixed cousins. On the other hand, however, many investors are concerned with the impact of inflation on their retirement income. They know that, whatever the nominal value of their income, it is the purchasing power that buys groceries.

But is a payout arrangement where the amount of each payment varies, not with the cost of living, but with the performance of the annuity investments, truly the best way to keep pace with inflation? If keeping pace with inflation is the sole objective, probably not. After all, the investments could suffer a loss—resulting in a decrease in the amount of the annuity payment—at the same time that inflation is increasing, further eroding the purchasing value of each dollar of that payment. A better solution would be a life annuity where the amount of each annual payment is adjusted in accordance with some index of inflation, such as the Consumer Price Index. Unfortunately, very few insurance companies offer such a contract. A few insurers offer fixed annuities where the amount of each year's payment will be increased by a specified percentage, typically, 1% - 3%; at the time of this writing the authors know of no company offering an annual adjustment of more than 5%. For the inflation fearful, a guaranteed increase of a few percentage points each year is better than nothing, but it is probably not what they would prefer. Of course, the initial payment of the increasing annuity will be lower than that of the level one. The greater the guaranteed annual increase, the greater this difference will be.

For those individuals, the choice, at the present time, comes down to purchasing a truly inflation-indexed annuity from an insurer that offers one which may not contain all the features the investor wants, or electing a variable payout in the hope that the performance of the annuity investments chosen will enable annuity payments to rise with, or even beyond, the rate of inflation. The authors hope that more insurers will choose to offer genuinely inflation indexed annuities, both as immediate contracts and as payout options in deferred ones.

The scenario described above is one in which the investor's goal is for an income that is guaranteed both to last a lifetime—or for the lifetime of investor and someone else—and to keep pace with inflation. But what if the goal is to outperform inflation? Many consumers, and probably all advisors, know that lifestyles are not carved in stone. Some retirees wish to do better every year—in real dollar terms. For these individuals, an inflation-indexed payout may not be so attractive. If they believe that a properly designed portfolio, which probably consists mostly of equities, is more likely than not to outperform inflation, a variable payout may make more sense. In any event, the guarantee that the income, whether level or varying with investment performance or inflation rate, cannot be outlived is a powerful benefit.

But annuity payout factors are not the only mechanism by which a variable annuity can generate income for the investor. Living benefits can do so as well. The Guaranteed Minimum Income Benefit (GMIB) guarantees a minimum income based on a guaranteed benefit base that is unaffected by any investment losses within the annuity. The cost of this benefit is, however, not only the contractual charge assessed, but also the fact that the GMIB income stream usually requires annuitization using payout factors less attractive than those available to contract holders not electing this benefit (see Chapter 5).

The guaranteed partial withdrawal benefit also provides a guarantee of a minimum income, but it is really a guarantee of principal irrespective of adverse investment performance, provided that principal—or benefit base, if higher—is accessed via withdrawals not exceeding a certain limit each year.

Passing Wealth to Those Intended

Annuity proceeds are paid to the contract owner's designated beneficiary. They generally pass outside of probate, avoiding the potential cost and time delays that may be associated with that process. In addition, annuity proceeds usually enjoy special creditor protection—the level of protection varying with state law.

Furthermore, special restrictive beneficiary designations offered by some carriers can allow the contract owner to limit the beneficiary's access to proceeds, either by requiring a fixed systematic withdrawal schedule or imposing limits on the amount that the insurer will release each year.[8]

The variable annuity, viewed strictly as an investment, is a remarkably potent vehicle. While many proponents and critics see it purely as an accumulation device, it offers benefits designed to address the needs implicit in all three legs of the financial and estate planning stool.

Endnotes

1. Two of the best demonstrations of this conclusion are in "Making Retirement Distributions Last A Lifetime," by Ameriks, Veres, and Warshawsky, *Journal of Financial Planning*, Dec. 2001, and "Merging Asset Allocation and Longevity Insurance: An Optimal Perspective On Payout Annuities," by Chen and Milevsky, *Journal of Financial Planning*, June 2003.

2. These variable subaccounts are sometimes referred to as separate accounts.

3. For purposes of projecting possible future values, the arithmetic mean is generally considered to be a better factor than the geometric mean. Published historical performance figures generally report the geometric mean, which is always equal or lower—often, significantly lower—than the arithmetic mean.

4. As noted earlier, most historical returns information, when including mean return, use the geometric mean—as that is the best measure of average performance in historical data. If that geometric mean is used as an input in an optimizer software program that expects the user to supply an arithmetic mean—a better measure of the average when forecasting future values—the results will be theoretically inaccurate.

5. R-Squared (R2) is a measure of the extent to which change in one variable can be explained by changes in another, the model. It is often said to be a measure of goodness of fit.

6. Many contracts limit the number of transfers that may be made without cost per year. A few allow switching as often as daily.

7. Deferred annuities are commonly exchanged for SPIAs when the annuity owner decides to annuitize and the current payout factors in the deferred annuity are less attractive than those available from a SPIA. Because this practice is so common, the authors suggest that the often-cited statistic that "only about 2% of deferred annuities are ever annuitized" is probably misleading—perhaps very misleading. Any deferred annuity exchanged for a SPIA would be considered as not annuitized, although the result of the Section 1035 exchange produces that result.

8. Such options are particularly appealing for deferred annuity owners that do not necessarily want to deal with the cost and hassle of using a trust to accomplish the same goals. In addition, the use of an individual beneficiary, albeit with restrictions, may be more income-tax-favorable that naming a trust as a beneficiary.

Chapter 7

Index Annuities

In Chapter 1, we observed that one of the ways to classify annuities is to distinguish how the cash value is invested between fixed annuities and variable annuities. Some commentators suggest that that there is also a third type—index annuities. While this might seem reasonable—after all, index annuities certainly look different—it is not correct. An index annuity is a type of fixed annuity. Indeed, it is, in every respect, a fixed annuity, because its value is expressed in dollars, not units that vary in value according to the underlying investments. It is not, in any respect, a variable annuity. To understand why, we must examine how an index annuity works.

But first, it is important to understand the sometimes troublesome matter of its name. Index Annuities (IAs) are also referred to as Equity Index Annuities (EIAs) or Equity-Linked Index Annuities (ELIAs). This is because the interest[1] credited to an IA is linked to an external index, which is usually, but not always, an equity index; typically, but not always, the S&P 500.[2] The nature of this linkage—that is, the extent to which changes in the index will be reflected in the amount of interest credited to the index annuity—varies, and often greatly from one IA product to another. There are several—or many, depending upon how closely one wishes to differentiate—basic index annuity designs and dozens of methods of crediting interest. But all of them link the interest to be credited to the annuity contract to changes in the index used for that contract.

A serious problem with the terms equity index annuity and equity-linked index annuity, according to Jack Marrion, probably the foremost expert in IAs, is that both imply a greater degree of correspondence between movement of the underlying index and interest credited to the index annuity than actually exists in any of the IA designs. Holders of IA contracts may, in attending to those two terms, come to expect the same level of returns—specifically, positive returns—that they could enjoy by holding a more nearly direct investment in the index, such as an index mutual fund, or an exchange traded fund such as the S&P 500 SPDR.[3] Moreover, both terms virtually ignore two of the most attractive benefits enjoyed by IA owners by virtue of the fact that an IA is a fixed annuity, namely: (1) a guarantee of principal and (2) a guarantee —in most, but not all, IA contracts—of a minimum rate of interest.

For these reasons, Marrion prefers to use the term index annuity, or, better yet, Fixed Index Annuity (FIA). In the authors' opinion, Marrion's concerns are valid. The last thing any advisor should want is a label for any savings or investment product that is misleading. So, we will dispense with both equity index annuity and equity-linked index annuities. But, with all due respect to Jack, we'll stick with the term index annuity because it is in common usage. It's also shorter.

Basics of Index Annuities

An index annuity is a fixed deferred annuity. Like all fixed deferred annuities, it offers a guarantee of principal and a guaranteed minimum rate of interest.[4] However, unlike traditional fixed annuities, the IA offers the potential for excess interest based, not on whatever the insurer decides to declare, but on the performance of the underlying index. An index annuity gives the buyer some of the gains achieved by the stock index and none of the losses. What do we mean by some? The extent to which the annuity owner participates in the gains realized by the underlying index and when those gains are credited to the annuity, in the form of interest, depends upon the design of the annuity. We will examine the basic designs later in this chapter, but, first, we need to clarify some of the special terminology used in index annuities and to understand the various moving parts that go into the construction of these contracts.

Index Annuity Terminology[5]

Indexing Method

The indexing method is the approach used to calculate the change in the underlying index, for the purpose of determining the interest to be credited to the annuity.

Term, or Index Term

The term or index term of an IA is the period over which index-linked interest is calculated. It is important to understand that term does not mean the duration of the annuity contract itself.

Participation Rate

The participation rate is a method—but not the only method—used to determine how much of the increase in the underlying index will be credited as interest to the annuity. For example, if the index growth over the index term was 10% and the participation rate is 70%, the interest credited will be 7% (10% x 70%). The participation rate may be guaranteed by the issuer for a period of time, from one year to the entire term, or may be changeable by the insurer at any time.

Some contracts guarantee that this rate will never fall below a stated minimum. The participation rate is one of the moving parts in an index annuity, allowing the issuing insurer to adjust the interest crediting formula to reflect changes in interest rates and the cost of equity options[6] over the term period.

Yield Spread or Term Asset Fee

The yield spread is another method of reducing the amount of index gain that will be credited as interest to the annuity, thus reducing the risk to the insurer, another of the moving parts. If the annualized growth of the index, over the index term, was 10% and the yield spread is 3%, the interest credited will be 7% (10% - 3%). Yield spread is simply another way of limiting the insurer's risk and annuity owner's gain—an alternative to the participation rate.

Cap Rate or Cap

Some index annuities put a maximum value on either the interest rate that will be credited, known as the interest rate cap, or the amount of index gain recognized in calculating the equity-linked interest, or index cap. The marketing material for some IAs that use a cap do not make entirely clear whether an interest rate cap or an index cap is being used. It is vitally important that the advisor, discussing an IA with a cap, understand which method is being employed. Here's why. Assume the underlying index gains 20% in a given year:

1. An IA with a 70% participation rate and a 12% interest rate cap will credit 12%. 20% x 70% = 14%, but the cap limits the interest credited to 12%; therefore, the interest credited is 12%.

2. An IA with a 3% yield spread and a 12% interest rate cap will credit 12%. 20% - 3% = 17%, but the cap limits the interest credited to 12%; therefore, the interest credited is 12%.

3. An IA with a 70% participation rate and a 12% index cap will credit 8.4% interest. The cap recognizes no more than 12% of the index movement—12% x 70% = 8.4%.

4. An IA with a 3% yield spread and a 12% index cap will credit 9% interest. The cap recognizes no more than 12% of the index movement—12% - 3% = 9%.

Does this mean that IAs with index caps are not as good as those with interest rate caps? Not necessarily, because IAs with index caps frequently offer higher participation rates or lower yield spreads than contracts with interest rate caps. As Marrion and Olsen explain, "caps are used to boost participation rates or minimize yield spreads. Since they limit upside exposure, the cost [to the insurer] of providing the index-linked interest is less, so participation in caps up to the cap are higher. Caps enable one to get 'more of most' instead of 'less of more.'"[7]

Index Annuity Designs

There are several different IA designs in common usage. However, as Marrion and Olsen observe, there are really two ways to credit index-linked interest to an annuity. One can either measure index movement over a year or two—an annual reset method—or measure movement over a period of years, or a term end point method.[8]

Annual Reset

Like a fixed rate annuity—a conventional fixed annuity—the annual reset, or annual ratchet method, credits interest each year. The amount of interest credited each year is based on the movement of the underlying index during that year, calculated from the ending balance of the index for the previous year. An essential characteristic of annual reset index annuities is that losses are ignored. If the index movement in any year is negative, the contract treats that loss as a zero percent gain and credits zero interest for that year. Another essential characteristic is that, because gain is measured from the index value at the end of the previous year, an annual reset IA can credit interest based on index gain even if the index value, after that gain, is less than it was at some earlier point in the contract.

Figures 7.1 and 7.2 illustrate the hypothetical performance of a $100,000 annual reset annuity with a 100% participation rate, and a 12% interest rate cap. In the first year, the index gained 15.63% and the contract credited 12% interest (due to the cap), resulting in a cash value of $112,000. In the second year, the index lost 17.37%. The contract credited 0% interest, and the cash value remained at $112,000. In the third year, the index lost another 29.72%, but, again, that loss was not recognized, and the cash value stayed at $112,000.

Figure 7.1

Figure 7.2

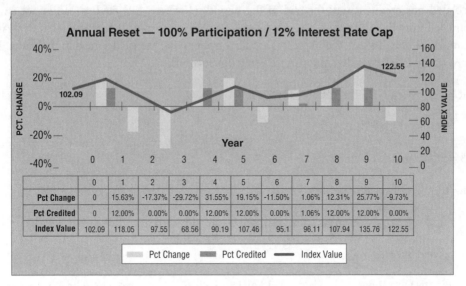

In the fourth year, however, the index gained 31.55%, resulting in crediting of 12% interest to the annuity. That gain was credited, despite the fact that the index balance, at the end of the fourth year (90.19), was less than its value at the inception of the annuity (102.09). The fourth year gain merely re-traced prior years' losses. At the end of 10 years, the index had gained 1.84%, while the annuity produced an annualized return of 5.94%. Does this mean that one can expect an annual reset IA, or any IA, for that matter, to outperform the underlying index? Definitely not. First, stocks in an equity index may produce dividends, which are not taken into account in IAs, but would be received by investors holding a mutual fund or exchange traded fund (ETF) based on that index. Moreover, this hypothetical illustration, which uses actual values of the S&P 500 Index from December 31, 1971 through December 31, 1981, is of a highly volatile period. Annual reset index annuities do very well in such climates, if an investor should be lucky enough to be invested when one occurs.

Point-to-Point

The point-to-point, or term end point, design measures index movements over a period greater than one or two years and does not calculate or credit interest each year. The investor's return is not known, and cannot be estimated, until the end of the term period, which is typically seven to ten years. The index gain is calculated by dividing the index value at the end of the term by its value at the beginning and then subtracting 1. For example, if the index is 100 at the outset of the contract, and ten years later is 180, the index gain is 80% [(180 ÷ 100) – 1]. That gain is then adjusted by applying any participation rate and the resulting interest percentage is multiplied by the initial contract value to produce the interest to be credited. For example, at a 70% participation rate, the cumulative interest credited would be 56% (80% x 70%). Such an annuity, purchased for $100,000, would be worth $156,000 at the end of the 10 years.

A variation of this design, called Term Yield Spread, works similarly, in that interest is neither calculated nor credited until the end of the period. However, the yield spread is not simply subtracted from the index gain, because the yield spread is an annual figure and the index gain is a cumulative one. Instead, the interest is credited by applying the yield spread to the annualized return of the index over the time period, using this formula:

$R = (E \div S)1/n - 1$; Interest Credited $= R - Y$

E = Ending Index Value

S = Starting Index Value

n= number of years in period

R = Index Return (the annualized compound rate of return over the period)

Y = Yield Spread

Using the facts above and a yield spread of 3%, the interest credited would be 3.054% per year $[(180 \div 100)^{1/10} - 1 = 6.054; 6.054 - 3.00 = 3.054]$. The annuity, at the end of 10 years would be worth \$135,098 $[100,000 \times (1 + .0354)^{10}]$. What if the index were lower at the end of 10 years than at the outset (or higher, but less than the guaranteed value)? Then the contract would not use that final index value, but would, instead credit the guaranteed interest rate to the initial index value for each year of the term.

The Annual Reset and Point-to-Point designs are the two basic types of index annuities. However, there are many variations on those themes. We will not attempt to describe all of the variations out there,[9] but we will look now at certain features that are common to several, or even all, index annuities.

High Water Mark

In this variation on the Term End Point design, index-linked interest,if any, is credited based on the difference between the starting index value and the highest value of the index—usually, at policy anniversaries—during the period. This method is rarely used in currently issued contracts because the cost of the options is higher, and so index participation would have to be much lower than for other interest crediting types.[10]

Averaging

Another method to protect the annuity owner from the impact of a severe decline in the index value at the end of the term is averaging index values for the purpose of calculating index-based gains. Most index annuities today—Jack Marrion estimates that more than

75%—average at least some portion of index values. Many point-to-point contracts will use the average of the last year's values, and most index annuities sold are annual reset contracts that use averaging. Averaging has the effect of driving numbers to the middle and smoothing index performance, but its true impact on that performance is often misunderstood. Clearly, it prevents the annuity owner from finishing a year locked into the lowest index point of that year, but it also guarantees that he will never hit the highest point. Less obvious, however, is the fact that, while averaging always drives values to the middle, this does not mean that index annuities using averaging will have half the return of an index annuity with a point-to-point design because averaging structures typically have higher rates or higher caps or lower spreads than unaveraged ones.[11]

Guaranteed Interest Rates

Some index annuities guarantee the crediting of a minimum amount of interest to the owner's entire investment. Others guarantee it to only a percentage—often, 80% or 90%—of that investment. The latter arrangement can produce confusion as to the minimum interest the annuity owner is guaranteed to receive. For example, many contracts guarantee 3% interest on 90% of the amount invested. This may appear to mean that the interest rate guaranteed is an annual compound rate of 2.7% credited to the amount invested. This is not correct! The principal on which the 3% interest is credited is only 90 cents for each dollar invested. Thus, on a $100,000 single premium, the guaranteed future value at the end of 10 years would be $FV = PV \times (1 + i)^n$ or $90,000 \times 1.03^{10} = $120,952$. The compound rate of return required to produce $120,952 at the end of 10 years, if one invests $100,000 today, is 1.92% $[(120,952 \div 100,000)^{1/10} - 1]$. The effective guaranteed minimum rate on the entire amount invested is, thus, 1.92%, not 2.7%.

Will that guaranteed minimum interest be paid if the owner of the annuity surrenders the contract before the end of the term? No, because guaranteed interest is almost always credited at the end of the surrender period and not each year. The owner surrendering an annuity that is not an annual reset design, or one that otherwise vests interest—as some high water mark designs do—will generally receive no index-linked interest, if surrender occurs prior to the end of the term. In this case, the individual would simply receive a return of the original premiums paid, and any guaranteed interest payable if applicable. Moreover, surrender charges may apply.

Surrender Charges

Surrender charges in index annuities work just like the surrender charges in other annuity contracts. However, the size of the charges, and the length of time during which they apply, is generally higher in index annuities. Some IAs do not impose surrender charges as such, but base the surrender value on the guaranteed minimum amount, based on crediting of interest to less than the full investment. This has the same effect as a declining surrender charge over the first few years of the contract.

Free Withdrawals

As is typically the case with both conventional fixed and variable annuities, IAs usually permit withdrawals of up to a specified percentage of the cash value each year without imposing surrender charges.

However, if the client feels that there is a significant likelihood of a need to tap the money in the index annuity before the expiration of the surrender charge period, we suggest that an annuity may not be appropriate in the first place. As was noted, surrender charges in index annuities typically are higher and last longer than those in other annuity contracts, so an early distribution in excess of the amount permitted under the free withdrawal feature could be subjected to a stiff penalty. Moreover, any distribution, whether surrender charges apply or not, could be subject to the 10% early distribution penalty. Furthermore, as discussed earlier, an early partial surrender could cause forfeiture of any accumulated equity-linked interest, or guaranteed minimum interest, to the extent attributable to the withdrawal taken. In short, the authors believe that annuities in general, and index annuities in particular, are of questionable appropriateness when liquidity is an issue.

Premium Bonus

Many index annuities offer a premium bonus, whereby the contract owner is credited with an additional percentage of the premium actually paid, which will earn interest on the same basis as paid premium, provided that the contract is not surrendered before the end of the term. However, this bonus is not free. Often, contracts offering a premium bonus require higher surrender charges, longer surrender charge periods, or a lower participation rate compared to contracts without the bonus. In some contracts, the difference is not reflected in lower benefits for the owner, but rather, in a lower commission paid to the selling agent. See the discussion on bonus annuities in Chapter 4.

Required Annuitization

Some index annuities require the contract to be annuitized for certain benefits to be payable, or provide lower levels of benefits, such as participation rate, for contracts that are surrendered for a lump sum—even if held to the end of the required term. The value of annuitization is, as will be discussed in a later chapter, a very controversial issue in the financial services community. The authors do not subscribe to the widespread belief that it is always a bad decision. However, it seems only logical to observe that, whatever value the annuity owner places on annuitization, an obligation to take proceeds in that form would not be attractive to a rational investor in the absence of some benefit not available without that requirement. A few contracts not only require annuitization for the contract holder to receive the entire account balance; that is, they impose on withdrawals and lump sum surrenders, surrender charges that never expire, but impose that same requirement upon beneficiaries. Fortunately for consumers—and, in the authors' opinion, for the insurance industry, too—such contracts are becoming increasingly rare.

How Can the Insurance Company Do All This?

A question often asked by consumers is, "how can the insurance company do all this?" This, meaning the guarantee principal plus a minimum rate of interest and participation in exceptional upside movements in the underlying index. Where's the catch? When this question is asked, it usually means that the advisor has done a poor job of explaining how the index annuity works. It may look too good to be true. This is certainly true when the advisor has said something like "with this annuity, you get the upside of the equity market, but with no downside risk."

That is just not true! The index annuity owner does not "get the upside of the equity market," but only a portion of that growth. The portion of any index growth an individual gets is determined by the various limiting factors, or the moving parts, in the contract design. These moving parts are essential for the issuing insurer to limit its loss exposure. After all, it is guaranteeing the purchaser's principal from any loss of principal and a minimum rate of return, if the contract is held for the full term.

Typically, the insurer purchases a combination of bonds and call options on the underlying index to guarantee the funds required to meet its obligations under the contract. The greatest part of the purchaser's premium is invested in bonds, in sufficient amount to provide the dollars needed to meet the insurer's minimum obligations. The remainder is used to buy those call options. The price of the call options, to fund the indexed-linked interest, and the cost and yield of the bonds, to fund the contractual guarantees, together determine how many options the insurer can purchase with a given premium. If option prices at a particular time are low—because expected index volatility is low—and bond yields are high, it might be possible for the insurer, at that time, to purchase enough index options to provide the annuity owner with 100% of the performance of the index, in addition to guaranteeing principal and the minimum interest rate.

But as of the time of this writing, such is not the case. Interest rates are near historic lows and option prices are relatively high, because index performance is expected to be more than usually volatile. So, at this time, insurers do not have enough left over from an index annuity purchaser's premium, after purchasing the bonds required, to buy enough index options to give that purchaser 100% of the index performance on the premium invested. For that reason, today's participation rates and cap rates are relatively low and yield spreads are relatively high. Issuers of index annuities are not purchasing options for all possible growth at this time because they can't. But they don't need to because today's participation rates, caps, and yield spreads limit the amount of that growth they're obliged to credit to their annuities.

This is precisely why, when an annuity owner is limited to a 70% participation rate or a cap of, say, 9%, and the index goes up 15%, the insurer does not keep the excess return above the 10.5% it would credit under a 70% participation rate or the 9% it would credit under the cap. And it does not purchase enough options to get 100% of the growth on the entire amount of that annuity owner's premium. There is no need to do so, nor is there enough paid-in premium left over, after purchase of the bonds, to do so. The insurer does not keep that excess because it does not receive it.

Why can't the insurer guarantee the level of the various moving parts (e.g., the cap rate, participation rate, and yield spread)? It may guarantee some of these factors, but it cannot guarantee all of them and expect to remain in business. Why?

It is because financial markets change. Interest rates change, and with them, the cost of the bonds the insurer will purchase to meet minimum contractual guarantees. Likewise, the cost of index options also change, increasing with the volatility, or expected volatility, of the index and the length of time over which they are exercisable. If an insurer chooses to guarantee the participation rate, cap rate, or yield spread for the entire term, it cannot offer as high a participation rate and cap rate, or as low a yield spread, as if it reserves the right to adjust those factors periodically because it will not be able to purchase as many options since the cost of those options will be higher. For these reasons, nearly all index annuities do not guarantee all of the moving parts for the entire term. This is particularly true of annual reset contracts, where the insurer will need to continue purchasing call options in the future at an unknown cost.

Because the issuing insurer can adjust these moving parts periodically, to reflect changing economic realities, it is essential that the advisor choose an insurer with a good record of renewing these rates so as to treat existing contract holders fairly. The authors strongly suggest that advisors ask the issuer of any index annuity, or fixed annuity, for that matter, they are considering for a history of renewal rates.

Which Index Annuity Design Is Best?

Perhaps the most common question asked by advisors who are considering index annuities for their clients is, "which kind is best?". In the authors' opinion, the only reasonable answer is, "it depends". As Marrion and Olsen point out, any crediting method can produce the best return for a given period. There are, however, certain general observations that one can make regarding index annuity policy designs.

Annual Reset

With an annual reset index annuity, the purchaser knows how much her annuity is worth at the end of each year. Interest is calculated, credited, and locked-in each year. Future decreases in the index will not reduce the annuity value. The biggest trade-off to this is that the participation rate, cap rate, or yield spread is likely to be lower than in other designs. These contracts generally excel in markets with high volatility, although such volatility tends to increase option costs and reduce participation rate or increase yield spread.

High Water Mark

The high water mark design protects the annuity owner from a decline in the index at the end of the term, which could wipe out much, or even all, of the gain previously experienced, but not credited. However, the rates for the various moving parts are likely to be less attractive than for a contract with a point-to-point design with the same term.

Point-to-Point

The point-to-point design does not allow the purchaser to know the value of the annuity until the end of the term. However, the rates for the moving parts are likely to be greater than for other policy designs with the same term. In addition, because many or all of the bonds and call options are put in place when the contract is acquired, point-to-point contracts tend to have fewer moving parts that may be changed after the contract is initially acquired.

Guaranteed Living Benefit Riders

Given the enormous popularity of Guaranteed Living Benefit riders in variable deferred annuity contracts, it was just a matter of time before issuers of fixed annuities—including index annuities—got into the game. In 2006, the first Guaranteed Lifetime Withdrawal Benefit was offered as a rider on an index annuity. By the end of that year, seven index annuity carriers were offering GLWBs, with more carriers considering the addition of these benefits.[12] As of December, 2011, GLWB riders are offered in many index annuities and are very popular. See "Guaranteed Lifetime Withdrawal Benefit in Index Annuities", in Chapter 5. As to other living benefits in index annuities no index annuity, to the authors' knowledge, offers any of the other two basic types of guaranteed living benefits (GMIB or GMWB).

In the authors' opinion, though, neither of those benefits really makes much sense in a fixed annuity—and an index annuity is a fixed annuity—because both are designed to offset the loss of a significant decline in the annuity's cash value. Conventional fixed annuities are never susceptible to this loss; neither are index annuities of the annual reset or high water mark types. A Final End Point-type index annuity might be, except that most contracts of this type employ averaging, which provides considerable protection against significant end-of-term declines.

Endnotes

1. The gain realized in an index annuity is interest, not dividends or capital gains.

2. The S&P 500, or S&P 500 Composite Price Index, was created by the Standard & Poor's Company in 1923. The S&P 500 is "calculated using a base-weighted aggregate methodology, meaning the level of the Index reflects the total market value of all component stocks relative to a particular base period. Total market value is determined by multiplying the price of its stock by the number of shares outstanding." See "S&P 50th Anniversary" at at: http://www2.standardandpoors.com/portal/site/sp/es/la/page.topic/indices_500anniv/2,3,2,2,0,0,0,0,0,1,1,0,0,0,0,0.html.

3. SPDR is the exchange symbol for the S&P 500 Index Fund, an exchange traded fund, and stands for Standard & Poor's Depository Receipt.

4. Some index annuities guarantee only a 0% rate of return. Most guarantee a rate of at least 3%, which might be credited to only a percentage, such as 80% or 90%, of the premiums received.

5. Some of the material in this section was taken from the *Buyer's Guide To Equity-Indexed Annuities*, prepared by the National Association of Insurance Commissioners, reprinted by the Illinois Division of Insurance at: www.ins.state.il.us/Life_Annuities/equityindex.htm.

6. Purchase of equity call options is the usual mechanism used by issuers of index annuities to guarantee the funds to pay the equity-linked interest. However, other methods may be used, or the insurer may go naked and self-insure that equity-linked interest payment liability [see Marrion & Olsen, *Index Annuities: A Suitable Approach* (Olsen & Marrion, LLC, 2010, www.indexannuitybook.com), Chapter 2.

7. Marrion & Olsen, *Ibid*, p.59

8. Ibid.

9. *Ibid.*

10. Ibid. p. 51

11. Ibid, p. 59

12. Jack Marrion, *A Look At Annuity And Securities GLWBs* (Advantage Compendium, August, 2008, available at www.indexannuity.org).

Chapter 8

Annuities and Trusts

As a financial asset, an annuity is necessarily part of the overall financial and estate plan of its purchaser. However, it is sometimes not well coordinated with the other components. Indeed, the ownership and beneficiary arrangement of an annuity may be inconsistent with—or even in conflict with—the rest of a client's plan. Not uncommonly, this results from an advisor's decision to employ the annuity in connection with a trust without a full understanding of the rules governing both. In the following discussion, we will examine some of the problems advisors may encounter when annuities are owned by, or made payable to, a trust, and the rules (i.e., the tax rules and the contractual provisions and administrative policies of annuity issuers) that are not well understood.

For most of the following discussion, we will be concerned only with deferred annuities. Not only are most annuities sold of this type, but the Internal Revenue Code (IRC) provisions that cause most of the difficulties where annuities are owned by or payable to a trust (Section 72(u) and certain paragraphs of Section 72(s)) do not apply to immediate annuities. We will also be concerned only with nonqualified contracts, because qualified annuities, or annuities used to fund IRAs, cannot be owned by a trust other than the trust for the type of plan being funded.

Problematic Annuity Structuring with Trusts

Problems can arise when a deferred annuity is:

- owned by and payable to a trust;

- owned by a trust and payable to another party;

- owned by another party and payable to a trust.

When an annuity is owned by a trust, the holder of the annuity is deemed by Section 72(s)(6)(A)[1] to be the primary annuitant.[2] It is vital that the advisor understand that this provision applies with regard to distributions required to be made from the annuity upon the death of the holder by Section 72(s), if the annuity is to be considered an annuity for income tax purposes. However, what if a particular annuity does not provide for payment upon the primary annuitant's death when the annuity is owned by a trust? The result is a conflict—an incongruity, which can pose serious problems as will be discussed later in this chapter.

Also, as was discussed in Chapter 2, an annuity owned by a trust, or other nonnatural person, will not be considered an annuity for income tax purposes unless the owning entity is acting as the agent of a natural person.[3] This requirement, too, is a source of potential problems. Although many trusts qualify as such agents, not all do (see Chapter 2).

When a trust is the beneficiary of an annuity, that annuity is subject to distribution requirements different from those applying when the beneficiary is an individual, or a natural person. These requirements apply whether or not the trust is also the holder of the annuity.

Annuity-Trust Situations

Where Trust Owns Annuity

1. The Annuity Is Owned by a Revocable Living Trust.

A curiosity that advisors frequently encounter is a deferred annuity contract owned by a client's Revocable Living Trust (RLT). It is curious, because there is often little reason for it. Sometimes, the annuity was transferred into the RLT because someone felt that everything ought to be in the trust. But there can be some problems with this arrangement.

First, we should ask, what is to be gained by owning a deferred annuity inside an RLT? RLTs avoid probate, of course, which is often a main reason for establishing these trusts. But annuity death benefits pass to beneficiaries outside probate anyway by operation of the annuity contract; so probate avoidance is not a good reason for putting an annuity in an RLT. Another, and better, reason might be a desire to have annuity death proceeds distributed under the terms of that trust, which terms can be far more flexible than a normal beneficiary designation. But that does not require that the annuity be owned by the trust, merely that it be payable to the trust under the beneficiary designation. Another reason might be to avoid problems that could arise upon the annuity owner's becoming incompetent. Yet a properly drafted durable power of attorney may suffice for this purpose.

Thus, nearly all of the benefits just described can be achieved by other means or by virtue of the annuity itself, without inviting the problems connected with naming the RLT as the annuity owner.

2. The Annuity Is Transferred to Owner's Irrevocable Trust.

A common reason for an owner to transfer ownership of a deferred annuity to his irrevocable trust is to remove its value from his taxable estate. Can this create problems? Perhaps. Section 72(e)(4)(C) says that:

> "If an individual who holds an annuity contract transfers it without full and adequate consideration, such individual shall be treated as receiving an amount equal to the excess of:
>
> (I)   the cash surrender value of such contract at the time of transfer; over
>
> (II) the investment in such contract at such time,under the contract as an amount not received as an annuity."

In other words, such a transfer will trigger recognition of all the gain in the contract. The only statutory exception to this rule is a gift to holder's spouse.[4]

What if the receiving trust is a grantor trust? Under the original grantor trust rules and subsequent rulings, a sale of property from an individual to his/her grantor trust does not trigger recognition of gain because it is not deemed to be an income tax event, because the trust is not viewed as a separate entity from the grantor capable of entering into a taxable sales transaction.[5] Section 72 is an income tax provision. Thus, under those rules, an individual holding a highly appreciated deferred annuity could theoretically transfer ownership of that annuity to a grantor trust and avoid income tax gain recognition, and the value of the annuity will also not be includible in the estate for federal estate tax purposes if the trust is otherwise not includible (e.g., in the case of a so-called Intentionally Defective Grantor Trust).

However, such a transfer for less than adequate consideration is probably a gift—certainly, in the case of a IDGT—and thus may trigger the aforementioned language of IRC Section 72(e) (4)(C) simply on the basis that a transfer has occurred, and by definition it was without full and adequate consideration because it triggered a gift tax event. In essence, the interpretive challenge is whether the word transfer is to be applied using an income tax framework, or a gift tax framework. From an income tax perspective, a transfer to a grantor trust should be exempt from the income tax event by virtue of the principle that a transaction between a taxpayer and his/her grantor trust is a transaction between the same tax entities and thus does not constitute an income tax transfer. However, if the term transfer is interpreted from a gift tax perspective, than any transfer that would be construed as a transfer for gift tax purposes (e.g., a gift to an IDGT) would cause an income tax event under 72(e)(4)(C). In point of fact, under the gift tax framework, in theory even an incomplete gift due to a retained interest may still trigger income taxes upon the transfer of an annuity, because the transfer would still be for less than full and adequate consideration.

Moreover, it is not clear that a grantor trust transaction would apply in the case of a transfer of an annuity to an intentionally defective grantor trust, in the manner that it applied to a sale of property to a grantor trust under Revenue Ruling 85-13. It is significant—in the authors' opinion—that the Ruling cited Sect. 1.675-1 of the Income Tax Regulations, noting that the Section "treats the grantor as the owner of a trust if, under the terms of the trust instrument, or the circumstances attendant to its operation, administrative control is exercisable primarily for the benefit of the grantor rather than the beneficiaries of the trust." In reviewing the applicability of Sect. 675, the Ruling observed that "In all of these cases, the justification for treating the grantor as owner is evidence of substantial grantor dominion and control over the trust."

In the authors' opinion, such justification is arguably not present when a taxpayer gifts a deferred annuity to an irrevocable trust of which he is not trustee. Prior to making the gift, that taxpayer could exercise unfettered control over the annuity; afterwards, he cannot. Control of the annuity has shifted, but the tax liability should not. Gary Underwood argues[6] that the most common sensible approach would be to assume that the grantor trust provisions prevail, and that Sect. 72(e)(4)(C) simply doesn't apply because no transfer has taken place, for income tax purposes. We are not so sure that the grantor trust provisions of the Code and Rev. Rul. 85-13 can be safely stretched to cover the facts of the present scenario and that the plain language rule of IRC. Sect. 72(e)(4)(C) can be ignored.

Unfortunately, neither the IRS nor the Treasury have issued definitive interpretation or guidance on this particular issue. To say the least, however, practitioners should be extremely cautious about any transfer of an annuity to an irrevocable trust that may constitute some form of gratuitous transfer.

An alternative to avoid these rules might be the sale of the annuity to the trust, perhaps in exchange for a balloon note, private annuity, or self-canceling installment note (SCIN). Such a sale would more clearly not trigger recognition of any gains in the annuity under the grantor trust rules[7] as it is clearly not treated as a sale for income tax purposes—under Revenue Ruling 85-13—nor a gratuitous transfer, and furthermore would allow the owner to avoid gift tax consequences on the transfer in exchange for the cash flow and estate tax consequences of using such devices. On the other hand, this transaction structure, too, may have its risks, as Revenue Ruling 85-13 viewed the exchange of property for a promissory note between a grantor and grantor's trust as an indirect borrowing of the property, and IRC Section 72(e)(4)(A) states that a loan—even indirect—against an annuity, as well as the pledge or assignment of an annuity as collateral for a loan, triggers income tax consequences as though the amount were withdrawn. To say the least, there is no clear consensus about the proper treatment even in this context, with plausible arguments on both sides of the case.

It is also worth noting that the transfer of an annuity to the owner's trust might produce different results with regard to the death benefit of the annuity, especially in the case where the owner is not the annuitant. We will examine this scenario later as we consider the implications of having a trust named as beneficiary of a nonqualified annuity.

3. The Annuity Is Owned by an Irrevocable Grantor Trust and the Grantor Is Not the Annuitant.

Let us suppose that George establishes an irrevocable grantor trust and that the trust purchases a deferred annuity. The trust is named owner and beneficiary. The primary annuitant is George's daughter, Sally. Whose death triggers payout of the contract? The answer is not clear. Some authorities state that Sally's death must cause payout. Others insist that George's death must do so.

Does Sally's death trigger payout? IRC Sect. 72(s)(6)(A) declares that when an annuity is owned by a nonnatural person, the primary annuitant shall be deemed, for purposes of post death distribution requirements, to be the holder, or owner. Thus, the death of Sally, the imputed owner, will trigger payout under the provisions of Sect. 72(s). Of course, if the annuity contract is annuitant-driven, the contract will be paid out upon Sally's death—that is, the death of the annuitant—even if 72(s)(6)(A) were not implicated.

Does George's death trigger payout? Some authorities insist yes, that the grantor trust rules require that the annuity be paid out upon George's death, even though George is neither the annuitant nor the owner named in the annuity contract or deemed owner by application of Sect. 72(s)(6)(A). Gary Underwood observes that:

> "Alternatively, one might argue that the death of a nongrantor annuitant triggers the death distribution rules, even for grantor trusts. Although no authority explicitly addresses this issue, distribution at the death of the grantor is the most logical choice. Since the grantor is the owner of grantor trust assets for income tax purposes, and the death of the owner is the primary trigger for annuity distributions at death, then the death of the grantor should trigger the death distribution requirements. It seems incorrect to assert that the grantor is the owner of the annuity for income tax purposes, but the grantor is not the owner for the income tax requirement of distributions at death under IRC Sec. 72. Although some insurance companies treat the death of the grantor as a distribution event, it is possible that other insurance companies may not be aware of the death of a nonannuitant grantor and may not have reporting procedures in place to trigger a distribution."[8]

The authors have been unable to find any authority as to which position is correct, or even any case law dealing with this issue. In practical terms, it appears that the correct answer is whatever the issuing insurer decides is correct, because that insurer will take action, or not take action, depending upon its interpretation, and if the trustee disagrees, the trustee will be compelled to request a Private Letter Ruling to dispute the reporting the insurer issues on the Form 1099-R. Thus, if it is the policy of that insurer to distribute the value of the annuity on the death of the primary annuitant, as Sect. 72(s)(6)(A) mandates, it will make such distribution, and apply the restrictions of Sect. 72(s), even if Mr. Underwood's interpretation is correct. Moreover, if the trust is beneficiary of the annuity as well as the owner—which many insurers require— most insurers will require full distribution of the contract within five years, as the trust is not a designated beneficiary under IRC Section 72(s)(4), as discussed further below.

If, on the other hand, the issuing insurer's policy follows Mr. Underwood's interpretation, it will not require payout upon Sally's death unless the annuity is annuitant-driven, but will do so upon George's death. In conversations with representatives of several insurers, the authors have learned that some insurers follow the rule of Sect. 72(s)(6)(A) and will require payout on George's death, while others agree with Mr. Underwood's interpretation, and will require payout if Sally dies first.

It is vital that everyone involved in such a scenario—in this case, George, Sally, the Trustee of George's trust, and all advisors offering counsel regarding the annuity—know, before anyone dies, what the issuing insurer will require in the event of either George's or Sally's death.

Where a Trust Is Beneficiary of an Annuity

Naming a trust as beneficiary of a nonqualified deferred annuity is even more common than naming the trust as owner of that annuity. As was noted above, the transfer is sometimes for no other reason than a belief that everything should be in the trust. Often, however, the reason is deliberate: because trusts allow greater dispositive freedom. The settlement provisions of most annuity contracts are fairly standardized; a trust can provide far greater flexibility.

What is often not well understood—or, in some instances, understood at all—is that when an annuity is payable to a trust, or to any beneficiary other than a natural person, the Internal Revenue Code imposes special restrictions as to when and how distributions must be made and a special rule as to whose death will trigger such distributions. We noted, in Chapter 3, that Section 72(h) governs payments to beneficiaries of annuities and when those payment elections must be made. However, Section 72(h) is not the only subsection that addresses beneficiary payments. As also mentioned in Chapter 3, Section 72(s) imposes its own requirements. So let's review the rules of Section 72(s) that apply to all payments of annuity proceeds to any beneficiaries.

Section 72(s) says that any annuity contract issued since January 18, 1985, in order to be considered an annuity in the first place, must provide that, upon death of the annuity holder, proceeds will be distributed in accordance with the following rules.

Distribution Requirements for Annuity Contracts

Section 72(s)(4) states that the proceeds of a deferred annuity not yet annuitized must be distributed within five years of the holder's death, unless one of the exceptions applies, as discussed in Chapter 3.[9] The exceptions include allowing the beneficiary to take proceeds over life expectancy, or a period not exceeding life expectancy;[10] however, this requires that the annuity be payable to, or for the benefit of, a designated beneficiary.[11] Section 72(s)(4) says, quite plainly, that "for purposes of this subsection, the term 'designated beneficiary' means any individual designated a beneficiary by the holder of the contract."

The key word, here, is individual. An individual is a natural person, and a trust is not a natural person.

Trusts under the Annuity Distribution Rules

So what happens if the deferred annuity is payable to a trust? A trust is not an individual and, thus, cannot be a designated beneficiary, and it certainly cannot be a spouse eligible for spousal continuation. Thus, must a trust that is the beneficiary of a nonqualified annuity take proceeds within five years, with no opportunity for stretching out payments based on a life expectancy?

Some commentators believe that other alternatives are available. One argument asserts that because Section 72(s)(2)(A)—in defining when the annuitization option of Section 72(s)(2)(B) will be permitted—requires only that the holder's interest be "payable to (or for the benefit of) a designated beneficiary," then (1) if the trust is acting as the agent of a natural person, and (2) if that natural person is the sole beneficiary of the trust, it follows that the trust is acting for the benefit of that designated beneficiary. Therefore, the trust should be able to take proceeds over a period not exceeding the life expectancy of that designated beneficiary, so long as payments commence within one year of death.

However, the authors believe that the agency argument just stated, however elegant, avoids the fact that Section 72(s)(4) is really quite precise. It says:

> "For purposes of this subsection, the term 'designated beneficiary' means any individual designated a beneficiary by the holder of the contract."

There is no opportunity for agency here. To be a designated beneficiary, an individual must be designated as such by the holder of the contract. He or she may not acquire that status by imputation. Section 72(s)(4) does not state that a designated beneficiary may be "any individual, or a nonnatural agent for that individual." If the beneficiary shown in the annuity contract and appearing on the application for that annuity is a trust, the trust is the party designated as a beneficiary. But a trust cannot be a designated beneficiary because that term, in the very specific context of Section 72(s)(4), must be an individual. As the trust, the only entity that was actually designated by the holder to be the beneficiary, is not an individual, and, therefore, not a designated beneficiary, the annuity has no designated beneficiary. Therefore, the annuitization option of Section 72(s)(2) is unavailable.

Another argument for the availability of the Section 72(s)(2) option holds that Congress, in enacting Section 72(s), intended to provide parity between the rules governing distributions from qualified plans and IRAs and those governing distributions from nonqualified annuities. The legislative history of Section 72 shows such intent, and the structure of that section certainly resembles that of Section 401(a)(9). Therefore, it is only logical that we look-through the trust to the individual trust beneficiaries in applying the required distribution rules, in the same manner that existing regulations permit a look-through of a trust named as beneficiary of a qualified plan or IRA.

It may be logical for us to want to look-through to the individual trust beneficiaries for an annuity, but the authors do not believe that existing rules offer any authority for such a position.

Unfortunately, the IRS has not seen fit to provide much guidance in this area, and there are no conforming Treasury Regulations for Section 72 to match those promulgated under 1.401(a)(9)-4 for the see-through treatment of trusts payable to IRAs. In addition, it is important to note that the existing Treasury regulations that allow look-through trust treatment are fairly new[12] in the context of a section of the Internal Revenue Code that has existed for much longer. Furthermore, the IRS has explicitly noted other situations where the provisions that apply to retirement accounts are intended to apply to annuities,[13] and its failure to announce any such parity regarding look-through trust treatment should inspire caution.

However, there is one holding[14] that affirms not only the availability of the annuitization option Section 72(s)(2), but also the spousal continuation option of Section 72(s)(3), where the beneficiary was a trust. However, the fact situation was extremely unusual. The surviving spouse/grantor/trustee had, according to the ruling, such complete control and dominion over the trust assets, which included two annuity contracts, that she was permitted to treat herself, individually, as the designated beneficiary of the annuities and exercise the spousal continuation option of Section 72(s)(3).[15]

What does this ruling suggest about the willingness of the IRS to ignore the existence of other trusts named as annuity beneficiaries and to look through to the trust beneficiaries in applying Section 72(s) rules? In the authors' opinion, very little. This ruling is an anomaly. The fact situation was, as we noted, very unusual. In a normal context, trusts established for other individuals will not allow complete dominion and control over the trust and consequently will not be able to apply the facts of this ruling. Otherwise, one might contend, why establish the trust in the first place? Moreover, we have been unable to locate any other ruling regarding annuities that arrived at a similar conclusion. Despite arguments that Congress intended parity between the rules governing nonqualified annuities and qualified plans, and that a trust as a beneficiary is merely an agent acting for the benefit of individuals who should be deemed to be designated beneficiaries, in the authors' opinion existing law and rulings support only a conclusion that a trust named as beneficiary of a nonqualified annuity will not be able to elect the annuitization option of Section 72(s)(2) or the spousal continuation option of Section 72(s)(3). Moreover, most insurance companies are unwilling to permit trust beneficiaries to elect these options.

A few insurers have taken the position that where a trust having certain characteristics is named as beneficiary of one of their deferred annuities, those companies will honor a request by the trustee to pay death proceeds of the annuity to the trust over the lifetime of the oldest trust beneficiary. These companies effectively believe that it is safe to interpret the implied parity between Section 401(a)(9) and Section 72(s) as being sufficiently reliable as to authorize treating trust beneficiaries similarly, whether those beneficiaries are receiving distributions from a retirement account or a nonqualified annuity. Whether this represents the beginning of a trend, we do not speculate. Most insurers insist that death proceeds payable to a trust be fully paid out within five years of the annuitant's death, and will not cooperate with a beneficiary that wishes to stretch through a trust until the IRS issues more definitive guidance allowing such treatment, or unless the trust submits its own Private Letter Ruling to request guidance based on a specific fact pattern at the time of death. In any event, it is important to note that even where an insurer will comply with a more favorable interpretation and allow a trust beneficiary to stretch out payments, there is no guarantee that the IRS will acquiesce to that treatment on discovering it, given that the IRS still has not definitively provided final guidance on the issue.

At this point, the authors want to make clear—and emphasize—that Section 72(s) does not say how death benefits will be paid from any particular annuity contract. The contract itself will govern, and Section 72(s) merely dictates what provisions must be in an annuity contract— issued since January 18, 1985—if that contract is to qualify as an annuity for income tax purposes in the first place. It is entirely possible that an annuity contract may contain provisions that are perfectly legal and enforceable (i.e., they do not violate principles of contract law, public policy, etc.), but that might violate the requirements of Section 72(s), such that the contract would not qualify as an annuity under that subsection.

Let's look at an example of such a potential conflict—specifically of the congruity or incongruity between when death distributions from an annuity owned by a trust must be made by law and when they will be made under terms of the annuity contract.

Annuities and Consistency with Section 72(s)

Annuity contracts issued since January 18, 1985, must require distribution of proceeds, in accordance with the rules of Section 72(s), upon the death of the holder. All annuities issued since that date require distribution of the annuity proceeds to the beneficiary upon the death of the owner of the annuity contract.[16] These are called owner-driven contracts. Some, but not all, annuities will also pay a death benefit upon the death of the annuitant. These are called annuitant-driven contracts. In actuality, they are both owner-driven and annuitant-driven.

When either type of annuity is owned by an individual, the death of the owner will always trigger payment of a death benefit[17] under the terms of the annuity contract (i.e., by the terms of a provision the annuity contract must contain under the death-of-holder rules of Section 72(s)). Here, owner and holder refer to the same individual, and when that individual dies and a payout occurs, the requirements of Section 72(s) that the owner's entire interest in the contract be distributed at the owner's death are satisfied.

But where the annuity is owned by a trust, the triggering event for the distribution required under Section 72(s) may not be the same as the event causing payment of any death benefit under the terms of the annuity contract. Section 72(s) mandates a distribution upon the death of the holder of an annuity. Where an annuity is owned by a trust or other nonnatural person, Section 72(s)(6)(A) deems the holder of the annuity to be the primary annuitant for purposes of this subsection.[18] Thus, for Section 72(s) purposes, that is, for purposes of Required Distributions Where Holder Dies Before Entire Interest Is Distributed, an annuity owned by a trust, must, by its terms, require that the entire interest in the annuity will be distributed upon the death of the annuitant.

The problem—the incongruity—is that some annuity contracts do not contain this requirement. Some annuities state that where the contract is owned by a trust, the contract value—but not necessarily the guaranteed minimum death benefit—will be distributed upon the death of the primary annuitant. No problem here. But at least one contract the authors have read contains language that appears to contravene the rule stated above, that an annuity owned by a trust, must, by its terms, require that the entire interest in the annuity will be distributed upon the death of the annuitant. In the section on Death Benefit in the prospectus, this particular contract states:

> "If the Annuity is owned by one or more natural persons, the Death Benefit is payable upon the first death of an Owner. If the Annuity is owned by an entity, the Death Benefit is payable upon the Annuitant's death, if there is no Contingent Annuitant. If a Contingent Annuitant was designated before the Annuitant's death and the Annuitant dies, then the Contingent Annuitant becomes the Annuitant and a Death Benefit will not be paid at that time. The person upon whose death the Death Benefit is paid is referred to below as the 'decedent'."

Note that while this provision does direct that the death benefit be paid upon the death of the primary annuitant if no contingent annuitant had been named, it denies a payment when a contingent annuitant had been named, and elevates that contingent annuitant to the status of primary annuitant. Whatever the reason for this provision, the authors believe that it clearly violates the requirements of Section 72(s) and that the IRS could, as a consequence, declare that every annuity issued with these terms fails to qualify as an annuity for income tax purposes.[19] Is this likely? The contract in question has been marketed since 2000, and the IRS has not, to the authors' knowledge, raised this issue. Moreover, the legal department of the issuing insurance company evidently believes that the provision does not violate the Section 72(s) rules.

Is this merely nit-picking on the part of the authors of this book? Perhaps it is. But we believe it is more than that. Whether the contract provision cited above actually does violate the required distribution rules of Section 72(s) or not, is just one issue and perhaps the authors' conclusion is wrong. But that cited provision is also an example of another issue—one that is absolutely vital to the financial well being of financial advisors who sell or offer counsel about annuities and the clients of those advisors. That issue is this:

> The contractual provisions of every annuity you deal with will determine how the various benefits of that annuity will be provided or not provided. If you, the advisor, do not understand what those provisions say—and what they mean—you cannot tell your client when—or whether—he will receive those benefits.

When a Deferred Annuity Is Purchased by a Special Needs Trust

A deferred annuity is sometimes recommended as an investment for a Special Needs Trust. This may be a suitable recommendation for several tax and nontax reasons. If the trust qualifies as the agent of a natural person, the annuity would enjoy tax-deferral; given the compressed tax rates to which trusts are often subject, such deferral may be a significant advantage.

However, in the case of so-called (d)(4)(A) Medicaid payback trusts, the situation is more complicated. To the extent there are required paybacks to the state by the trust of Medicaid benefits made to the trust beneficiary, the state could be held to constitute a beneficiary's interest. If the state is a remainder beneficiary of the trust, such a trust may not qualify as the agent of a natural person under 72(u), causing annual gains in the annuity to be taxable as earned—as ordinary income, at compressed trust tax rates.

Thus, generally speaking, third-party special needs trusts that do not require Medicaid payback—and therefore should only have natural persons as beneficiaries—are more likely to withstand scrutiny as the owner of an annuity that can be deemed an agent of a natural person.

When a Deferred Annuity Is Owned by a QTIP Trust

A deferred annuity presents unique complications as an investment for a QTIP trust, because undistributed gains in the annuity may not, in the laws of some states, be considered income and thus may not have to be distributed to the spouse beneficiary. If the purpose of the QTIP was to maximize income to the spouse, this may be an issue; conversely, the spouse may potentially force the liquidation of the annuity, to convert it to income-producing property. Otherwise, the trustee may potentially be caught in a conflict between a spouse who wants to increase income distributions from the trust, and a remainder beneficiary who wants to maximize the expecting corpus remaining behind.

Either way, though, if the beneficiary of the QTIP is under the age of 59½, the early withdrawal penalty tax of Sect. 72(q) may apply, making a QTIP trust with a younger-than-59½ beneficiary unappealing, even if the income aforementioned allocation rules are not an issue.

Best Practices When an Annuity Is Used In Connection with a Trust

Many advisors rely upon the marketing materials, home office marketing representatives, or external wholesalers of insurance companies for their understanding of those companies' insurance products. To be sure, these sources can be very helpful. But they may not be sufficient. Sometimes, they are either unclear or just plain wrong.[20] Those of us who are not licensed attorneys cannot, and should not, practice law. But we can, should, and must exercise due care in our advisory activities. Therefore, with regard to annuities, the authors strongly recommend that advisors consider the following caveats:

1. Avoid naming a trust as annuity owner unless:

    a. there is very good reason for doing so; and

    b. you are sure of all of the results of the designation—including when the insurance company will pay a benefit and under what conditions any death benefit enhancements will be payable.

2. Avoid naming a trust as beneficiary, for the same reasons.

3. Avoid naming different individuals as owner and annuitant, for the same reasons.[21] This is a good rule to observe, whether a trust is involved or not.

4. If the owner and annuitant will be two different individuals, know whether the contract you are considering is annuitant-driven or not.

The above list is not a complete recitation of things to know and avoid about annuities, but merely the authors' suggestions of the most vital caveats to consider when annuities and trusts are both involved. A better general caveat might be:

Be sure that you understand how, and under what conditions, the annuity you are considering will deliver, or not deliver, all the benefits provided by that annuity.

Endnotes

1. This provision applies to any annuity owned by an entity other than a natural person, including a corporation, partnership, or trust.

2. Primary annuitant is defined by IRC Section 72(s)(6)(B) as "the individual, the events in the life of whom are of primary importance in affecting the timing or amount of the payout under the contract."

3. IRC Sec. 72(u).

4. IRC Sec. 72(e)(4)(c)(ii).

5. IRC Sections 671-677; Revenue Ruling 85-13.

6. Underwood, "Trust Ownership of Nonqualified Annuities: General Consideration for Trustees", Journal of Financial Service Professionals, May, 2010, footnote 45.

7. There are no income or gift tax consequences of transfers from a taxpayer to himself, whether by gift or sale.

8. Underwood, Ibid.

9. IRC Sec. 72(s)(1)(B).

10. IRC Sec. 72(s)(2).

11. IRC Sec. 72(s)(2)(A).

12. Amendments to Treasury Regulation §1.401(a)(9)-4 became effective on April 15, 2002.

13. For example, IRS Notice 2004-15, 2004-9 IRB 526, explicitly established cross-application of the rules under IRC Section 72(t)(2)(A)(iv) regarding substantially equal periodic payments from retirement accounts to the same type of payments under annuities and IRC Section 72(q)(2)(D).

14. Let. Rul. 200323012.

15. In addition, the spouse was permitted to make a tax-free exchange of the annuities, under IRC Section 1035, for new annuity contracts owned by herself.

16. An exception to this general rule exists where an annuity is jointly owned. See Chapter 3.

17. We have said a death benefit, rather than the death benefit because annuitant-driven contracts typically pay the contractually-guaranteed guaranteed minimum, or enhanced death benefit only upon the death of the annuitant. In these contracts, the amount payable to the beneficiary upon the death of the owner is only the cash value of the annuity, and, in some contracts, a surrender charge may apply.

18. "This subsection" refers to IRC Section 72(s).

19. Presumably, the most immediate consequence would be that all these contracts were not in fact tax-deferred, and that income attributable to the contract for prior years should be declared as taxable income, with retroactive interest, and potential penalties, applicable to any years not closed by the statute of limitations.

20. Most experienced advisors have at least a few horror stories of home office marketing reps or wholesalers who made statements about the operation or tax treatment of an insurance product that were totally inaccurate. The authors have more than a few of these stories as well.

21. The potential problems resulting from different individuals named as the annuitant and owner are so common and serious that some insurance companies refuse to issue contracts on this basis.

Chapter 9

Annuities in Estate Planning

Chapter 8 examined the annuity as an investment, in the context of a 3-legged stool model. This chapter will focus on how various kinds of annuities can work in a more specific context— that of estate planning.

Avoidance of Probate

One of the estate planning reasons often cited for buying, or recommending, an annuity is that values in such contracts generally pass to beneficiaries directly, through the beneficiary designation, and are not subject to the probate process. This is true, but one does not need to purchase an annuity to achieve this result. Assets held in trust or taxable accounts titled as Payable On Death (POD) or Transfer On Death (TOD) also bypass probate.[1]

However, annuity beneficiary designations and the beneficiary designations permitted by state laws regulating POD and TOD accounts typically do not allow the degree of dispositive flexibility offered by a well-drafted trust. Moreover, values in an annuity may be includable, under state law, in the owner's augmented estate and subject to a surviving spouse's elective share.[2] If includable, an election by such spouse to take such share could cause the annuity value to be subject to probate, and to pass other than by the beneficiary designation to someone besides the named beneficiary. To determine whether this issue is a matter of state law, advisors should check the rules in those jurisdictions in which they practice.

That said, the fact that annuity values do generally pass directly to named beneficiaries, outside of probate, is significant, and may be a valuable advantage for many clients.

Providing Guaranteed Income to Heirs

A principal goal of many estate plans is to provide income to the estate owner's heirs. This goal can often be achieved by using either immediate or deferred annuities. Where the goal is to provide heirs with an immediate income, an immediate annuity may be the ideal mechanism, especially if the income is to continue for the recipient's lifetime. The certainty afforded by such a contract is sometimes more important than the amount of each income payment or the fact that the annuity income does not preserve principal. This may be particularly appropriate to satisfy specific beneficiary lifetime income bequests from a portion of assets while the remainder passes to another beneficiary.[3]

Where the desire is for the heir's income to increase over time—perhaps to keep pace with inflation—an immediate annuity providing for known annual increases is often attractive. While most insurers do not offer immediate annuities with cost of living increases tied to some index such as the consumer price index, some do, and more are likely to be offering such contracts in the future in response to a demand that appears to be increasing. An additional attraction is that annuities enjoy creditor protection in most jurisdictions.

A disadvantage to immediate annuities, in this context and others, is their inflexibility. Most immediate annuities, once begun, do not permit modification of the payment amount or commutation, although an increasing number of contracts do.

Purchase of a Single Premium Immediate Annuity (SPIA) by a Credit Shelter Trust

One application of immediate annuities which may be of interest to estate planners is their use to solve the trustee's investment dilemma. Often, a trust (e.g., a credit shelter trust) is established to provide both an income to an income beneficiary, perhaps the surviving spouse, and growth of principal, for the benefit of remainder beneficiaries, perhaps the children and/or grandchildren. The dilemma for the trustee is satisfying the opposing desires of these beneficiaries. The income beneficiary wishes to receive as much income as possible, and would prefer that trust monies be invested to provide that goal. Remainder beneficiaries are interested in capital accumulation, and prefer that the trust be funded with growth investments. The problem, of course, is that investments which provide high current income rarely offer good long term growth, and vice versa.

This conflict has always presented problems for trustees. A possible solution might be for the trust to purchase an immediate annuity, naming the income beneficiary as annuitant, in an amount sufficient to provide the income the beneficiary requires—perhaps increasing over time—and to invest all remaining trust assets solely for growth, without regard for whether they produce any current income. Adverse results in the growth investments will have no effect upon the income beneficiary. This strategy does not always work, of course. Financially, its attractiveness may appear to be directly proportional to the age of the income beneficiary/

annuitant, because, the older the annuitant, the greater the income that each dollar of premium will purchase; or, viewed another way, the less premium required to produce each dollar of income. This is assuming that the annuity is to continue for the annuitant's life. However, it's also arguable that older income beneficiaries are likely to die sooner, and that an annuity which expires without value at the beneficiary's death may be perceived as a bad deal. The existence of a refund element may reduce this objection.

Whether a refund feature should be included in the annuity is, however, problematic. A life-only annuity will require a smaller premium than one providing a benefit to another beneficiary if the annuitant, or the income beneficiary of the trust, should die prematurely. This would allow a greater percentage of the trust corpus to be allocated to growth investments, for the benefit of remainder beneficiaries. However, many people, including many advisors, find an annuity that provides no further benefit if an annuitant dies shortly after income payments commence unacceptable. The perception is that the insurance company keeps this extra money. This perception is false; the money is not retained by the insurer, but is paid out by that insurer to other members of the risk sharing pool, or annuitants who lived longer than their expected lifetimes. That said, the perception may be its own reality. Most people will not buy a life-only annuity and would probably prefer that such an annuity not be purchased for anyone of whom they might become remainder beneficiary.

Purchase of an Immediate Annuity for Heirs Outside a Trust

Sometimes, an estate owner's goals include providing a specific and certain income for specified heirs, apart from the overall dispositive provisions of the estate plan. Here, an immediate annuity is arguably the perfect instrument. Without the certainty of the annuity, a trustee or executor must take into account the market risk involved when invested assets must be accessed each year to make payments to the beneficiary. Thus, the use of an annuity may allow the trustee/executor to invest more money immediately on behalf of the other beneficiaries while still guaranteeing that the income beneficiary will receive all promised payments.

Purchase of a Deferred Annuity for Heirs

Where estate planning goals include providing a certain income for heirs to begin at some future time, a deferred annuity may make sense. Advantages include tax deferral of current gains, which can be of considerable importance if the annuity is owned by a trust subject to the compressed tax rates applicable to nongrantor trusts,[4] creditor protection (to the extent allowed by relevant law) where the annuity is owned outside a trust, and the risk management and investment characteristics of deferred annuities discussed at length in earlier chapters of this book. Disadvantages include the overhead cost of the annuity, which may be higher than that of alternative investments, surrender charges (if applicable), the fact that all distributions from an annuity are taxed at ordinary income rates, and the unavailability of a step-up in basis for annuities owned by a decedent.

Purchase of a SPIA by the Estate Owner for the Estate Owner and Spouse

Impact on the Attractiveness of Making Lifetime Gifts to Heirs

A primary goal of many, if not all, estate owners is to ensure income for themselves for their lifetimes. This goal often surfaces in discussions between clients and advisors when considering lifetime gifts. "I might need that money" is perhaps the most common objection raised by many clients to suggestions that they utilize the gift tax annual exclusion[5] in making lifetime gifts to heirs. To the extent that the estate owner is guaranteed that he or she—and his/her spouse, if applicable—can be assured of required income no matter what, annual gifts to heirs, whatever the reason for making them, may be far less worrisome. If, having secured this required income, perhaps by purchasing an immediate annuity, a client feels able to make more lifetime gifts than he or she otherwise would, the result can be both greater net wealth transferred to heirs—due to lower transfer tax and estate clearance costs—and greater emotional satisfaction. One can live to see his heirs enjoy lifetime gifts. One can also see how well such gifts are managed. For the parent or grandparent concerned that sizeable inheritances might spoil the kids, being able to see how well those kids deal with the money can be both gratifying and informing. If the kids mishandle such gifts, estate plans can be changed, perhaps by adding additional spendthrift provisions.

Implications for the Estate Owner's Asset Allocation Decisions

Even where lifetime gifts are not a concern, adequate income for the estate owner(s) is usually a key estate planning goal. "We want to provide for the kids and grandkids, but first we've got to take care of ourselves" is a refrain familiar to all estate planners. Allocating a portion of one's retirement portfolio to an instrument designed specifically to produce income can help one achieve this key planning objective, to the extent of making the allocation of remaining assets easier, or at least, less worrisome. This can be done using either a deferred annuity or an immediate annuity.

Using a Variable Deferred Annuity to Provide Death Benefit to an Uninsurable Estate Owner

A deferred annuity is not life insurance. A contract qualifying as life insurance under Section 7702 of the Internal Revenue Code has a death benefit that is taxed differently (under Section 101) from a contract qualifying as an annuity under Section 72. The two chief differences are:

1. All gain, or excess of contract value over adjusted basis, in an annuity will be taxed as Ordinary Income, either to the living contract holder or to the beneficiary.[6] By contrast, the death benefit of a life insurance policy is generally received income tax free by the beneficiary.[7]

2. Distributions to the living owner of a life insurance policy are generally taxed under a first in, first out basis. All distributions are considered a return of principal until all contract gain has been distributed.[8] Distributions from an annuity (issued since 8/13/82) are taxed on a last in, first out basis, or as gain until all gain has been

distributed. This same treatment also applies to life insurance policies that are modified endowment contracts.[9]

That said, a variable deferred annuity often provides a death benefit in excess of the contract's cash value, whereas the death benefit of most fixed deferred annuities is limited to the cash value. The advantage of this additional death benefit in a variable annuity can be significant, especially for an individual who cannot obtain life insurance, or for whom the rates would be unacceptably high. This is for one simple reason: while the contract owner does not escape taxation on that death benefit, he or she does escape insurance underwriting. The annuity death benefit is available to anyone who is willing to pay the standard cost charged for it.

How large might that benefit be? Some variable annuities offer an enhanced death benefit that pays the greatest of: (a) the contract value at death; (b) total contributions, accumulated at a specified rate of interest (often, 6%) until a maximum age, which is sometimes, as late as age 91, this is often called the rollup value; or (c) the contract value as of the highest annual, monthly, or even daily, valuation date, prior to some maximum age.

If investment performance of the annuity is good, the resulting death benefit can be far greater than the amount invested, or the cash value otherwise available at the individual's death. Even if performance is poor, the second of those two factors produces a constantly rising floor under the contract death benefit.

Many advisors recommend variable annuities with strong enhanced death benefit guarantees for this reason. Yet even this strategy might be improved by splitting the annuity investment into more than one annuity contract, as can be seen from the following examples:

1.   Ms. A invests $100,000 in a single variable deferred annuity with an enhanced death benefit. She selects a diversified asset allocation model, consisting of 50% equities and 50% bonds. At Ms. A's death six years later, the account balance at her death is larger than at any prior valuation date and is also larger than her contribution of $100,000, compounded at 6%—despite the fact that in the two years prior to her death, the stock market dropped significantly, while the bond market flourished. Her beneficiaries will receive the date-of-death account balance as a death benefit.

      That balance includes, not just the appreciated value of those subaccounts that did well (the bonds), but also the value of those equity subaccounts that lost money. The losses of the latter are netted against the gains of the former to produce the total account balance.

2.   Mr. B splits his $100,000 into $50,000 contributions for each of two different variable deferred annuities, each with the same enhanced death benefit and also allocates his overall annuity holdings in a 50% equities/50% bond mix. He allocates all the equities to the first $50,000 annuity and all the bonds to the second. At

his death, the account balance of the first contract is lower than at a prior valuation date—due to the decline in the stock market—so that greater prior value is paid as a death benefit. The date-of-death balance of the second contract containing the bonds which did well, becomes the death benefit of the second contract.

The losses in the first contract are not netted against the gains in the second. Indeed, the losses in the first are ignored, because the rollup death benefit value is used. Thus, Mr. B's heirs receive more money at Mr. B's death, because they receive all of the appreciation from the contract holding bonds, and the rollup death benefit of the contract holding equities.

Sadly, many advisors are unaware of this strategy. Some even insist that an advisor's sale of two annuities instead of one is inherently bad. Often, this is because they believe it results in a higher commission, which it does not.

There is yet another reason why two deferred annuities can be better than one. This one works with both fixed and variable contracts and has nothing to do with death benefit.

Example: Ms. A invests $100,000 in a single deferred annuity. Two years later, she decides to withdraw $20,000 from the contract, which is now worth $120,000. Her entire withdrawal consists of gain and is, therefore, fully taxable. Had she bought two contracts, each for $50,000 and gotten the same investment results, she would now have two contracts of $60,000 each. She could withdraw the $20,000 from only one, whereupon only half ($10,000) of the withdrawal would be taxable as gain, with the other half being considered a return of principal. It is important to note that due to the annuity anti-abuse rules, all annuities purchased from the same insurance company in the same calendar year will be treated as one contract, requiring gains to be aggregated for withdrawal purposes.[10] Consequently, a $20,000 withdrawal would still be treated as being withdrawn from an aggregate contract worth $120,000, resulting in the same $20,000 gain as the first scenario. Thus, to apply this strategy, the annuity purchaser would need to purchase each annuity from different insurance companies, or in different calendar years.

Using the Guarantees in a Deferred Annuity to Provide Portfolio Insurance

A fixed deferred annuity provides three guarantees to its owner:

1. A guarantee of principal. The money invested in a fixed deferred annuity is guaranteed against loss by the insurer.

2. A guaranteed minimum rate of return.

3. Guaranteed annuity payout factors.

The first two guarantees provide a known minimum return, on the portion of one's portfolio allocated to the annuity, which has the effect of lowering the overall principal and interest rate risks of the entire portfolio. Moreover, the assurance that this known future value can be converted into an income stream that will provide at least a certain amount of money each year can make projections of one's future cash flows less problematic.

A variable deferred annuity does not offer the first two guarantees to the living policy owner, except to the extent that annuity values are invested in the fixed account. However, it provides others. The guaranteed death benefit always provides assurance that heirs—not the living policy owner—will receive, at a minimum, the amount originally invested or the account balance at death, if greater. Enhanced death benefit guarantees, common in newer variable contracts, can assure heirs of the greater of that original investment or account balance at death or some other potentially higher minimum amount; perhaps the account balance at some policy anniversary prior to death or the original investment, compounded at some specified rate of return. If the minimum amount that will pass to heirs is a serious estate planning concern, the guaranteed death benefit may be worth its cost.

The guaranteed living benefits in today's variable deferred annuities may provide even more comfort for the estate owner in making his asset allocation decisions, precisely because of the refrain noted earlier, namely: "we want to provide for the kids and grandkids, but first we've got to take care of ourselves." The guaranteed minimum income benefit, guaranteed minimum withdrawal benefit, guaranteed minimum accumulation benefit, and provisions combining all three features can assure the estate owner that, irrespective of the performance of the investments in the annuity, certain minimum income and/or future lump sum values will be available.

Many critics contend that the costs for these provisions outweigh the benefits that they are likely to provide. The mathematics supporting such a conclusion—if any are supplied—often rely upon historical averages and probable life expectancies. This is not to say that all such criticisms are invalid, or that the logic and mathematics are never valid or persuasive. They may be both. However, it is the authors' contention that the certainties these riders provide can be very important to many estate owner clients on an emotional level. These certainties, with regard to that part of a client's portfolio invested in annuities providing them, can enable the client to make asset allocations with regard to money that the client might not otherwise feel comfortable making. In addition, it's important to note that even though the client may come out with less money in the long run on average, the client is still guaranteeing that a particular minimum amount will be available, which may be more consistent with a client's goals than merely having the most dollars at death by investing heavily in equities.

Many clients, especially older ones, are often wary of putting too much in the stock market, even though they know that equities have historically provided significantly better returns than fixed dollar investments such as CDs and bonds. To the extent that such a conservative (read: risk-intolerant) client's equity investments can be held in an investment account which

guarantees minimum future lump sum and present and future income values, the client may
be willing to allocate more of his portfolio to such equities, and remain invested in them longer
than if no such guarantees were available. For the client whose portfolio is not large enough to
generate required income with reasonable certainty if invested very conservatively, this increased
equity exposure might make the difference between an adequate income and just getting by,
or even running out of money. Why might this be? The client might only be willing to invest
substantially in equities if there are underlying guarantees, and would otherwise choose a much
more conservative portfolio, with lower expected risk and return.

Using the Guaranteed Income of an Immediate Annuity
to Reduce Retirement Portfolio Failure Rate

As noted, the risk management benefits of either a fixed or variable deferred annuity may
allow some clients to invest their retirement portfolios—the portion invested in those annuities,
but also, perhaps, more of the nonannuity portion—more aggressively, and with more
confidence, than they might in the absence of these guarantees. The result of such a change in
allocation should, over time, be an increase in the income produced, despite the expenses of the
annuity. For retirees living on less than the amount their portfolios earn, this translates to greater
capital accumulation, ultimately providing more wealth to transfer to heirs.

Yet many retirees do not live on less than what their investments earn. For all too many
clients, the most important issue is not how much will be left to heirs after they die, but whether
their portfolios will produce enough for them to live on, for as long as they live. Indeed, this
uncertainty represents what one of the authors refers to as the one big risk in retirement income
planning, namely: "what are the chances that my account balance will fall to zero before my
blood pressure does?". This risk can be managed, with considerable effectiveness, by use of
immediate annuities. As was noted in the last chapter, there is mounting evidence that allocating
a portion of one's retirement portfolio to a mechanism providing immediate, certain income
can produce a significant increase in the probability that the portfolio as a whole will be able to
provide required income for the retiree's entire lifetime, however long that may be. The purchase
of a life annuity, either for a level or an increasing annual benefit, can offset—to an extent
proportional to the percentage of required retirement income provided by the annuity—the
effects of negative dollar cost averaging, where more shares must be liquidated to provide a set
amount of income after a decline in the value of those shares than would have had to be sold if
the share price remained level or increased. A life annuity is not the only way to implement this
strategy. Laddered bonds or laddered period certain annuities may also be used. Whatever the
implementation, this strategy can offset negative dollar cost averaging, decrease the probability
that the retirement portfolio will be exhausted during retiree's lifetime—or produce declining
income levels—and provide greater emotional comfort, although only an annuity guarantees
that payments will continue even if an individual lives much longer than anticipated. In addition,
this strategy may foster greater willingness to make lifetime gifts to heirs and/or gifts—lifetime,
testamentary, or both—to charities.

Using Annuities to Maintain Tax Deferral, and Control, from Beyond the Grave

Ensuring Tax Deferral of Gain Beyond the Annuity Owner's Lifetime

The income tax on annual gain in a deferred annuity is generally deferred until it is distributed (see Chapter 2). Distributees of annuity proceeds can benefit from even further tax deferral if those distributions are considered amounts received as an annuity (see Chapter 3). If so, a portion of each payment is excluded from tax as a return of principal under the regular annuity rules of IRC Section 72(b). This treatment applies to annuity payments whether made to an annuitant or to a beneficiary. Thus, if a deferred annuity is structured so as to ensure that the beneficiary or beneficiaries can, or perhaps must, take proceeds in the form of an annuity, the benefits of tax deferral will survive the annuity owner. This can be done utilizing a concept known as the stretch annuity.

What is a stretch annuity? In its broadest sense, one might say the term describes any annuity where the beneficiary designation allows, or requires the beneficiary to stretch death proceeds, and the benefits of tax deferral of undistributed gain, over as long a period as possible. Deferred annuity contracts nearly always allow the beneficiary to take proceeds in the form of an annuity, either over lifetime or for a period of years. If the beneficiary is the surviving spouse of the owner, he or she is typically granted a spousal continuation option, allowing an election to treat the contract as if it were his/her own from inception,[11] and to name new beneficiary(ies), who will, themselves, be able to choose to take proceeds as an annuity. Moreover, many contacts permit the owner to ensure that death proceeds will be eligible for the favorable tax treatment of the regular annuity rules by allowing the owner to require that death proceeds be taken by the beneficiary(ies) as an annuity. This election is usually made on the beneficiary designation form, or by election of a special contract option. Such election is usually revocable by the contract owner at any point before death, but not by the beneficiary after the owner dies.

However, election of a regular annuity payout option, whether by the owner or beneficiary, is not necessarily the only way to achieve this post-death tax deferral. As was noted in Chapter 3, the IRS has privately ruled that payment of annuity death benefits to a beneficiary where the amount of each payment is determined by the life expectancy fraction method, rather than by the payout factors of a regular annuity option, can satisfy the requirements of IRC Section 72(s). The undistributed gain would not be constructively received (and would, therefore, enjoy tax deferral until it is distributed).[12] In other words, the private ruling allowed a beneficiary to take systematic withdrawals as the beneficiary of an annuity, without annuitizing, and still stretch the payments—and tax on the gain—over the beneficiary's lifetime.

In a subsequent letter ruling the IRS went even further, to hold that, under certain circumstances, payout to a beneficiary using this method or the amortization or annuity factor methods[13] will qualify as amounts received as an annuity.[14] As such, the regular annuity rules of IRC Section 72(b) would be applicable, whereby a portion of each annuity payment is excluded from tax as a return of principal. It must be noted that the ruling which permitted this tax result did so on the basis of case-specific facts. Advisors should not assume that this result is available for any particular client without a ruling from the Internal Revenue Service. Moreover, many annuity contracts do not permit the life expectancy fraction method to be used.[15] Finally, insurers that do permit this option may issue a Form 1099-R to beneficiaries indicating that the payments made are amounts not received as an annuity. That is, they may not apply the regular annuity rules exclusion ratio, but will report such payments as fully taxable, to the extent of any remaining gain in the contract.

Of the three optional methods referred to previously (amortization, annuity factor, and life expectancy fraction), the last offers the most stretch of tax deferral, because it permits smaller payments in the early payout years. It also offers beneficiaries the greatest flexibility. Most annuitizations are irrevocable. The beneficiary is stuck with the arrangement for the duration of the payout, which may be for that beneficiary's entire lifetime.

By contrast, the fractional method permits the beneficiary to take only the relatively small amounts required under that method and the freedom to take amounts over and above those required at any time. Moreover, undistributed proceeds will remain invested in the chosen subaccounts and any gains earned will continue to enjoy the benefit of tax deferral.

As noted, the life expectancy fraction method of payout offers the most stretch. Thus, a more restrictive—but, in the authors' opinion, better—definition of stretch annuity is any annuity contract that guarantees for the beneficiaries the right to take proceeds according to this life expectancy fraction method. This definition might be refined even further, to include only contracts that waive surrender charges upon death.

A few caveats should be noted. First, as was noted above, not all deferred annuity contracts allow the beneficiary to use the life expectancy fraction method or, for that matter, the other two optional methods described in Notice 89-25. Many, especially older contracts, restrict the beneficiary to the use of regular annuity options. Second, not all contracts that do make the life expectancy fraction method payout arrangement available to beneficiaries permit the policy owner to restrict beneficiaries to using only that option. But is that necessarily a bad thing?

An annuity owner's right to restrict beneficiaries to some form of stretched payout of death proceeds does offer the benefit of post-death tax deferral. But it does so at the cost of flexibility. What if the beneficiary has extraordinary, unanticipated financial needs such as uninsured medical bills? An irrevocable annuity income will be of little help in meeting such expenses.[16]

Some flexibility and post-death control may be offered by the use of special beneficiary designations or contractual options. One key benefit of these is that annuity owners can place certain limitations on how beneficiaries receive the money after death, without having to go through the cost and trouble of having a lawyer draft a trust to accomplish that goal. Of course, it should be noted that a trust can provide much greater flexibility to accomplish goals than use of a beneficiary designation, which, no matter how special, cannot.

However, a nonqualified annuity payable to a trust will be required to make a full distribution under the 5-year rule (as discussed in Chapter 2), while the same annuity payable to an individual beneficiary with a restricted beneficiary designation may provide for similar restrictions while still allowing the beneficiary to stretch withdrawals and income tax consequences over his/her lifetime. Consequently, as long as trusts cannot be designated beneficiaries, owners and their advisors must weigh the income tax consequences with the flexibility allowed by trusts in determining an appropriate course of action.

Example: One major insurer offers a Predetermined Beneficiary Payout Option that permits the owner to restrict the beneficiary to a payout over his/her lifetime calculated only in accordance with the Single Life table of Treasury Regulation Section 1.401(a)(9)-9, Q&A 1, and, upon reaching a specified age, access to any distributions above the minimum specified by that table.

However, some deferred annuities do not offer such provisions. It is essential that the advisor know what stretch provisions are permitted by the annuity contract being considered. Whether the law permits a payout option is a moot point if the issuing insurer does not offer it. It is also crucial that the advisor knows whose death will result in the payment of the contractually guaranteed death benefit of the annuity being considered. In annuitant-driven contracts, the death of a nonannuitant owner will force distribution (per the requirements of IRC Section 72(s)), but any guaranteed death benefit exceeding the cash value in the contract will not be payable. See Chapters 1 and 3.

Using a SPIA to Provide for a Longtime Household Employee

Often, wealthy clients wish to provide benefits, at their deaths, to longtime household help. They may be concerned that the employee might lack the skills to manage a lump sum bequest, or might squander it. A direction, in the estate planning documents, to purchase an immediate annuity for the benefit of that employee can address these concerns, without the hassle of establishing a standalone subtrust for such purposes. A SPIA would ensure an income for that employee for lifetime; moreover, the cost of a life-contingent immediate annuity for a specified amount of income decreases with the age of the annuitant at issue. Thus, the longer the estate owner lives, the older the employee will be when the annuity is purchased, and the lower the cost of the annuity.[17]

Using a SPIA to Fund a Small Bequest

Similarly, a SPIA might be used to fund a small bequest to someone not a beneficiary under the client's trusts, where there is concern that the recipient might be unable or unwilling to manage the bequest prudently and where the amount of the bequest is less than the minimum that professional trust managers will accept. Of course, this assumes that the SPIA bequest itself would still produce a large enough monthly or annual payment to be a meaningful bequest in the eyes of the decedent.

Purchase of a SPIA by a Trust for the Benefit of Children not His and Hers

As Mancini, Olsen, & Warshaw note[18], "when a trust is created at the death of an individual for the benefit of his or her spouse and children, if the children are not also the surviving spouse's children, tension can develop over the trust's investments." One solution might be for the trustee to be directed to purchase one or more immediate annuities for the benefit of that deceased spouse's children and manage the balance for the benefit of the other trust beneficiaries. Of course, this does separate out the trust principal at the time of first death, making such principal, and its interest, unavailable to the surviving spouse while he/she is still alive, but it avoids the cost of drafting multiple trusts to accommodate all the heirs.

Using a Deferred Annuity to Fund a QTIP Trust

In some estate planning situations involving trusts, the use of an annuity may be problematic. Gary Underwood writes:

> "Annuities may not be appropriate investments for QTIP trusts for a reason associated with state law definitions of income. In most states, the undistributed gains inside of an annuity are not defined as income, and therefore may not have to be distributed to the income beneficiary. Income would only be recognized to the extent the trustee made withdrawals of gains from the annuity. If the trustee made no withdrawals, then there may be significantly less trust income to distribute to the surviving spouse. The trustee could be placed in an unenviable position between the surviving spouse who may want to maximize income and the children who want to maximize principal for later distribution. Unless the trustee and all beneficiaries agree on specific parameters for any annuity withdrawals, an annuity may present problems."[19]

Some of the aforementioned problems highlighted by Underwood can be mitigated by a clear drafting of the QTIP trust before the first death (i.e., to clearly state what constitutes income and whether/how income with respect to the annuity will be classified for income distribution purposes). In some cases, the treatment of an annuity may be preferable to alternatives, if the specific goal is actually to minimize income distributions to the surviving spouse. On the other hand, if the spouse is not happy with such an arrangement, the spouse could potentially have the annuity liquidated, under the required right of a spouse under a QTIP trust, compelling the trustee to convert QTIP assets to income-producing property. If such a conversion occurs after many years, the trust could be compelled to recognize significant accrued taxable gains in a single year. Accordingly, it may ultimately be wise to avoid the use of deferred annuities inside of a QTIP trust, unless the spouse income beneficiary is clearly supportive of the arrangement, and unlikely to have his/her mind changed.

Using a Variable Annuity to Fund a Charitable Remainder Unitrust

One commonly used application of a variable annuity is in funding a charitable remainder unitrust (CRUT). In fact, the variable annuity has often been touted as the perfect funding instrument for the so-called spigot NIMCRUT—especially by those marketing variable annuities. Is it? The following discussion will examine the pros and cons of such a strategy. But first, some terms need to be defined. What is a spigot NIMCRUT?

A CRUT is a type of Charitable Remainder Trust (CRT)—a split-interest trust with a charitable remainder beneficiary and one or more noncharitable beneficiaries with rights to payments each year during the term of the trust. Often, the estate-owner client is the noncharitable beneficiary. The CRUT provides that the noncharitable beneficiaries will receive a unitrust amount each year (i.e., a certain percentage of the trust value, as revalued each year). CRTs that pay specified amounts each year are called Charitable Remainder Annuity Trusts.

The NIM stands for Net Income with Makeup. Net income means that each year the trust will pay the lesser of the net income or the payout percentage specified in the trust to the noncharitable beneficiary. The makeup part means that whenever net income is less than the payout percentage, the shortfall is credited to a makeup account, which can be tapped later on if the trust's net income exceeds the specified payout percentage, but only to the extent of that excess.

The spigot part means that the payment stream can be turned on and off, as with a spigot. Typically, this works by having a special independent trustee instruct the trust administrator to turn the payment stream on or off, as needed by the noncharitable beneficiary.

Proponents of the variable annuity-funded spigot NIMCRUT sometimes assert that only with a variable annuity can the noncharitable beneficiary be sure of being able to tap the makeup account, which may have been created deliberately by having the trust invest in the early years in vehicles which produce only capital gains, but no trust income.

This is not necessarily true. First, the Principal and Income Act of the state in which the trust is sited may permit allocation of post-contribution capital gains as either income or principal, each year, as the trustee sees fit. Secondly, there are certain types of investments that can produce income on demand, so to speak, such as a Limited Liability Company (LLC). Some commentators have described a one person LLC as the ideal spigot NIMCRUT instrument, where state law permits such entities.

There are also some fundamental disadvantages to using variable annuities to fund this type of CRT. First, there's the fact that, beneficiaries of a CRT are generally taxed under a four-tier system in which trust income is deemed to be (1) ordinary income, (2) realized capital gains, (3) tax-exempt income, or (4) principal, in Worst In, First Out (WIFO) order. All distributions from an annuity are always ordinary income. A CRT funded with an annuity can never receive capital gains treatment on any gains from that annuity.

A second disadvantage is that a variable annuity owned by a NIMCRUT is not considered to be owned as an agent for a natural person.[20] Consequently, annual gain in the annuity—even if not distributed—is taxable. Although the NIMCRUT itself is a tax-deferred entity, insurance companies have recently adopted the practice of issuing a Form 1099-R to the CRT/owner, showing the annuity gain to be currently taxable. Previously, many insurers did not issue a Form 1099-R to report undistributed gain if the contract owner was a CRT, since it is already a tax-exempt entity. For this reason, and because charitable trust accounting is very complex, advisors recommending or considering a variable annuity to fund a NIMCRUT should be aware that the services of an accountant experienced in charitable trust accounting will be essential.

A third disadvantage is the wrapper cost of the annuity, which was discussed earlier. These overhead costs can serve as a drag on investment performance, especially if the insurance charges produce benefits only for the charitable remainder beneficiary and if the client's interest in benefiting the charity is secondary. It should be mentioned, here, that the first word in the term charitable remainder trust is charitable, and that advisors and clients probably ought to keep that in mind.

Critics of using variable annuities to fund spigot NIMCRUTs often harp on these disadvantages, often without acknowledging that there might be advantages in the bargain. This is neither fair nor accurate.

Ordinary trust accounting rules treat realized capital gains as additions to trust corpus, not as income. However, a CRT can be drafted so as to allow the trustee to treat capital gains as income. Regardless of which rule is applicable, if the trust investments include, say, a stock which has appreciated in value in the trust, but which is now performing poorly, the trustee, or a special trustee, of a spigot NIMCRUT may have an unpleasant decision to make if the income beneficiary doesn't happen to want income at the time. If the stock is sold, the gains are additions to principal, which will not benefit the income beneficiary; or, the trustee treats the capital gain as income, but at a time when the beneficiary doesn't want income.

On the other hand, a spigot NIMCRUT funded by an annuity can be drafted so as to define distributable income as any distribution from the annuity used to fund the trust, provided state law permits such language. Buys and sells within the annuity aren't income unless actually distributed. When income is desired, the distribution may be taken in the amount desired—limited, of course, by the actual gain the annuity has produced—provided that there is gain in the annuity. There can be no distributable income from the annuity unless its value exceeds its basis (the amount originally invested). If no gain exists in the annuity, no income exists to be distributed to the income beneficiary, because of how trust accounting rules define income. This last point is all too often not fully understood by clients, or advisors.

It's also important to understand that when a spigot NIMCRUT defines distributable income, that definition of income—or the definition under the state's Principal and Income Act—may be different than taxable income earned by the trust. This is specifically applicable when a NIMCRUT owns a variable annuity, because the trust's nonnatural person ownership causes annual gains on the contract to be taxable. Consequently, even when a NIMCRUT receives a Form 1099-R for taxable income attributable to annual gains on the contract, it does not necessarily mean that the trust must distribute that amount of income under its net income requirements, if the definition of income states otherwise.

The bottom line answer to the question of whether a variable annuity is the best funding instrument for a spigot NIMCRUT or not is, as one might expect, it depends on several factors. These include: what the client's state Principal and Income Act permits, how flexible a spigot the client requires, and the size of the annuity wrapper costs, just to name three factors.

Endnotes

1. POD and TOD are types of financial accounts with designated beneficiaries, where account values pass directly to those beneficiaries, generally bypassing the probate process. POD accounts are often bank accounts, while securities or investment accounts are typically TOD.

2. That share which, by state law, is the surviving spouse's by right, regardless of decedent spouse's provisions to the contrary.

3. For example, a decedent wants to leave $50,000/year, for life, to one beneficiary while leaving the remaining estate assets to other beneficiaries (e.g., children).

4. Such tax deferral is possible only if the trust owning the annuity can qualify as an agent of a natural person. See Chapter 2.

5. IRC Sec. 2503(b).

6. See Chapter 2 for further discussion of the taxation of annuities.

7. IRC Sec. 101(a)(1).

8. IRC Sec. 72(e)(5)(C).

9. IRC Secs. 72(e)(5)(C), 72(e)(10), and 72(e)(2)(B).

10. IRC Sec. 72(e)(11).

11. For the tax implications of this decision, see Chapter 3.

12. PLR 200151038.

13. These are the three methods set forth in Q&A-12 of Notice 89-25, 1989-1 CB 662, 666, as modified by Rev. Rul. 2002-62, 2002-2 CB 710.

14. PLR 200313016.

15. According to Rick Bueter (www.rickbueter.com), an industry expert on stretch annuities, only a fraction of contracts currently available permit the use of the life expectancy fraction option.

16. It should be noted that firms exist which will purchase an annuitant's right to an annuity income—or a structured settlement—for a lump sum, but the lump sum is usually discounted at a rate of interest much greater than the rate used to create that income stream. Moreover, such a purchase may be barred by contractual provisions or local law.

17. Mancini, Mary Ann; Olsen, John; & Warshaw, Mel, "Annuities in Estate Planning" *Private Wealth,* Nov., 2011

18. Mancini, Olsen, & Warshaw, *Ibid.*

19. Gary Underwood, "Trust Ownership of Nonqualified Annuities: General Consideration for Trustees", *Journal of Financial Service Professionals,* May, 2010

20. PLR 9009047.

Chapter 10

The Great Debate:
Are Annuities Good or Bad?

Part One: Arguments in Favor of Annuities

Annuities have, for many years, been the subject of considerable debate among financial planners, insurance agents, financial journalists, and academics. While some of this discussion is dispassionate, a surprising amount of it is not. Much of what is written on the subject—especially by those opposed to annuities—is outright polemic. The debate has become, for many, a feud—as if one must either be for annuities or against them.

This is both unfortunate and absurd. It is unfortunate because the tone and level of discussion regarding the appropriateness and value of annuities in financial planning often sinks to the point of mere diatribe, in which the search for genuine understanding is abandoned for the sake of making one's case. In that sort of debate, as in war, the first casualty is truth. It is absurd because it rests upon an absurd premise—that an annuity, which is simply a financial tool, can be, in and of itself, inherently good or bad.

The authors of this book are neither in favor of, nor opposed to, annuities. They view, and strongly encourage the reader to view an annuity, or any annuity, as a tool; the appropriateness and value of which necessarily depends upon how well it does the job to be done, and how well it accomplishes the planning objectives compared to other tools that are available. In these two chapters we will evaluate some of the more commonly advanced arguments for and against annuities and attempt to supply some balance.

Arguments in Favor of Deferred Annuities

The Benefits of Tax Deferral

Many proponents of deferred annuities point to tax-deferral as a great advantage of these instruments. Indeed, many commentators have stated, flatly, that tax deferral is the main attraction of deferred annuities—implying that it must be the main reason for purchasing one. Others have argued that the real value to such deferral is the control it gives the contract owner. Because there are no required minimum distributions applicable to deferred annuities, and because the contract owner can decide when, and in what amounts, to take distributions, the deferred annuity has been labeled by some as the perfect tax control device.

Certainly, tax deferral has value. Some commentators have observed that it enhances even further, the miracle of compound interest. Jack Marrion refers to this enhancement as "triple interest crediting."

> Money that remains inside an annuity grows free from current income taxes. Not only does the principal earn interest (simple interest at work), and the interest earns interest (compound interest at work), but the money that would have gone to Uncle Sam also earns interest (tax-advantaged interest at work). [1]

Moreover, the control over the timing of taxation of gain enjoyed by the owner of a deferred annuity is unquestionably worthwhile. The annuity owner may choose to take distributions in years of unusually low income or when such distributions can be netted against ordinary income losses. Moreover, the income earned in an annuity, but not yet distributed, is not countable for purposes of the alternative minimum tax or the taxability of Social Security benefits.

Yet the tax deferral and tax control provided by a deferred annuity are not entirely free. There are costs to these benefits, and the costs are not always acknowledged by those who proclaim the benefits. What are these costs?

Insurance Charges. These apply only to variable annuities. The insurance charges, or the sum of the mortality and expense (M&E) charge and any separate administrative expense charge, are usually the largest component of the overhead cost in a variable annuity. These charges are discussed in detail in Chapter 4.

Surrender Charges. Many deferred annuities assess surrender charges for distributions exceeding a specified amount or a percentage of the account value, if taken during the surrender charge period. These charges are a limitation upon control the annuity owner enjoys over the money invested in his annuity.

Early Distribution Penalty. In addition to any contractual surrender charges, the Internal Revenue Code imposes a penalty tax on distributions taken from a nonqualified annuity by an annuity owner who is under age 59½, unless the distributions qualify under certain very specific exceptions (see Chapter 2). The penalty is equal to 10% of the taxable amount of such distributions.[2] Like surrender charges, this penalty tax is a limitation on the tax control enjoyed by the annuity owner.

Ordinary Income Treatment. All distributions from an annuity are taxed as ordinary income. The preferential tax treatment of long-term capital gains, and qualified dividends, enjoyed by many other investment alternatives, is not applicable to the gain in an annuity. This is true for all distributions—partial withdrawals, total contact surrenders, or death benefits—to the extent that there is gain in the contract, and it applies whether a distribution is taken as a lump sum or in the form of annuity income.

Does ordinary income treatment constitute a disadvantage of deferred annuities? If someone is comparing a deferred variable annuity to investments such as stocks, commodities, or mutual funds, the answer might be yes. Much of the gain derived from these investments will, if the investment is held for at least one year, qualify as long-term capital gains, and/or may receive qualified dividend treatment, both of which enjoy taxation at rates significantly lower than ordinary income rates—especially for high-income investors. In addition, qualified dividends on stocks—or mutual funds holding stocks—may also be eligible for preferential tax treatment lower than ordinary income tax rates. The difference in net, after-tax, accumulated wealth and net after-tax income, wrought by the differential between these two tax regimes, can be profound. See Chapter 12 for a comparison of a deferred variable annuity with a nonqualified mutual fund portfolio. On the other hand, it's important to note that one material benefit of the tax-deferral structure for annuities holding equities is the fact that the investor can change equity allocations without realizing capital gains and generating a current income tax liability. Thus, for portfolios with high enough turnover, the benefits of tax deferral can still theoretically outweigh the less favorable ordinary income treatment.

On the other hand, when comparing a deferred fixed annuity to investments such as certificates of deposit or bonds, the ordinary income treatment of annuity distributions may not represent a disadvantage at all, simply because the interest earned on CDs and bonds is taxed in exactly the same way. In such a scenario, taxation will be subject to ordinary income treatment either way, yet the annuity's ordinary income gains are at least tax deferred.

It should be noted that the benefit of tax deferral in a deferred annuity is not limited to the accumulation phase, or the period from contract inception to the point where the owner begins taking distributions. Distributions taken as an annuity are taxable only to the extent that the annuity payment exceeds the excludible portion, calculated according to the annuity rules of Section 72(b). Gain not yet received, by this method, continues to enjoy tax-deferral until all gain has been distributed, which occurs when the annuitant reaches life expectancy or the end of a period certain term.

This opportunity for tax deferral of annuity growth, even during the distribution phase of a deferred annuity is often overlooked by critics of annuities, who often compare the annuity to some investment alternative assuming that both will be surrendered at some future point in a lump sum. The advantage of continuing tax deferral during the distribution period can be very substantial, as was noted in a study conducted in 2002 by Price Waterhouse Cooper, entitled "The Value of Lifetime Annuitization."[3]

> **No Step-up in Basis for Inherited Annuities.** As was noted above, the gain in a deferred annuity is always taxed as ordinary income, even when distributed to a beneficiary as death proceeds, with the exception of original pre-1979 contracts, as discussed in Chapter 3. When received by a beneficiary, such gain is considered income in respect of a decedent. Most other types of investments held by a decedent at death enjoy, under current law, a treatment known as step-up in basis, in which the cost basis, for income tax purposes, of the investment passing to an heir is stepped-up to its value as of the date of decedent's death.[4] Thus, a stock, which the decedent paid $1,000 for, but which is worth $2,000 at his death, passes to his heir with an income tax cost basis of $2,000. If that heir subsequently sells the stock for $2,500, he will pay tax only on a gain of $500.

If, however, the decedent had bought a deferred annuity for $1,000 and died without taking any distributions, when the annuity was worth $2,000, the beneficiary would be liable for the tax on the entire $1,000 of untaxed gain, at ordinary income rates.[5]

The authors suggest that, where net wealth passing to heirs is a major planning goal, far better instruments than a deferred annuity may be available. For example, life insurance offers far better tax treatment, if the individual is insurable. The beneficiary of a life insurance policy can receive, free of income tax, not just the full cash value of the policy, but the greater—often, far greater—death benefit.

An Annuity Is the Only Vehicle that Can Guarantee an Income for Life

One of the most commonly advanced arguments in favor of an annuity is that it is the only vehicle guaranteeing, for a given investment amount, an income that (a) is certain as to amount and (b) cannot be outlived. Strictly speaking, this is not true. Perpetual bonds guarantee an interest rate in perpetuity, in addition to invested principal, but these bonds are sufficiently rare as to qualify as exotic investments. Ordinary bonds cannot guarantee an income indefinitely, because all ordinary bonds have a fixed duration. Most instruments considered by investors desiring a certain income either have fixed durations or generate income only through dividends or interest that are not absolutely guaranteed. Deferred annuities also have a maximum maturity date, by which the owner must either surrender or annuitize the contract, so the claim stated above really applies only to immediate annuities or deferred annuities that will be annuitized.

That being said, there is a huge difference between the income generated by an immediate annuity, or a deferred annuity that has been annuitized, and that produced by any nonannuity alternative. By definition, an annuity is an income stream representing both earnings and the systematic liquidation of principal. To compare the income produced by an annuity with the income produced by some alternative using only earnings on principal is to compare totally dissimilar instruments. Unless it is made clear that one alternative preserves principal while the other exhausts it, such a comparison is utterly misleading.

Yet if income is the only goal for a particular investor, the fact that no principal will remain at the annuitant's death—or at the end of the annuity period, if a period certain payout is contemplated—may not be as important as the amount of the income. For older clients, the annual annuity payment may be significantly greater than that realistically obtainable from any alternative, given the same lump sum investment. The additional income may, for these clients, be worth the cost of spending the kids' inheritance. Moreover, a comparison of a life annuity with an alternative investment need not contemplate that all of the investor's capital will be placed under either alternative. Allocating part of someone's assets to a life annuity might, in some situations, produce an income that is both certain—with all the emotional satisfaction that certainty provides—and sufficiently larger than might otherwise be achievable. The investor then might feel comfortable allocating his remaining assets to more conservative investments, to reduce investment risk, or to more aggressive ones, to achieve even greater total income or final wealth. In either scenario, the annuity would be performing, not only as an investment, but also—the authors would say primarily—as a risk management tool.

If one grants the advantages to annuitization just described, there remains the question of when the annuity needs to be purchased to achieve these advantages. Would it not make sense for our investor to put his money into some instrument that offers more growth opportunity than a fixed annuity or lower overhead costs than a variable one and simply sell that instrument to purchase an immediate annuity when the time comes to begin taking income?

Many commentators and advisors will answer yes. Supporting this conclusion is the fact that the annuity payout factors guaranteed in a deferred annuity have rarely been as attractive as the payout factors available in the immediate annuity marketplace. Moreover, many investment alternatives may be taxed at Long-Term Capital Gains (LTCG) rates and may even enjoy some degree of tax deferral. For example, the profit from an investment in a nondividend-paying growth stock will be taxed only when that stock is sold, and, then, at LTCG rates.

These are valid points. Tax deferral is not the sole province of annuities, and annuities never get capital gains treatment. However, the guarantee of principal, of a minimum rate of return in fixed annuities, and the guaranteed living benefits available in today's variable contracts provide a degree of downside risk protection that should not be overlooked. Whether that protection is worth the tradeoffs involved is a question well worth serious consideration. But it is not actually an investment question, even though most critics view it as such. It is really a risk management question.

As to whether investing in some alternative which perhaps offers LTCG tax treatment, during someone's wealth accumulation phase and then surrendering that investment to purchase an immediate annuity is preferable to locking in guaranteed annuity rates is a question we should consider in the light of longevity trends. Americans are living longer with each passing decade. Is it not possible that medical breakthroughs may so lengthen the life expectancy of the average American that immediate annuity rates, decades hence, will be less attractive than those payout rates guaranteed in today's deferred annuity contracts? If so—and, especially, if those future annuity payout factors are significantly lower than today's guaranteed ones—the result could be a significantly lower income, for every year of the investor's retirement, for each dollar annuitized.

Can we know which scenario is more likely? Not unless we have a functioning crystal ball. Absent that, we can either make a bet that future Single Premium Immediate Annuity (SPIA) rates will be at least as attractive as today's guaranteed rates and that the risk management features of the deferred annuity will cost us more than the benefits they guarantee, or we can insure against those risks.

Furthermore, it is important to remember that if the alternative investment has created substantial gains over the years, a tax liability will be due upon the conversion of that asset from its nonannuity form to an annuitized payout. This foregoes the opportunity for additional tax deferral. Consequently, it may be more beneficial to accumulate funds within an annuity with the plan of future annuitization, because of the tax-deferral achieved not only during the accumulation phase, but also the tax further deferred by spreading the income recognition treatment across a lifetime of annuity payments.

The Guaranteed Death Benefit in a Variable Annuity
Provides Protection Alternative Investments Do Not Offer

A feature of modern variable deferred annuity contracts often cited by their proponents is the guaranteed death benefit. It offers the annuity investor assurance of a minimum amount which will pass to his heirs, regardless of the performance of the underlying investment subaccounts. If the annuity owner happens to pass away after a severe market decline, the beneficiaries will not suffer from that decline, but will receive a guaranteed minimum amount. The standard minimum death benefit is typically the greater of: (a) the account balance at death; or (b) the amount originally invested, less cumulative withdrawals. Most contracts also offer an enhanced death benefit for an additional charge. The enhanced death benefit may provide that the beneficiary will receive the greater of: (a) the amount originally invested, less any withdrawals; (b) the account balance at death; (c) the original investment, less withdrawals, compounded at some specified rate of interest; or (d) the highest account balance at any of certain specified prior policy anniversaries. Some contracts will include only one of the last two factors.

For investors who are greatly concerned with maximizing the amount passing to their heirs, this guarantee may be very important. It is further argued that this investor might, having the assurance of the minimum death benefit guarantee, allocate his investments more aggressively than he would without that guarantee. If so, the argument goes, the historical risk premium of equities investments, or the amount by which equities returns have exceeded returns on more conservative investments to compensate their owners for the additional risk involved, should offer opportunity both for a greater death benefit—because the guarantee typically is the largest of the account balance at death or other specified amounts—and greater wealth accumulation for the annuity owner during his lifetime.

The authors believe that this argument has merit. However, fairness obliges us to point out that the same objective could be accomplished with life insurance. If the investor is able to obtain life insurance, of a type that is likely to be in force when death occurs, the cost for the coverage could be less than the cost of the guaranteed minimum death benefit. Moreover, the life insurance death proceeds will be payable regardless of how the annuity, or other investment alternative, performs. If the alternative investment never experiences a decline in value, the combination of a life insurance policy and the investment will pay both the face amount of the insurance plus the (appreciated) value of the investment. The premium for the life insurance will always produce more wealth passing to heirs than would be the case if no insurance were purchased. This is assuming that the insurance death benefit exceeds the total premiums paid into the policy.[6]

By contrast, the annuity death benefit guarantee is not certain to produce more money for the owner's beneficiaries than they would receive without it. If the account balance at death is greater than the other factors taken into account in the guarantee (e.g., the amount contributed to the annuity, that amount compounded at a certain rate of interest, or account balance at some prior policy anniversary), the beneficiaries will receive only the accumulated account balance. The presence of the guaranteed minimum death benefit will produce no additional value, unless the owner happened to achieve a greater return with higher risk (and return) investments because of the presence of the guarantee.

Some critics of variable annuity death benefit guarantees believe that the historical upside bias of equity investments means that if the annuity is held long enough, the probability that the death benefit guarantee will exceed the account balance at death is too small to justify the cost of that guarantee. Over the long haul, it is sometimes said, equity investments have historically returned an average of, say, 10% per year. Even after reducing that average return by, say, 2.5%—to reflect the total expense ratio, including subaccount expenses, of a typical variable annuity—the result is an average return of 7.5%. That should, or so the argument goes, produce an account balance at death greater than the original contribution compounded at the 5% or 6% rate typically used in a variable annuity (VA) guaranteed death benefit formula, and far greater than the original contribution. Thus, the argument concludes, the cost of the death benefit guarantee is merely wasted money, nothing more than an annual drag on investment performance.

In the authors' opinion, there are two serious flaws to this argument. First, it amounts to the notion that the market always goes up... eventually. It is certainly true that the long-term trend of equities markets has generally been upward[7]. However, prolonged bear markets happen, and one cannot be certain that one will not die during, or at the end of, one of them. Second, many death benefit guarantee formulas include as a factor—of which the highest will be paid to beneficiaries—the account balance as of certain prior policy anniversaries. Even the most bullish critic must concede that the upward trend of equities markets is not constant. Corrections happen, and markets often take years to return to a prior high point. A death benefit guarantee that locks in a prior all time high may be of significant value, especially in a period of high market volatility.

With regard to the cost of the guaranteed death benefit provisions in today's variable annuity contracts, one criticism that is rarely voiced, but which deserves the advisor's serious attention, is how that cost is calculated. Most, but not all, contracts assess the charge for both the standard and enhanced death benefit against the accumulated account balance in the annuity.[8] The additional charge for the enhanced death benefit varies considerably (as of December, 2011, charges from 20–120 basis points per year, as a percentage of account balance).[9] As the account balance increases, so does the cost for the guaranteed minimum death benefit. Yet, as the account balance and the amount of gain in the contract increases, the probability that the beneficiary will receive more than that account balance from one of the death benefit guarantees decreases. This occurs because the more that the account balance grows beyond the amount originally invested, the less chance there is that it will fall below that amount. The same is true, though to a lesser degree, of the chance that the account balance will fall below the value of that original investment, accumulated at the rate of return specified in the death benefit guarantee—for death benefits that have this option. To the extent that the annual growth in the annuity exceeds this specified rate, the accumulated value will exceed the death benefit guaranteed using that rate. The greater this excess, the less likelihood that the account balance will later fall below that future contributions, accumulated at N% value. Thus, in a situation where the annuity performs well, the contract owner will incur an increasing annual cost for a benefit increasingly unlikely to be payable. The cost/benefit ratio actually decreases with the annuity value.

This pattern does not hold true, however, for the account balance at a prior policy anniversary component. If someone believes that the magnitude of a possible market decline, and thus, a decline in the value of the annuity value, increases with the size of the account balance. The higher the market goes, the bigger the correction is likely to be. The reverse may even be true.

When considering the enhanced death benefit as a whole, however, the fact that the cost of the death benefit guarantee is based on the account balance, rather than upon the value guaranteed, appears—to the authors, at least—to be unattractive, from a cost/benefit perspective. A few insurers have recognized this, and now offer guaranteed death benefit provisions where the cost is more directly related to the amount at risk.

Whether the guaranteed death benefit in a variable annuity (either standard or enhanced) is worth its cost is, ultimately, a risk management question. Regrettably, many critics of annuities insist upon treating it as an investment; one where the cost of what is clearly an insurance feature is seen simply as an overhead cost. In the authors' view, this makes sense only if the insurance benefits are dismissed as valueless—or, at the very least, unimportant.

They may, for some investors, be just that. For the client who has no heirs, or who dislikes those he has, a guaranteed minimum death benefit is likely to be of little or no interest, and the cost of that benefit would, indeed, be merely a drag on investment performance. For this individual, a variable annuity—because it charges for insurance he does not want or need—is arguably a poor choice.

The Case for Guaranteed Living Benefits in Variable Annuities

In recent years, the emergence of guaranteed living benefits has made variable annuities increasingly attractive to many investors. As guaranteed death benefits offer beneficiaries the assurance of minimum values, irrespective of the performance of the underlying investment subaccounts, living benefits guarantee minimum values, no matter how the annuity investments perform, to living contract owners. Four basic types are currently available:

1. Guaranteed Minimum Income Benefit (GMIB)

2. Guaranteed Minimum Accumulation Benefit (GMAB)

3. Guaranteed Minimum Withdrawal Benefit (GMWB)

4. Guaranteed Lifetime Withdrawal Benefit (GLWB)

These guaranteed living benefits (described extensively in Chapter 5) assure different things. The first guarantees a minimum income. The second guarantees a minimum future lump sum value. The third guarantees that the contract owner will receive, at a minimum, a benefit base, or the amount invested, or that amount, plus specified interest, in installments, while enjoying the potential figure growth on undistributed amounts. The fourth type guarantees that the contract owner will receive, at a minimum, a specified percentage of that benefit base for life, or for the life of the client and his/her spouse.

While the mechanics and specific guarantees offered by these provisions vary widely from contract to contract, the fundamental issue to be aware of is that they are risk management features, not investment features.

They Are Risk Management Features

Guaranteed living benefits are not designed to maximize the investor's profit; they are risk management features, designed to control loss. In a best case scenario (e.g., where the investment subaccounts produce double-digit returns in each and every year), living benefits can never be worth their cost, because those benefits will never be triggered. In other scenarios, the costs of the living benefits may increase—because the account balance increases—in all but the final year or two of the contract, but the benefits themselves, when triggered, will be comparatively small. In these scenarios, someone might view these costs, from a purely investment perspective, as excessive, or even wasted money.

In the authors' opinion, such a view is mistaken because it applies a perspective that is inappropriate. A variable annuity, especially one that provides guaranteed living benefits, is not purely an investment and should not be analyzed as if it were. The purpose of guaranteed living benefits is not to maximize wealth, or investment success and future account balance, but to minimize the chance of failure—that the future account balance will be insufficient to meet a client's needs. Electing these benefits is a choice, by the client, to give up some potential excess return as a cost of insurance against the risk that the returns will produce less than the amounts guaranteed. It is a prudent choice for the client who assigns a greater economic value to the risks that are shifted to the insurance company than to the total annual costs for the transfer— including the opportunity cost of those dollars. One might also argue that there is also economic value to peace of mind, quite apart from mathematical probabilities of failure or success.

The Guaranteed Minimum Income Benefit assures a minimum amount of income (for whatever payout period is elected, including lifetime), based on the greater of the actual future account balance or a guaranteed minimum balance. If that guarantee of minimum income is worth the cost,[10] electing it makes sense.

The Guaranteed Minimum Accumulation Benefit assures the contract owner of a minimum future lump sum account balance, even if actual investment performance produces a lower one. If this assurance is worth the cost, electing it makes sense.

The Guaranteed Minimum Withdrawal Benefit assures that the contract owner will be able to recover his investment (by periodic withdrawals), irrespective of adverse investment performance, and be able to participate in investment gains earned by funds not withdrawn. If that guarantee of return of principal is worth the drag on investment performance represented by its cost, electing it makes sense.

The Guaranteed Lifetime Withdrawal Benefit assures the contract owner of at least a certain percentage of the benefit base, as an income which will persist for the client's entire lifetime or the joint lifetime of the client and his/her spouse, regardless of adverse investment performance. If this guarantee of a lifetime income is worth the cost, then including it in the policy benefits makes sense.

Whatever the decision with regard to these options, it must be understood that they are insurance options, not investment ones, and that their costs will necessarily produce a lower future account balance, on average, than would result from the same annuity's performance if these options were not elected, and the costs for them not incurred. This is because the issuing insurance company has expenses associated with its operations, and prices its products to make a profit. For the entire risk pool of contract holders with access to these living benefits, the insurer knows that the premiums paid for them should, over time, be greater than the benefits the insurer will pay out. However, this actuarial certainty has no application to a single individual. For the contract owner concerned about having too small a future account balance, too little income, or losing principal due to investment losses, the experience of his or her account is all that matters.

That the cost of these insurance benefits makes the contract offering them less optimal as an investment vehicle may be less worrisome than the prospect of not having those benefits.

The authors suggest that what really matters is not whether the advisor thinks the guarantees represent a good deal, but whether the client, who is assisted by the advisor in making an informed and educated choice, feels that they provide a good value for the client's goals and the desire to ensure those goals are achieved.

Arguments in Favor of Immediate Annuities

An Annuity is the Only Device that Can Guarantee
a Stated Income for a Stated Period or for Life

An annuity is the only financial instrument that can guarantee a stated level of income for a specific time period or for the life of the recipient. This point was discussed earlier in this chapter.

The Income Produced by an Immediate Annuity is Greater than
that Achievable from any Investment Alternative, on a Guaranteed Basis

Because an annuity consists both of earnings and the systematic amortization of principal, the amount of income produced by an annuity is virtually certain to exceed that of an investment alternative producing an income consisting solely of earnings or interest. Conceivably, there may be some device guaranteeing an interest rate high enough that its interest income would exceed an immediate annuity payout over the same guarantee period, but it is exceedingly unlikely. For example, as of December 24, 2011, one insurer offers a life annuity with no refund element, that will pay a 55 year old annuitant $483 for life, for a single premium of $100,000. The yield required to produce that income for as long as the recipient lives, if principal must be preserved, is about 6%. No investment, that the authors are aware of, can guarantee such a return, as of December, 2011. Although a rise in future interest rates might allow an interest only investment to produce such a return, the payments from the above annuity example would almost certainly be more as well, reflecting the same higher interest rate environment.

Of course, principal is not preserved in an immediate annuity payment stream. To equate the income produced by an immediate annuity with that produced solely from earnings is not a valid comparison, unless the only factor of importance is the amount of income. For example, a 71-year-old male, having that same $100,000 to invest, could—using a different company's SPIA, as of December, 2011—receive an income of $536 month from one insurer's SPIA with a cash refund option, of which approximately 80% ($429/month) will be excluded from taxable income until he has recovered his entire investment tax-free, which would take over 19 years. As of December, 2011, that investor might be able to buy an A rated 20 year tax free bond offering a 4.2% yield. That bond would produce less income; $350 per month versus $429. It would also preserve that investor's principal. The investor could then pass $100,000 to his heirs, assuming that the bond valued at par at his death. If having as much income as possible on an absolutely certain basis, for as long as he lives is this man's chief concern, the huge difference in the income of which he can be certain may be worth the tradeoffs, or loss of access to principal, spending the kids' inheritance. In addition, this investor also faces the risk that the tax-free bond may eventually mature, forcing him to reinvest at potentially lower future interest rates; the immediate annuity's guaranteed payment stream does not face any such reinvestment risk.

The Certain Income of an Annuity May Allow
a Client to Act Differently with Regard to His Other Assets

One of the curiosities of the Great Debate over annuities is that it often presumes an either-or scenario. Consider, for example, the following two assertions:

- Don't invest your retirement money in an immediate annuity

- An immediate annuity is the ideal retirement investment

The unspoken implication in both statements is that it applies to a person's entire retirement portfolio—that one should either avoid buying an immediate annuity with any of that money or that one should do so with every dollar. Neither scenario necessarily makes good sense.

What often does make sense is the purchase of an immediate annuity with part of a retirement portfolio. There are several benefits to this strategy:

1. The estate owner who wishes to use lifetime gifting may be more willing to do so having the assurance of a certain income for life.

2. A risk averse investor, having invested a portion of his retirement portfolio in an immediate annuity to secure income, may be more comfortable allocating more of the rest of his portfolio to higher return—but higher risk—instruments than he would in the absence of those annuity guarantees.

3. For the client concerned with outliving his retirement portfolio, annuitizing a portion of it may increase the probability that the portfolio as a whole will provide a required income level given the uncertainties of future market performance.

4. The emotional value of a certain income for life is not necessarily limited to that calculable by investment algebra. The confidence that such a client gains from the certainty of his annuity income, like the peace of mind many homeowners gain by paying off the mortgage, may be worth more than a computation of return on investment would indicate.

Endnotes

1. Jack Marrion, www.indexannuity.org.

2. IRC Sec. 72(q).

3. Available from www.navanet.org.

4. A potential exception to these general step-up in basis rules applied for some decedents who passed away in 2010.

5. An itemized income tax deduction for the federal estate tax attributable to this gain is available to the beneficiary, under IRC Sec. 691(c).

6. One might argue—and the authors do—that this statement is strictly true only if the insurance proceeds exceed the total premiums paid, accumulated at an appropriate time value of money.

7. It should surprise no one that the argument just presented is offered less often now, after the "black swan" market decline of 2008-2009, than it was previously.

8. The standard death benefit guarantee is usually a part of the standard mortality and expense charge.

9. The more generous the death benefit, the higher the charge.

10. The cost of the Guaranteed Minimum Income Benefit should be considered to include the reduced annuity payout factors that are often applicable to its exercise, as well as any annuitization age setback required. See Chapter 5.

Chapter 11

The Great Debate:
Are Annuities Good or Bad?

Part Two: Arguments Against Annuities

They're Too Expensive

Perhaps the most common argument heard against deferred annuities is that they are too expensive. Usually, this criticism refers to variable contracts, as most fixed annuities assess no front-end or annually recurring charges.[1] We have seen in Chapter 10 how the costs for the insurance offered by the guaranteed living benefits of variable annuities can be, and often are, seen as excessive, and that this judgment may result from the application of investment analysis methodology to an insurance problem.[2] One example of this misapplication appearing frequently in the financial press is the side-by-side comparison of a variable annuity with a mutual fund, assuming the same gross investment return and liquidation of the investment in a lump sum at the end of a specified period. Even where the analyst attempts to be fair and reasonable with income tax assumptions (e.g., taking into account the turnover rate in the mutual fund portfolio and the fact that not all distributions are taxed at long-term capital gains rates), assuming that both alternatives will earn a specific positive rate of return each year renders the death benefit guarantees of the annuity inoperative. Moreover, the stipulation that the investor will cash out both alternatives in a lump sum obviates the advantages of the taxation of annuitized proceeds and assumes that the annuity payout factors guaranteed in the annuity can never be of any value. The costs for these insurance features are taken into account each year by reducing the gross return assumed on the annuity by the mortality and expense charge. The potential benefits purchased by those costs are precluded from ever being realized. Such a comparison may be side-by-side, but it is not truly apples to apples.

An even more egregious example of unfairness occurs when the comparison pits a fully commissionable Variable Annuity (VA) against a no-load mutual fund. On the VA side of the ledger, the costs include compensation to the financial advisor, including ongoing renewal commissions. These commissions pay—not simply for the advisor's selling the annuity—but for the financial counsel that the advisor renders to the investor as part of the sale. This includes the initial asset allocation and ongoing servicing, portfolio rebalancing, etc. On the mutual fund side, there are no commission costs—which necessarily implies that the investor is receiving no financial advice. In the authors' opinion, such an analysis is no more fair than a comparison of the bill presented to a client by a competent estate planning attorney with the cost of do it yourself legal software such as Quicken WillMaker Plus.® The product in both cases may be a valid legal instrument, but the attorney's documents were informed by individual professional counseling and the attorney's client will have recourse for liabilities caused by errors or problems through the attorney's actions or work.

If the investor does not want or need any counsel, he should not be required to pay for it. But where advice is both wanted and needed—where it has clear value—both the benefit of that advice and its cost should be reflected on both sides of the comparison. Thus, if the mutual fund considered, hypothetically, of course, is a no-load product, and where the annuity cost includes compensation to the investment advisor, fairness would require that the mutual fund side of the ledger include a separate cost for advice. That sort of comparison is rarely seen.

With regard to the notion that variable annuities are too expensive, it should be noted that a few insurers have recently released contracts with very low annual expenses. Some of these contracts offer guaranteed living benefit riders, yet their annual expense ratio is less than the typical VA.

They're Too Complicated

The values guaranteed by living benefit provisions in variable annuities are often the result of formulas and conditions. Rarely can one point to a dollar figure and say "this is the amount guaranteed by this benefit." Perhaps most painfully, the terms under which the guaranteed amounts themselves are payable can be quite complicated. The result is a serious potential for misunderstanding and confusion—both by those purchasing these contracts and by those selling them.

For example, a Guaranteed Minimum Income Benefit (GMIB) provision may apply a guaranteed interest rate of 6% to amounts invested, to produce a benefit base from which GMIB payments will be calculated. This does not mean that the contract owner is guaranteed a minimum of a 6% return on his investment, as would be the case if the guaranteed cash value of the contract could never be less than contributions compounded at 6%. Yet the authors have heard this provision explained in just that way on several occasions—not only by policy owners, but also by professional advisors. Clearly, these individuals had no idea how the GMIB provision they were describing actually worked. Jack Marrion, in a recent study of Guaranteed Living Benefits, writes that he has received many emails from VA purchasers who state that "they were receiving, or were told they would receive, a guaranteed 7% a year payout for 14 years and then they would still get at least 100% of their money back at that time,"[3] despite the fact that the GMWB guarantees only that 7% payment for 14 years.

In the authors' view, this is potentially a very serious problem, for both advisors and their clients. Any competent decision as to whether a guaranteed living benefit is worth, to a particular client, what the insurer charges for it necessarily requires that all parties to that decision fully understand what they are assessing. Some insurers, recognizing this, have instituted special training programs to ensure that those recommending these complex products understand them. The NAIC has also recognized this problem, and included, in its Suitability in Annuity Transactions Model Regulation of 2010 (SATMR) a mandate that agents recommending any annuity complete a four-hour continuing education course specifically devoted to annuities (see discussion of SATMR in Chapter 14). In the authors' experience, far too many agents selling annuities do not thoroughly understand the complexities of the annuity contracts they are selling, and the SATMR-required training is long overdue. Some, but certainly not all, agents know about the products they offer only by what they read in point-of-sale brochures and hear from product wholesalers. Far too many have never read the annuity contracts.

Similarly, many advisors fail to understand the complexity underlying at least some types of equity-indexed annuity contracts. Although some use formulas that are relatively straightforward and easy to understand, others do not. A failure to understand the implications of crediting formulas in all potential return environments— not simply the one illustrated in the marketing materials, which is often not merely an average scenario, but an optimal one—can lead to a mismatch between client expectations and reality.

The authors strenuously recommend a serious study, both of the marketing brochures and the actual contract language describing policy provisions—especially, the descriptions of guaranteed living benefits for variable annuities and the crediting formulas for equity-indexed annuities—to anyone who intends to provide recommendations regarding annuities with such provisions. We also recommend that any advisor who intends to sell, or offer advice concerning these benefits take advantage of special training classes on the subject, even if these classes are not yet mandated in the states in which they work.

Guaranteed living benefit riders, and equity-indexed annuities, when properly understood, can be of significant value to many clients, but both advisor and client must be capable of wading through the complexity to know what the annuities will, and will not do. It's not impossible to understand the sometimes complex provisions contained in annuity contracts. Although, arguably, there are a few exceptions where the contracts are so complex only that the actuaries who designed them may ever fully comprehend how they work! If an advisor and their client are not willing to get a handle on the complexity involved, it may be better to select an alternative route.

Annuities Should Never Be Used to Fund an IRA or Qualified Plan

A generalization often made about annuities claims that they should never be used to fund an IRA or qualified plan. This sweeping pronouncement has met with surprisingly wide acceptance among financial journalists, attorneys, accountants, and many financial planners. It has become virtually accepted wisdom for many, despite the facts that: (a) it ignores the huge differences that exist between immediate and deferred annuities and between the fixed and variable varieties of the latter; and (b) the arguments most commonly made in its support are grievously and obviously flawed.

Those who argue that annuities are inappropriate instruments for funding IRAs or qualified plans are almost always referring to deferred annuities, and, usually, to variable deferred annuities. The three most common of these arguments are:

1. "You're paying for tax deferral you're not getting." This is simply nonsense. While it is true that an annuity offers no additional tax advantages over any other investment vehicle when used to fund an IRA or qualified, no annuity assesses any charge for the benefit of tax deferral. To be sure, variable deferred annuities impose charges that alternatives such as mutual funds do not. Those are, as we have seen, insurance charges. They have absolutely nothing whatsoever to do with the tax treatment enjoyed by the annuity. The tax treatment of an annuity used to fund an IRA or qualified plan is identical to that applicable to any other IRA investment. The treatment which would apply to a deferred annuity, if it were not used to fund such a plan, is irrelevant when the annuity is so used.

    The insurance charges of a variable deferred annuity may or may not be worthwhile to a particular investor, based upon that investor's need for the risk management benefits the charges pay for; but this is true whether the annuity is funding an IRA or is a non-qualified annuity. If the insurance benefits are not worth the cost to a particular client, then they should not be paid for, whether the money in question is qualified or not.

2. "The tax deferral of an annuity used to fund an IRA is wasted." This one is doubly flawed. First, because the tax deferral enjoyed by nonqualified annuities flows from provisions of the Internal Revenue Code that apply only to nonqualified annuities, that deferral cannot be wasted by an IRA annuity because it does not apply to an IRA annuity. Second, the argument rests upon an assumption that the tax treatment which a particular type of investment property would enjoy if it were held in a taxable account is somehow relevant to whether it is an appropriate funding vehicle for an IRA or qualified account. To illustrate the absurdity of this assumption, let us consider the question of whether small cap growth stocks, or a fund investing in these stocks,

might be appropriate for an IRA. The investment returns produced by these stocks, or funds, will generally be taxed at long-term capital gain (LTCG) rates if held for longer than one year. LTCG rates are, of course, significantly lower than the rates for ordinary income. Inasmuch as all non-Roth IRAs and qualified plans, except for basis, are taxed at higher ordinary income rates, it would follow that funding an IRA with small cap growth stocks—or a fund investing in the same—would be a waste of capital gains treatment. Obviously, the appropriateness of a small cap growth stock for an IRA or qualified plan has nothing to do with how it would be taxed if it were held otherwise. The same holds true for an annuity.

Furthermore, a small cap growth stock held in a taxable account receives the same tax-deferral benefit as one held in a retirement account, if you assume that it is held until some future point when it is sold or liquidated for a lump sum, as is commonly the case with annuity comparisons. Although individual stocks can be held indefinitely, with no recognition of annual gain until liquidation—not unlike a nonqualified annuity—one rarely sees arguments that stocks are an inappropriate investment for retirement accounts, despite the fact that the tax benefit of holding individual stocks outside of a retirement account is even more beneficial than that applying to a nonqualified annuity. This is because the stock receives preferential tax treatment; through the application of LTCG rates, and the opportunity for a step-up in basis if held until death. To the extent that it is clearly inappropriate to suggest that retirement accounts should not hold individual stocks because of the benefits foregone by not purchasing them in taxable accounts, the same holds true for annuities.

3.   "They're Too Expensive." As we have said, if the insurance benefits of the annuity, which are the source of the excessive costs cited by critics, are neither needed nor wanted, they should not be purchased. A deferred annuity, especially a deferred variable annuity with guaranteed death and living benefits, is chiefly a risk management tool. If the risk management features are not desired, an instrument providing and charging for them is, indeed, too expensive. If they are desired, the charges for them must be viewed for what they are—insurance costs.

Annuities Are Sold Mostly because of the High Commissions They Pay

This argument may be accurate to some degree, but it is also an ad hominem logical fallacy. It is true that the commissions paid on deferred annuities are often higher than those paid on mutual funds, and common sense suggests that a commissioned advisor, in choosing among alternatives to recommend to a client, will be influenced by the amount of compensation each alternative provides him. However, the benefit of any investment to its owner consists in what can be realized from it. The value of that investment must, of course, be reckoned by relating the benefits received to the cost paid. If a deferred annuity offers benefits not available from alternatives, but its cost to purchase and maintain is higher, the value of that contract depends upon whether the additional benefits are worth the additional cost.

The Advisor's Guide to Annuities

A particular annuity contract that pays 3.5% of the investor's contribution to one selling agent, but 6% to another—because those agents have different contracts with their respective broker-dealers—will have the same value to the purchaser, assuming that the advisors are equally competent and diligent. The agents' commissions will be of significance to those agents, and, arguably, may affect their recommendations. But the value of that annuity to its purchaser will be the same, whichever agent makes the sale.

The value of the annuity relative to its costs depends on the features and benefits of the contract and the costs to the client, regardless of where or how those costs may be subsequently allocated. As an extreme and entirely imaginary example, consider an investment that charges the purchaser an overhead cost of 5% per year, but provides a guaranteed return of between 15%-25%. Although the annual cost of the investment is absurdly high, so is the return. This would probably be an extremely good investment, if it existed. Moreover, the decision as to whether this is or is not a good investment depends solely on the costs and benefits of the contract. Whether the issuer uses the 5% per year it collects from the purchaser to compensate a salesman with 2%, 5%, 10%, or 20% of the purchase price has no bearing on the value of the investment to the client.

Some annuities do not pay commissions and generally offer lower charges as a result. These low load contracts account for only a small fraction of the annuities sold each year. Does this mean that most annuity purchasers are being abused? That conclusion does not follow, for two reasons:

1. The guaranteed death benefits, and especially the guaranteed living benefits offered by low load, deferred annuity contracts are often less attractive—though, of course, less costly—than those offered by fully loaded annuities. Where these guarantees are important to the client, the lesser benefits offered by low load contracts may be unattractive, even if the annuity includes a total lower annual cost.[4]

2. Noncommissionable products are sold chiefly by fee-based or fee-only advisorsadvisors who charge for advisory services. When adding the advisory fee to the annual cost of a low load annuity, the resulting total annual cost—while it may or may not be less than the annual cost of a fully-commissionable contract—may still be unattractive, as the benefit of that cost will be limited to the generally less attractive guarantees of the low load annuity.

Only 2% or a Low Percentage of Deferred Annuities Are Ever Annuitized

There are two flaws implicit in this argument. First, the right to annuitize is just that—a right. It is not an obligation. The opportunity to avail oneself of either the payout factors currently available to holders of a deferred annuity, or to elect annuitization using the factors guaranteed in the contract, is just that. It is an opportunity, a choice, and a risk management decision, much more than an investment one. A decision not to exercise an option does not make the option valueless.

An even more serious flaw to this argument is that it is a statistic which is utterly unreliable. Even conceding the accuracy of data on annuitized contracts, the flaw lies in the definition of annuitized. That term means an election, by the owner of a deferred annuity contract, to accept an annuitization option in that contract. In that literal sense, the statistic—of 2% or whatever percentage one happens to use—of contracts that are annuitized may be accurate, but it is entirely meaningless as an indication of how many owners of deferred annuity contracts have chosen to convert their accumulated value to an income stream.

One of the authors has been selling annuities for over 38 years and has very rarely recommended that a client exercise any annuity option in his contract. He has recommended to many clients that they exchange an existing deferred annuity for a single premium immediate annuity from whatever highly rated insurer happened, at the time, to offer the highest annuity payout rate for the option chosen. But, as it occurred, the current annuity payout rate in the client's existing deferred annuity was almost never as attractive as the payout rate in a competing company's SPIA.

This procedure (i.e., going shopping for annuity rates on behalf of a client, and recommending a tax-free exchange of that client's existing deferred annuity for an immediate annuity) is a very common practice. It could be argued that the failure to offer this option to a client constitutes a breach of advisor responsibility, since by accepting a payout rate higher than the one guaranteed in his deferred contract, the client cannot fail to benefit so long as the issuer of the immediate annuity is at least as financially strong and viable as the issuer of the deferred contract. These exchanges are done every day both because they are in the client's interest and because the agent selling the immediate annuity earns a commission. They are not reflected in the statistic quoted above. It is certain that the total number of annuity contract holders electing to convert a deferred annuity to an income stream—a number that must include both annuitizations and exchanges of deferred annuities for immediate ones—is far higher than the 2% or so reported. How much higher is anyone's guess.

Arguments Against Immediate Annuities

Those who argue against the purchase of immediate annuities usually do so for one or more of the following reasons:

1. **Inflexibility.** Nearly all immediate annuities are inflexible. Once begun, the arrangement may not be modified, nor may remaining payments be commuted to a lump sum. This is certainly a valid concern. The inability of a planning strategy to adapt to changing goals and circumstances is, by definition, a disadvantage. Moreover, an irrevocable annuitization has an emotional component. One loses control over that part of one's wealth that has been annuitized. The feeling of this loss may exact a price not measurable in investment terms. That said, a few newer immediate annuity contracts allow for some modification in the payout arrangement, including commutation of remaining payments. There is, of course, a cost to this benefit, perhaps in the form of

a lower initial payout than would be offered without it. Many consumers will find this flexibility worth the price.

The authors suggest that an alternative might be to consider a conventional immediate annuity—without the flexibility benefits or the cost for same—only for that portion of one's portfolio that one is prepared to lock into an income stream. As noted earlier, the decision whether or not to purchase an immediate annuity need not be all or nothing.

2. **Immediate Annuities Lock In Low Interest Rates.** This argument is usually advanced during periods of low prevailing interest rates, but it has merit at any time. The interest rate used to compute the amount of payments in an immediate annuity contract is always conservative. It has to be because the issuing insurer must make those payments regardless of future changes in the returns the insurer will earn on invested premiums and how long the annuitant lives, in the case of life annuities. When interest rates change, so do annuity payout rates. Although immediate annuities with longer payout periods do not necessarily experience the same level of decline as those with longer period payouts, a decline in the general interest rate environment will generally reduce the current payout factors of all annuities.

    That said, the argument that the buyer of an immediate annuity is locking in low interest rates for the duration of the annuity period misses the whole point. The point, and the whole purpose of an immediate annuity is not to earn a return on invested principal, but to convert that invested principal into income that is certain as to amount and duration; in the case of life annuities, for as long as the annuitant lives. It is those certainties that constitute the real benefit, not the rate of return used to compute the payments. An immediate annuity is an insurance vehicle that transfers risks from the contract owner to the issuing insurer. The risks transferred are: (a) the risk that future changes in the financial markets might cause future income payments to decline; and (b) the risk that the annuitant might outlive the income payments. If an investor is willing to assume those risks, other investments offer potentially higher income, from potentially higher interest rates or investment yields, than an immediate annuity, but at the costs of no assurance of either the amount of income or its duration. For someone considering a period certain annuity—for a specified period of years, whether the annuitant outlives that period or not—alternatives may not provide the same initial level of income, but may offer access to principal, and potentially higher returns in later years, due to principal growth. In the end, if the guarantees offered by the annuity produce the actual dollars needed to secure one's goals, the fact that interest rates or investment returns may be higher in the future is not necessarily even relevant to the client.

3. **No Inflation Protection.** Most immediate annuities are fixed in amount. Although a few contracts offer the option of either a fixed amount or an annuity increasing at a set

percentage each year (usually no more than 3%-5%), most do not. For those that do, the amount of the first year's annuity payment will always be less than that of contracts, offered by the same insurers, without this option. The greater the guaranteed annual increase, the lower the initial payment for any amount invested. A very few SPIAs offer an option that annuity payments will vary directly with the unknown future fluctuations in the rate of inflation, as measured by an index such as the Consumer Price Index. Why such a contract is not more available, or popular, is bewildering. It may be that insurers are having difficulty determining how to hedge their own exposure to inflation if such a contract is offered, especially given the current (as of the time of this writing) near-zero real yields on TIPs. Alternatively, the authors have heard, repeatedly, that there is very little market for this type of product, which seems unpersuasive, given the almost universal recognition of the devastating impact that inflation can have on those living on a fixed income. To be sure, the first year's income from an inflation-adjusted annuity—especially an annuity guaranteed for the life of the annuitant—will be less, or possibly a great deal less, than that guaranteed by an un-indexed product. It may be that most consumers would not be willing to accept that trade-off. Nevertheless, in the authors' opinion at least, a contract offering the purchaser a choice between fixed payments and payments that will keep pace with inflation ought to be attractive.

Arguments Against Guaranteed Living Benefits in Variable Annuities

The two most commonly advanced criticisms of guaranteed living benefits are: (a) that they promise benefits which are unlikely to be realized; and (b) that they're too expensive. In fact, the two reasons are inseparable. No critic, to the authors' knowledge, asserts that there is no chance of a GLB's ever producing value. The two criticisms amount, in essence, to a single charge: that the possible benefit derived from a GLB is not worth the certain cost. See Chapter 5 for a detailed discussion of GLBs and attempts to value them.

Notwithstanding the criticism from some that GLBs are too expensive for the benefits they provide, other critics have charged that insurers issuing these guaranteed living benefits may not be able to pay them because these insurers either: (1) do not really know how much financial risk they are underwriting, (2) are not charging enough for these benefits, or (3) have not set aside sufficient reserves to pay them. Some critics believe all three conditions are true, implying that insurers should be charging more for the guarantees they offer to ensure that claims can be paid in the face of an uncertain future. In 2007, Moshe Milevsky, a long-time critic of the cost of VA death benefit guarantees, wrote that he believed many of these guaranteed living benefits to be underpriced, which implies a good value for the consumer, as long as the insurance company doesn't lose so much money that it fails to make good on its guarantees.[5] Clearly, he was right, as insurers offering guaranteed living benefits have, in the five years since Prof. Milevsky wrote that article, either reduced the benefit levels of these riders, increased their cost, or both. Several major insurers have discontinued issuing guaranteed living benefits altogether. Indeed, a few insurers have exited the variable annuity marketplace. Ironically, this means that as long as the insurer doesn't actually default on their annuity guarantees, the GLBs offered over the past decade may have actually represented a uniquely mispriced guarantee in the favor of consumers who bought them.

As we observed in Chapter 5, one type of guaranteed living benefit, the Guaranteed Lifetime Withdrawal Benefit (GLWB) has recently become an increasingly popular option available in index annuities. While the cost of this rider is generally less in index annuities than in variable annuities, the potential benefit is arguably greater in the latter, due to the greater upside potential of market-based growth not reduced by a participation rate or cap rate. Fairness obliges us to acknowledge that there is considerable debate on this issue.

Whether in the context of index annuities, or their more volatile variable annuity cousins, the question of whether the issuer of a guaranteed living benefit can be relied upon to pay the guarantees is a serious issue. Although the separate accounts in a variable annuity are secure from financial failure of the issuing—because they are, in fact, separate accounts, not subject to creditors of that insurer—the contractual guarantees made in the annuity, including those of guaranteed living and death benefits, are backed only by the financial solvency of the insurance company. If a particular insurer has greatly underpriced its guarantees and/or has not set aside adequate reserves for paying them, the contract holder could, if that insurer fails, find herself with guarantees that are meaningless. In the case of an index annuity, both the underlying contract value and the guaranteed living benefit features are subject to the credit risk of the insurer.

How can an advisor know if the guarantees he describes are truly safe? In the authors' opinion, there's only one way to be reasonably sure: do your due diligence! Ask for details of how your company is assessing the risks that it bears under these provisions, how—and if—it hedges those risks, and how it is reserving to pay the benefits associated with them. Don't expect a lot of specifics! Much of this information will be both proprietary and closely-guarded, especially hedging strategies. However, a responsible insurer will be willing to address these concerns, at least generally.

The authors also suggest the following guidelines and caveats:

1. The more financially sound the insurer, the better. Check an insurer's ratings from at least three ratings services and stick with a company that holds at least the third-highest rating from at least three services.

2. The less exposure an insurer has to losses from exercise of guaranteed living benefits, as a percentage of its overall business, the better. If a large chunk of the insurer's book of variable annuity business includes exercisable guaranteed living benefits, there should be some offsetting factor, such as a large volume of nonvariable annuity business.

3. If an insurer issues both indexed annuities and variable annuities with guaranteed living benefits, that's a positive. Index annuities are call-based instruments, where the

derivative providing the nonguaranteed benefit is usually a series of calls on an equity index, typically the S&P 500. By contrast, guaranteed living benefits are basically put-based instruments, where the insurer's risk increases, not with a rise in the value of the underlying investments, but with a decline. Where an insurer has a sizeable block of business in both product types, the basic risks tend to offset one another. There are numerous academic studies on this subject available on the Internet, and accessible via a browser search on hedging variable index annuities. Many of these are highly technical and employ mathematical analysis beyond the average person's understanding. However, for the advisor interested in responding to a question such as, "how can I be sure that this insurance company will be able to pay the benefits you just described?" with something more than just "trust me," this is a research project worth undertaking.

At the very least, the authors suggest an advisor pose that "how can I be sure?" question to each insurer whose VA products, with guaranteed living benefits, he or she intends to recommend.

As to the general question posed at the beginning of this chapter, "Are Annuities Good or Bad?", the debate will continue. One component of this debate of vital importance to financial advisors is the regulatory responses it provokes. The question of variable annuity suitability has brought forth rulings from the SEC, FINRA, state departments of securities and insurance, and broker-dealers that advisors may ignore only at their peril. The latest of these rulings (as of the publication of this book), FINRA Rule 2330, is included in the appendices to this book.

Endnotes

1. This does not mean, of course, that there are no annual expenses in fixed annuities, but only that those expenses are paid for out of the interest rate spread, rather than by direct charges to the contract owner. See Chapter 4.

2. While a few critics arrive at the conclusion that insurance costs in VAs are too high from a risk management analysis—comparing the death benefit guarantee cost to term life insurance rates, for example—most inappropriately, in the authors' opinion treat these costs as investment overhead.

3. Marrion, Jack, *A Look At Securities And Securities GLWBs* (Advantage Compendium, August, 2008, available at: www.indexannuity.org.

4. It is quite possible that some low load deferred annuity contracts will begin offering both guaranteed living and guaranteed death benefits comparable to their fully loaded cousins. However, this will increase—substantially—the cost of these contracts. As the chief appeal of low load annuities appears to be access to the annuity wrapper and the tax treatment that goes with it, at the least annual cost, providers of low load contracts may be reluctant to increase costs of those contracts—particularly those companies that offer both commissionable and noncommissionable products.

5. Milevsky, Moshe, "Confessions of a VA Critic," *Research* (January, 2007).

Chapter 12

Summary: The Annuity as a Planning Tool

We have examined, in this and preceding chapters, how annuities work, how they are taxed, their special provisions, and some of the arguments made in favor of, and in opposition to, the use of annuities in financial, estate, and retirement planning. The authors have tried to treat the subject fairly, and to present the pros and cons of annuities as planning tools as objectively as we know how. It is, of course, up to the reader to decide whether we have been successful in that effort. The authors are neither for nor against annuities. Annuities are merely tools, and are appropriate or inappropriate to the extent that they do the job better or worse than available alternatives.

The value of any annuity, as a planning tool, depends upon the planning objective. Where that objective involves managing certain risks, the annuity may well be the right tool, for an annuity is not only an investment but also a risk management instrument. As such, its performance should be assessed in the light of how well it performs in both areas. If a particular investor has no want or need for some of the risk management features of an annuity, the cost for those features can reasonably be considered to be investment overhead cost. However, where the benefits provided by these features have value to the investor, the cost of those benefits should not be charged against investment performance, as is often done, especially when the annuity is compared to an instrument that neither provides these benefits nor charges for them. The risk management benefits, to the extent that they are wanted and needed, should be related to the charges for that benefit and a cost/benefit decision should be made. If, for example, the guaranteed death benefit in a variable annuity costs 25 basis points per year, its value might be ascertained by the consumer asking, "would I rather have the investment performance of the contract without this benefit, and risk leaving my heirs with whatever the account balance happens to be on the day I die, or is having the guaranteed values I've just examined worth my giving up one-quarter of one percent of investment returns every year?"

This procedure can be done with each of the risk management features of the annuity that are not offered by an alternative investment. Where the benefit is perceived to be worth less than its contractual cost, that difference may be viewed as an additional cost of the annuity. However, where the investor values the benefit, and has determined that it is worth so many basis points per year in reduced returns, a proper comparison of the annuity with an alternative would require that the return for that alternative be reduced by the cost of the valued benefit, which is not provided for on the alternative side of the ledger. On the other hand, the assumption by many marketers of annuities, that the risk management features of these contracts are worth the charges imposed for them is no more valid than the assumptions of critics that such features are of little or no value. Value is in the eye of the beholder, and should be measured as it applies to any unique client situation.

Variable Deferred Annuities

Not all variable deferred annuities offer the same risk management features. Some offer no guaranteed living benefit riders and/or only a basic return of principal guaranteed death benefit. These contracts typically assess often, much lower annual costs than contracts offering living benefits and enhanced death benefits and, in some cases, impose no surrender charges. In the extreme, some variable deferred annuities do not even provide a death benefit guarantee at all, and simply provide the current cash value to a beneficiary and the feature of tax deferral.

The authors believe that these bare-bones variable annuities represent a cost/benefit proposition fundamentally different from that offered by their all-the-whistles-and-bells counterparts. While the investment benefits and costs are similar in both types, the risk transfer benefits, or the insurance benefits, and the costs of those benefits in the bare-bones contracts are far smaller. In a deferred annuity having no living benefits and offering only a return of principal as a guaranteed death benefit—or in some cases not even a death benefit guarantee—the only risk that the purchaser is transferring to the insurance company is superannuation, when that the contract owner might outlive his/her money. The insurer underwrites this risk by including guaranteed annuity payout factors in the contract. The contract owner may annuitize the contract, using these payout factors, at any time, even if then-current payout rates for immediate annuities are less favorable. If life expectancies continue to lengthen, it is certainly possible that these guaranteed annuity payout factors will become valuable, but they have not proven so in the past. There has rarely been a time, to the authors' knowledge, when the payout factors guaranteed in a deferred annuity were as attractive as factors for the same payout arrangement available in the immediate annuity marketplace. But we cannot say, with certainty, that this will hold true in the future. The purchaser of any deferred annuity transfers to the insurer the risk that later economic conditions might not permit a regular annuity amount as high as that guaranteed in the contract, by application of those payout factors. If there are any death benefit guarantees associated with one of these bare-bones contracts, those risks are also transferred to the insurance company on behalf of the beneficiaries.

A bare-bones variable deferred annuity gives very minimal and basic risk transfer opportunities, for which the contract owner pays a typically very modest M&E charge.

A whistles-and-bells contract gives the contract owner those same opportunities, as well as the risk transference afforded by its guaranteed living benefits and enhanced guaranteed death benefits. For all of that, the owner pays both the M&E charge and the costs of any additional guaranteed living and death benefits selected.

The total risk transfer benefits and costs of these two types of variable annuities can be hugely different. Yet the investment benefits—the variety and quality of investment subaccounts, the opportunity for dollar cost averaging, portfolio rebalancing, etc.—are basically the same.

Regrettably, many comparisons of annuities with investment alternatives either assume that the special annuity benefits are worth their cost or that they are not. Some proponents of annuities assume that tax deferral is always better than as earned taxation even when the trade-off is the unavailability of capital gains taxation. Often, the unattractive tax implications for beneficiaries of nonqualified annuities are either ignored or dismissed as unimportant. Critics of annuities frequently assume that the investor will take his accumulated money in a lump sum at the end of the comparison period, which implicitly condemns both the guaranteed payout factors as worthless and ignores the favorable taxation of annuitized benefits. Even worse, many comparisons contain serious analytical errors, including stacking the deck by applying one set of assumptions on the annuity side of the ledger and different assumptions on the other side.

The problem with The Great Annuity Debate is that it is, all too often, less a debate than a feud. Balance and logic give way to mere polemic, and the result is not analysis, but diatribe. No one benefits by this, least of all, the consumer seeking honest and impartial advice and a decent understanding.

When, and In What Planning Situation, Does an Annuity Make Sense? When Does it Not?

As advisors who often talk about annuities to financial advisors, the authors are often asked whether we like annuities. To that question, our standard answer is that we neither like nor dislike them—because they're just tools, which work well in certain circumstances and do not work well in others. Occasionally, that response will elicit what may appear to be a better follow-up question:

"When—that is: in what planning situations—does an annuity make good sense and when does it not make good sense?"

That's a core question, and one that might be in the mind of you, our reader, as you hold this book. What's our answer? One answer might be that "it depends… on the specific facts and circumstances of the case." That's a reasonable and rather obvious reply, and what our audiences often expect to hear. But it's not our answer. Our answer to that question is that the question is unanswerable—until we know what the questioner means by an annuity. Are we talking about a variable deferred annuity; a fixed immediate annuity? As we've seen in earlier chapters, those contracts are hugely different. Each is an annuity but the two contract forms are designed to meet completely opposite needs. Generalizations, always hazardous, are especially unproductive when used with annuities. A true statement about fixed annuities is likely to be false when applied to variable ones, and vice versa. The same is true when the annuities are immediate versus deferred. Yet many, if not most, consumers—and all too many advisors—routinely generalize about annuities, often to the extent that their conclusions are so flawed as to be worthless.

This is not to say that all generalizations about annuities are without value, but merely that we should avoid lumping together, in a summary judgment, things that are more different than alike. "Immediate annuities are usually inflexible" is a fair statement because most immediate annuities do not permit either a change in the pattern of payouts or commutation of the contract, or surrender for a lump sum in lieu of remaining annuity payments. By contrast, the statement that "deferred annuities are risky" is misleading at best, because the risks borne by the owner of a fixed deferred annuity are mostly, but not entirely, different from those borne by a variable annuity owner. Both generally assume a temporary liquidity risk, due to surrender charges, but the former enjoys a guarantee of principal while the latter does not, with regard to amounts invested in variable subaccounts.[1] The former is subject to interest rate risk while the latter must shoulder market risk.

If we bear in mind this caveat—that we must generalize only when our assessment can be generally accurate—we can now attempt to answer the question posed earlier: "When, and in what planning situations does an annuity make good sense and when does it not make good sense?" The authors believe that we can, and should, construct bright line tests to help us determine when an annuity is likely to be suitable for our client. In the following discussion,[2] we'll examine some of the most common goal situations and how well or poorly annuities may work in those situations. Where a particular type of annuity is clearly suitable or unsuitable, the authors suggest suitability rules, or bright line tests.

Where the Goal is Immediate Income

When immediate income is the primary goal, an immediate annuity may be appropriate, so long as it is understood that it may provide no benefit at the annuitant's death. Indeed, if the annuitant lives beyond the point where any refund element is payable, an immediate annuity will not provide any death benefit. As an immediate annuity consists of the amortized distribution of both earnings and principal, and as it will terminate without value at the later of the annuitant's death or the end of the period certain, if elected, it is not appropriate when all—or even some—of the amount invested must remain at the end of the income period.

A deferred annuity is not designed to produce income immediately. Indeed, many deferred annuities do not permit distributions during the first contract year. Those contracts that do permit distributions in the first year generally limit such distributions to contract gain. Thus, if income must commence within a year of the investment, a deferred annuity is usually inappropriate. There are, of course, exceptions. For example, if the contract permits withdrawals of up to 10% of contract value each year without penalty, and the purchaser does not anticipate needing more than that level of income, a deferred annuity may make sense. If the contract contains a Guaranteed Minimum Withdrawal Benefit, or Lifetime Benefit, that is designed to support withdrawals which commence immediately, a deferred annuity may make more sense than an immediate one. As always, individual facts and circumstances trump rules of thumb.

Where the Income Amount Must Be as High as Possible on a Guaranteed Basis

Where the primary goal is income and where the amount of that income must be as high as possible on a guaranteed basis, an immediate annuity is ideal. The key word, here, is guaranteed. Where the income period is a fixed number of years, a Period Certain fixed immediate annuity will generally provide a greater amount than can be assured from any investment alternative because the nonannuity alternative must preserve principal. Where the income period is for the entire lifetime of the recipient and where no part of principal must remain at the expiry of that period, and where the amount of each income payment must be assured in advance and be as high as possible, a fixed immediate annuity is not just the most appropriate solution; it is the only solution.

This is true not only when the amount of each payment must be the same, but also when the amount of each year's payment must increase, by either a fixed percentage or by an index such as the Consumer Price Index (CPI). It should be noted that not all fixed immediate annuities offer such an increasing amount option and that very few offer increases tied to an external index such as the CPI.

Where the amount of income payments must be guaranteed in advance and be as high as possible, and where no principal must remain, a fixed immediate annuity is the ideal solution.

Where the Goal Is Accumulation of Capital

Where the goal is capital accumulation, an immediate annuity is clearly not suitable, but a deferred annuity may be. If preservation of principal is a requirement, a fixed deferred annuity might be appropriate, but a variable one, in the absence of a Guaranteed Living Benefit rider,[3] might not. This is because a variable annuity, except to the extent that its cash value is invested in the fixed account, does not offer safety of principal.

With the addition of this rider—or, if the purchaser is willing to regard a return of purchase payments in installments as a guarantee of principal, a Guaranteed Minimum Withdrawal Benefit (GMWB)—a variable deferred annuity can serve as an instrument for capital accumulation with safety of principal. Indeed, the GMWB provision of many contracts includes a step-up feature that not only assures the return of the original investment in installments, but also any contract gain accrued as of the point where the step-up option may be exercised. However, it is important to emphasize that in this context, the safety of principal provided by the deferred annuity exists only if the annuity owner accesses the principal according to the terms of the guarantee. In the context of a GMWB, this means that principal is not guaranteed, unless the annuity owner is willing to extract that principal as a series of periodic payments over a span of many years.

If safety of principal is not required, or if the riders described have been added, and the timing and nature of the principal guarantee fit the client's protection goals, a variable annuity can certainly serve as an instrument for capital accumulation. Whether it's the right instrument, however, depends upon several factors.

First, we must account for and evaluate both its protection (insurance) and accumulation (investment) features. If the protection features offered, and charged for, in a variable deferred annuity are desired, then we must decide whether the cost of those features is acceptable. If it is, then the cost of those protections should be accounted for on both sides of any comparison with an alternative. As described above, we might adjust our comparison ledger by adding those annual costs to the annual expense ratio of the alternative—which neither offers nor charges for those protection benefits—or by deducting them from its assumed return.

If we do not value the protection features or consider them overpriced, the extent of the overcharge could be reckoned as overhead cost of the annuity, requiring no adjustment on the other side of our comparison ledger.

> *Example:* If the enhanced guaranteed death benefit of the annuity is something we want, but we believe it's worth only 25 basis points (bps) per year rather than the 60 basis points actually charged, we might, in comparing the projected value of the annuity with some alternative, add 25 basis points to the expense ratio of the alternative or reduce its assumed return by that same amount.

Second, we must understand how the costs—both explicit and implicit—of deferred annuities impact investment returns and pay for insurance protection.

In a variable annuity, the Mortality & Expense (M&E) charge pays for both the basic death benefit guarantee, or guarantee of principal, and the guaranteed annuity payout factors. In a fixed annuity, these insurance features are not charged for directly, but are paid for from the interest rate spread, or the difference between what the insurer realizes by investing the premium and what it pays the contract owner. In comparing the variable annuity with alternatives, we can account for those insurance features and their impact on returns in the manner described above. But as a fixed annuity doesn't charge us directly for these features, we must look to the difference between the interest rate we expect to receive from the annuity and what we might otherwise get from a comparable alternative (e.g., a CD or bond). If the expected return from the fixed annuity exceeds that of the alternative, we might consider that the insurance provided by the annuity payout factors is free.

It's not free, of course—not literally. Rather, it's paid for, ultimately, from the difference between what the insurer expects to get from investing our premium and what we would expect to get by investing those same dollars. Yet where such a difference exists, where the expected return from the annuity exceeds that of our comparable investment, one might argue that the insurance benefit of the guaranteed annuity payout factors in a fixed annuity is pure value added, and in effect, free.

A variable annuity, on the other hand, charges us directly for both the basic guaranteed death benefit and the guaranteed annuity payout factors, neither of which is typically available from a comparable alternative investment. Here, as with an enhanced death benefit, we can determine what we believe these combined protections are worth to us. If we decide that's 60 bps/year and the M&E charge of the variable annuity is 140 bps/year, we can adjust the annual expense of the alternative upward by 80 bps or reduce its assumed return by the same amount.

Some critics of variable annuities ask why an M&E charge is even necessary. After all, they assert, a fixed annuity offers both a guarantee of principal, of all accrued and credited interest, and guaranteed annuity payout factors. The answer is simple. In a fixed annuity, the issuing insurer invests the contract owner's premium and is entitled to whatever return it can earn on those dollars. As was noted, it is from those investment earnings that the insurer pays for the guarantees of principal and minimum annuity payout it offers, and is also where the insurer earns some of its profits.

The issuer of a variable annuity, on the other hand, receives no return from investing the contract owner's premium except to the extent that the premium is invested in the insurer's fixed account. Investments in the separate accounts are, literally, separate. They are invested directly with the managers of those accounts. The insurer cannot pay for insurance benefits from the earnings it receives on those dollars; it must charge for them directly, and it does.

But the dollars invested in the fixed account do generate investment earning for the insurer, which is precisely why no variable annuity contract assesses the M&E charge against funds invested in the fixed account.

All variable deferred annuities offer a fixed account and many advisors recommend allocating a portion of the client's money to them. There are two advantages to this strategy, in addition to the obvious diversification advantage. First, holding a portion of one's annuity money in a fixed account guarantees both safety of principal and a minimum interest rate with respect to that portion. Second, as was noted, M&E charges and any optional rider charges are assessed only against the value of separate, nonfixed accounts. That said, it should be noted that the current interest rate of the fixed account in some variable annuities is less than the current interest rate offered by the same insurer in its fixed deferred annuities. Funding a variable annuity entirely with the fixed account may be less attractive than simply buying a fixed annuity.

With regard to comparisons, it should also be noted that, in variable contracts, the net return available to the purchaser is the gross rate earned by the underlying investments, less the operating costs at the investment subaccount level—comparable to the expense ratio of mutual funds—less the contractual charges. If one assumes, for purposes of comparison, that the gross return on a portfolio of variable annuity subaccounts is the same as that of a comparable portfolio of mutual funds, the annuity imposes an additional level of costs, which inevitably results in a lower net return in the annuity.

Where All That Is Wanted Is Capital Accumulation

Where the goal is purely accumulation of capital, with no concern for assuring a minimum income later on or for a guaranteed minimum death benefit, a fixed deferred annuity may be appropriate, but, in the authors' opinion, a variable annuity is probably not.

As discussed earlier, this is primarily because variable annuities impose additional charges to pay for mortality and other guarantees. These costs, and the benefits they provide, must be carefully assessed when considering a variable annuity for accumulation purposes. If the insurance benefits are not desired—that is, that the investor does not value the annuity guarantees or the basic death benefit guarantee—then the charges for those benefits should be considered overhead costs that will inexorably drive down investment returns. Of course, not all investors consider annuity and minimum death benefit guarantees to be meaningless. For those who do, however, a bright line test emerges with regard to variable deferred annuities that do not include Guaranteed Living Benefits:

- To the extent that the investor considers the insurance benefits purchased by the M&E cost of a variable annuity, that cost is more overhead, or a drag on investment performance.

- An analogous bright line test for the suitability of a fixed deferred annuity might be:

  To the extent that the investor can obtain a fixed deferred annuity with a rate comparable to available fixed income alternatives, and is willing to take on the reduced liquidity of the annuity—in terms of pre-59½ tax treatment and potential surrender charges—a fixed deferred annuity may be appropriate for capital accumulation.

But what about those investors who wish the upside potential of returns possible from a portfolio of equity, or equity and bond, investments, but with some downside guarantees? That's where the newer Guaranteed Living Benefits, available in newer variable deferred annuity contracts, can be very attractive. These benefits are discussed further in Chapter 5.

Where the Goal Is Tax Deferral

The true value of tax deferral in a deferred annuity is a subject of considerable debate. Annuity proponents have argued for years that tax deferral is an unalloyed good thing. The authors agree that, where all other factors are equal, the opportunity to pay a dollar of tax next year is certainly preferable than a requirement to pay that dollar of tax today. But is that really the choice? Critics of variable deferred annuities point out that all taxable distributions from these contracts, whenever and to whomever made, must, under current law, be taxed at ordinary income rates. By contrast, they insist, investors in stocks, real estate, mutual funds, and other instruments that qualify for long-term capital gains taxation often enjoy much lower tax rates on a significant portion of their profits. The real choice, such a critic might suggest, is not paying a dollar of tax today versus paying that dollar of tax later, but, rather, paying tax on a dollar of income today, versus paying tax on that dollar of income later.

The difference, of course, is that in the latter case, the rate at which the tax is payable may be different. Long-Term Capital Gains (LTCG) rates are, for all investors, lower than ordinary income rates. A taxpayer holding a stock or share of a stock mutual fund will enjoy LTCG rates on much, or, in some cases, all profit from that investment. A taxpayer holding a stock or share of a stock mutual fund will enjoy LTCG rates on much of, or, in some cases, all of the profit from that annuity. In addition, regardless of whether some income may be taxed as ordinary income, taxpayers face the risk that their marginal tax rates will be higher in the future, resulting in potentially higher tax burden by deferring income.

Moreover, tax deferral of investment gain can be obtained from buying an investment other than an annuity. If one buys a share of stock and holds it, there is no current tax liability in any year, other than on the stock dividend, if any, which may still be taxed at preferential qualified dividend rates under current tax law. If one holds a stock mutual fund, there may be current capital gains liability, due to turnover in the fund, and dividends, if any. However, some mutual funds are managed for tax efficiency—to reduce short-term or overall capital gains distributions, and commensurate current tax liability, and increase the percentage of total return eligible for LTCG taxation and/or for overall tax deferral.

Of course, not all gain from investments in a nonannuity account will get such treatment. Some dividends are not eligible for qualified dividend treatment, and interest never received such favorable treatment. Even those distributions from a mutual fund that are eligible for LTCG treatment are taxable in the year received.

The choice, then, is not simply "pay a dollar now or pay it later," but instead is more complicated. In a comparison of a variable deferred annuity with a nonqualified mutual fund invested partly or wholly in equities. It's a trade-off between the total tax deferral offered by a variable annuity, regardless of the types of investment subaccounts held, with all gains receiving all ordinary income treatment and tax deferral until the funds are withdrawn, versus mutual fund gains that at least receive some LTCG treatment and potential for deferral until those gains are turned over and distributed by the mutual fund and that are never subject to the 10% penalty imposed on annuity distributions by IRC Sect. 72(q).

It should be noted that this tax deferral vs. all ordinary income treatment trade-off exists for a variable annuity, but not for a fixed annuity. This is because the alternatives reasonably comparable to a fixed annuity (e.g., CDs, bonds) are, themselves, subject to all ordinary income treatment. Of course, the Sect. 72(q) penalty tax applies to distributions from both fixed and variable deferred annuities.

Where the Goal Is Market-Like Returns With Downside Guarantees

Amounts invested in the separate accounts of a variable deferred annuity[4] enjoy neither safety of principal nor a guaranteed minimum return. The value of these accounts varies directly with the performance of the underlying investments chosen. The purchaser assumes the investment risk inherent in these accounts, in exchange for the potential reward associated with such holdings. However, many investors want and need the returns possible when their money is in the market, but are unwilling to assume all the risks commensurate with that choice. To satisfy these investors, issuers of variable deferred annuities have developed optional riders to their contracts, the so-called Guaranteed Living Benefits. See Chapter 5 for a further discussion of these contract riders and how they may be applied in certain client situations.

Endnotes

1. Some guaranteed living benefit riders provide a guarantee of principal, or principal plus specified interest, either in a lump sum or through periodic withdrawals or regular annuity payments.

2. The material in this section was adapted from "*Annuities and Suitability: Reflections On The State of the Debate,*" by John L. Olsen, *Journal of the Society of Financial Service Professionals* (November, 2006).

3. While the Guaranteed Minimum Withdrawal Benefit rider available in most variable deferred annuity contracts guarantees the purchaser at least a return of the amount originally invested, that return must be taken in installments. In the authors' opinion, most consumers equate guarantee of principal with the right to take that principal in a lump sum. An assurance that one will receive, in installments, one's original investment is not the same thing. Moreover, it ignores the time value of money.

4. Separate accounts—sometimes termed investment subaccounts—are invested in pooled equity and/or bond accounts the value of which can, and usually does, change daily. There is no safety of principal or Minimum Guaranteed Return in such accounts. Amounts invested in the fixed account of such contracts are invested in the general account of the issuing insurer and do enjoy guarantees, both of principal and of a minimum interest rate.

Chapter 13

Longevity Annuities

The longevity annuity is a relatively new type of annuity contract, different from both the deferred and immediate types. Like an immediate life annuity, it provides only a guaranteed stream of income for life and typically has no account balance that may be accessed other than by annuitization. However, where income payout from an immediate annuity must commence within one year of purchase, the payout from a longevity annuity is generally not available until, perhaps many years after purchase.

The longevity annuity appeared as a concept called the high protection annuity in a 1978 paper by James Stephenson.[1] Nearly 30 years later, it emerged as a concept product in a paper by Moshe Milevsky.[2] Milevsky's term for the product was Advanced Life Deferred Annuity, (ALDA). In 2006, Scott, Watson and Hu called it a delayed payout annuity and argued that it affords the buyer with far more efficient annuitization than an immediate annuity.[3] In 2007, Webb, Gong, and Sun described this product as an annuity that people might actually buy.[4]

How Does a Longevity Annuity Work?

A longevity annuity might be viewed as a hybrid of a deferred annuity and an immediate annuity. Like the former, it is purchased in advance of the annuity starting date—typically, well in advance. However, like an immediate annuity, it offers no accumulation benefits and may provide for no benefits at all unless and until the annuitant reaches a certain age. Although the longevity annuity has existed for several years, it is very much a work in progress. Few insurers currently offer longevity annuities, although several are considering adding it to their portfolios. It is virtually certain that the product will evolve over time, as market forces, or the demands of consumers and advisors in the distribution channel, dictate. At this time, there are two basic versions. The first is what the authors call a pure longevity annuity, providing no benefits until the annuitant reaches the annuity starting age. The second provides for some benefits before that event—either a death benefit, a cash value, or both—and may allow the contract owner to commute remaining annuity payments after the annuity starting date.

One contract, currently offered by a major U.S. insurer, requires annuitization only at age 85 or later and provides no death benefit or commutation feature. This is an example of the pure longevity annuity and is similar to Milevsky's concept product, except that Milevksy envisioned that annuity payments would be inflation-adjusted.[5]

Another contract, offered by that same insurer, allows annuitization at the earlier of age 50 or two years after purchase, with a maximum annuitization age of age 85, includes a death benefit equal to premiums paid plus 3% interest if the investor dies prior to annuitization, and permits the investor to commute the annuity, or to take a lump sum in lieu of remaining income payments, within 60 days following the annuity starting date. This one time only commutation feature is the only way in which the contract owner may liquidate the contract for a lump sum.

Not all longevity annuities permit only a single purchase payment and require payout at a specified, usually advanced, age. A few carriers offer contracts which permit ongoing premiums and/or allow payout at an age chosen by the purchaser, either for life—which is typically a requirement in most longevity annuities offered today—or for a specified period of years (Period Certain).

A few years ago, one of the authors talked with several financial advisors, none of whom was familiar with longevity annuities, about the pure version. The almost unanimous opinion of these advisors, on first hearing of the general provisions of this pure type, was a mix of incredulity and distaste. "Why would anybody buy one of those?" was the consensus.

Why, indeed? What's it good for?

Milevsky writes that the longevity annuity, his ALDA, "is a close relative of a defined benefit pension, and intended for those who don't have one."[6] This is an utterly vital observation, one that goes to the heart of the longevity annuity. It's all about the assurance of a known level of income, starting in the investor's old age. Yet the advisors who, on hearing that the annuity will terminate without value if the investor fails to live to age 85, and who found that provision unacceptable, were employing a very different mindset. They were applying investment thinking to a risk management problem. Milevsky speaks to this difference. "From a slightly different perspective," he writes, "this type of product is akin to buying car, home or health insurance with a large deductible, which is also the optimal strategy—and common practice—when dealing with catastrophic risk."[7] Walter Updegrave, a senior editor at *Money* magazine, describes the product in similar terms, observing that, "In effect it's like buying a homeowners or health insurance policy that has a very large deductible. You're insuring yourself against a catastrophic risk you can't handle on your own—in this case, running out of money late in life—while holding your premium to a minimum."[8]

The risk is the possibility of running out of money at a time in the investor's life when she probably cannot generate money. The benefit of the longevity annuity is that it enables her to insure against that risk at a deep discount. Obviously, an insurer can offer an annuity purchaser a far greater guaranteed income, per dollar invested, if it owes nothing, or if she fails to live to the annuity starting date, than if it would if the insurer were required to return the amount invested (plus interest) as a death benefit.

Jason Scott, in his article *The Longevity Annuity: An Annuity For Everyone?* [9] distinguishes between funding a retirement income by saving (or investing) in a portfolio that will provide that income and purchasing insurance that will do so. He makes the point that funding a retirement income portfolio with investment assets amounts to setting aside the full replacement cost of the income stream, which is essentially self insurance. He observes that "with self insurance, the money is set aside whether or not the insurance event occurs."[10] The longevity annuity—the insurance solution, if you will—differs in that the payout, or the benefit, is contingent upon the insured's survival, without which, the risk in question does not occur.

Because it offers little or no benefit until the annuity starting date, the longevity annuity allows the purchaser to secure a substantial level of late retirement income very cheaply, compared to alternatives. It can do so because it insures against the risk of not having that income, if the purchaser lives long enough to experience late retirement; it does not ensure that same income if she does not.

In the conventional model of retirement income funding, we save for an event—reaching late retirement age, when we'll need the money—rather than insure against it. In this savings model, the money we save is ours, and is always available—either to us or to our heirs—whether the event for which we're saving, or reaching late retirement age, occurs or not. When we purchase a pure longevity annuity, we invoke a different model. In this insurance model, we buy a contract that will pay off only if the event insured against actually occurs, that is, if we reach late retirement age. It is this contingency of payoff that makes the longevity annuity so cost-effective.

One problem with this two model view is that it characterizes the investor during the savings period wholly as an accumulator. When we save for an event, the money we save is available to us, whether the event occurs or not, because it's always been our money. When we insure against an event, we pay a premium to an insurance policy in exchange for a promise to pay us a much larger sum in the event that the event actually occurs. We do not accumulate that larger sum, because it is not ours until it is paid to us. If it is never paid to us, the insurance company uses our funds to pay the claims for someone else in the pool, making the overall cost of pure protection lower for everyone involved. Our clients are not mere accumulators; they're also consumers. They have lifestyles, and those lifestyles cost money.

Should we not take into account that certain asset allocation, income distribution strategies, and spending choices could be attractive to an investor who is assured of a certain income on reaching the annuity starting age but unattractive to an investor having no such assurance?

What lifestyle choices may become available to our investor if she has an assurance that her retirement portfolio need not persist beyond age 85 because the longevity annuity will take it from there?

It is this certainty—that once the investor reaches a certain age, the retirement income need will be met, to the extent of the benefit purchased, for the rest of that investor's life—that totally reconfigures the retirement income planning problem. Without the longevity annuity in place, the problem is one of ensuring an adequate income over an indefinite period. With the longevity annuity, the period to be funded by withdrawals from a retirement portfolio is known in advance. It begins at the age of retirement and ends at the longevity annuity's starting date. These are not merely different scenarios; they are wholly different paradigms.

One might argue that there is another risk in play here. If one buys a pure longevity annuity and does not survive until benefits are payable, the purchase payment may be viewed as lost. But that is the same risk borne by anyone who purchases an automobile, medical expense, disability income, or term life insurance policy. If the insured peril does not occur, no benefit is payable. The purchaser, in that situation, will still have received value—the absolute assurance of the specified benefit had the insured peril materialized.

That said, some advisors will insist upon viewing the premium paid for a pure longevity annuity as a loss in the event of the insured's death prior to annuitization. For this reason, some insurers offer contracts with a pre-annuitization death benefit. The cost of this benefit is the difference between the income guaranteed by that contract and the income guaranteed by the pure variant. In any such product, this difference is significant, and the greater the period between purchase and annuitization date, the greater the difference in the annual benefit provided by the two variants. If you require a refund of your investment if you don't live to age 85, for example, you'll get possibly much less income if you do reach that age. That income reduction will last as long as you do.

In the authors' opinion, buying a longevity annuity with a pre-annuitization death benefit is like buying term life or disability income insurance with a return of premium benefit. One is not only insuring against the occurrence of a specified peril (death or disability), but also insuring the economic value of the premium payments themselves. By adding an ancillary benefit, one reduces, inexorably, the leverage in the underlying insurance. To some purchasers and some advisors, this may make sense. To the authors, though, it is not prudent risk management. Theoretically, the purpose of insurance is to protect only against risks that the individual otherwise could not afford to manage without such protection. If the premium is so unaffordable that it would require its own insurance just for the cost of the premium, it may be time to revisit the decision to purchase longevity, or any other kind, of insurance in the first place.

Another way of viewing the potential loss of premium would be to compare the current purchase of a pure longevity annuity with saving for the purchase of an immediate annuity at the age when the longevity annuity begins to pay off.

Example (June, 2008): A 60-year-old client can purchase a pure longevity annuity today for $50,000 and be assured of receiving $5,211 per month, or $62,532 per year, for life upon reaching age 85. An immediate annuity at today's rates, paying $5,211 per month for life, for an 85-year-old male, would cost $365,837.[11] What rate of return must we earn on the $50,000 we are considering using to buy the longevity annuity to produce $365,811—that will produce the same annual income as the annuity—in 25 years? The answer is 8.29%. Taxes are ignored for simplicity.

Example (December, 2011): Same client, same age. His $50,000 will now purchase, from the same insurer, a longevity annuity of $3,255 per month, or $39,060 per year,[12] commencing at age 85. An immediate annuity for an 85-year-old male, at December, 2011 rates, would cost $251,254. What rate of return would be required for $50,000 to grow to that amount in 25 years? 6.67%.

What does this answer tell us? It does not tell us that the longevity annuity produces the same result we'd get if we could be assured of earning that computed interest rate every year from investing that $50,000, because, in the save for scenario, the invested funds are ours. We can take that money at any time, or leave it to our heirs. The longevity annuity has no cash surrender value or, indeed, any value whatsoever unless and until we reach age 85.

On the other hand, the goal—an income for life, commencing at age 85—is guaranteed in the annuity scenario. It is merely projected in the save for scenario, and our projection makes two huge assumptions. First, that we will, in fact, earn the projected return each and every year. However, this is exceedingly unlikely.

Second, even if we were to grant that our earnings assumption will be realized, we cannot be sure that the save for scenario will produce the required income at 85, because immediate annuity rates are sensitive to both interest and longevity rates. This is readily apparent from the differences in the costs and benefits of both the longevity annuity and the SPIA from the summer of 2008, when the first example was created, to December, 2011. Interest rates declined significantly during that interval. If, 25 years from now, long-term interest rates are lower than they are today, a single premium immediate annuity (SPIA) purchased at that time with $251,254 might not buy the anticipated $3,255 per month of guaranteed income. The same may also be true if life expectancy is greater, which is likely. If interest rates are lower and life expectancy is greater 25 years from now, SPIA rates could be much less attractive. A longevity annuity purchased today locks in both today's annuity payout rates and the underlying guaranteed internal rate of return, during the deferral period, that is derived from those guaranteed rates.

Is the certainty that $50,000 today will buy us $3,255 per month, or whatever income could be purchased at the time you read this chapter, for life, if and only if we reach age 85, worth locking away that money, perhaps never to get it back? That's not an easy question to answer. Our quantification example provides a baseline for the comparable return we must earn on our investments over the next 25 years to achieve the future lump sum required, which obliges us to note that earning an average return as high as 6.67% will entail some investment risk itself. When we employ that baseline, we should remember that the longevity annuity pays off, if and only if.

Part of the difficulty stems from the fact that our computation makes the valuation of the longevity annuity an investment problem. We've compared how much money our investor would need to have accumulated at age 85 to obtain the amount of income that could be guaranteed today by a longevity annuity if she really does live that long. Only one of the two alternatives can occur. The real risk against which the longevity annuity provides insurance is that our investor will live longer than anticipated, and that her assets may not be enough to produce a sufficient income over an unexpectedly long life. Arguably, if she doesn't live to that age, she won't need the money, because that long-life, or superannuation, risk never materializes. To put it bluntly, dead people don't require income.

From a practical standpoint, we ought to note that the cost of a longevity annuity that might be lost if the investor doesn't live to the target age, or the annuity starting date, should never be more than a fraction of that investor's total portfolio for at least two reasons.

First, because a higher cost is not necessary. The amount of premium required to guarantee a given level of income, commencing at age 85, with a longevity annuity is but a fraction of the money that would be required to accumulate sufficient capital to produce that same income at age 85. Scott states that "the spending benefit a retiree could achieve with a 10% allocation to a longevity annuity typically exceeds the benefit from a 50% allocation to an immediate annuity."[13] Our earlier example showed similar results. This significant difference occurs because the insurance company can pool the money for all those who don't live to age 85 with those who do receive payments past age 85, allowing the insurer to transform the liquidity that the purchaser gives up into an increased guaranteed benefit amount. This is what actuaries call a morality credit, and it's what makes the longevity annuity so efficient.

Second, because retirement income might not be the investor's only goal. The individual may also have estate planning and legacy goals for heirs. In this case, the authors recommend that the client can best maximize both retirement and legacy goals by obtaining a pure longevity annuity to minimize the expense of insuring against an unexpectedly long life, while locking in the maximum leverage inherent in such a contract. The money freed up by this strategy is thus available for other uses, such as legacies.

What About Inflation?

One major carrier offers two versions of its longevity annuity—one with a death benefit and one without—but both provide only a level annual benefit. That is, there is no inflation increase or Cost-Of-Living-Adjustment (COLA) feature. Another insurer's product offers consumers a choice of an annual increase ranging from 1%-5% of the annual benefit, but the increase begins only in the second year of payout.

In other words, there is no protection against unexpected inflation occurring from policy purchase until the first payout year, which may render the first payment already insufficient to provide for the desired purchasing power of the retiree. Moreover, an individual longevity annuity owner who receives annuity payments over many years will see the value of those payments eroded by the inflation occurring during that payout period.

The lack of inflation protection in most of the longevity contracts currently offered is worrisome. The authors encourage advisors to be very cautious in recommending longevity annuities that may, ultimately, fail to provide a sufficient level of real (after inflation) income to meet the client's entire future needs.

One method of dealing with this problem, where the longevity annuity being considered offers no inflation protection for the deferral period, might be to compute, first, the future, or inflated, amount of income required and to recommend that inflated amount. If, however, the contract recommended offers no inflation increases during the payout period, this is only a partial solution.

Another might be to purchase a series of longevity annuities, buying additional protection as the need for it becomes apparent. Although, this too may not produce adequate inflation protection if the contracts purchased provide none.

One U.S. insurer offers a longevity rider to one of its variable annuity contracts in which the rider premium is paid by installments, as a percentage of the total premiums paid into the annuity contract.

None of these solutions is, in the authors' opinion, as satisfactory as choosing a longevity annuity that offers protection against inflation occurring during both the payout and deferral periods. The authors hope that we will see such contracts as the market for this product matures.

The Importance of a Death Benefit Feature

In conversations with marketing executives at two major insurers currently offering longevity annuities, one of the authors has been told that the overwhelming majority of advisors considering these products prefer a version offering a death benefit. In conversations with dozens of financial planners and insurance agents, the authors have heard the same thing. Apparently, most advisors believe that a client will not pay money for a product guaranteeing a substantial income at, say age 85, if it pays no benefit if the client dies beforehand.

Viewed one way, this makes sense. Why would one invest one's money in something that might never pay off? Yet this viewpoint is, in the authors' opinion, fundamentally misdirected for a very simple reason: a longevity annuity is not, in any way whatsoever, an investment. It is wholly a risk transfer instrument, a pure insurance play.[14]

What is the risk in question? It is the possibility that your income might decline, perhaps to zero, in your old age, because you lived longer than expected—at a time when you will almost certainly be unable to generate more income. That's the risk. If that possibility so concerns you that you're willing to part with a substantial insurance premium now to preclude it, even if that will mean losing that money if you never reach old age, then transferring that risk to an insurer by making that premium may make good sense to you—just as you find it sensible to buy medical expense insurance knowing that if you don't get sick, that insurance will never pay off.

The reason that advisors don't like longevity annuities without a death benefit is they're applying investment analysis to a product that isn't an investment, or even an insurance product with investment features. In the authors' opinion, the longevity insurance purchase decision should be, functionally speaking, identical to the thought process involved in purchasing a property and casualty product, where a premium is paid purely to insure a risk with no other benefit but the risk protection—and it should be viewed as such.

Regrettably, that is not how it is being marketed, if the brochures from the few insurers offering it are any indication. Both the point-of-sale and the agent training materials typically speak of the longevity annuity as an income investment product, which is half right and half dead wrong. A longevity annuity is all about income, but it's nothing about investment. Until insurance marketers understand this, their producers, orinsurance agents and financial advisors, never will. Until we advisors do, our clients won't either.

Implications of the Longevity Annuity
for Retirement Income Planning in General

In the authors' opinion, the Longevity Annuity concept has the potential to redefine the landscape of retirement income planning. Traditionally, the problem facing planners is to construct and manage a portfolio which will provide, at least to a minimum level of confidence, required levels of income throughout retirement. We make projections to model how various asset allocations and income distribution patterns will perform to that end. In doing so, we take into account numerous variables. That, by itself, isn't hard, given the formidable computer software tools now available. The difficulty lies, of course, in the uncertainties. Even when we prescribe the levels of net real income required and assume particular tax and inflation rates, we're left to deal with two fundamental uncertainties: (1) the level and sequence of investment returns; and (2) the length of the period over which income will be required.

Various methodologies have been developed to help us do this. Stochastic techniques, such as Monte Carlo simulation, historical backtesting, which uses actual returns over a specified earlier period, and historical bootstrapping, or using actual historical returns, chosen randomly for each analysis year are all in common use. Each method has its proponents and critics, but each must acknowledge that we do not know for certain: (1) what investment returns our client will earn each year; or (2) for how many years returns will be needed. The influence of each of these uncertainties upon our overall confidence is considerable, but the product of both—of these uncertainties compounded, if you will—exerts a profound impact upon the confidence we feel about our results.

How much more confident might we be if one of these two uncertainties were removed—if we knew that, while we're still guessing, however scientifically, about future investment returns each year, we knew, for certain, for how many years we would need those returns to generate retirement income from the portfolio?

To the extent that a longevity annuity will provide, with surety, the level of income our client needs on reaching a particular age—age 85, for example—it transforms our period uncertain problem to one of a period certain. Now we know the client's remaining assets will be required to last only until age 85, because the longevity annuity will take it from there.

What kind of asset allocation decisions can now be made with regard to those remaining assets in the light of this new certainty? Even more importantly, what kind of lifestyle choices may the client now make, with confidence?

Longevity annuities are still very new to the marketplace. Most insurers do not offer one. To the authors' knowledge none offers a pure longevity annuity that is adjusted for inflation by use of an index such as the CPI, which, in the authors' opinion, presents a substantial risk for the longevity annuity buyer. Almost no one is buying them; chiefly because very few advisors are recommending them. Yet the potential these contracts offer for retirement income planning is huge. Just how, and how much, they will be employed remains to be seen.

In February, 2012, the U.S. Treasury Department and the Internal Revenue Service proposed a package of rules designed to make it easier for participants in employer-sponsored retirement plans and IRAs to invest in longevity annuities. These rules would, among other things, ease the Required Minimum Distribution aggregation of accounts rules and, under certain circumstances, postpone the application of those rules until the longevity annuities begin payout. These proposals represent a good start, but widespread acceptance of these tools has a long way to go.

The Contingent Annuity

Recently, a number of Private Letter Rulings[15] have addressed an entirely new type of annuity: the contingent annuity. Essentially a stand-alone guaranteed lifetime withdrawal benefit rider, the contingent annuity is a contract between an issuing insurance company and a customer, or the annuitant holding an investment account at a sponsoring organization, or the sponsor. The customer is guaranteed the right to make withdrawals of up to a specified amount from a benefit base for life. The benefit base may, as with the GLWB in an annuity, be the greatest of the account balance, the account balance at specified prior dates (i.e., a high water mark structure), or the account balance at inception, accumulated at a specified rate of interest. As with the GLWB, if withdrawals under this benefit result in the account balance falling below zero, the insurance element of the contingent annuity would come into play, and the insurance company will continue payments of the same amount to the annuitant for life; or, if a joint benefit is elected, the joint lifetime of the annuitant and his/her spouse.

Unlike payments under the GLWB, payments by the insurer under a contingent annuity will, based on the PLRs cited, enjoy regular annuity rules taxation, or a portion of each payment is considered a tax-free return of principal. Moreover, the investment account would not be considered an annuity contract, and returns would be eligible for capital gains taxation.

As of January 2012, there is considerable confusion as to whether a contingent annuity is, in fact, an annuity contract. Contingent annuity contracts have been filed with insurance regulators in many states; in some states, they have been approved as annuity contracts. In others, they have not. In November 2011, the NAIC formed a working group to study the marketing of these instruments.

Endnotes

1. Stephenson, James B., "The High Protection Annuity," *Journal of Risk And Insurance*, Vol. 45, Issue 4 (December 1978).

2. Moshe Milevsky, "Real Longevity Insurance with a Deductible: Introduction to Advanced-Life Delayed Annuities," Managing Retirement Assets Symposium, 2004, published in *North American Actuarial Journal* (9)(4), 109-122.

3. Jason S. Scott, John G. Watson & Wei-Yin Hu, *Efficient Annuitization With Delayed Payout Annuities*, November 2006.

4. Anthony Webb, Guan Gong & Wei Sun, *An Annuity That People Might Actually Buy,* (Center for Retirement Research at Boston College) July, 2007.

5. As of July 2008, one major insurer's longevity annuity offers inflation protection, via a purchaser-selected annual increase percentage; another offers no such option, but is considering adding it.

6. Milevsky, *Ibid.*

7. Milevsky, *Ibid.*

8. Updegrave, Walter, "*Sure Income For The Very (Very) Long Haul,*" *Money* Magazine (January 21, 2008).

9. Jason Scott, *The Longevity Annuity: An Annuity For Everyone?* (Financial Engines, Inc., 2007).

10. Scott, *Ibid.*

11. Rates for both immediate and longevity annuities vary considerably by age and sex and by insurer. The results of this comparison might be very different for a client of a different age and/or sex, or if contracts from a different insurer were used.

12. The decrease from the prior example appears to be attributable primarily to the dramatic decline in long-term interest rates over the intervening time period

13. Scott, *Ibid.*

14. See Olsen, "Longevity Annuities Could Redefine the Retirement Income Planning Landscape", *Life Insurance Selling,* January, 2009.

15. PLRs 200949007, 201002016, 201129029.

Chapter 14

Suitability: The Changing Nature of the Standard of Care

Overview

Annuities are hybrid financial products. They are insurance products, and, as such, are regulated by state insurance departments. Some annuities are also considered to be securities, subject to regulation by federal and state securities agencies. Furthermore, some rules are applied by federal regulatory bodies, while others are established and administered by states. Thus, the rules governing the sale and marketing of annuities are a matter of jurisdiction, and the rules are not entirely consistent from one jurisdiction to another. This can make compliance with relevant rules complicated and difficult. Adding to the difficulty is the fact that the standard of care required of those who recommend annuities is not uniform. At the present time, there are actually two standards of care in the financial services industry: suitability and the fiduciary standard.

Suitability can be defined as "the quality of having the properties that are right for a specific purpose or situation." That is a general definition, but the term suitability has a more specific meaning when applied to recommendations of insurance, investment, and annuity products, a meaning which is evolving constantly. Until recently, there was little, if any, precision as to when the sale or recommendation of an annuity would be considered suitable. Virtually no jurisdictions offered rules with any intentional definitions—that is, specifications of the necessary and sufficient conditions that must apply for the transaction in question to be qualified as suitable—or providing concrete examples. Many state statutes were simply self-recursive; they simply defined a suitable transaction as one that is suitable.

These suitability standards generally apply, at the present time, both to: (a) insurance agents recommending insurance and annuity products that are not securities and to; (b) registered representatives recommending insurance, annuity, and/or investment products that are securities so long as the advice that they render, in the course of making those securities recommendations, is solely incidental to their activities as securities salespersons—in many regulations, the term used is brokers.

The other standard of care that may apply when an annuity is recommended is the fiduciary standard. This is a much higher standard, and applies to investment advisers under the Investment Advisers Act of 1940. Section 202(a)(11) of that Act generally defines an investment adviser as any person or firm that: (1) for compensation; (2) is engaged in the business of; (3) providing advice, making recommendations, issuing reports, or furnishing analyses on securities, either directly or through publications. It does not generally apply to registered representatives to whom the broker exclusion of Section 201(a)(11)(C) of the Act applies. Section 201 excludes from the Act's definition of investment advisor, registered representatives offering advice in connection with the recommendation of a security, provided that two conditions are satisfied:

(a) No special compensation is received (for the advice)

(b) The advice is solely incidental to the broker's brokerage activities

The Standard of Care Debate

There has been, for some time, a strong demand, by many consumer advocates, regulators, members of Congress, and financial service professionals, for financial services reform, which includes a reworking of the standards of care that should apply to those who provide financial services to consumers. This demand has already produced new regulations at state and federal levels and continues to inspire debate as to whether additional regulations are needed and, if so, what those regulations should require. At the heart of this debate is the issue of financial advice, and on this issue, participants fall generally into one of three broad groups.

The Unified Standard Group holds that the current arrangement, in which some advisors are held to a fiduciary standard while others are subject to a lesser one, is unworkable. Consumers, they insist, cannot reasonably know the nature of the duty owed to them by any particular financial service professional, as some must act as fiduciaries, others need not, and yet others may or may not bear that duty, depending upon the capacity in which they are acting—and even including what type of policy, if insurance, they're recommending or selling. As the fiduciary standard: (a) requires that an advisor must act in the consumer's best interest and subordinate his or her own self-interest to that goal; (b) requires that the advisor disclose all conflicts of interest; and (c) is clearly a higher standard than that of suitability, members of this group believe that the uncertainty now faced by consumers should be resolved by holding all advisors to this higher standard.

The "Let the Current Rules Continue" Group believes that such a resolution will create more problems than the resolution is worth. Members of this group point out that not all those who render advice of a financial nature give investment advice, that some financial professionals are legally precluded from doing so, and that many who are not so precluded may offer advice which is merely ancillary to the sale of financial products. They often insist that the adoption of a universal fiduciary standard will create increased costs of doing business and may result in reduced access to financial products and expertise by many consumers—chiefly, those who do not now, and do not wish to, deal with investment advisors.

The "Changes Are Needed, but a Unified Fiduciary Standard Goes Too Far" Group acknowledges that some reform is clearly required, but insists that a single standard is neither needed nor desirable.

A thorough discussion of the standard of care debate, and the extent to which it will impact those who recommend annuities, is beyond the scope of this chapter. That said, readers should be aware that there is widespread interest, in the regulatory and consumerist communities, in extending the fiduciary standard of care to those who sell annuities. In the remainder of this chapter, we will focus on the issue of the suitability of annuity transactions using the suitability standard as that is the standard of care currently applicable to most annuity sales.

The Regulatory Players

As noted above, sales of annuities are subject to regulation by both state and Federal agencies. Any annuity sale must meet the requirements of insurance regulations in the state in which the sale is made. Typically, state insurance regulations are consistent with, and often identical to, the Model Regulations adopted by the National Association of Insurance Commissioners (NAIC), the standards-setting and regulatory support organization created and governed by the chief insurance regulators of the 50 states, the District of Columbia, and five U.S. territories.

Variable annuities are regulated as securities, in addition to being regulated as insurance, and, as such, are subject to regulation by the Securities and Exchange Commission (SEC) and the Financial Industry Regulatory Authority (FINRA). FINRA is a private corporation that acts as a self-regulatory authority having oversight over all securities firms that do business with U.S customers. It was created in 2007, in a merger of the National Association of Securities Dealers and NYSE Regulation, Inc., the enforcement arm of the New York Stock Exchange. Many of the rules and regulations of FINRA are adaptations of, or identical to, earlier NASD rules. One of the difficulties financial advisors encounter in attempting to locate and understand the rules to which they are subject is that FINRA often restates earlier NASD rules but with a different numbering. For example, the current FINRA rule 2330, dealing with the suitability of variable annuity transactions, is a restatement of the earlier NASD rule 2821.

While regulation of insurance and annuity products that are not securities is generally left to the states, the Federal Government is a player, especially since the enactment of the Dodd-Frank Wall Street Reform and Consumer Protection Act of 2010. As will be discussed later, Section 989J of the Dodd-Frank Act prescribes that recommendations of insurance and annuity products must meet the suitability rules of an NAIC regulation dealing with annuities adopted in 2010.

Suitability Rules Dealing Specifically with Annuities[1]

Suitability rules dealing with annuities can be divided into three groups:

1. Rules dealing with annuities that are not deemed securities

2. Rules dealing with annuities that are deemed securities

3. Rules dealing with annuities that may be securities because the status of those contracts is not yet clear.

Rules Dealing with Annuities that Are Not Securities

Each state insurance department prescribes rules governing the sale of annuities in that state. Annuity contracts must contain certain required language dealing with such things as nonforfeiture provisions, the period of time during which the buyer of an annuity contract may cancel the sale, often termed free look provisions, interest rate guarantees, etc. Annuity sales must be suitable. Often, the state rules are drafted to comport with Model Regulations adopted by the NAIC.

NAIC regulations dealing with annuities suitability have evolved over time. The current NAIC Model Regulation is the Suitability in Annuity Transactions Model Regulation #275, which we will refer to as SATMR.

NAIC Suitability in Annuity Transactions
Model Regulation #275 of 2010 (SATMR)

As explained in the NAIC's Executive Summary, this Model Regulation was adopted "to set standards and procedures for suitable annuity recommendations and to require insurers to establish a system to supervise recommendations so that the insurance needs and financial objectives of consumers are appropriately addressed." The Executive Summary states:

"Specifically, this Model Regulation was adopted to:

1. Establish a regulatory framework that holds insurers responsible for ensuring that annuity transactions are suitable based on the criteria in Section 5I [of the Model

Regulation], whether or not the insurer contracts with third-party to supervise or monitor the recommendations made in the marketing and sales of annuities;

2.   Require that producers be trained on the provisions of annuities in general, and the specific products they are selling.

3.   Where feasible and rational, to make these suitability standards consistent with the suitability standards imposed by the Financial Industry Regulatory Authority (FINRA)." [2]

The Model Regulation requires all producers, or insurance agents selling annuity contracts, to have adequate product specific training, including compliance with the insurer's standards for product training, prior to soliciting the sale of an annuity product. It mandates that such producers complete a one-time, for credit hour, course in general annuity training.

Section 6A, entitled *Duties of Insurer and of Insurance Producers*, provides a general four-part test of suitability, with subparts, and states:

"A. In recommending to a consumer the purchase of an annuity or the exchange of an annuity that results in another insurance transaction or series of insurance transactions, the insurance producer, or the insurer where no producer is involved, shall have reasonable grounds for believing that the recommendation is suitable for the consumer on the basis of facts disclosed by the consumer as to his or her investments and other insurance products and as to his or her financial situation and needs, including the consumer's suitability information, and that there is reasonable basis to believe all of the following:

(1) The consumer has been reasonably informed of various features of the annuity, such as the potential surrender period and surrender charge, potential tax penalty if the consumer sells, exchanges, surrenders or annuitizes the annuity, mortality and expense fees, investment advisory fees, potential charges for and features of riders, limitations on interest returns, insurance and investment components and market risk;

(2) The consumer would benefit from certain features of the annuity, such as tax-deferred growth, annuitization or death or living benefit;

(3) The particular annuity as a whole, the underlying subaccounts to which funds are allocated at the time of purchase or exchange of the annuity, and riders and similar product enhancements, if any, are suitable (and in the case of an exchange or replacement, the transaction as a whole is suitable) for the particular consumer based on his or her suitability information; and

(4) In the case of an exchange or replacement of an annuity, the exchange or replacement is suitable including taking into consideration whether:

(a) The consumer will incur a surrender charge, be subject to the commencement of a new surrender period, lose existing benefits, such as death, living or other contractual benefits, or be subject to increased fees, investment advisory fees or charges for riders and similar product enhancements;

(b) The consumer would benefit from product enhancements and improvements; and

(c) The consumer has had another annuity exchange or replacement and, in particular, an exchange or replacement within the preceding 36 months.[3]"

Section 5I of the Model Regulation lists 12 factors which must be considered in any recommendation of an annuity. These factors are:

1. Age

2. Annual income

3. Financial situation and need, including the financial resources used for the funding of the annuity

4. Financial experience

5. Financial objectives

6. Intended use of the annuity

7. Financial time horizon

8. Existing assets, including investment and life insurance holdings

9. Liquidity needs

10. Liquid net worth

11. Risk tolerance

12. Tax status [4]

The recitation of these 12 factors, as elements that must be considered prior to the sale of any annuity product, represents a significant—and, in the authors' opinion, much needed—clarification of suitability rules for annuity transactions. On the other hand, such recitation might be seen as an assumption that the producer does not have discretion in determining the factors that must be considered in any suitability analysis. Nor does SATMR offer a rebuttable presumption of suitability. Interestingly, both discretion about which factors are appropriate for suitability, and a rebuttable presumption of suitability, were included in an earlier NAIC model regulation which was never adopted. That Model Regulation, OR NAIC Life Insurance and Annuity Model Regulation of 2002, included the following guidance:

> that "Insurance producers shall have reasonable discretion... To determine what information is relevant or necessary for any specific insurance transaction" [Section 6] and that [Section 7] "a rebuttable presumption that a recommendation was suitable is created if the insurer or insurance producer can demonstrate:
>
> 1.   collection and consideration of relevant information;
>
> 2.   conformance with an insurer's guidelines and procedures, prior to making a recommendation; and
>
> 3.   that the insurance transaction assisted the consumer in meeting the consumer's insurable needs or financial objectives."

As of December, 2011, more than 20 states have adopted a form of SATMR, and it is virtually certain that all states will eventually do so, particularly as section 989J of Dodd-Frank practically compels this. The impact of Dodd-Frank will be discussed later in this chapter.

Rules Dealing with Annuities that Are Securities

Variable annuities, as annuity contracts, are subject to regulation by state insurance departments—and, indirectly, by the NAIC—and, as securities, are subject to regulation by state securities departments and Federal securities regulators. Over the years, rulings by the NASD and FINRA have sought to provide guidance as to when a variable annuity is suitable."

FINRA Rule 2090

The FINRA Rule 2090 Know Your Customer rule, announced in FINRA's Regulatory Notice 11–02 in January, 2010, is modeled after NYSE Rule 405(1). It requires FINRA members to use reasonable diligence and to know the essential facts concerning their customers. The Rule explains that essential facts are: "those required to (a) effectively service the customer's account, (b) act in accordance with any special handling instructions for the account, (c) understand the authority of each person acting on behalf of the customer and (d) comply with applicable laws, regulations, and rules.[5]"

The know-your-customer obligation arises at the beginning of the customer-broker relationship and does not depend on whether the broker has made a recommendation.

FINRA Rule 2111

FINRA rule 2111 is both a know your customer and suitability rule. Announced in regulatory notice 11–02, and effective on October 7, 2011, it requires that registered representatives and the firms for which they work have a reasonable basis to believe that a recommended transaction or investment strategy involving a security is suitable for the customer, based upon "the information obtained through the reasonable diligence of the [FINRA] member or associated person to ascertain the customer's investment profile." It is significant that this rule, unlike previous rulings, applies both to recommendations of product and of investment strategy.

The Rule declares that investment profile "includes, but is not limited to, the customer's age, other investments, financial situation and needs, tax status, investment objectives, investment experience, investment time horizon, liquidity needs, risk tolerance, and any other information the customer may disclose to the member or associated person in connection with such recommendation." The factors identified in that list are very similar to those identified in SATMR. This is a common condition in regulatory language. Often, the authors of an NAIC rule will adopt the language of rules previously issued by other regulatory authorities such as FINRA.

FINRA Rule 2330

The current FINRA suitability rule applicable to deferred variable annuities "to recommended purchases and exchanges of deferred variable annuities and recommended initial subaccount allocations," is FINRA rule 2330, modeled after NASD rule 2821. It provides that:

"No member or person associated with a member shall recommend to any customer the purchase or exchange of a deferred variable annuity unless such member or person associated with a member has a reasonable basis to believe

(A) that the transaction is suitable in accordance with NASD Rule 2310 and, in particular, that there is a reasonable basis to believe that

(i)   the customer has been informed, in general terms, of various features of deferred variable annuities, such as the potential surrender period and surrender charge; potential tax penalty if customers sell or redeem deferred variable annuities before reaching the age of 59½; mortality and expense fees; investment advisory fees; potential charges for and features of riders; the insurance and investment components of deferred variable annuities; and market risk;

(ii) the customer would benefit from certain features of deferred variable annuities, such as tax-deferred growth, annuitization, or a death or living benefit; and

(iii) the particular deferred variable annuity as a whole, the underlying subaccounts to which funds are allocated at the time of the purchase or exchange of the deferred variable annuity, and riders and similar product enhancements, if any, are suitable (and, in the case of an exchange, the transaction as a whole also is suitable) for the particular customer based on the information required by paragraph (b)(2) of this Rule; and

(B) in the case of an exchange of a deferred variable annuity, the exchange also is consistent with the suitability determination required by paragraph (b)(1)(A) of this Rule, taking into consideration whether

(i)   the customer would incur a surrender charge, be subject to commencement of a new surrender period, lose existing benefits (such as death, living, or other contractual benefits), or be subject to increased fees or charges (such as mortality and expense fees, investment advisory fees, or charges for riders and similar product enhancements);

(ii) the customer would benefit from product enhancements and improvements; and

(iii) the customer has had another deferred variable annuity exchange within the preceding 36 months.[6"]

Like the NAIC's "Suitability in Annuities Transactions Model Regulation" of 2010 (SATMR), FINRA Rule 2330 provides guidance as to the factors that should be considered before the recommendation of an annuity. Indeed, the factors that it cites are virtually identical to those cited in SATMR, which took them from the earlier NASD Rule 2821. Rule 2330's text states that:

"Prior to recommending the purchase or exchange of a deferred variable annuity, a member or person associated with a member shall make reasonable efforts to obtain, at a minimum, information concerning the customer's age, annual income, financial situation and needs, investment experience, investment objectives, intended use of the deferred variable annuity, investment time horizon, existing assets (including investment and life insurance holdings), liquidity needs, liquid net worth, risk tolerance, tax status, and such other information used or considered to be reasonable by the member or person associated with the member in making recommendations to customers."

Notwithstanding the similarity of language in FINRA rule 2330 and SATMR, the regulatory implications are very different. SATMR applies, in those states which have adopted it, to the sale of all annuities, while the FINRA rule applies only to the sale of variable contracts. As we shall see, however, Sect.989J of Dodd-Frank will apply the suitability rules of SATMR, including these suitability factors, to the sale not only of all annuity contracts, but, perhaps, to the sale of insurance products other than annuities.

The reader will have noted, by this point, that there are a lot of rules, from different agencies, at different jurisdictional levels, governing the sale of an annuity, and he or she might well be asking "which ones affect me? Do I have to comply with all of them?" The answer is "if you're a registered representative selling a variable annuity, you're subject to all of them." Why? Because, as an insurance agent selling an annuity, you are subject to state rules governing annuity sales, and, as a registered rep selling a registered product, you're subject to FINRA rules, and any additional rules that may be imposed by your State Department of Securities. A more practical answer might be "observe all the rules, even those that may not apply to you right now, just to be safe."

As the 12 suitability factors cited in SATMR and FINRA Rule 2330 and, as we shall see, incorporated by reference into Section 989J of Dodd-Frank, must be considered by any advisor prior to recommending an annuity, we will now look at each of these factors in more detail.

The Twelve Suitability Factors of SATMR / FINRA Rule 2330 In Detail.

1. Age. The age of the buyer of an annuity is an extremely important factor in any determination of whether that annuity is suitable. In the case of an immediate annuity payable for life, the age of the annuitant will determine the amount of each annuity payment. If the proposed annuitant is not in good health or if his or her family health history suggests a shorter than average life expectancy, the advisor should question whether a nonunderwritten life annuity is appropriate. For such an applicant, a fully-underwritten annuity—where the amount of annuity payments would take into account the annuitant's health status—might offer a substantially greater benefit than a nonunderwritten contract.

If the contract being proposed is a deferred annuity, the age of the prospective owner and of the prospective annuitant, if different, are relevant factors. Many insurers will not issue a deferred annuity contract if the proposed annuitant is older than a certain age, which, in the authors' experience, accounts for many contracts where the annuitant and owner are different individuals. As was noted in Chapter 2, this can create problems.

Even where the prospective owner and annuitant are the same individual, the age of that person is relevant to the suitability of a deferred annuity. The NAIC and insurance regulators of many states have issued consumer alerts, warning seniors of deceptive sales practices, and, in many states, special suitability requirements apply when the applicant of a deferred annuity is a senior citizen. That said, no state regulation of which the authors are aware states that an annuity is inappropriate merely because the prospective buyer has reached a certain age.

Where the proposed deferred annuity includes either a guaranteed minimum death benefit or a living benefit rider, the age of the owner and/or annuitant often determines the availability or the terms of that benefit.

2. Annual Income. The annual income of the buyer of an annuity is relevant to the suitability of that contract for several reasons. If the contract is a flexible premium one, contemplating ongoing contributions, the applicant should be able to make those contributions.

3. Financial Situation and Needs, Including the Financial Resources Used for the Funding of the Annuity. An annuity is a tool designed to meet specific financial needs; therefore, the nature and extent of those needs are relevant to the annuity's suitability to do the job. Moreover, the source of funds is of particular concern when securities are involved. The agent recommending the annuity must be appropriately licensed, not only for the annuity contract being proposed, but also for securities, if the source of funds for the annuity is securities and if he or she is recommending that those securities be sold to fund the annuity.

It is widely believed that if the source of funds includes securities, that anyone recommending an annuity must necessarily be registered to sell the type of securities involved. Sources such as the *Joint Bulletin No. 14-2009* issued by the Arkansas Insurance and Securities departments in September, 2009, are often cited to support this position. However, a close reading of the ruling in question may indicate otherwise. For example, the Arkansas ruling states:

> "The recommendation to replace securities such as mutual funds, stocks, bonds and various other investment vehicles defined as securities under the Arkansas Securities Act is the offering of investment advice. It is unlawful to offer investment advice unless one is registered (licensed) with the Arkansas Securities Department as an investment adviser or investment adviser representative."

This does not say that the proceeds of the sale of securities may never be used to purchase an annuity unless the agent recommending that annuity is securities registered. It says only that the agent may not recommend such liquidation without being registered as an investment advisor, or investment advisor representative. Even a Series 6 or Series 7 registration would not suffice in Arkansas because the regulators in that state have defined a recommendation to replace securities as the rendering of investment advice. In another state, that same recommendation might be considered to fall within the solely incidental exception of Sect. 202(a)(11)(C) of the Investment Advisers Act of 1940. Generally, however, an advisor recommending a nonvariable annuity, to be funded with the proceeds of securities sales, must be registered to sell the type of securities involved, but need not be securities registered if he or she does not actually recommend the sale of securities to purchase the annuity. But this may not be a reliable safe harbor. Can an advisor whose client purchased the annuity he recommended with funds from securities sales rely upon the defense that "I did not know where the money was coming from"? If he or she is obliged to consider "Financial Situation and Needs, Including the Financial Resources Used for the Funding of the Annuity", and SATMR imposes that obligation, the answer would appear to be a flat "no", absent evidence that the client deliberately misled the advisor as to the source of funds.

4. Financial Experience. The financial experience of a consumer is important, especially if the financial product being recommended is complicated or appropriate only for sophisticated buyers. A complaint often made by plaintiffs in annuity-related litigations, is "I did not understand what I was buying." The more complicated the annuity, the more likely this complaint—or, at the least, the more reasonable it may sound to a jury or arbitrator.

5. Financial Objectives. As the authors have noted earlier, an annuity is just a tool. Any assessment of its suitability must necessarily consider the job to be done. It is vital that everyone involved in the sale of an annuity; the applicant, the recommending advisor, and the insurance company issuing the annuity— understand what financial objectives that annuity is being purchased to achieve. In the authors' opinion, it is probably impossible to over-emphasize the importance of this factor or to over-document its consideration. A thorough documentation of why the annuity is, in the opinion of the advisor, the right tool for the job can be invaluable to the defendant in litigation alleging a bad sale. More importantly, it may prevent that litigation by ensuring both that the consumer buys the right product and that he or she understands as much.

6. Intended Use of the Annuity. This is a variation on the theme addressed by factor #5, focusing less on, "is the annuity the right tool for the job?" and more on, "how will that tool be used to do the job?". Consideration of this factor can produce useful, and possibly unexpected, results. For example, if the proposed annuity includes a guaranteed minimum death benefit and the purchaser shows a special interest in this feature, a discussion of life insurance, which is usually a more efficient delivery instrument for death benefits than an annuity, may be in order.

7. Financial Time Horizon. Time horizon can be a confusing term. It can be used to mean the maximum period during which this investment will be held. It can also be used to mean the number of years before which distributions, or income, are expected to be needed. Both are relevant to a proper determination of suitability, and the authors suggest that the advisor and consumer understand how long the annuity will be held, which is particularly important when surrender charges are considered, and over what period of time distributions—whether in the form of withdrawals or regular annuity payments—will be made.

8. Existing Assets, Including Investment and Life Insurance Holdings. Existing assets are important, not only because they are part of that client's financial situation (Factor #3), but because the nature and extent of those assets will help the advisor to determine the extent to which the financial objectives, identified in Concern #5, are likely to be met. A review of existing assets can also help the advisor assess the accuracy of the client's responses to the advisor's questions regarding the other suitability factors. For example, a client claiming to have extensive financial experience and sophistication and a great desire for tax-favored treatment of his investments, yet who holds only certificates of deposit, may not understand the extent to which the expressed concerns are inconsistent with his prior financial decisions and current holdings.

9. Liquidity Needs. The liquidity of an asset refers to how quickly and cheaply it can be converted to cash. While a deferred annuity that imposes surrender charges (as most do) can be surrendered for cash relatively quickly, the cash received might, because of those charges, be significantly less than the annuity's value just prior to surrender. In a few index annuities, surrender charges never expire, and may even apply to death proceeds taken in a lump sum; those annuities may be considered relatively illiquid. That does not necessarily make them unsuitable, as long as the annuity purchaser is comfortable that the illiquidity is still reasonable, given his or her goals. On the other hand, it's important to note that even those contracts whose charges do expire after a term of years may have a high cost for early liquidity during that surrender charge period, especially in the early years of that period.

10. Liquid Net Worth. After learning the liquid net worth of the annuity applicant, the advisor can compare that figure with the applicant's liquidity needs. If it appears that the liquid net worth is not sufficient to meet the liquidity needs during the surrender charge period, the advisor may wish to recommend that some of the funds being considered for investment in the annuity be placed in a highly liquid account to meet that potential shortfall.

11. Risk tolerance. Risk tolerance is an essential factor in the determination of the suitability of an annuity because annuities are risk management instruments. Unfortunately, this simple fact is not widely, or well understood by many financial advisors and, sad to say, regulators. Moreover, the very notion of risk is largely misunderstood and, often, misapplied.

What is risk? Textbooks in Finance tell us that there are many different kids of risk, including market risk, interest rate risk, inflation risk, currency risk, credit risk, liquidity risk, etc. Yet many risk tolerance questionnaires used by financial advisors—and often required by insurers and/or broker/dealers to be completed prior to the sale of an annuity, especially a variable annuity—focus only on one of these: market risk, which is commonly defined in either of two very different ways.

One definition says that market risk is "the risk that market pressures may cause the value of an investment to fluctuate." In that sense, market risk means volatility. Another, equally widely-held, says that market risk is the possibility that market pressures will cause the value of an investment to decline. In that sense, market risk equals principal risk. Both involve uncertainty—which, the authors believe, is the central element of risk—as to the future value of one's capital.

Certainly, that's an important consideration to any investor; but it's not all-important. The widespread use of risk tolerance assessment tools, such as a questionnaire, that identifies risk only as the possibility of losing one's capital, or principal, focuses attention only on the capital preservation and wealth accumulation potential of the product being considered, concerning which tool is employed.

That can be a problem when one is assessing the suitability of an annuity because the risk that is of greatest concern to a prospective annuity purchaser may not be "that I might lose some principal" but, rather, that "I might run out of income". Moreover, principal risk is never a factor in an immediate annuity, because an immediate annuity is an income stream, and has no principal. It may not be a factor when the product proposed is a fixed deferred annuity, because all fixed deferred annuities guarantee principal, except to the extent that surrender charges or a market value adjustment may erode principal if the contract is surrendered early. Indeed, principal risk may not be a great concern even when the proposed product is a variable deferred annuity if a guaranteed living benefit has been chosen because the income guaranteed with such benefits is often immune to adverse market performance.

The authors do not suggest that market risk should not be a concern in determining the suitability of any proposed investment, including an annuity, but only that many risk tolerance measurement tools focus only on market risk—and, in doing so, marginalize, or ignore completely, the applicant's tolerance for other risks that may be of far greater concern. We believe that any discussion of risk tolerance should be informed by the applicant's responses to the other eleven factors in this list, and by the advisor's understanding of the client's total picture.

12. Tax Status. The tax status of the applicant for an annuity is obviously important because annuities receive special tax treatment. The tax deferral that is enjoyed by a deferred annuity comes with a cost, orall ordinary income treatment of all distributions and a 10% penalty tax on any distribution not qualifying for an exception under IRC Sect. 72(q)(2). The benefit of such tax deferral is much greater for applicants in high tax brackets than for applicants in very low brackets, for whom the benefit may be outweighed by its cost.

Some Observations on Liquidity and Deferred Annuity Surrender Charges

Surrender charges should always be considered in any recommendation of a deferred annuity. The ethical advisor will always want to ensure that the client fully understands both the benefits and the costs of what he or she is buying, and surrender charges are part of the cost of the contract. They are also the most commonly cited factor in complaints about allegedly improper annuity sales. Complaints to regulators and lawsuits over annuity sales typically allege that the buyer did not understand either the amount of surrender charges or the conditions under which they would be imposed. Of course, those charges are disclosed in every annuity contract and in most point-of-sale brochures. However, such disclosure is not always in the clearest of language. The conditions under which surrender charges will be waived are not always fully explained in product brochures and, indeed, are sometimes difficult to find in the contracts themselves, even for an expert. How might an advisor improve the chances that a buyer truly understands surrender charges—or that he or she can demonstrate to regulators, arbitrators, or a jury that they were fully explained? The authors suggest a few techniques:

- Where the annuity proposed is a variable contract, the advisor can review the sections in the prospectus detailing surrender charges. Of course, he or she should never underline or highlight the prospectus. For nonvariable contracts, the authors strongly recommend that the advisor obtain a specimen contract, which is sometimes also known as a sample contract, of every product he or she intends to recommend and to review the appropriate specimen contract with every applicant, prior to closing the sale. Sadly, many advisers we have spoken with have never obtained, or even seen, a single specimen contract.

- Many insurers and annuity marketing organizations now require the submission of a risk tolerance questionnaire with every application for an annuity. Often, these documents require that the applicant initial those paragraphs explaining surrender charges and other relevant factors. This is an excellent practice, one which the authors strongly commend. If the insurer offering an annuity or the marketing organization through which that annuity will be submitted does not offer such a document, the advisor may wish to create one and submit it, after completion by the client, along with the annuity application.

- When reviewing point-of-sale material with the client, the advisor may wish to ask the client to initial the paragraphs explaining the various features and costs of the product being recommended, on both the copy being left with the client and the copy to be retained, by the advisor, in the client's file.

- The authors strongly believe that any discussion of annuity surrender charges is incomplete without an explanation of why those charges exist. As explained earlier in this book, surrender charges are not entirely a drawback or disadvantage to the client. Clients who understand why surrender charges are imposed, that they are imposed only on those purchasers who surrender annuities before the issuing insurer has had an opportunity to recover its costs, and that, absent those charges, the benefits offered by the annuity would probably be less, are more likely to be satisfied with their purchase and less likely to complain afterwards.

- The authors believe that many annuity complaints could be avoided if the advisor, prior to closing the sale, tests the willingness of the client to pay surrender charges. This might be accomplished by asking the applicant "is there any chance at all that you'll need access to the funds you're considering putting into this annuity during the next N years (where N = the surrender charge period), given the fact that you have access to the other liquid funds you've told me about? If the answer is "yes", the advisor should not recommend funding the annuity with the amount originally contemplated, but recommend that a portion of that money be allocated to a liquid account (e.g., a money market, checking, or savings account). That done, the process should be repeated— and again, if necessary—until the purchaser's response is "no". At that point, the advisor could ask "so you're telling me that you're comfortable locking up this amount of money in this annuity for N years in order to obtain the benefits we've discussed?"

Some advisors might object that this technique ignores the fact that most deferred annuities permit penalty-free withdrawals of up to a certain amount of percentage of the annuity value during the surrender charge period and withdrawals in excess of those amounts under certain conditions, such as nursing home confinement. That is true. But how many purchasers, told of a 10% free withdrawal privilege, can be sure that they won't need, say, 15%? In the authors' opinion, beginning the discussion of surrender charges by verifying that the purchaser has liquid funds sufficient to pay for emergencies or unexpected expenses during the entire surrender charge period, and then, and only then, reviewing the free withdrawal provisions will go a long way toward ensuring that the annuity is suitable from a liquidity perspective.

Continuing our discussion of FINRA Rule 2330, it should be noted that many annuity contracts, both variable and nonvariable, are sold through broker-dealers, some of which require their registered representatives to submit even nonvariable contracts through them. As the suitability rules for variable annuities are not identical to those imposed by the NAIC and state insurance regulators upon sales of nonvariable annuities, inconsistencies can occur. This issue is addressed in SATMR. Section 6H of that regulation, the so-called safe harbor, as the Executive Summary states, is:

"… intended to prevent duplicative suitability standards being applied to sales of annuities through FINRA broker-dealers. Sales of insurance products which are securities under federal law, such as variable annuities, are required to meet FINRA suitability rules, and sales in compliance with FINRA rules would comply with NAIC suitability regulation. Broker-Dealers may subject fixed annuity sales to FINRA suitability and supervision rules, and sales made in compliance with such rules would also qualify as complying with the NAIC suitability regulation. However, since FINRA does not have authority to enforce its rules on the sale of fixed annuities, broker-dealers supervising fixed annuity sales may be subject to more intensive insurance examination than for sale of security insurance products. Representatives of a broker-dealer, who are not required by the broker-dealer to comply with the FINRA requirements on the sale of fixed annuities, will have to comply with the insurance suitability regulation adopted by the state. In any case, insurers are responsible for any unsuitable annuity transactions no matter what suitability regulation or rule is applied by a broker-dealer."

Rules Dealing with Annuities that May Be Securities

Variable annuities are securities. Declared rate fixed annuities are not, at least under current rules. The status of index annuities is less clear. Despite the fact that index annuities share the common defining characteristics of fixed annuities—a guarantee of principal and a minimum rate of interest—the SEC published, in 2008, Rule 151A, which declared these contracts to be securities, subject to its jurisdiction. The rule was successfully challenged and vacated [7] on a technicality; the SEC subsequently withdrew Rule 151A. While many believed, even after those events, that index annuities were still, properly speaking, securities, a position still held by many thoughtful observers, the issue was arguably put to rest by Sect. 989J of the Dodd-Frank financial reform act of 2010.

Section 989J of Dodd-Frank: The Federal Extension
of NAIC Rules for Annuity Transactions to
Transactions Involving Annuity and Insurance Products

The language of this section often known as the Harkin amendment after the Senator who proposed it—was designed to keep regulation of indexed annuities with the states and not with the SEC. Interestingly, it did so by making such exemption from SEC jurisdiction contingent upon compliance with a new test of suitability.

To qualify for the Sect. 3(a)(8) exemption of the 1933 Act, any insurance or annuity contract must either:

a. [Sect. 989J(a)(3)(A)] if issued on or after June 16, 2013, be issued in a state, or by an insurer domiciled in a state, that has adopted suitability rules governing sale of such policies that substantially meet or exceed the minimum requirements of the NAIC Suitability in Annuity Transactions Model Reg #275, adopted in March, 2010 (SATMR) and any further successions thereto within 5 years of the NAIC's adoption of such successors; or

b. be issued by an insurer that has adopted and implemented sales practices on a nationwide scale that substantially meet or exceed those same minimum requirements, including the successors thereto provision. This condition (Sect. 989J(a)(3)(B)) does not specify a date by which it must be met, which could mean the only way in which such an insurance or annuity contract issued prior to 6/16/13 can meet the suitability requirements of Sect. 989J would be if the issuing insurer had adopted and implemented sales practices meeting those requirements prior to such issue—even if the state in which the contract is issued had already adopted suitability rules satisfying those same requirements.[8]

There are many uncertainties connected with Sect. 989J, including:

• Must the insurance comply with SATMR for all its products, or only the products seeking to rely on the safe harbor of Sect. N989J?

• Must all elements of SATMR be met in all states in which the product is offered, even in those states that have not adopted that Model Regulation?

These questions and others await clarification from the SEC. For the advisor who recommends or gives advice about annuities, however, no clarification is needed; compliance with the suitability rules of SATMR is clearly the best course of action for at least two reasons. First, because many states have already adopted rules at least as stringent as those of SATMR and it's a very safe bet that all states will do so within a fairly short time. Second, because it's both ethically and practically the right thing to do.

The Neasham Case

On December 8, 2010, Glenn Neasham, a California insurance agent, was charged with a criminal offense by the prosecuting attorney of Lake County, California. The charge alleged that Neasham had, in selling an index annuity to Fran Schuber, an 83-year-old woman, engaged in felony theft from a senior. On October 21, 2011, a jury found Mr. Neasham guilty. Since the announcement of the verdict, the Neasham case has been the subject of daily discussion in the financial services industry. While the authors believe that there is much to criticize in the handling of this affair by the California Department of Insurance and the Lake County California prosecutor's office, we are not attorneys and it is not the business of this book to dissect the court's decision after the fact. That said, we believe that this case presents issues that affect everyone who may become involved in the recommendation of an annuity contract. We will look now at some of those issues.

- The Neasham case involved the sale of a deferred annuity to an aged person who, it was alleged, suffered from cognitive impairment at the time of the sale. The California Department of Insurance determined, in its investigation in 2009–2010, that Ms. Schuber "lacked the mental capacity to enter into this contract and that the terms and conditions of the annuity contract were not in her best financial interest." [9]

- The Lake County prosecutor argued, at Mr. Neasham's trial, that Mr. Neasham should have known of this alleged cognitive impairment at the time he presented the annuity proposal.

That argument, and the fact that it was successful in the Neasham case, should raise concerns for any advisor involved in the sale or recommendation of an annuity. What obligation does an advisor have in this situation? Few, if any, states have enacted statutes that specifically identify an agent's duty to assess the mental competence of a prospective buyer, or how he or she should do so. The charge that a reasonable person, in the agent's position, should have known of an applicant's impaired mental state begs the question of how. Cognitive impairment is not always easy to observe, much less to quantify, especially for someone with no training in this area. That said, the authors suggest that a pro-active approach makes good business sense. The advisor should be especially alert to the possibility of mental confusion when dealing with individuals of an advanced age. It may be good practice to address this issue directly with all applicants over a certain age. For example, the advisor might ask such an applicant if he or she has experienced difficulty in reading financial documents or understanding the costs and benefits of investment or insurance products. One technique that the authors believe ought to be used in all presentations is to ask the buyer who has heard an explanation of the proposed product to explain, in her own words, her understanding of its costs and benefits. This may be especially useful if some time has elapsed since that earlier explanation. Other tools and techniques for ascertaining the cognitive state of an individual are available; tests such as the Blessed Orientation-Memory-Concentration Test.[10]

Agents, of course, are not psychologists, but if advisers, including insurance agents, are to be held accountable for judging whether their prospects and clients are mentally competent or not, they should be provided with the tools necessary to make that judgment.

The authors suggest that issuers of financial products, including annuities, consider providing their sales forces who will be selling to the elderly with both assessment tools (point of sale questionnaires, etc.) and the training to use those tools. Alternatively, insurers may decide that the risks of marketing to the elderly outweigh the benefits. Of course, there is considerable profit in selling annuities to senior citizens and the Neasham case may be simply an anomaly that does not justify so drastic a marketing decision. But if it is not; if advisors and the insurers whose products they recommend are likely to be held accountable in both civil and criminal actions for selling products to elderly consumers whose competence is later questioned, one might well ask if such sales are worth pursuing. In a conversation with one of the authors, Dr. Jack Marrion, whose doctoral work was in cognitive biases in decision-making, addressed this very point when he said:

> "According to research conducted by Plassman and others on the prevalence of dementia, one in four people in their 80s (ages 80-89) have dementia. This raises the question as to whether agents should accept any annuity buyers over age 80. It is unfair to place the burden on determining what is acceptable cognitive ability on an agent. If a carrier decides to accept annuity buyers over age 79 perhaps it should be required to conduct appropriate cognitive testing to determine whether the buyer is acceptable."

Both the California Department of Insurance and the Lake County prosecutor argued that the size and duration of surrender charges of the annuity purchased by Ms. Schuber made that contract unsuitable for her. Yet the annuity in question had been approved by the California Department of Insurance for sale to applicants up to age 85 and Ms. Schuber had signed a disclosure of those surrender charges and had not complained about them—or, indeed, made any complaint regarding the annuity to any authority.

What does this suggest that an advisor must do when presenting a contract, especially to a senior citizen, that includes surrender charges? Are a thorough, and documented, discussion of those charges and a signed disclosure sufficient? The authors believe that, in this climate of increasing litigiousness and regulatory scrutiny, they may well not be. We offer the following as suggested practices:

A. Before describing the size and duration of surrender charges, the advisor may wish to explain why such charges exist in the first place. One of the authors uses the following method in his practice:

"Mr. Prospect, you know that insurance companies sell annuities to make a profit. You may not know that any insurer will lose money if the buyer surrenders the annuity before the company has had a chance to recover the costs it incurred in putting that contract in force. Those costs include commissions, of course, but also the costs of issuing and administering the contract and of setting aside the monies required by law to back the guarantees of that contract. Basically, an insurer can recover such costs in only three ways: first, it could assess a front-end sales charge. That is, it could take a percentage of the buyer's investment immediately, and those dollars would never earn interest or be available to the contract owner. Second, it could reduce the interest it would otherwise be able to pay to the buyer each year or assess an annual recovery charge, which amounts to the same thing. Third, it could recognize that the only annuity buyers who would keep it from recovering its acquisition costs are those buyers who surrender their contracts early and charge only those buyers, by imposing a surrender charge. Which method would you want the insurance company to use for your annuity?"

In decades of selling annuities, one of the authors has never had a prospective buyer answer other than "the third one". Once a prospective buyer understands the reason for surrender charges, a discussion of the size and duration of those charges can proceed.

B.   Merely showing a document describing the surrender charge schedule and asking the applicant to sign it offers, in the authors' opinion, no assurance that the buyer truly understands those charges. We suggest that, following that presentation, the advisor ask the client to state what the charges would be in various surrender years. If an illustration showing projected contract values is used, the client could be handed a calculator and asked to compute the dollar value of the surrender charge in those years. The surrender charge could then be compared with the projected contract gain in those same years.

C.   If the annuity being presented is of the bonus type—that is, it offers an initial interest crediting, over and above the anticipated annual interest—it is, in the authors' opinion, utterly essential that the client understand the conditions under which that bonus interest will be available to the client. Is it available only if the contract is annuitized? Is it subject to a vesting schedule? A thorough discussion of these conditions and documentation of the client's understanding of them may take time, but it is in everyone's interest.

D.   If a bonus annuity is being presented, the authors strongly urge that the advisor also show to the client a nonbonus alternative—a contract having as nearly the same features and benefits as the bonus alternative, including, if possible, current interest crediting and, for index annuities, participation rate, cap rate, etc. apart from the surrender charge schedule. A side-by-side comparison should be shown and the client's preference should be documented. We suggest that such a comparison document should include a section with blank lines on which the client should be asked to write, in his or her own words, in his or her own handwriting, the reasons for his/her preference.

The Neasham case involved an elderly client who elected to name, as beneficiary, someone other than a relative. Indeed, this choice of beneficiary was chiefly responsible for the case's being referred to authorities in the first place. The authors suggest that when a client's beneficiary designation is unusual, the prudent advisor will address, with the client, the implications of that designation. This inquiry need not look like an inquisition, nor need the advisor appear to be critical of the client's choice. But some beneficiary designations can present problems. For example, naming a trust as beneficiary may well require a more rapid payout, upon death, than would be required if individuals were named. When a nonfamily member is named, and when the client is elderly, the issue of undue influence may later be raised, as, indeed, it was in the Neasham case.

Suitability is, as we have seen, not a simple matter to determine. Authorities, at various jurisdictional levels, have provided rules and guidelines that the advisor must take into account when making an annuity recommendation. As the Neasham case has demonstrated, adherence to such published rules and guidelines may not be enough. The authors suggest that the prudent advisor will, when making any recommendation for any annuity to any prospective buyer, keep in the back of his or her mind the possibility that his or her words and actions will be later scrutinized in adversarial proceedings.

A Final Note

The issue of suitability, as it applies to the recommendation of annuity products, is a complex one; not only are the rules not entirely consistent from one jurisdiction to another, but the rules of the individual jurisdiction are in almost constant revision, though a few elements will persist.

- The suitability of a particular annuity in a particular situation will always be a matter of facts and circumstances. That said, if the factors cited in SATMR are properly considered by the agent/advisor before recommending an annuity, unsuitability should be minimized, and egregiously unsuitable sales could become a rarity.

- The present suitability standard is almost certain to become more stringent. The current push for harmonization of the two standard of care regimes or for a single fiduciary standard applying to all those who give financial advice will, in the authors' opinion, inevitably produce a standard of care for annuity advisors incorporating elements now confined to the fiduciary standard. Disclosure of commissions will, we believe, probably become obligatory, which should not adversely affect those advisors who are already employing the kind of diligent suitability practices that the regulations we've examined seek to mandate.

- For those advisors who are subject to more than one standard of care (e.g.: registered representatives who are also registered investment advisors or advisory associates), it is possible, if not likely, that they will be held to the highest standard that would apply to them, regardless of the type of case. In other words, a broker who, when selling a fixed annuity is currently held only to the standard of suitability may, if he is also an investment advisor, or associate, be held in future to the fiduciary standard applicable when he acts as an investment advisor, even when he is merely selling product. Broker/Dealers are unlikely to be willing to guess, when overseeing the activities of their representatives, which hat those representatives are wearing in any given interaction with consumers.

Education requirements will continue to stiffen. SATMR requires any agent who sells any annuity to complete at least a four-hour course on annuities. Many Broker/Dealers and insurers also require such training. Given the growing complexity of annuity products and a litigious consumer population, increased competency is both ethically laudable and very good business.

Endnotes

1. NAIC Model Reg. 275.
2. Ibid.
3. Ibid.
4. Ibid.
5. FINRA Reg. Not. 1102.
6. FINRA Rule 2330.
7. *American Equity Investment Life Insurance Co. v. S.E.C. 2009 WL 2152351* (D.C. Cir. July 21, 2009).
8. As the safe harbor language in Sect. 989J(a)(3)(A) - providing that such a contract will be deemed an exempt security if the issuing state has adopted suitability rules consistent with SATMR (and its successors)—refers only to contracts issued on or after 6/16/13, it is arguable that contracts issued earlier cannot claim its protection.
9. CA Dept of Insurance announcement, quoted in senioradvisor.com, December, 2010.
10. See Katzman R, Brown T, Fuld P, et al. Validation of a short orientation- memory-concentration test of cognitive impairment. Am J Psychiatry 1983;140:734-9. Copyright 1983, American Psychiatric Association.

Appendix A

Actuarial Tables for Taxing Annuities

As referenced in various places throughout the text of this publication, the tables used for taxing annuities appear on the following pages. Included here are gender-based Tables I, II, IIA, and III and unisex Tables V, VI, VIA, and VII. The gender-based tables are to be used if the investment in the contract does not include a post-June 30, 1986 investment in the contract. The unisex tables are to be used if the investment in the contract does include a post-June 30, 1986 investment in the contract.

However, even if there is no investment in the contract after June 30, 1986, an annuitant receiving annuity payments after June 30, 1986 (regardless of when they first began) may elect to treat his entire investment in the contract as post-June 30, 1986 and apply Tables V-VII. This election may be made for any taxable year in which such amounts are received by the taxpayer; it is irrevocable and applies with respect to all amounts the taxpayer receives as an annuity under the contract in the taxable year for which the election is made or in any subsequent tax year.

If investment in the contract includes both a pre-July 1986 investment and a post-June 1986 investment, an election may be made to make separate computations with respect to each portion of the aggregate investment in the contract using with respect to each portion the tables applicable to it. The amount excludable is the sum of the amounts determined under the separate computations. However, the election is not available (i.e., the entire investment must be treated as post-June 1986 investment) if the annuity starting date is after June 30, 1986 and the contract provides an option, whether or not it is exercised, to receive amounts under the contract other than in the form of a life annuity (Reg. §1.72-6(d)).

Treasury regulations extend some of the tables to higher and lower ages, but the partial tables contained here are adequate for all practical purposes. The multiples in Tables I, II, and IIA or V, VI, and VIA need not be adjusted for monthly payments. For quarterly, semi-annual or annual payments, they must be adjusted according to the Frequency of Payment Adjustment Table, below. Table III and Table VII multiples, giving the percentage value of refund features, are never adjusted.

All tables are entered with the age of the annuitant at his or her birthday nearest the annuity starting date.

Frequency of Payment Adjustment Table

If the number of whole months from the annuity starting date to the first payment date is	0-1	2	3	4	5	6	7	8	9	10	11	12
And payments under the contract are to be made:												
Annually	+0.5	+0.4	+0.3	+0.2	+0.1	0	0	-0.1	-0.2	-0.3	-0.4	-0.5
Semiannually	+ .2	+ .1	0	0	- .1	- .2	....	....	....	....	....	....
Quarterly	+ .1	0	- .1	....	....	....	....	....	....	....	....	....

Example. Ed Black bought an annuity contract on January 1 which provides him with an annual payment of $4,000 payable on December 31st of each year. His age on birthday nearest the annuity starting date (January 1) is 66. The multiple from Table V for male age 66, is 19.2. This multiple must be adjusted for annual payment by subtracting .5 (19.2 - .5 = 18.7). Thus, his total expected return is $74,800 (18.7 x $4,000). See Treas. Reg. §1.72-5(a)(2).

Table I — Ordinary Life Annuities — One Life — Expected Return Multiples

Male	Ages Female	Multiples	Male	Age Female	Multiples
6	11	65.0	59	64	18.9
7	12	64.1	60	65	18.2
8	13	63.2	61	66	17.5
9	14	62.3	62	67	16.9
10	15	61.4	63	68	16.2
11	16	60.4	64	69	15.6
12	17	59.5	65	70	15.0
13	18	58.6	66	71	14.4
14	19	57.7	67	72	13.8
15	20	56.7	68	73	13.2
16	21	55.8	69	74	12.6
17	22	54.9	70	75	12.1
18	23	53.9	71	76	11.6
19	24	53.0	72	77	11.0
20	25	52.1	73	78	10.5
21	26	51.1	74	79	10.1
22	27	50.2	75	80	9.6
23	28	49.3	76	81	9.1
24	29	48.3	77	82	8.7
25	30	47.4	78	83	8.3
26	31	46.5	79	84	7.8
27	32	45.6	80	85	7.5
28	33	44.6	81	86	7.1
29	34	43.7	82	87	6.7
30	35	42.8	83	88	6.3
31	36	41.9	84	89	6.0
32	37	41.0	85	90	5.7
33	38	40.0	86	91	5.4
34	39	39.1	87	92	5.1
35	40	38.2	88	93	4.8
36	41	37.3	89	94	4.5
37	42	36.5	90	95	4.2
38	43	35.6	91	96	4.0
39	44	34.7	92	97	3.7
40	45	33.8	93	98	3.5
41	46	33.0	94	99	3.3
42	47	32.1	95	100	3.1
43	48	31.2	96	101	2.9
44	49	30.4	97	102	2.7
45	50	29.6	98	103	2.5
46	51	28.7	99	104	2.3
47	52	27.9	100	105	2.1
48	53	27.1	101	106	1.9
49	54	26.3	102	107	1.7
50	55	25.5	103	108	1.5
51	56	24.7	104	109	1.3
52	57	24.0	105	110	1.2
53	58	23.2	106	111	1.0
54	59	22.4	107	112	.8
55	60	21.7	108	113	.7
56	61	21.0	109	114	.6
57	62	20.3	110	115	.5
58	63	19.6	111	116	.0

Table II — Ordinary Joint Life and Last Survivor Annuities — Two Lives — Expected Return Multiples

Male	Ages Male / Female	35 / 40	36 / 41	37 / 42	38 / 43	39 / 44	40 / 45	41 / 46	42 / 47	43 / 48	44 / 49	45 / 50	46 / 51	47 / 52
35	40	46.2	45.7	45.3	44.8	44.4	44.0	43.6	43.3	43.0	42.6	42.3	42.0	41.8
36	41	...	45.2	44.8	44.3	43.9	43.5	43.1	42.7	42.3	42.0	41.7	41.4	41.1
37	42	...	...	44.3	43.8	43.4	42.9	42.5	42.1	41.8	41.4	41.1	40.7	40.4
38	43	...	...	...	43.3	42.9	42.4	42.0	41.6	41.2	40.8	40.5	40.1	39.8
39	44	...	...	...	...	42.4	41.9	41.5	41.0	40.6	40.2	39.9	39.5	39.2
40	45	...	...	...	...	...	41.4	41.0	40.5	40.1	39.7	39.3	38.9	38.6
41	46	...	...	...	...	...	...	40.5	40.0	39.6	39.2	38.8	38.4	38.0
42	47	...	...	...	...	...	...	...	39.6	39.1	38.7	38.2	37.8	37.5
43	48	...	...	...	...	...	...	...	...	38.6	38.2	37.7	37.3	36.9
44	49	...	...	...	...	...	...	...	...	...	37.7	37.2	36.8	36.4
45	50	...	...	...	...	...	...	...	...	...	...	36.8	36.3	35.9
46	51	...	...	...	...	...	...	...	...	...	...	...	35.9	35.4
47	52	...	...	...	...	...	...	...	...	...	...	...	...	35.0

Male	Ages Male / Female	48 / 53	49 / 54	50 / 55	51 / 56	52 / 57	53 / 58	54 / 59	55 / 60	56 / 61	57 / 62	58 / 63	59 / 64	60 / 65
35	40	41.5	41.3	41.0	40.8	40.6	40.4	40.3	40.1	40.0	39.8	39.7	39.6	39.5
36	41	40.8	40.6	40.3	40.1	39.9	39.7	39.5	39.3	39.2	39.0	38.9	38.8	38.6
37	42	40.2	39.9	39.6	39.4	39.2	39.0	38.8	38.6	38.4	38.3	38.1	38.0	37.9
38	43	39.5	39.2	39.0	38.7	38.5	38.3	38.1	37.9	37.7	37.5	37.3	37.2	37.1
39	44	38.9	38.6	38.3	38.0	37.8	37.6	37.3	37.1	36.9	36.8	36.6	36.4	36.3
40	45	38.3	38.0	37.7	37.4	37.1	36.9	36.6	36.4	36.2	36.0	35.9	35.7	35.5
41	46	37.7	37.3	37.0	36.7	36.5	36.2	36.0	35.7	35.5	35.3	35.1	35.0	34.8
42	47	37.1	36.8	36.4	36.1	35.8	35.6	35.3	35.1	34.8	34.6	34.4	34.2	34.1
43	48	36.5	36.2	35.8	35.5	35.2	34.9	34.7	34.4	34.2	33.9	33.7	33.5	33.3
44	49	36.0	35.6	35.3	34.9	34.6	34.3	34.0	33.8	33.5	33.3	33.0	32.8	32.6
45	50	35.5	35.1	34.7	34.4	34.0	33.7	33.4	33.1	32.9	32.6	32.4	32.2	31.9
46	51	35.0	34.6	34.2	33.8	33.5	33.1	32.8	32.5	32.2	32.0	31.7	31.5	31.3
47	52	34.5	34.1	33.7	33.3	32.9	32.6	32.2	31.9	31.6	31.4	31.1	30.9	30.6
48	53	34.0	33.6	33.2	32.8	32.4	32.0	31.7	31.4	31.1	30.8	30.5	30.2	30.0
49	54	...	33.1	32.7	32.3	31.9	31.5	31.2	30.8	30.5	30.2	29.9	29.6	29.4
50	55	...	...	32.3	31.8	31.4	31.0	30.6	30.3	29.9	29.6	29.3	29.0	28.8
51	56	...	...	...	31.4	30.9	30.5	30.1	29.8	29.4	29.1	28.8	28.5	28.2
52	57	...	...	...	...	30.5	30.1	29.7	29.3	28.9	28.6	28.2	27.9	27.6
53	58	...	...	...	...	...	29.6	29.2	28.8	28.4	28.1	27.7	27.4	27.1
54	59	...	...	...	...	...	...	28.8	28.3	27.9	27.6	27.2	26.9	26.5
55	60	...	...	...	...	...	...	...	27.9	27.5	27.1	26.7	26.4	26.0
56	61	...	...	...	...	...	...	...	...	27.1	26.7	26.3	25.9	25.5
57	62	...	...	...	...	...	...	...	...	...	26.2	25.8	25.4	25.1
58	63	...	...	...	...	...	...	...	...	...	...	25.4	25.0	24.6
59	64	...	...	...	...	...	...	...	...	...	...	...	24.6	24.2
60	65	...	...	...	...	...	...	...	...	...	...	...	...	23.8

Table II — Ordinary Joint Life and Last Survivor Annuities — Two Lives —
Expected Return Multiples — Continued

Ages Male / Female		61/66	62/67	63/68	64/69	65/70	66/71	67/72	68/73	69/74	70/75	71/76	72/77	73/78
35 / 40		39.4	39.3	39.2	39.1	39.0	38.9	38.9	38.8	38.8	38.7	38.7	38.6	38.6
36 / 41		38.5	38.4	38.3	38.2	38.2	38.1	38.0	38.0	37.9	37.9	37.8	37.8	37.7
37 / 42		37.7	37.6	37.5	37.4	37.3	37.3	37.2	37.1	37.1	37.0	36.9	36.9	36.9
38 / 43		36.9	36.8	36.7	36.6	36.5	36.4	36.4	36.3	36.2	36.2	36.1	36.0	36.0
39 / 44		36.2	36.0	35.9	35.8	35.7	35.6	35.5	35.5	35.4	35.3	35.3	35.2	35.2
40 / 45		35.4	35.3	35.1	35.0	34.9	34.8	34.7	34.6	34.6	34.5	34.4	34.4	34.3
41 / 46		34.6	34.5	34.4	34.2	34.1	34.0	33.9	33.8	33.8	33.7	33.6	33.5	33.5
42 / 47		33.9	33.7	33.6	33.5	33.4	33.2	33.1	33.0	33.0	32.9	32.8	32.7	32.7
43 / 48		33.2	33.0	32.9	32.7	32.6	32.5	32.4	32.3	32.2	32.1	32.0	31.9	31.9
44 / 49		32.5	32.3	32.1	32.0	31.8	31.7	31.6	31.5	31.4	31.3	31.2	31.1	31.1
45 / 50		31.8	31.6	31.4	31.3	31.1	31.0	30.8	30.7	30.6	30.5	30.4	30.4	30.3
46 / 51		31.1	30.9	30.7	30.5	30.4	30.2	30.1	30.0	29.9	29.8	29.7	29.6	29.5
47 / 52		30.4	30.2	30.0	29.8	29.7	29.5	29.4	29.3	29.1	29.0	28.9	28.8	28.7
48 / 53		29.8	29.5	29.3	29.2	29.0	28.8	28.7	28.5	28.4	28.3	28.2	28.1	28.0
49 / 54		29.1	28.9	28.7	28.5	28.3	28.1	28.0	27.8	27.7	27.6	27.5	27.4	27.3
50 / 55		28.5	28.3	28.1	27.8	27.6	27.5	27.3	27.1	27.0	26.9	26.7	26.6	26.5
51 / 56		27.9	27.7	27.4	27.2	27.0	26.8	26.6	26.5	26.3	26.2	26.0	25.9	25.8
52 / 57		27.3	27.1	26.8	26.6	26.4	26.2	26.0	25.8	25.7	25.5	25.4	25.2	25.1
53 / 58		26.8	26.5	26.2	26.0	25.8	25.6	25.4	25.2	25.0	24.8	24.7	24.6	24.4
54 / 59		26.2	25.9	25.7	25.4	25.2	25.0	24.7	24.6	24.4	24.2	24.0	23.9	23.8
55 / 60		25.7	25.4	25.1	24.9	24.6	24.4	24.1	23.9	23.8	23.6	23.4	23.3	23.1
56 / 61		25.2	24.9	24.6	24.3	24.1	23.8	23.6	23.4	23.2	23.0	22.8	22.6	22.5
57 / 62		24.7	24.4	24.1	23.8	23.5	23.3	23.0	22.8	22.6	22.4	22.2	22.0	21.9
58 / 63		24.3	23.9	23.6	23.3	23.0	22.7	22.5	22.2	22.0	21.8	21.6	21.4	21.3
59 / 64		23.8	23.5	23.1	22.8	22.5	22.2	21.9	21.7	21.5	21.2	21.0	20.9	20.7
60 / 65		23.4	23.0	22.7	22.3	22.0	21.7	21.4	21.2	20.9	20.7	20.5	20.3	20.1
61 / 66		23.0	22.6	22.2	21.9	21.6	21.3	21.0	20.7	20.4	20.2	20.0	19.8	19.6
62 / 67		...	22.2	21.8	21.5	21.1	20.8	20.5	20.2	19.9	19.7	19.5	19.2	19.0
63 / 68		...	...	21.4	21.1	20.7	20.4	20.1	19.8	19.5	19.2	19.0	18.7	18.5
64 / 69		...	...	...	20.7	20.3	20.0	19.6	19.3	19.0	18.7	18.5	18.2	18.0
65 / 70		...	...	...	...	19.9	19.6	19.2	18.9	18.6	18.3	18.0	17.8	17.5
66 / 71		...	...	...	...	...	19.2	18.8	18.5	18.2	17.9	17.6	17.3	17.1
67 / 72		...	...	...	...	...	...	18.5	18.1	17.8	17.5	17.2	16.9	16.7
68 / 73		...	...	...	...	...	...	...	17.8	17.4	17.1	16.8	16.5	16.2
69 / 74		...	...	...	...	...	...	...	...	17.1	16.7	16.4	16.1	15.8
70 / 75		...	...	...	...	...	...	...	...	...	16.4	16.1	15.8	15.5
71 / 76		...	...	...	...	...	...	...	...	...	...	15.7	15.4	15.1
72 / 77		...	...	...	...	...	...	...	...	...	...	...	15.1	14.8
73 / 78		...	...	...	...	...	...	...	...	...	...	...	...	14.4

Ages Male / Female		74/79	75/80	76/81	77/82	78/83	79/84	80/85	81/86	82/87	83/88	84/89	85/90
35 / 40		38.6	38.5	38.5	38.5	38.4	38.4	38.4	38.4	38.4	38.4	38.3	38.3
36 / 41		37.7	37.6	37.6	37.6	37.6	37.6	37.5	37.5	37.5	37.5	37.5	37.4
37 / 42		36.8	36.8	36.7	36.7	36.7	36.7	36.6	36.6	36.6	36.6	36.6	36.6
38 / 43		36.0	35.9	35.9	35.8	35.8	35.8	35.8	35.8	35.7	35.7	35.7	35.7
39 / 44		35.1	35.1	35.0	35.0	35.0	34.9	34.9	34.9	34.9	34.8	34.8	34.8
40 / 45		34.3	34.2	34.2	34.1	34.1	34.1	34.1	34.0	34.0	34.0	34.0	34.0
41 / 46		33.4	33.4	33.3	33.3	33.3	33.2	33.2	33.2	33.2	33.1	33.1	33.1
42 / 47		32.6	32.6	32.5	32.5	32.4	32.4	32.4	32.4	32.3	32.3	32.3	32.3
43 / 48		31.8	31.8	31.7	31.7	31.6	31.6	31.5	31.5	31.5	31.5	31.4	31.4
44 / 49		31.0	30.9	30.9	30.8	30.8	30.8	30.7	30.7	30.7	30.6	30.6	30.6
45 / 50		30.2	30.1	30.1	30.0	30.0	29.9	29.9	29.9	29.8	29.8	29.8	29.8
46 / 51		29.4	29.4	29.3	29.2	29.2	29.2	29.1	29.1	29.0	29.0	29.0	28.9
47 / 52		28.7	28.6	28.5	28.5	28.4	28.4	28.3	28.3	28.2	28.2	28.2	28.1
48 / 53		27.9	27.8	27.8	27.7	27.7	27.6	27.6	27.5	27.5	27.5	27.4	27.4
49 / 54		27.2	27.1	27.0	26.9	26.9	26.8	26.8	26.7	26.7	26.6	26.6	26.6
50 / 55		26.4	26.3	26.3	26.2	26.2	26.1	26.1	26.0	26.0	25.9	25.9	25.8
51 / 56		25.7	25.6	25.5	25.5	25.4	25.3	25.3	25.2	25.2	25.1	25.1	25.0
52 / 57		25.0	24.9	24.8	24.7	24.7	24.6	24.5	24.5	24.4	24.4	24.3	24.3
53 / 58		24.3	24.2	24.1	24.0	23.9	23.9	23.8	23.7	23.7	23.6	23.6	23.5
54 / 59		23.6	23.5	23.4	23.3	23.2	23.2	23.1	23.0	23.0	22.9	22.9	22.8
55 / 60		23.0	22.9	22.8	22.7	22.6	22.5	22.4	22.3	22.3	22.2	22.2	22.1
56 / 61		22.3	22.2	22.1	22.0	21.9	21.8	21.7	21.6	21.6	21.5	21.5	21.4
57 / 62		21.7	21.6	21.5	21.3	21.2	21.1	21.1	21.0	20.9	20.8	20.8	20.7
58 / 63		21.1	21.0	20.8	20.7	20.6	20.5	20.4	20.3	20.2	20.2	20.1	20.0
59 / 64		20.5	20.4	20.2	20.1	20.0	19.9	19.8	19.7	19.6	19.5	19.4	19.4
60 / 65		19.9	19.8	19.6	19.5	19.4	19.3	19.1	19.0	19.0	18.9	18.8	18.7
61 / 66		19.4	19.2	19.1	18.9	18.8	18.7	18.5	18.4	18.3	18.3	18.2	18.1
62 / 67		18.8	18.7	18.5	18.3	18.2	18.1	18.0	17.8	17.7	17.7	17.6	17.5
63 / 68		18.3	18.1	18.0	17.8	17.6	17.5	17.4	17.3	17.2	17.1	17.0	16.9
64 / 69		17.8	17.6	17.4	17.3	17.1	17.0	16.8	16.7	16.6	16.5	16.4	16.3
65 / 70		17.3	17.1	16.9	16.7	16.6	16.4	16.3	16.2	16.0	15.9	15.8	15.8
66 / 71		16.9	16.6	16.4	16.3	16.1	15.9	15.8	15.6	15.5	15.4	15.3	15.2
67 / 72		16.4	16.2	16.0	15.8	15.6	15.4	15.3	15.1	15.0	14.9	14.8	14.7
68 / 73		16.0	15.7	15.5	15.3	15.1	15.0	14.8	14.6	14.5	14.4	14.3	14.2
69 / 74		15.6	15.3	15.1	14.9	14.7	14.5	14.3	14.2	14.0	13.9	13.8	13.7
70 / 75		15.2	14.9	14.7	14.5	14.3	14.1	13.9	13.7	13.6	13.4	13.3	13.2
71 / 76		14.8	14.5	14.3	14.1	13.8	13.6	13.5	13.3	13.1	13.0	12.8	12.7
72 / 77		14.5	14.2	13.9	13.7	13.5	13.2	13.0	12.9	12.7	12.5	12.4	12.3
73 / 78		14.1	13.8	13.6	13.3	13.1	12.9	12.7	12.5	12.3	12.1	12.0	11.8
74 / 79		13.8	13.5	13.2	13.0	12.7	12.5	12.3	12.1	11.9	11.7	11.6	11.4
75 / 80		...	13.2	12.9	12.6	12.4	12.2	11.9	11.7	11.5	11.4	11.2	11.0
76 / 81		...	...	12.6	12.3	12.1	11.8	11.6	11.4	11.2	11.0	10.8	10.7
77 / 82		...	...	...	12.1	11.8	11.5	11.3	11.1	10.8	10.7	10.5	10.3
78 / 83		...	...	...	...	11.5	11.2	11.0	10.7	10.5	10.3	10.1	10.0
79 / 84		...	...	...	...	...	11.0	10.7	10.5	10.2	10.0	9.8	9.6
80 / 85		...	...	...	...	...	...	10.4	10.2	10.0	9.7	9.5	9.3
81 / 86		...	...	...	...	...	...	...	9.9	9.7	9.5	9.3	9.1
82 / 87		...	...	...	...	...	...	...	...	9.4	9.2	9.0	8.8
83 / 88		...	...	...	...	...	...	...	...	...	9.0	8.7	8.5
84 / 89		...	...	...	...	...	...	...	...	...	...	8.5	8.3
85 / 90		...	...	...	...	...	...	...	...	...	...	...	8.1

Table IIA—Annuities for Joint Life Only — Two Lives — Expected Return Multiples

Ages Male	Ages Female	35 40	36 41	37 42	38 43	39 44	40 45	41 46	42 47	43 48	44 49	45 50	46 51	47 52
35	40	30.3	29.9	29.4	29.0	28.5	28.0	27.5	27.0	26.5	26.0	25.5	24.9	24.4
36	41	...	29.5	29.0	28.6	28.2	27.7	27.2	26.7	26.2	25.7	25.2	24.7	24.2
37	42	...	...	28.6	28.2	27.8	27.3	26.9	26.4	25.9	25.5	25.0	24.4	23.9
38	43	...	...	...	27.8	27.4	27.0	26.5	26.1	25.6	25.2	24.7	24.2	23.7
39	44	...	...	...	...	27.0	26.6	26.2	25.8	25.3	24.8	24.4	23.9	23.4
40	45	...	...	...	...	...	26.2	25.8	25.4	25.0	24.5	24.1	23.6	23.1
41	46	...	...	...	...	...	...	25.4	25.0	24.6	24.2	23.8	23.3	22.9
42	47	...	...	...	...	...	...	...	24.6	24.2	23.8	23.4	23.0	22.6
43	48	...	...	...	...	...	...	...	...	23.9	23.5	23.1	22.7	22.2
44	49	...	...	...	...	...	...	...	...	...	23.1	22.7	22.3	21.9
45	50	...	...	...	...	...	...	...	...	...	...	22.4	22.0	21.6
46	51	...	...	...	...	...	...	...	...	...	...	...	21.6	21.2
47	52	...	...	...	...	...	...	...	...	...	...	...	...	20.9

Ages Male	Ages Female	48 53	49 54	50 55	51 56	52 57	53 58	54 59	55 60	56 61	57 62	58 63	59 64	60 65
35	40	23.8	23.3	22.7	22.1	21.6	21.0	20.4	19.8	19.3	18.7	18.1	17.5	17.0
36	41	23.6	23.1	22.5	22.0	21.4	20.8	20.3	19.7	19.1	18.6	18.0	17.4	16.9
37	42	23.4	22.9	22.3	21.8	21.2	20.7	20.1	19.6	19.0	18.4	17.9	17.3	16.7
38	43	23.2	22.6	22.1	21.6	21.1	20.5	20.0	19.4	18.9	18.3	17.8	17.2	16.7
39	44	22.9	22.4	21.9	21.4	20.9	20.3	19.8	19.3	18.7	18.2	17.7	17.1	16.6
40	45	22.7	22.2	21.7	21.2	20.7	20.1	19.6	19.1	18.6	18.0	17.5	17.0	16.5
41	46	22.4	21.9	21.4	20.9	20.4	19.9	19.4	18.9	18.4	17.9	17.4	16.9	16.3
42	47	22.1	21.6	21.2	20.7	20.2	19.7	19.2	18.7	18.2	17.7	17.2	16.7	16.2
43	48	21.8	21.4	20.9	20.5	20.0	19.5	19.0	18.6	18.1	17.6	17.1	16.6	16.1
44	49	21.5	21.1	20.6	20.2	19.8	19.3	18.8	18.4	17.9	17.4	16.9	16.4	15.9
45	50	21.2	20.8	20.4	19.9	19.5	19.1	18.6	18.1	17.7	17.2	16.7	16.3	15.8
46	51	20.9	20.5	20.1	19.7	19.2	18.8	18.4	17.9	17.5	17.0	16.6	16.1	15.6
47	52	20.5	20.1	19.8	19.4	19.0	18.5	18.1	17.7	17.3	16.8	16.4	15.9	15.5
48	53	20.2	19.8	19.4	19.1	18.7	18.3	17.9	17.5	17.0	16.6	16.2	15.7	15.3
49	54	...	19.5	19.1	18.8	18.4	18.0	17.6	17.2	16.8	16.4	16.0	15.5	15.1
50	55	...	...	18.8	18.4	18.1	17.7	17.3	16.9	16.6	16.2	15.8	15.3	14.9
51	56	...	...	...	18.1	17.8	17.4	17.0	16.7	16.3	15.9	15.5	15.1	14.7
52	57	...	...	...	...	17.4	17.1	16.8	16.4	16.0	15.7	15.3	14.9	14.5
53	58	...	...	...	...	...	16.8	16.4	16.1	15.8	15.4	15.1	14.7	14.3
54	59	...	...	...	...	...	...	16.1	15.8	15.5	15.1	14.8	14.4	14.1
55	60	...	...	...	...	...	...	...	15.5	15.2	14.9	14.5	14.2	13.9
56	61	...	...	...	...	...	...	...	...	14.9	14.6	14.3	13.9	13.6
57	62	...	...	...	...	...	...	...	...	...	14.3	14.0	13.7	13.4
58	63	...	...	...	...	...	...	...	...	...	...	13.7	13.4	13.1
59	64	...	...	...	...	...	...	...	...	...	...	...	13.1	12.8
60	65	...	...	...	...	...	...	...	...	...	...	...	...	12.6

Ages Male	Ages Female	61 66	62 67	63 68	64 69	65 70	66 71	67 72	68 73	69 74	70 75	71 76	72 77	73 78
35	40	16.4	15.8	15.3	14.7	14.2	13.7	13.1	12.6	12.1	11.6	11.1	10.7	10.2
36	41	16.3	15.8	15.2	14.7	14.1	13.6	13.1	12.6	12.1	11.6	11.1	10.6	10.2
37	42	16.2	15.7	15.1	14.6	14.1	13.6	13.0	12.5	12.0	11.5	11.1	10.6	10.1
38	43	16.1	15.6	15.1	14.5	14.0	13.5	13.0	12.5	12.0	11.5	11.0	10.6	10.1
39	44	16.0	15.5	15.0	14.5	13.9	13.4	12.9	12.4	11.9	11.5	11.0	10.5	10.1
40	45	15.9	15.4	14.9	14.4	13.9	13.4	12.9	12.4	11.9	11.4	11.0	10.5	10.0
41	46	15.8	15.3	14.8	14.3	13.8	13.3	12.8	12.3	11.8	11.4	10.9	10.5	10.0
42	47	15.7	15.2	14.7	14.2	13.7	13.2	12.7	12.3	11.8	11.3	10.9	10.4	10.0
43	48	15.6	15.1	14.6	14.1	13.6	13.1	12.7	12.2	11.7	11.3	10.8	10.4	9.9
44	49	15.5	15.0	14.5	14.0	13.5	13.1	12.6	12.1	11.7	11.2	10.8	10.3	9.9
45	50	15.3	14.8	14.4	13.9	13.4	13.0	12.5	12.0	11.6	11.1	10.7	10.3	9.8
46	51	15.2	14.7	14.2	13.8	13.3	12.9	12.4	12.0	11.5	11.1	10.6	10.2	9.8
47	52	15.0	14.6	14.1	13.7	13.2	12.8	12.3	11.9	11.4	11.0	10.6	10.1	9.7
48	53	14.9	14.4	14.0	13.5	13.1	12.6	12.2	11.8	11.3	10.9	10.5	10.1	9.7
49	54	14.7	14.3	13.8	13.4	13.0	12.5	12.1	11.7	11.3	10.8	10.4	10.0	9.6
50	55	14.5	14.1	13.7	13.3	12.8	12.4	12.0	11.6	11.2	10.7	10.3	9.9	9.5
51	56	14.3	13.9	13.5	13.1	12.7	12.3	11.9	11.5	11.1	10.7	10.3	9.9	9.5
52	57	14.1	13.7	13.3	12.9	12.5	12.1	11.7	11.3	10.9	10.6	10.2	9.8	9.4
53	58	13.9	13.6	13.2	12.8	12.4	12.0	11.6	11.2	10.8	10.5	10.1	9.7	9.3
54	59	13.7	13.4	13.0	12.6	12.2	11.9	11.5	11.1	10.7	10.3	10.0	9.6	9.2
55	60	13.5	13.2	12.8	12.4	12.1	11.7	11.3	11.0	10.6	10.2	9.9	9.5	9.1
56	61	13.3	12.9	12.6	12.2	11.9	11.5	11.2	10.8	10.5	10.1	9.8	9.4	9.0
57	62	13.0	12.7	12.4	12.1	11.7	11.4	11.0	10.7	10.3	10.0	9.6	9.3	8.9
58	63	12.8	12.5	12.2	11.8	11.5	11.2	10.9	10.5	10.2	9.8	9.5	9.2	8.8
59	64	12.6	12.3	11.9	11.6	11.3	11.0	10.7	10.4	10.0	9.7	9.4	9.1	8.7
60	65	12.3	12.0	11.7	11.4	11.1	10.8	10.5	10.2	9.9	9.6	9.3	8.9	8.6
61	66	12.0	11.8	11.5	11.2	10.9	10.6	10.3	10.0	9.7	9.4	9.1	8.8	8.5
62	67	...	11.5	11.2	11.0	10.7	10.4	10.1	9.8	9.6	9.3	9.0	8.7	8.4
63	68	...	...	11.0	10.7	10.5	10.2	9.9	9.7	9.4	9.1	8.8	8.5	8.2
64	69	...	...	...	10.5	10.2	10.0	9.7	9.5	9.2	8.9	8.7	8.4	8.1
65	70	...	...	...	...	10.0	9.8	9.5	9.3	9.0	8.8	8.5	8.2	8.0
66	71	...	...	...	...	...	9.5	9.3	9.1	8.8	8.6	8.3	8.1	7.8
67	72	...	...	...	...	...	...	9.1	8.9	8.6	8.4	8.1	7.9	7.7
68	73	...	...	...	...	...	...	...	8.6	8.4	8.2	8.0	7.7	7.5
69	74	...	...	...	...	...	...	...	...	8.2	8.0	7.8	7.6	7.3
70	75	...	...	...	...	...	...	...	...	...	7.8	7.6	7.4	7.2
71	76	...	...	...	...	...	...	...	...	...	...	7.4	7.2	7.0
72	77	...	...	...	...	...	...	...	...	...	...	...	7.0	6.8
73	78	...	...	...	...	...	...	...	...	...	...	...	...	6.7

Table IIA — Annuities for Joint Life Only — Two Lives —
Expected Return Multiples — Continued

Ages Male	Male Female		74 79	75 80	76 81	77 82	78 83	79 84	80 85	81 86	82 87	83 88	84 89	85 90	86 91
35	40	....	9.7	9.3	8.9	8.5	8.1	7.7	7.3	6.9	6.6	6.2	5.9	5.6	5.3
36	41	....	9.7	9.3	8.9	8.4	8.0	7.7	7.3	6.9	6.6	6.2	5.9	5.6	5.3
37	42	....	9.7	9.3	8.8	8.4	8.0	7.6	7.3	6.9	6.5	6.2	5.9	5.6	5.3
38	43	....	9.7	9.2	8.8	8.4	8.0	7.6	7.2	6.9	6.5	6.2	5.9	5.6	5.3
39	44	....	9.6	9.2	8.8	8.4	8.0	7.6	7.2	6.9	6.5	6.2	5.9	5.6	5.3
40	45	....	9.6	9.2	8.8	8.4	8.0	7.6	7.2	6.9	6.5	6.2	5.9	5.5	5.2
41	46	....	9.6	9.2	8.7	8.3	7.9	7.6	7.2	6.8	6.5	6.2	5.8	5.5	5.2
42	47	....	9.5	9.1	8.7	8.3	7.9	7.5	7.2	6.8	6.5	6.2	5.8	5.5	5.2
43	48	....	9.5	9.1	8.7	8.3	7.9	7.5	7.2	6.8	6.5	6.1	5.8	5.5	5.2
44	49	....	9.5	9.0	8.6	8.2	7.9	7.5	7.1	6.8	6.4	6.1	5.8	5.5	5.2
45	50	....	9.4	9.0	8.6	8.2	7.8	7.5	7.1	6.8	6.4	6.1	5.8	5.5	5.2
46	51	....	9.4	9.0	8.6	8.2	7.8	7.4	7.1	6.7	6.4	6.1	5.8	5.5	5.2
47	52	....	9.3	8.9	8.5	8.1	7.8	7.4	7.1	6.7	6.4	6.1	5.8	5.5	5.2
48	53	....	9.3	8.9	8.5	8.1	7.7	7.4	7.0	6.7	6.4	6.0	5.7	5.4	5.1
49	54	....	9.2	8.8	8.4	8.1	7.7	7.3	7.0	6.7	6.3	6.0	5.7	5.4	5.1
50	55	....	9.1	8.8	8.4	8.0	7.7	7.3	7.0	6.6	6.3	6.0	5.7	5.4	5.1
51	56	....	9.1	8.7	8.3	8.0	7.6	7.3	6.9	6.6	6.3	6.0	5.7	5.4	5.1
52	57	....	9.0	8.6	8.3	7.9	7.6	7.2	6.9	6.6	6.2	5.9	5.6	5.4	5.1
53	58	....	8.9	8.6	8.2	7.9	7.5	7.2	6.9	6.5	6.2	5.9	5.6	5.3	5.1
54	59	....	8.9	8.5	8.2	7.8	7.5	7.1	6.8	6.5	6.2	5.9	5.6	5.3	5.0
55	60	....	8.8	8.4	8.1	7.7	7.4	7.1	6.8	6.4	6.1	5.8	5.6	5.3	5.0
56	61	....	8.7	8.4	8.0	7.7	7.3	7.0	6.7	6.4	6.1	5.8	5.5	5.3	5.0
57	62	....	8.6	8.3	7.9	7.6	7.3	7.0	6.7	6.4	6.1	5.8	5.5	5.2	5.0
58	63	....	8.5	8.2	7.9	7.5	7.2	6.9	6.6	6.3	6.0	5.7	5.5	5.2	4.9
59	64	....	8.4	8.1	7.8	7.5	7.1	6.8	6.5	6.3	6.0	5.7	5.4	5.2	4.9
60	65	....	8.3	8.0	7.7	7.4	7.1	6.8	6.5	6.2	5.9	5.6	5.4	5.1	4.9
61	66	....	8.2	7.9	7.6	7.3	7.0	6.7	6.4	6.1	5.9	5.6	5.3	5.1	4.8
62	67	....	8.1	7.8	7.5	7.2	6.9	6.6	6.4	6.1	5.8	5.5	5.3	5.0	4.8
63	68	....	8.0	7.7	7.4	7.1	6.8	6.6	6.3	6.0	5.7	5.5	5.2	5.0	4.7
64	69	....	7.8	7.6	7.3	7.0	6.7	6.5	6.2	5.9	5.7	5.4	5.2	4.9	4.7
65	70	....	7.7	7.4	7.2	6.9	6.6	6.4	6.1	5.9	5.6	5.4	5.1	4.9	4.7
66	71	....	7.6	7.3	7.1	6.8	6.5	6.3	6.0	5.8	5.5	5.3	5.1	4.8	4.6
67	72	....	7.4	7.2	6.9	6.7	6.4	6.2	6.0	5.7	5.5	5.2	5.0	4.8	4.6
68	73	....	7.3	7.0	6.8	6.6	6.3	6.1	5.9	5.6	5.4	5.2	4.9	4.7	4.5
69	74	....	7.1	6.9	6.7	6.4	6.2	6.0	5.8	5.5	5.3	5.1	4.9	4.7	4.5
70	75	....	7.0	6.8	6.5	6.3	6.1	5.9	5.7	5.4	5.2	5.0	4.8	4.6	4.4
71	76	....	6.8	6.6	6.4	6.2	6.0	5.8	5.6	5.3	5.1	4.9	4.7	4.5	4.3
72	77	....	6.6	6.4	6.3	6.1	5.9	5.7	5.5	5.3	5.0	4.9	4.7	4.5	4.3
73	78	....	6.5	6.3	6.1	5.9	5.7	5.5	5.3	5.1	5.0	4.8	4.6	4.4	4.2
74	79	....	6.3	6.1	6.0	5.8	5.6	5.4	5.2	5.0	4.9	4.7	4.5	4.3	4.1
75	80	....	..	6.0	5.8	5.6	5.5	5.3	5.1	4.9	4.8	4.6	4.4	4.2	4.1
76	81	....	..	..	5.6	5.5	5.3	5.2	5.0	4.8	4.7	4.5	4.3	4.1	4.0
77	82	....	..	..	..	5.3	5.2	5.0	4.9	4.7	4.5	4.4	4.2	4.1	3.9
78	83	....	..	..	..	..	5.0	4.9	4.7	4.6	4.4	4.3	4.1	4.0	3.8
79	84	....	..	..	..	..	..	4.7	4.6	4.5	4.3	4.2	4.0	3.9	3.7
80	85	....	..	..	..	..	..	..	4.5	4.3	4.2	4.1	3.9	3.8	3.6
81	86	....	..	..	..	..	..	..	..	4.2	4.1	3.9	3.8	3.7	3.6
82	87	....	..	..	..	..	..	..	..	..	4.0	3.8	3.7	3.6	3.5
83	88	....	..	..	..	..	..	..	..	..	..	3.7	3.6	3.5	3.4
84	89	....	..	..	..	..	..	..	..	..	..	..	3.5	3.4	3.3
85	90	....	..	..	..	..	..	..	..	..	..	..	..	3.3	3.2
86	91	....	..	..	..	..	..	..	..	..	..	..	..	..	3.1

Table III — Percent Value of Refund Feature

Ages		Duration of guaranteed amount											
Male	Female	1 Yr %	2 Yrs %	3 Yrs %	4 Yrs %	5 Yrs %	6 Yrs %	7 Yrs %	8 Yrs %	9 Yrs %	10 Yrs %	11 Yrs %	12 Yrs %
6	11	..	..	..	..	..	..	..	..	1	1	1	1
7	12	..	..	..	..	..	..	..	..	1	1	1	1
8	13	..	..	..	..	..	..	..	1	1	1	1	1
9	14	..	..	..	..	..	..	..	1	1	1	1	1
10	15	..	..	..	..	..	..	..	1	1	1	1	1
11	16	..	..	..	..	..	..	..	1	1	1	1	1
12	17	..	..	..	..	..	..	..	1	1	1	1	1
13	18	..	..	..	..	..	..	..	1	1	1	1	1
14	19	..	..	..	..	..	..	..	1	1	1	1	1
15	20	..	..	..	..	..	..	..	1	1	1	1	1
16	21	..	..	..	..	..	..	..	1	1	1	1	1
17	22	..	..	..	..	..	..	..	1	1	1	1	1
18	23	..	..	..	..	..	..	..	1	1	1	1	1
19	24	..	..	..	..	..	..	..	1	1	1	1	1
20	25	..	..	..	..	..	..	..	1	1	1	1	1
21	26	..	..	..	..	..	..	..	1	1	1	1	1
22	27	..	..	..	..	..	..	1	1	1	1	1	1
23	28	..	..	..	..	..	..	1	1	1	1	1	1
24	29	..	..	..	..	..	..	1	1	1	1	1	1
25	30	..	..	..	..	..	..	1	1	1	1	1	1
26	31	..	..	..	..	..	1	1	1	1	1	1	1
27	32	..	..	..	..	..	1	1	1	1	1	1	1
28	33	..	..	..	..	..	1	1	1	1	1	1	1
29	34	..	..	..	..	..	1	1	1	1	1	1	1
30	35	..	..	..	..	1	1	1	1	1	1	1	2
31	36	..	..	..	..	1	1	1	1	1	1	1	2
32	37	..	..	..	..	1	1	1	1	1	1	2	2
33	38	..	..	..	1	1	1	1	1	1	1	2	2
34	39	..	..	..	1	1	1	1	1	1	2	2	2
35	40	..	..	..	1	1	1	1	1	2	2	2	2
36	41	..	..	..	1	1	1	1	1	2	2	2	2
37	42	..	..	1	1	1	1	1	2	2	2	2	3
38	43	..	..	1	1	1	1	1	2	2	2	2	3
39	44	..	..	1	1	1	1	2	2	2	2	3	3
40	45	..	..	1	1	1	1	2	2	2	3	3	3
41	46	..	..	1	1	1	1	2	2	2	3	3	3
42	47	..	..	1	1	1	2	2	2	3	3	3	4
43	48	..	1	1	1	1	2	2	2	3	3	4	4
44	49	..	1	1	1	1	2	2	3	3	3	4	4
45	50	..	1	1	1	2	2	2	3	3	4	4	5
46	51	..	1	1	1	2	2	3	3	3	4	4	5
47	52	..	1	1	1	2	2	3	3	4	4	5	5
48	53	..	1	1	2	2	2	3	3	4	5	5	6
49	54	..	1	1	2	2	3	3	4	4	5	5	6
50	55	..	1	1	2	2	3	3	4	5	5	6	7
51	56	..	1	1	2	3	3	4	4	5	6	6	7
52	57	1	1	2	2	3	3	4	5	5	6	7	8
53	58	1	1	2	2	3	4	4	5	6	7	7	8
54	59	1	1	2	2	3	4	5	5	6	7	8	9
55	60	1	1	2	3	3	4	5	6	7	8	8	9
56	61	1	1	2	3	4	4	5	6	7	8	9	10
57	62	1	1	2	3	4	5	6	7	8	9	10	11
58	63	1	2	2	3	4	5	6	7	8	9	10	12
59	64	1	2	3	4	5	6	7	8	9	10	11	12
60	65	1	2	3	4	5	6	7	8	10	11	12	13
61	66	1	2	3	4	5	6	8	9	10	12	13	14
62	67	1	2	3	4	6	7	8	10	11	12	14	15
63	68	1	2	4	5	6	7	9	10	12	13	15	16
64	69	1	3	4	5	7	8	9	11	13	14	16	17
65	70	1	3	4	6	7	9	10	12	13	15	17	19
66	71	1	3	4	6	8	9	11	13	14	16	18	20
67	72	2	3	5	6	8	10	12	14	15	17	19	21
68	73	2	3	5	7	9	11	13	14	16	18	21	23
69	74	2	4	6	7	9	11	13	16	18	20	22	24
70	75	2	4	6	8	10	12	14	17	19	21	23	26
71	76	2	4	6	9	11	13	15	18	20	22	25	27
72	77	2	5	7	9	12	14	16	19	21	24	26	29
73	78	2	5	7	10	12	15	18	20	23	25	28	30
74	79	3	5	8	11	13	16	19	22	24	27	30	32
75	80	3	6	8	11	14	17	20	23	26	29	31	34
76	81	3	6	9	12	15	18	21	24	27	30	33	36
77	82	3	7	10	13	16	20	23	26	29	32	35	38
78	83	4	7	11	14	17	21	24	28	31	34	37	40
79	84	4	8	11	15	19	22	26	29	33	36	39	42
80	85	4	8	12	16	20	24	27	31	34	38	41	44
81	86	4	9	13	17	21	25	29	33	36	40	43	46
82	87	5	9	14	18	23	27	31	35	38	42	45	48
83	88	5	10	15	19	24	28	33	37	40	44	47	50
84	89	5	11	16	21	26	30	34	38	42	46	49	52
85	90	6	11	17	22	27	32	36	41	44	48	51	55

Table III — Percent Value of Refund Feature — Continued

Ages			Duration of guaranteed amount											
Male	Female		13 Yrs %	14 Yrs %	15 Yrs %	16 Yrs %	17 Yrs %	18 Yrs %	19 Yrs %	20 Yrs %	21 Yrs %	22 Yrs %	23 Yrs %	24 Yrs %
6	11	....	1	1	1	1	1	1	1	1	1	1	1	2
7	12	....	1	1	1	1	1	1	1	1	1	1	1	2
8	13	....	1	1	1	1	1	1	1	1	1	1	1	2
9	14	....	1	1	1	1	1	1	1	1	1	1	1	2
10	15	....	1	1	1	1	1	1	1	1	1	1	2	2
11	16	....	1	1	1	1	1	1	1	1	1	1	2	2
12	17	....	1	1	1	1	1	1	1	1	1	1	2	2
13	18	....	1	1	1	1	1	1	1	1	1	2	2	2
14	19	....	1	1	1	1	1	1	1	1	1	2	2	2
15	20	....	1	1	1	1	1	1	1	1	1	2	2	2
16	21	....	1	1	1	1	1	1	1	1	2	2	2	2
17	22	....	1	1	1	1	1	1	1	1	2	2	2	2
18	23	....	1	1	1	1	1	1	1	2	2	2	2	2
19	24	....	1	1	1	1	1	1	2	2	2	2	2	2
20	25	....	1	1	1	1	1	1	2	2	2	2	2	2
21	26	....	1	1	1	1	1	2	2	2	2	2	2	2
22	27	....	1	1	1	1	1	2	2	2	2	2	2	3
23	28	....	1	1	1	1	2	2	2	2	2	2	2	3
24	29	....	1	1	1	2	2	2	2	2	2	2	3	3
25	30	....	1	1	1	2	2	2	2	2	2	3	3	3
26	31	....	1	1	2	2	2	2	2	2	3	3	3	3
27	32	....	1	2	2	2	2	2	2	3	3	3	3	3
28	33	....	1	2	2	2	2	2	3	3	3	3	3	4
29	34	....	2	2	2	2	2	2	3	3	3	3	4	4
30	35	....	2	2	2	2	2	3	3	3	3	4	4	4
31	36	....	2	2	2	2	3	3	3	3	4	4	4	5
32	37	....	2	2	2	3	3	3	3	4	4	4	5	5
33	38	....	2	2	3	3	3	3	4	4	4	5	5	5
34	39	....	2	3	3	3	3	4	4	4	5	5	5	6
35	40	....	2	3	3	3	4	4	4	5	5	5	6	6
36	41	....	3	3	3	4	4	4	5	5	5	6	6	7
37	42	....	3	3	3	4	4	4	5	5	6	6	7	7
38	43	....	3	3	4	4	4	5	5	6	6	7	7	8
39	44	....	3	4	4	4	5	5	6	6	7	7	8	8
40	45	....	4	4	4	5	5	6	6	7	7	8	8	9
41	46	....	4	4	4	5	6	6	7	7	8	8	9	9
42	47	....	4	5	5	5	6	6	7	8	8	9	9	10
43	48	....	4	5	5	6	6	7	8	8	9	9	10	11
44	49	....	5	5	6	6	7	7	8	9	9	10	11	12
45	50	....	5	6	6	7	7	8	9	9	10	11	12	12
46	51	....	5	6	7	7	8	9	9	10	11	12	12	13
47	52	....	6	7	7	8	9	9	10	11	12	12	13	14
48	53	....	6	7	8	8	9	10	11	12	12	13	14	15
49	54	....	7	8	8	9	10	11	11	12	13	14	15	16
50	55	....	7	8	9	10	11	11	12	13	14	15	16	17
51	56	....	8	9	10	10	11	12	13	14	15	16	17	18
52	57	....	8	9	10	11	12	13	14	15	16	17	18	20
53	58	....	9	10	11	12	13	14	15	16	17	19	20	21
54	59	....	10	11	12	13	14	15	16	17	18	20	21	22
55	60	....	10	11	13	14	15	16	17	18	20	21	22	24
56	61	....	11	12	13	15	16	17	18	20	21	22	24	25
57	62	....	12	13	14	16	17	18	20	21	22	24	25	27
58	63	....	13	14	15	17	18	19	21	22	24	25	27	28
59	64	....	14	15	16	18	19	21	22	24	25	27	28	30
60	65	....	15	16	18	19	20	22	24	25	27	28	30	32
61	66	....	16	17	19	20	22	23	25	27	28	30	32	33
62	67	....	17	18	20	22	23	25	27	28	30	32	33	35
63	68	....	18	20	21	23	25	26	28	30	32	33	35	37
64	69	....	19	21	23	24	26	28	30	32	33	35	37	39
65	70	....	20	22	24	26	28	30	32	33	35	37	39	41
66	71	....	22	24	26	28	29	31	33	35	37	39	41	43
67	72	....	23	25	27	29	31	33	35	37	39	41	43	45
68	73	....	25	27	29	31	33	35	37	39	41	43	45	47
69	74	....	26	28	30	33	35	37	39	41	43	45	47	48
70	75	....	28	30	32	34	37	39	41	43	45	47	49	50
71	76	....	29	31	34	36	39	41	43	45	47	49	51	52
72	77	....	31	34	36	38	41	43	45	47	49	51	53	54
73	78	....	33	35	38	40	43	45	47	49	51	53	55	56
74	79	....	35	37	40	42	45	47	49	51	53	55	57	58
75	80	....	37	39	42	44	47	49	51	53	55	57	58	60
76	81	....	39	41	44	46	49	51	53	55	57	59	60	62
77	82	....	41	43	46	48	51	53	55	57	59	61	62	64
78	83	....	43	45	48	50	53	55	57	59	61	62	64	65
79	84	....	45	48	50	53	55	57	59	61	63	64	66	67
80	85	....	47	50	52	55	57	59	61	63	64	66	67	69
81	86	....	49	52	54	57	59	61	63	65	66	68	69	70
82	87	....	51	54	56	59	61	63	65	66	68	69	71	72
83	88	....	53	56	58	61	63	65	66	68	70	71	72	73
84	89	....	55	58	60	63	65	67	68	70	71	73	74	75
85	90	....	57	60	62	65	67	68	70	71	73	74	75	76

Table III — Percent Value of Refund Feature — Continued

Ages		Duration of guaranteed amount										
Male	Female	25 Yrs %	26 Yrs %	27 Yrs %	28 Yrs %	29 Yrs %	30 Yrs %	31 Yrs %	32 Yrs %	33 Yrs %	34 Yrs %	35 Yrs %
6	11	2	2	2	2	2	2	2	2	2	2	2
7	12	2	2	2	2	2	2	2	2	2	2	3
8	13	2	2	2	2	2	2	2	2	2	2	3
9	14	2	2	2	2	2	2	2	2	2	3	3
10	15	2	2	2	2	2	2	2	2	3	3	3
11	16	2	2	2	2	2	2	2	2	3	3	3
12	17	2	2	2	2	2	2	2	3	3	3	3
13	18	2	2	2	2	2	2	2	3	3	3	3
14	19	2	2	2	2	2	2	3	3	3	3	3
15	20	2	2	2	2	2	3	3	3	3	3	3
16	21	2	2	2	2	3	3	3	3	3	3	4
17	22	2	2	2	2	3	3	3	3	3	4	4
18	23	2	2	2	3	3	3	3	3	4	4	4
19	24	2	2	3	3	3	3	3	4	4	4	4
20	25	2	3	3	3	3	3	4	4	4	4	5
21	26	3	3	3	3	3	4	4	4	4	5	5
22	27	3	3	3	3	4	4	4	4	5	5	5
23	28	3	3	3	3	4	4	4	5	5	5	5
24	29	3	3	3	4	4	4	5	5	5	5	6
25	30	3	3	4	4	4	5	5	5	6	6	6
26	31	3	4	4	4	5	5	5	6	6	6	7
27	32	4	4	4	5	5	5	6	6	6	7	7
28	33	4	4	5	5	5	6	6	6	7	7	8
29	34	4	5	5	5	6	6	6	7	7	8	8
30	35	5	5	5	6	6	6	7	7	8	8	9
31	36	5	5	6	6	6	7	7	8	8	9	9
32	37	5	6	6	7	7	7	8	8	9	10	10
33	38	6	6	7	7	7	8	8	9	10	10	11
34	39	6	7	7	8	8	9	9	10	10	11	12
35	40	7	7	8	8	9	9	10	10	11	12	12
36	41	7	8	8	9	9	10	10	11	12	13	13
37	42	8	8	9	9	10	11	11	12	13	13	14
38	43	8	9	9	10	11	11	12	13	13	14	15
39	44	9	9	10	11	11	12	13	14	14	15	16
40	45	9	10	11	11	12	13	14	15	15	16	17
41	46	10	11	11	12	13	14	15	16	16	17	18
42	47	11	12	12	13	14	15	16	17	18	18	19
43	48	12	12	13	14	15	16	17	18	19	20	21
44	49	12	13	14	15	16	17	18	19	20	21	22
45	50	13	14	15	16	17	18	19	20	21	22	23
46	51	14	15	16	17	18	19	20	21	22	24	25
47	52	15	16	17	18	19	20	21	23	24	25	26
48	53	16	17	18	19	20	22	23	24	25	26	28
49	54	17	18	19	21	22	23	24	25	27	28	29
50	55	18	20	21	22	23	24	26	27	28	29	31
51	56	20	21	22	23	25	26	27	28	30	31	32
52	57	21	22	23	25	26	27	29	30	31	33	34
53	58	22	24	25	26	28	29	30	32	33	34	36
54	59	24	25	26	28	29	31	32	33	35	36	38
55	60	25	26	28	29	31	32	34	35	36	38	39
56	61	27	28	29	31	32	34	35	37	38	40	41
57	62	28	30	31	33	34	36	37	39	40	41	43
58	63	30	31	33	34	36	37	39	40	42	43	45
59	64	31	33	35	36	38	39	41	42	44	45	47
60	65	33	35	36	38	40	41	43	44	46	47	48
61	66	35	37	38	40	41	43	44	46	47	49	50
62	67	37	38	40	42	43	45	46	48	49	51	52
63	68	39	40	42	44	45	47	48	50	51	52	54
64	69	41	42	44	46	47	49	50	52	53	54	55
65	70	42	44	46	47	49	50	52	53	55	56	57
66	71	44	46	48	49	51	52	54	55	56	58	59
67	72	46	48	50	51	53	54	56	57	58	59	61
68	73	48	50	52	53	55	56	57	59	60	61	62
69	74	50	52	53	55	56	58	59	60	62	63	64
70	75	52	54	55	57	58	60	61	62	63	64	65
71	76	54	56	57	59	60	61	63	64	65	66	67
72	77	56	58	59	60	62	63	64	65	66	67	69
73	78	58	59	61	62	64	65	66	67	68	68	70
74	79	60	61	63	64	65	66	67	68	69	70	71
75	80	62	63	64	66	67	68	69	70	71	72	72
76	81	63	65	66	67	68	69	70	71	72	73	..
77	82	65	66	68	69	70	71	72	73	74	..	..
78	83	67	68	69	70	71	72	73	74	..	..	..
79	84	68	70	71	72	73	74	75	..	..	..	..
80	85	70	71	72	73	74	75	..	..	..	..	..
81	86	72	73	74	75	75	..	..	..	..	..	..
82	87	73	74	75	76	..	..	..	..	..	..	..
83	88	74	75	76	..	..	..	..	..	..	..	..
84	89	76	77	..	..	..	..	..	..	..	..	..
85	90	77	..	..	..	..	..	..	..	..	..	..

Table V — Ordinary Life Annuities — One Life — Expected Return Multiples

Age	Multiple	Age	Multiple	Age	Multiple
5	76.6	42	40.6	79	10.0
6	75.6	43	39.6	80	9.5
7	74.7	44	38.7	81	8.9
8	73.7	45	37.7	82	8.4
9	72.7	46	36.8	83	7.9
10	71.7	47	35.9	84	7.4
11	70.7	48	34.9	85	6.9
12	69.7	49	34.0	86	6.5
13	68.8	50	33.1	87	6.1
14	67.8	51	32.2	88	5.7
15	66.8	52	31.3	89	5.3
16	65.8	53	30.4	90	5.0
17	64.8	54	29.5	91	4.7
18	63.9	55	28.6	92	4.4
19	62.9	56	27.7	93	4.1
20	61.9	57	26.8	94	3.9
21	60.9	58	25.9	95	3.7
22	59.9	59	25.0	96	3.4
23	59.0	60	24.2	97	3.2
24	58.0	61	23.3	98	3.0
25	57.0	62	22.5	99	2.8
26	56.0	63	21.6	100	2.7
27	55.1	64	20.8	101	2.5
28	54.1	65	20.0	102	2.3
29	53.1	66	19.2	103	2.1
30	52.2	67	18.4	104	1.9
31	51.2	68	17.6	105	1.8
32	50.2	69	16.8	106	1.6
33	49.3	70	16.0	107	1.4
34	48.3	71	15.3	108	1.3
35	47.3	72	14.6	109	1.1
36	46.4	73	13.9	110	1.0
37	45.4	74	13.2	111	.9
38	44.4	75	12.5	112	.8
39	43.5	76	11.9	113	.7
40	42.5	77	11.2	114	.6
41	41.5	78	10.6	115	.5

Table VI — Ordinary Joint Life and Last Survivor Annuities — Two Lives — Expected Return Multiples

AGES	35	36	37	38	39	40	41	42	43	44	45	46	47	48	49	50
35	54.0	...	...	...	...	...	...	...	...	...	...	...	...	...	...	...
36	53.5	53.0	...	...	...	...	...	...	...	...	...	...	...	...	...	...
37	53.0	52.5	52.0	...	...	...	...	...	...	...	...	...	...	...	...	...
38	52.2	52.0	51.5	51.0	...	...	...	...	...	...	...	...	...	...	...	...
39	52.2	51.6	51.0	50.5	50.0	...	...	...	...	...	...	...	...	...	...	...
40	51.8	51.2	50.6	50.0	49.5	49.0	...	...	...	...	...	...	...	...	...	...
41	51.4	50.8	50.2	49.6	49.1	48.5	48.0	...	...	...	...	...	...	...	...	...
42	51.1	50.4	49.8	49.2	48.6	48.1	47.5	47.0	...	...	...	...	...	...	...	...
43	50.8	50.1	49.5	48.8	48.2	47.6	47.1	46.6	46.0	...	...	...	...	...	...	...
44	50.5	49.8	49.1	48.5	47.8	47.2	46.7	46.1	45.6	45.1	...	...	...	...	...	...
45	50.2	49.5	48.8	48.1	47.5	46.9	46.3	45.7	45.1	44.6	44.1	...	...	...	...	...
46	50.0	49.2	48.5	47.8	47.2	46.5	45.9	45.3	44.7	44.1	43.6	43.1	...	...	...	...
47	49.7	49.0	48.3	47.5	46.8	46.2	45.5	44.9	44.3	43.7	43.2	42.6	42.1	...	...	...
48	49.5	48.8	48.0	47.3	46.6	45.9	45.2	44.5	43.9	43.3	42.7	42.2	41.7	41.2	...	...
49	49.3	48.5	47.8	47.0	46.3	45.6	44.9	44.2	43.6	42.9	42.3	41.8	41.2	40.7	40.2	...
50	49.2	48.4	47.6	46.8	46.0	45.3	44.6	43.9	43.2	42.6	42.0	41.4	40.8	40.2	39.7	39.2
51	49.0	48.2	47.4	46.6	45.8	45.1	44.3	43.6	42.9	42.2	41.6	41.0	40.4	39.8	39.3	38.7
52	48.8	48.0	47.2	46.4	45.6	44.8	44.1	43.3	42.6	41.9	41.3	40.6	40.0	39.4	38.8	38.3
53	48.7	47.9	47.0	46.2	45.4	44.6	43.9	43.1	42.4	41.7	41.0	40.3	39.7	39.0	38.4	37.9
54	48.6	47.7	46.9	46.0	45.2	44.4	43.6	42.9	42.1	41.4	40.7	40.0	39.3	38.7	38.1	37.5
55	48.5	47.6	46.7	45.9	45.1	44.2	43.4	42.7	41.9	41.2	40.4	39.7	39.0	38.4	37.7	37.1
56	48.3	47.5	46.6	45.8	44.9	44.1	43.3	42.5	41.7	40.9	40.2	39.5	38.7	38.1	37.4	36.8
57	48.3	47.4	46.5	45.6	44.8	43.9	43.1	42.3	41.5	40.7	40.0	39.2	38.5	37.8	37.1	36.4
58	48.2	47.3	46.4	45.5	44.7	43.8	43.0	42.1	41.3	40.5	39.7	39.0	38.2	37.5	36.8	36.1
59	48.1	47.2	46.3	45.4	44.5	43.7	42.8	42.0	41.2	40.4	39.6	38.8	38.0	37.3	36.6	35.9
60	48.0	47.1	46.2	45.3	44.4	43.6	42.7	41.9	41.0	40.2	39.4	38.6	37.8	37.1	36.3	35.6
61	47.9	47.0	46.1	45.2	44.3	43.5	42.6	41.7	40.9	40.0	39.2	38.4	37.6	36.9	36.1	35.4
62	47.9	47.0	46.0	45.1	44.2	43.4	42.5	41.6	40.8	39.9	39.1	38.3	37.5	36.7	35.9	35.1
63	47.8	46.9	46.0	45.1	44.2	43.3	42.4	41.5	40.6	39.8	38.9	38.1	37.3	36.5	35.7	34.9
64	47.8	46.8	45.9	45.0	44.1	43.2	42.3	41.4	40.5	39.7	38.8	38.0	37.2	36.3	35.5	34.8
65	47.7	46.8	45.9	44.9	44.0	43.1	42.2	41.3	40.4	39.6	38.7	37.9	37.0	36.2	35.4	34.6
66	47.7	46.7	45.8	44.9	44.0	43.1	42.2	41.3	40.4	39.5	38.6	37.8	36.9	36.1	35.2	34.4
67	47.6	46.7	45.8	44.8	43.9	43.0	42.1	41.2	40.3	39.4	38.5	37.7	36.8	36.0	35.1	34.3
68	47.6	46.7	45.7	44.8	43.9	42.9	42.0	41.1	40.2	39.3	38.4	37.6	36.7	35.8	35.0	34.2
69	47.6	46.6	45.7	44.8	43.8	42.9	42.0	41.1	40.2	39.3	38.4	37.5	36.6	35.7	34.9	34.1
70	47.5	46.6	45.7	44.7	43.8	42.9	41.9	41.0	40.1	39.2	38.3	37.4	36.5	35.7	34.8	34.0
71	47.5	46.6	45.6	44.7	43.8	42.8	41.9	41.0	40.1	39.1	38.2	37.3	36.5	35.6	34.7	33.9
72	47.5	46.6	45.6	44.7	43.7	42.8	41.9	40.9	40.0	39.1	38.2	37.3	36.4	35.5	34.6	33.8
73	47.5	46.5	45.6	44.7	43.7	42.8	41.8	40.9	40.0	39.0	38.1	37.2	36.3	35.4	34.6	33.7
74	47.5	46.5	45.6	44.7	43.7	42.7	41.8	40.9	39.9	39.0	38.1	37.2	36.3	35.4	34.5	33.6
75	47.4	46.5	45.5	44.7	43.6	42.7	41.8	40.8	39.9	39.0	38.1	37.1	36.2	35.3	34.5	33.6
76	47.4	46.5	45.5	44.7	43.6	42.7	41.7	40.8	39.9	38.9	38.0	37.1	36.2	35.3	34.4	33.5
77	47.4	46.5	45.5	44.7	43.6	42.7	41.7	40.8	39.8	38.9	38.0	37.1	36.2	35.3	34.4	33.5
78	47.4	46.4	45.5	44.5	43.6	42.6	41.7	40.7	39.8	38.9	38.0	37.0	36.1	35.2	34.3	33.4
79	47.4	46.4	45.5	44.5	43.6	42.6	41.7	40.7	39.8	38.9	37.9	37.0	36.1	35.2	34.3	33.4
80	47.4	46.4	45.5	44.5	43.6	42.6	41.7	40.7	39.8	38.8	37.9	37.0	36.0	35.1	34.2	33.4
81	47.4	46.4	45.5	44.5	43.5	42.6	41.6	40.7	39.8	38.8	37.9	37.0	36.0	35.1	34.2	33.3
82	47.4	46.4	45.4	44.5	43.5	42.6	41.6	40.7	39.7	38.8	37.9	36.9	36.0	35.1	34.2	33.3
83	47.4	46.4	45.4	44.5	43.5	42.6	41.6	40.7	39.7	38.8	37.9	36.9	36.0	35.1	34.2	33.3
84	47.4	46.4	45.4	44.5	43.5	42.6	41.6	40.7	39.7	38.8	37.8	36.9	36.0	35.0	34.1	33.2
85	47.4	46.4	45.4	44.5	43.5	42.6	41.6	40.7	39.7	38.8	37.8	36.9	36.0	35.0	34.1	33.2
86	47.3	46.4	45.4	44.5	43.5	42.5	41.6	40.6	39.7	38.7	37.8	36.9	36.0	35.0	34.1	33.2
87	47.3	46.4	45.4	44.5	43.5	42.5	41.6	40.6	39.7	38.7	37.8	36.9	35.9	35.0	34.1	33.2
88	47.3	46.4	45.4	44.5	43.5	42.5	41.6	40.6	39.7	38.7	37.8	36.9	35.9	35.0	34.1	33.2
89	47.3	46.4	45.4	44.4	43.5	42.5	41.6	40.6	39.7	38.7	37.8	36.9	35.9	35.0	34.1	33.2
90	47.3	46.4	45.4	44.4	43.5	42.5	41.6	40.6	39.7	38.7	37.8	36.9	35.9	35.0	34.1	33.2

Table VI — Ordinary Joint Life and Last Survivor Annuities — Two Lives — Expected Return Multiples

AGES	51	52	53	54	55	56	57	58	59	60	61	62	63	64	65	66
51	38.2	...	...	...	...	...	...	...	...	...	...	...	...	...	...	...
52	37.8	37.3	...	...	...	...	...	...	...	...	...	...	...	...	...	...
53	37.3	36.8	36.3	...	...	...	...	...	...	...	...	...	...	...	...	...
54	36.9	36.4	35.8	35.3	...	...	...	...	...	...	...	...	...	...	...	...
55	36.5	35.9	35.4	34.9	34.4	...	...	...	...	...	...	...	...	...	...	...
56	36.1	35.6	35.0	34.4	33.9	33.4	...	...	...	...	...	...	...	...	...	...
57	35.8	35.2	34.6	34.0	33.5	33.0	32.5	...	...	...	...	...	...	...	...	...
58	35.5	34.8	34.2	33.6	33.1	32.5	32.0	31.5	...	...	...	...	...	...	...	...
59	35.2	34.5	33.9	33.3	32.7	32.1	31.6	31.1	30.6	...	...	...	...	...	...	...
60	34.9	34.2	33.6	32.9	32.3	31.7	31.2	30.6	30.1	29.7	...	...	...	...	...	...
61	34.6	33.9	33.3	32.6	32.0	31.4	30.8	30.2	29.7	29.2	28.7	...	...	...	...	...
62	34.4	33.7	33.0	32.3	31.7	31.0	30.4	29.9	29.3	28.8	28.3	27.8	...	...	...	...
63	34.2	33.5	32.7	32.0	31.4	30.7	30.1	29.5	28.9	28.4	27.8	27.3	26.9	...	...	...
64	34.0	33.2	32.5	31.8	31.1	30.4	29.8	29.2	28.6	28.0	27.4	26.9	26.4	25.9	...	...
65	33.8	33.0	32.3	31.6	30.9	30.2	29.5	28.9	28.2	27.6	27.1	26.5	26.0	25.5	25.0	...
66	33.6	32.9	32.1	31.4	30.6	29.9	29.2	28.6	27.9	27.3	26.7	26.1	25.6	25.1	24.6	24.1
67	33.5	32.7	31.9	31.2	30.4	29.7	29.0	28.3	27.6	27.0	26.4	25.8	25.2	24.7	24.2	23.7
68	33.4	32.5	31.8	31.0	30.2	29.5	28.8	28.1	27.4	26.7	26.1	25.5	24.9	24.3	23.8	23.3
69	33.2	32.4	31.6	30.8	30.1	29.3	28.6	27.8	27.1	26.5	25.8	25.2	24.6	24.0	23.4	22.9
70	33.1	32.3	31.5	30.7	29.9	29.1	28.4	27.6	26.9	26.2	25.6	24.9	24.3	23.7	23.1	22.5
71	33.0	32.2	31.4	30.5	29.7	29.0	28.2	27.5	26.7	26.0	25.3	24.7	24.0	23.4	22.8	22.2
72	32.9	32.1	31.2	30.4	29.6	28.8	28.1	27.3	26.5	25.8	25.1	24.4	23.8	23.1	22.5	21.9
73	32.8	32.0	31.1	30.3	29.5	28.7	27.9	27.1	26.4	25.6	24.9	24.2	23.5	22.9	22.2	21.6
74	32.8	31.9	31.1	30.2	29.4	28.6	27.8	27.0	26.2	25.5	24.7	24.0	23.3	22.7	22.0	21.4
75	32.7	31.8	31.0	30.1	29.3	28.5	27.7	26.9	26.1	25.3	24.6	23.8	23.1	22.4	21.8	21.1
76	32.6	31.8	30.9	30.1	29.2	28.4	27.6	26.8	26.0	25.2	24.4	23.7	23.0	22.3	21.6	20.9
77	32.6	31.7	30.8	30.0	29.1	28.3	27.5	26.7	25.9	25.1	24.3	23.6	22.8	22.1	21.4	20.7
78	32.5	31.7	30.8	29.9	29.1	28.2	27.4	26.6	25.8	25.0	24.2	23.4	22.7	21.9	21.2	20.5
79	32.5	31.6	30.7	29.9	29.0	28.2	27.3	26.5	25.7	24.9	24.1	23.3	22.6	21.8	21.1	20.4
80	32.5	31.6	30.7	29.8	29.0	28.1	27.3	26.4	25.6	24.8	24.0	23.2	22.4	21.7	21.0	20.2
81	32.4	31.5	30.7	29.8	28.9	28.1	27.2	26.4	25.5	24.7	23.9	23.1	22.3	21.6	20.8	20.1
82	32.4	31.5	30.6	29.7	28.9	28.0	27.2	26.3	25.5	24.6	23.8	23.0	22.3	21.5	20.7	20.0
83	32.4	31.5	30.6	29.7	28.8	28.0	27.1	26.3	25.4	24.6	23.8	23.0	22.2	21.4	20.6	19.9
84	32.3	31.4	30.6	29.7	28.8	27.9	27.1	26.2	25.4	24.5	23.7	22.9	22.1	21.3	20.5	19.8
85	32.3	31.4	30.5	29.6	28.8	27.9	27.0	26.2	25.3	24.5	23.7	22.8	22.0	21.3	20.5	19.7
86	32.3	31.4	30.5	29.6	28.7	27.9	27.0	26.1	25.3	24.5	23.6	22.8	22.0	21.2	20.4	19.6
87	32.3	31.4	30.5	29.6	28.7	27.8	27.0	26.1	25.3	24.4	23.6	22.8	21.9	21.1	20.4	19.6
88	32.3	31.4	30.5	29.6	28.7	27.8	27.0	26.1	25.2	24.4	23.5	22.7	21.9	21.1	20.3	19.5
89	32.3	31.4	30.5	29.6	28.7	27.8	26.9	26.1	25.2	24.4	23.5	22.7	21.9	21.1	20.3	19.5
90	32.3	31.3	30.5	29.5	28.7	27.8	26.9	26.1	25.2	24.3	23.5	22.7	21.8	21.0	20.2	19.4

Table VI — Ordinary Joint Life and Last Survivor Annuities — Two Lives — Expected Return Multiples

AGES	67	68	69	70	71	72	73	74	75	76	77	78	79	80	81	82
67	23.2	...	...	...	...	...	...	...	...	...	...	...	...	...	...	...
68	22.8	22.3	...	...	...	...	...	...	...	...	...	...	...	...	...	...
69	22.4	21.9	21.5	...	...	...	...	...	...	...	...	...	...	...	...	...
70	22.0	21.5	21.1	20.6	...	...	...	...	...	...	...	...	...	...	...	...
71	21.7	21.2	20.7	20.2	19.8	...	...	...	...	...	...	...	...	...	...	...
72	21.3	20.8	20.3	19.8	19.4	18.9	...	...	...	...	...	...	...	...	...	...
73	21.0	20.5	20.0	19.4	19.0	18.5	18.1	...	...	...	...	...	...	...	...	...
74	20.8	20.2	19.6	19.1	18.6	18.2	17.7	17.3	...	...	...	...	...	...	...	...
75	20.5	19.9	19.3	18.8	18.3	17.8	17.3	16.9	16.5	...	...	...	...	...	...	...
76	20.3	19.7	19.1	18.5	18.0	17.5	17.0	16.5	16.1	15.7	...	...	...	...	...	...
77	20.1	19.4	18.8	18.3	17.7	17.2	16.7	16.2	15.8	15.4	15.0	...	...	...	...	...
78	19.9	19.2	18.6	18.0	17.5	16.9	16.4	15.9	15.4	15.0	14.6	14.2	...	...	...	...
79	19.7	19.0	18.4	17.8	17.2	16.7	16.1	15.6	15.1	14.7	14.3	13.9	13.5	...	...	...
80	19.5	18.9	18.2	17.6	17.0	16.4	15.9	15.4	14.9	14.4	14.0	13.5	13.2	12.8	...	...
81	19.4	18.7	18.1	17.4	16.8	16.2	15.7	15.1	14.6	14.1	13.7	13.2	12.8	12.5	12.1	...
82	19.3	18.6	17.9	17.3	16.6	16.0	15.5	14.9	14.4	13.9	13.4	13.0	12.5	12.2	11.8	11.5
83	19.2	18.5	17.8	17.1	16.5	15.9	15.3	14.7	14.2	13.7	13.2	12.7	12.3	11.9	11.5	11.1
84	19.1	18.4	17.7	17.0	16.3	15.7	15.1	14.5	14.0	13.5	13.0	12.5	12.0	11.6	11.2	10.9
85	19.0	18.3	17.6	16.9	16.2	15.6	15.0	14.4	13.8	13.3	12.8	12.3	11.8	11.4	11.0	10.6
86	18.9	18.2	17.5	16.8	16.1	15.5	14.8	14.2	13.7	13.1	12.6	12.1	11.6	11.2	10.8	10.4
87	18.8	18.1	17.4	16.7	16.0	15.4	14.7	14.1	13.5	13.0	12.4	11.9	11.4	11.0	10.6	10.1
88	18.8	18.0	17.3	16.6	15.9	15.3	14.6	14.0	13.4	12.8	12.3	11.8	11.3	10.8	10.4	10.0
89	18.7	18.0	17.2	16.5	15.8	15.2	14.5	13.9	13.3	12.7	12.2	11.6	11.1	10.7	10.2	9.8
90	18.7	17.9	17.2	16.5	15.8	15.1	14.5	13.8	13.2	12.6	12.1	11.5	11.0	10.5	10.1	9.6

Table VI — Ordinary Joint Life and Last Survivor Annuities — Two Lives — Expected Return Multiples

AGES	83	84	85	86	87	88	89	90
83	10.8	...	...	...	...	...	...	...
84	10.5	10.2	...	...	...	...	...	...
85	10.2	9.9	9.6	...	...	...	...	...
86	10.0	9.7	9.3	9.1	...	...	...	...
87	9.8	9.4	9.1	8.8	8.5	...	...	...
88	9.6	9.2	8.9	8.6	8.3	8.0	...	...
89	9.4	9.0	8.7	8.3	8.1	7.8	7.5	...
90	9.2	8.8	8.5	8.2	7.9	7.6	7.3	7.1

Table VIA — Annuities for Joint Life Only — Two Lives — Expected Return Multiples

AGES	35	36	37	38	39	40	41	42	43	44	45	46	47	48	49	50
35	40.7	...	...	...	...	...	...	...	...	...	...	...	...	...	...	...
36	40.2	39.7	...	...	...	...	...	...	...	...	...	...	...	...	...	...
37	39.7	39.3	38.8	...	...	...	...	...	...	...	...	...	...	...	...	...
38	39.2	38.7	38.3	37.9	...	...	...	...	...	...	...	...	...	...	...	...
39	38.6	38.2	37.8	37.4	36.9	...	...	...	...	...	...	...	...	...	...	...
40	38.0	37.7	37.3	36.9	36.4	36.0	...	...	...	...	...	...	...	...	...	...
41	37.4	37.1	36.7	36.3	35.9	35.5	35.1	...	...	...	...	...	...	...	...	...
42	36.8	36.5	36.2	35.8	35.4	35.0	34.6	34.1	...	...	...	...	...	...	...	...
43	36.2	35.9	35.6	35.2	34.9	34.5	34.1	33.7	33.2	...	...	...	...	...	...	...
44	35.5	35.2	34.9	34.6	34.3	34.0	33.6	33.2	32.8	32.3	...	...	...	...	...	...
45	34.8	34.6	34.3	34.0	33.7	33.4	33.0	32.7	32.3	31.8	31.4	...	...	...	...	...
46	34.1	33.9	33.7	33.4	33.1	32.8	32.5	32.1	31.8	31.4	30.9	30.5	...	...	...	...
47	33.4	33.2	33.0	32.8	32.5	32.2	31.9	31.6	31.2	30.8	30.5	30.0	29.6	...	...	...
48	32.7	32.5	32.3	32.1	31.8	31.6	31.3	31.0	30.7	30.3	30.0	29.6	29.2	28.7	...	...
49	32.0	31.8	31.6	31.4	31.2	30.9	30.7	30.4	30.1	29.8	29.4	29.1	28.7	28.3	27.9	...
50	31.3	31.1	30.9	30.7	30.5	30.3	30.0	29.8	29.5	29.2	28.9	28.5	28.2	27.4	27.4	27.0
51	30.5	30.4	30.2	30.0	29.8	29.6	29.4	29.2	28.9	28.6	28.3	28.0	27.7	27.3	26.9	26.5
52	29.7	29.6	29.5	29.3	29.1	28.9	28.7	28.5	28.3	28.0	27.7	27.4	27.1	26.8	26.5	26.1
53	29.0	28.9	28.7	28.6	28.4	28.2	28.1	27.9	27.6	27.4	27.1	26.9	26.6	26.3	25.9	25.6
54	28.2	28.1	28.0	27.8	27.7	27.5	27.4	27.2	27.0	26.8	26.5	26.3	26.0	25.7	25.4	25.1
55	27.4	27.3	27.2	27.1	27.0	26.8	26.7	26.5	26.3	26.1	25.9	25.7	25.4	25.1	24.9	24.6
56	26.7	26.6	26.5	26.3	26.2	26.1	26.0	25.8	25.6	25.4	25.2	25.0	24.8	24.6	24.3	24.0
57	25.9	25.8	25.7	25.6	25.5	25.4	25.2	25.1	24.9	24.8	24.6	24.4	24.2	24.0	23.7	23.5
58	25.1	25.0	24.9	24.8	24.7	24.6	24.5	24.4	24.2	24.1	23.9	23.7	23.5	23.3	23.1	22.9
59	24.3	24.2	24.1	24.1	24.0	23.9	23.8	23.6	23.5	23.4	23.2	23.1	22.9	22.7	22.5	22.3
60	23.5	23.4	23.4	23.3	23.2	23.1	23.0	22.9	22.8	22.7	22.5	22.4	22.2	22.1	21.9	21.7
61	22.7	22.6	22.6	22.5	22.4	22.4	22.3	22.2	22.1	22.0	21.8	21.7	21.6	21.4	21.2	21.1
62	21.9	21.9	21.8	21.7	21.7	21.6	21.5	21.4	21.3	21.2	21.1	21.0	20.9	20.7	20.6	20.4
63	21.1	21.1	21.0	21.0	20.9	20.8	20.8	20.7	20.6	20.5	20.4	20.3	20.2	20.1	19.9	19.8
64	20.3	20.3	20.2	20.2	20.1	20.1	20.0	20.0	19.9	19.8	19.7	19.6	19.5	19.4	19.3	19.1
65	19.6	19.5	19.5	19.4	19.4	19.3	19.3	19.2	19.1	19.1	19.0	18.9	18.8	18.7	18.6	18.5
66	18.8	18.8	18.7	18.7	18.6	18.6	18.5	18.5	18.4	18.4	18.3	18.2	18.1	18.0	17.9	17.8
67	18.0	18.0	18.0	17.9	17.9	17.9	17.8	17.8	17.7	17.6	17.6	17.5	17.4	17.3	17.3	17.2
68	17.3	17.3	17.2	17.2	17.2	17.1	17.1	17.0	17.0	16.9	16.9	16.8	16.7	16.7	16.6	16.5
69	16.5	16.5	16.5	16.5	16.4	16.4	16.4	16.3	16.3	16.2	16.2	16.1	16.1	16.0	15.9	15.8
70	15.8	15.8	15.8	15.7	15.7	15.7	15.6	15.6	15.6	15.5	15.5	15.4	15.4	15.3	15.3	15.2
71	15.1	15.1	15.1	15.0	15.0	15.0	15.0	14.9	14.9	14.9	14.8	14.8	14.8	14.7	14.7	14.5
72	14.4	14.4	14.4	14.3	14.3	14.3	14.3	14.2	14.2	14.2	14.1	14.1	14.1	14.0	14.0	13.9
73	13.7	13.7	13.7	13.7	13.7	13.6	13.6	13.6	13.6	13.5	13.5	13.5	13.4	13.4	13.3	13.3
74	13.1	13.0	13.0	13.0	13.0	13.0	13.0	12.9	12.9	12.9	12.8	12.8	12.8	12.7	12.7	12.7
75	12.4	12.4	12.4	12.4	12.3	12.3	12.3	12.3	12.3	12.2	12.2	12.2	12.2	12.1	12.1	12.1
76	11.8	11.8	11.7	11.7	11.7	11.7	11.7	11.7	11.6	11.6	11.6	11.6	11.6	11.5	11.5	11.5
77	11.1	11.1	11.1	11.1	11.1	11.1	11.1	11.1	11.1	11.0	11.0	11.0	11.0	10.9	10.9	10.9
78	10.5	10.5	10.5	10.5	10.5	10.5	10.5	10.5	10.5	10.4	10.4	10.4	10.4	10.4	10.3	10.3
79	10.0	10.0	9.9	9.9	9.9	9.9	9.9	9.9	9.9	9.9	9.9	9.9	9.8	9.8	9.8	9.8
80	9.4	9.4	9.4	9.4	9.4	9.4	9.4	9.3	9.3	9.3	9.3	9.3	9.3	9.3	9.2	9.2
81	8.9	8.8	8.8	8.8	8.8	8.8	8.8	8.8	8.8	8.8	8.8	8.8	8.7	8.7	8.7	8.7
82	8.3	8.3	8.3	8.3	8.3	8.3	8.3	8.3	8.3	8.3	8.3	8.2	8.2	8.2	8.2	8.2
83	7.8	7.8	7.8	7.8	7.8	7.8	7.8	7.8	7.8	7.8	7.8	7.8	7.7	7.7	7.7	7.7
84	7.3	7.3	7.3	7.3	7.3	7.3	7.3	7.3	7.3	7.3	7.3	7.3	7.3	7.3	7.3	7.2
85	6.9	6.9	6.9	6.9	6.9	6.9	6.9	6.9	6.9	6.9	6.8	6.8	6.8	6.8	6.8	6.8
86	6.5	6.5	6.5	6.5	6.4	6.4	6.4	6.4	6.4	6.4	6.4	6.4	6.4	6.4	6.4	6.4
87	6.1	6.0	6.0	6.0	6.0	6.0	6.0	6.0	6.0	6.0	6.0	6.0	6.0	6.0	6.0	6.0
88	5.7	5.7	5.7	5.7	5.7	5.7	5.7	5.6	5.6	5.6	5.6	5.6	5.6	5.6	5.6	5.6
89	5.3	5.3	5.3	5.3	5.3	5.3	5.3	5.3	5.3	5.3	5.3	5.3	5.3	5.3	5.3	5.3
90	5.0	5.0	5.0	5.0	5.0	5.0	5.0	5.0	5.0	5.0	5.0	4.9	4.9	4.9	4.9	4.9

(Table VIA continues on the following page.)

Table VIA — Annuities for Joint Life Only — Two Lives — Expected Return Multiples

AGES	51	52	53	54	55	56	57	58	59	60	61	62	63	64	65	66
51	26.1	...	...	...	...	...	...	...	...	...	...	...	...	...	...	...
52	25.7	25.3	...	...	...	...	...	...	...	...	...	...	...	...	...	...
53	25.2	24.8	24.4	...	...	...	...	...	...	...	...	...	...	...	...	...
54	24.7	24.4	24.0	23.6	...	...	...	...	...	...	...	...	...	...	...	...
55	24.2	23.9	23.5	23.2	22.7	...	...	...	...	...	...	...	...	...	...	...
56	23.7	23.4	23.1	22.7	22.3	21.9	...	...	...	...	...	...	...	...	...	...
57	23.2	22.9	22.6	22.2	21.9	21.5	21.1	...	...	...	...	...	...	...	...	...
58	22.6	22.4	22.1	21.7	21.4	21.1	20.7	20.3	...	...	...	...	...	...	...	...
59	22.1	21.8	21.5	21.2	20.9	20.6	20.3	19.9	19.5	...	...	...	...	...	...	...
60	21.5	21.2	21.0	20.7	20.4	20.1	19.8	19.5	19.1	18.7	...	...	...	...	...	...
61	20.9	20.6	20.4	20.2	19.9	19.6	19.3	19.0	18.7	18.3	17.9	...	...	...	...	...
62	20.2	20.0	19.8	19.6	19.4	19.1	18.8	18.5	18.2	17.9	17.5	17.1	...	...	...	...
63	19.6	19.4	19.2	19.0	18.8	18.6	18.3	18.0	17.7	17.4	17.1	16.8	16.4	...	...	...
64	19.0	18.8	18.6	18.5	18.3	18.0	17.8	17.5	17.3	17.0	16.7	16.3	16.0	15.6	...	...
65	18.3	18.2	18.0	17.9	17.7	17.5	17.3	17.0	16.8	16.5	16.2	15.9	15.6	15.3	14.9	...
66	17.7	17.6	17.4	17.3	17.1	16.9	16.7	16.5	16.3	16.0	15.8	15.5	15.2	14.9	14.5	14.2
67	17.1	16.9	16.8	16.7	16.5	16.3	16.2	16.0	15.8	15.5	15.3	15.0	14.7	14.5	14.1	13.8
68	16.4	16.3	16.2	16.1	15.9	15.8	15.6	15.4	15.2	15.0	14.8	14.6	14.3	14.0	13.7	13.4
69	15.8	15.7	15.6	15.4	15.3	15.2	15.0	14.9	14.7	14.5	14.3	14.1	13.9	13.6	13.3	13.1
70	15.1	15.0	14.9	14.8	14.7	14.6	14.5	14.3	14.2	14.0	13.8	13.6	13.4	13.2	12.9	12.6
71	14.5	14.4	14.3	14.2	14.1	14.0	13.9	13.8	13.6	13.5	13.3	13.1	12.9	12.7	12.5	12.2
72	13.8	13.8	13.7	13.6	13.5	13.4	13.3	13.2	13.1	12.9	12.8	12.6	12.4	12.3	12.0	11.8
73	13.2	13.2	13.1	13.0	13.0	12.9	12.8	12.7	12.5	12.4	12.3	12.1	12.0	11.8	11.6	11.4
74	12.6	12.6	12.5	12.4	12.4	12.3	12.2	12.1	12.0	11.9	11.8	11.6	11.5	11.3	11.2	11.0
75	12.0	12.0	11.9	11.9	11.8	11.7	11.7	11.6	11.5	11.4	11.3	11.1	11.0	10.9	10.7	10.5
76	11.4	11.4	11.3	11.3	11.2	11.2	11.1	11.0	10.9	10.9	10.8	10.6	10.5	10.4	10.3	10.1
77	10.8	10.8	10.8	10.7	10.7	10.6	10.6	10.5	10.4	10.3	10.3	10.2	10.0	9.9	9.8	9.7
78	10.3	10.2	10.2	10.2	10.1	10.1	10.0	10.0	9.9	9.8	9.8	9.7	9.6	9.5	9.4	9.2
79	9.7	9.7	9.7	9.6	9.6	9.6	9.5	9.5	9.4	9.3	9.3	9.2	9.1	9.0	8.9	8.8
80	9.2	9.2	9.1	9.1	9.1	9.0	9.0	9.0	8.9	8.9	8.8	8.7	8.7	8.6	8.5	8.4
81	8.7	8.7	8.6	8.6	8.6	8.5	8.5	8.5	8.4	8.4	8.3	8.3	8.2	8.1	8.0	8.0
82	8.2	8.2	8.1	8.1	8.1	8.1	8.0	8.0	8.0	8.0	7.9	7.9	7.8	7.8	7.7	7.6
83	7.7	7.7	7.7	7.6	7.6	7.6	7.6	7.5	7.5	7.5	7.4	7.4	7.3	7.3	7.2	7.1
84	7.2	7.2	7.2	7.2	7.2	7.1	7.1	7.1	7.1	7.0	7.0	7.0	6.9	6.9	6.8	6.7
85	6.8	6.8	6.8	6.7	6.7	6.7	6.7	6.7	6.6	6.6	6.6	6.5	6.5	6.5	6.4	6.4
86	6.4	6.4	6.3	6.3	6.3	6.3	6.3	6.3	6.2	6.2	6.2	6.2	6.1	6.1	6.0	6.0
87	6.0	6.0	6.0	5.9	5.9	5.9	5.9	5.9	5.9	5.8	5.8	5.8	5.8	5.7	5.7	5.6
88	5.6	5.6	5.6	5.6	5.6	5.5	5.5	5.5	5.5	5.5	5.5	5.4	5.4	5.4	5.3	5.3
89	5.2	5.2	5.2	5.2	5.2	5.2	5.2	5.2	5.2	5.1	5.1	5.1	5.1	5.1	5.0	5.0
90	4.9	4.9	4.9	4.9	4.9	4.9	4.9	4.9	4.9	4.8	4.8	4.8	4.8	4.8	4.7	4.7

Table VIA — Annuities for Joint Life Only — Two Lives — Expected Return Multiples

AGES	67	68	69	70	71	72	73	74	75	76	77	78	79	80	81	82
67	13.5	...	...	...	...	...	...	...	...	...	...	...	...	...	...	...
68	13.1	12.8	...	...	...	...	...	...	...	...	...	...	...	...	...	...
69	12.8	12.5	12.1	...	...	...	...	...	...	...	...	...	...	...	...	...
70	12.4	12.1	11.8	11.5	...	...	...	...	...	...	...	...	...	...	...	...
71	12.0	11.7	11.4	11.2	10.9	...	...	...	...	...	...	...	...	...	...	...
72	11.6	11.4	11.1	10.8	10.5	10.2	...	...	...	...	...	...	...	...	...	...
73	11.2	11.0	10.7	10.5	10.2	9.9	9.7	...	...	...	...	...	...	...	...	...
74	10.8	10.6	10.4	10.1	9.9	9.6	9.4	9.1	...	...	...	...	...	...	...	...
75	10.4	10.2	10.0	9.8	9.5	9.3	9.1	8.8	8.6	...	...	...	...	...	...	...
76	9.9	9.8	9.6	9.4	9.2	9.0	8.8	8.5	8.3	8.0	...	...	...	...	...	...
77	9.5	9.4	9.2	9.0	8.8	8.6	8.4	8.2	8.0	7.8	7.5	...	...	...	...	...
78	9.1	9.0	8.8	8.7	8.5	8.3	8.1	7.9	7.7	7.5	7.3	7.0	...	...	...	...
79	8.7	8.6	8.4	8.3	8.1	8.0	7.8	7.6	7.4	7.2	7.0	6.8	6.6	...	...	...
80	8.3	8.2	8.0	7.9	7.8	7.6	7.5	7.3	7.1	6.9	6.8	6.6	6.3	6.1	...	...
81	7.9	7.9	7.7	7.5	7.4	7.3	7.1	7.0	6.8	6.7	6.5	6.3	6.1	5.9	5.7	...
82	7.5	7.4	7.3	7.2	7.1	6.9	6.8	6.7	6.5	6.4	6.2	6.0	5.9	5.7	5.5	5.3
83	7.1	7.0	6.9	6.8	6.7	6.6	6.5	6.4	6.2	6.1	5.9	5.8	5.6	5.5	5.3	5.1
84	6.7	6.6	6.5	6.4	6.4	6.3	6.2	6.0	5.9	5.8	5.7	5.5	5.4	5.2	5.1	4.9
85	6.3	6.2	6.2	6.1	6.0	5.9	5.8	5.7	5.6	5.5	5.4	5.3	5.2	5.0	4.9	4.7
86	5.9	5.9	5.8	5.8	5.7	5.6	5.5	5.4	5.4	5.3	5.1	5.0	4.9	4.8	4.7	4.5
87	5.6	5.6	5.5	5.4	5.4	5.3	5.2	5.2	5.1	5.0	4.9	4.8	4.7	4.6	4.4	4.3
88	5.3	5.2	5.2	5.1	5.1	5.0	5.0	4.9	4.8	4.7	4.6	4.5	4.4	4.3	4.2	4.1
89	5.0	4.9	4.9	4.8	4.8	4.7	4.7	4.6	4.5	4.5	4.4	4.3	4.2	4.1	4.0	3.9
90	4.7	4.6	4.6	4.6	4.5	4.5	4.4	4.4	4.3	4.2	4.2	4.1	4.0	3.9	3.8	3.8

Table VIA — Annuities for Joint Life Only — Two Lives — Expected Return Multiples

AGES	83	84	85	86	87	88	89	90
83	4.9	...	...	...	...	...	...	...
84	4.7	4.6	...	...	...	...	...	...
85	4.6	4.4	4.2	...	...	...	...	...
86	4.4	4.2	4.1	3.9	...	...	...	...
87	4.2	4.1	3.9	3.8	3.6	...	...	...
88	4.0	3.9	3.8	3.6	3.5	3.4	...	...
89	3.8	3.7	3.6	3.5	3.4	3.2	3.1	...
90	3.7	3.5	3.4	3.3	3.2	3.1	3.0	2.9

Table VII — Percent Value of Refund Feature
Duration of Guaranteed Amount

Age	1 Yr.	2 Yrs.	3 Yrs.	4 Yrs.	5 Yrs.	6 Yrs.	7 Yrs.	8 Yrs.	9 Yrs.	10 Yrs.	11 Yrs.	12 Yrs.	13 Yrs.	14 Yrs.	15 Yrs.	16 Yrs.	17 Yrs.	18 Yrs.	19 Yrs.	20 Yrs.
19	...	...	...	...	...	...	...	...	...	...	...	...	...	...	...	...	...	...	...	...
20	...	...	...	...	...	...	...	...	...	...	...	...	...	...	...	...	...	...	...	1
21	...	...	...	...	...	...	...	...	...	...	...	...	...	...	...	...	...	...	...	1
22	...	...	...	...	...	...	...	...	...	...	...	...	...	...	...	...	...	...	...	1
23	...	...	...	...	...	...	...	...	...	...	...	...	...	...	...	...	...	1	1	1
24	...	...	...	...	...	...	...	...	...	...	...	...	...	...	...	...	...	1	1	1
25	...	...	...	...	...	...	...	...	...	...	...	...	...	...	...	...	1	1	1	1
26	...	...	...	...	...	...	...	...	...	...	...	...	...	...	...	...	1	1	1	1
27	...	...	...	...	...	...	...	...	...	...	...	...	...	...	...	1	1	1	1	1
28	...	...	...	...	...	...	...	...	...	...	...	...	...	...	1	1	1	1	1	1
29	...	...	...	...	...	...	...	...	...	...	...	...	...	...	1	1	1	1	1	1
30	...	...	...	...	...	...	...	...	...	...	...	...	...	1	1	1	1	1	1	1
31	...	...	...	...	...	...	...	...	...	...	...	...	1	1	1	1	1	1	1	1
32	...	...	...	...	...	...	...	...	...	...	...	...	1	1	1	1	1	1	1	1
33	...	...	...	...	...	...	...	...	...	...	...	1	1	1	1	1	1	1	1	1
34	...	...	...	...	...	...	...	...	...	...	...	1	1	1	1	1	1	1	1	1
35	...	...	...	...	...	...	...	...	...	...	1	1	1	1	1	1	1	1	1	1
36	...	...	...	...	...	...	...	...	...	1	1	1	1	1	1	1	1	1	1	1
37	...	...	...	...	...	...	...	1	1	1	1	1	1	1	1	1	1	1	1	1
38	...	...	...	...	...	...	...	1	1	1	1	1	1	1	1	1	1	1	1	2
39	...	...	...	...	...	...	1	1	1	1	1	1	1	1	1	1	1	1	2	2
40	...	...	...	...	...	...	1	1	1	1	1	1	1	1	1	1	1	2	2	2
41	...	...	...	...	...	...	1	1	1	1	1	1	1	1	1	1	2	2	2	2
42	...	...	...	...	...	1	1	1	1	1	1	1	1	1	1	2	2	2	2	2
43	...	...	...	...	...	1	1	1	1	1	1	1	1	1	2	2	2	2	2	3
44	...	...	...	...	1	1	1	1	1	1	1	1	2	2	2	2	2	3	3	3
45	...	...	...	...	1	1	1	1	1	1	1	1	2	2	2	2	3	3	3	3
46	...	...	...	...	1	1	1	1	1	1	1	2	2	2	2	2	3	3	3	3
47	...	...	...	...	1	1	1	1	1	1	1	2	2	2	2	2	3	3	3	4
48	...	...	...	...	1	1	1	1	1	1	2	2	2	2	2	3	3	3	4	4
49	...	...	...	1	1	1	1	1	1	2	2	2	2	2	3	3	3	4	4	4
50	...	...	...	1	1	1	1	1	1	2	2	2	2	3	3	3	4	4	4	5
51	...	...	...	1	1	1	1	1	2	2	2	2	3	3	3	3	4	4	5	5
52	...	...	...	1	1	1	1	1	2	2	2	2	3	3	3	4	4	5	5	5
53	...	...	1	1	1	1	1	2	2	2	2	3	3	3	4	4	4	5	5	6
54	...	...	1	1	1	1	1	2	2	2	3	3	3	4	4	4	5	5	6	7
55	...	...	1	1	1	1	2	2	2	2	3	3	4	4	4	5	5	6	7	7
56	...	...	1	1	1	1	2	2	2	3	3	3	4	4	5	5	6	7	7	8
57	...	...	1	1	1	2	2	2	3	3	3	4	4	5	5	6	6	7	8	9
58	...	1	1	1	1	2	2	2	3	3	4	4	5	5	6	6	7	8	9	9
59	...	1	1	1	1	2	2	3	3	4	4	5	5	6	6	7	8	9	9	10
60	...	1	1	1	2	2	2	3	3	4	4	5	6	6	7	8	9	10	10	11
61	...	1	1	1	2	2	3	3	4	4	5	6	6	7	8	9	10	10	11	13
62	...	1	1	2	2	2	3	4	4	5	5	6	7	8	9	10	11	12	13	14
63	...	1	1	2	2	3	3	4	5	5	6	7	8	9	10	11	12	13	14	15
64	...	1	1	2	2	3	4	4	5	6	7	8	8	9	10	12	13	14	15	17
65	...	1	2	2	3	3	4	5	6	6	7	8	9	10	12	13	14	15	17	18
66	1	1	2	2	3	4	5	5	6	7	8	9	10	12	13	14	15	17	17	20
67	1	1	2	3	3	4	5	6	7	8	9	10	11	13	14	15	17	18	20	22
68	1	1	2	3	4	5	6	7	8	9	10	11	13	14	15	17	19	20	22	24
69	1	1	2	3	4	5	6	7	8	10	11	12	14	15	17	19	20	22	24	26
70	1	2	3	4	5	6	7	8	9	11	12	14	15	17	19	20	22	24	26	28
71	1	2	3	4	5	6	8	9	10	12	13	15	17	18	20	22	24	26	28	30
72	1	2	3	4	6	7	8	10	11	13	15	16	18	20	22	24	26	28	30	32
73	1	2	4	5	6	8	9	11	13	14	16	18	20	22	24	26	28	31	33	35
74	1	3	4	5	7	9	10	12	14	16	18	20	22	24	26	28	31	33	35	37
75	1	3	4	6	8	9	11	13	15	17	19	22	24	26	28	31	33	35	38	40
76	2	3	5	7	9	10	12	15	17	19	21	24	26	28	31	33	36	38	40	43
77	2	4	5	7	9	12	14	16	18	21	23	26	28	31	33	36	38	41	43	45
78	2	4	6	8	10	13	15	18	20	23	25	28	31	33	36	38	41	43	46	48
79	2	4	7	9	11	14	17	19	22	25	28	30	33	36	38	41	44	46	48	51
80	2	5	7	10	13	15	18	21	24	27	30	33	36	38	41	44	46	49	51	53
81	3	5	8	11	14	17	20	23	26	29	32	35	38	41	44	47	48	51	54	56
82	3	6	9	12	15	19	22	25	28	32	35	38	41	44	47	49	52	54	56	58
83	3	7	10	13	17	20	24	27	31	34	38	41	44	47	49	52	54	57	59	61
84	4	7	11	15	19	22	26	30	33	37	40	44	47	49	52	55	57	59	61	63
85	4	8	12	16	20	24	28	32	36	40	43	46	49	52	55	57	59	62	63	65
86	4	9	13	18	22	27	31	35	39	42	46	49	52	55	57	60	62	64	66	67
87	5	10	15	20	24	29	33	37	41	45	48	52	55	57	60	62	64	66	68	69
88	5	11	16	21	26	31	36	40	44	48	51	54	57	60	62	64	66	68	70	71
89	6	12	18	23	28	33	38	43	47	50	54	57	60	62	65	67	68	70	72	73
90	7	13	19	25	31	36	41	45	49	53	56	59	62	64	67	69	70	72	74	75

Table VII — Percent Value of Refund Feature
Duration of Guaranteed Amount

Age	21 Yrs.	22 Yrs.	23 Yrs.	24 Yrs.	25 Yrs.	26 Yrs.	27 Yrs.	28 Yrs.	29 Yrs.	30 Yrs.	31 Yrs.	32 Yrs.	33 Yrs.	34 Yrs.	35 Yrs.	36 Yrs.	37 Yrs.	38 Yrs.	39 Yrs.	40 Yrs.
5	...	...	...	...	...	...	...	...	...	...	...	1	1	1	1	1	1	1	1	1
6	...	...	...	...	...	...	...	...	...	...	...	1	1	1	1	1	1	1	1	1
7	...	...	...	...	...	...	...	...	...	...	1	1	1	1	1	1	1	1	1	1
8	...	...	...	...	...	...	...	...	...	1	1	1	1	1	1	1	1	1	1	1
9	...	...	...	...	...	...	...	...	1	1	1	1	1	1	1	1	1	1	1	1
10	...	...	...	...	...	...	...	1	1	1	1	1	1	1	1	1	1	1	1	1
11	...	...	...	...	...	...	1	1	1	1	1	1	1	1	1	1	1	1	1	1
12	...	...	...	...	...	...	1	1	1	1	1	1	1	1	1	1	1	1	1	1
13	...	...	...	...	...	1	1	1	1	1	1	1	1	1	1	1	1	1	1	1
14	...	...	...	...	1	1	1	1	1	1	1	1	1	1	1	1	1	1	1	1
15	...	...	...	1	1	1	1	1	1	1	1	1	1	1	1	1	1	1	1	1
16	...	...	1	1	1	1	1	1	1	1	1	1	1	1	1	1	1	1	1	1
17	...	...	1	1	1	1	1	1	1	1	1	1	1	1	1	1	1	1	1	1
18	...	1	1	1	1	1	1	1	1	1	1	1	1	1	1	1	1	1	1	2
19	1	1	1	1	1	1	1	1	1	1	1	1	1	1	1	1	1	1	2	2
20	1	1	1	1	1	1	1	1	1	1	1	1	1	1	1	1	1	2	2	2
21	1	1	1	1	1	1	1	1	1	1	1	1	1	1	1	1	1	2	2	2
22	1	1	1	1	1	1	1	1	1	1	1	1	1	1	1	1	2	2	2	2
23	1	1	1	1	1	1	1	1	1	1	1	1	1	1	1	2	2	2	2	2
24	1	1	1	1	1	1	1	1	1	1	1	1	1	2	2	2	2	2	2	2
25	1	1	1	1	1	1	1	1	1	1	1	2	2	2	2	2	2	2	2	3
26	1	1	1	1	1	1	1	1	1	1	2	2	2	2	2	2	2	2	3	3
27	1	1	1	1	1	1	1	1	1	2	2	2	2	2	2	2	2	3	3	3
28	1	1	1	1	1	1	1	1	2	2	2	2	2	2	2	2	3	3	3	3
29	1	1	1	1	1	1	1	2	2	2	2	2	2	2	3	3	3	3	3	4
30	1	1	1	1	1	1	1	2	2	2	2	2	2	3	3	3	3	3	4	4
31	1	1	1	1	1	2	2	2	2	2	2	3	3	3	3	3	3	4	4	4
32	1	1	1	1	2	2	2	2	2	2	2	3	3	3	3	3	4	4	4	5
33	1	1	1	1	2	2	2	2	2	2	3	3	3	3	3	4	4	4	5	5
34	1	1	2	2	2	2	2	2	2	3	3	3	3	3	4	4	4	5	5	5
35	1	2	2	2	2	2	2	3	3	3	3	3	3	4	4	4	5	5	5	6
36	2	2	2	2	2	2	2	3	3	3	3	4	4	4	4	5	5	5	6	6
37	2	2	2	2	2	3	3	3	3	4	4	4	4	4	5	5	6	6	6	7
38	2	2	2	2	2	3	3	3	3	4	4	4	5	5	5	6	6	7	7	8
39	2	2	2	2	3	3	3	4	4	4	4	5	5	5	6	6	7	7	8	8
40	2	2	3	3	3	3	3	4	4	4	5	5	5	6	7	7	7	8	8	9
41	2	3	3	3	3	3	4	4	4	5	5	5	6	6	7	7	8	8	9	10
42	3	3	3	3	4	4	4	5	5	5	6	6	7	7	8	8	9	9	10	11
43	3	3	3	4	4	4	5	5	6	6	7	7	8	8	9	9	10	11	11	12
44	3	3	4	4	4	5	5	6	6	7	7	8	8	9	9	10	11	12	12	13
45	3	4	4	4	5	5	5	6	6	7	7	8	8	9	10	10	11	12	13	14
46	4	4	4	5	5	5	6	6	7	7	8	9	9	10	11	11	12	13	14	15
47	4	4	5	5	5	6	6	7	7	8	9	9	10	11	11	12	13	14	15	16
48	4	5	5	5	6	6	7	7	8	9	9	10	11	12	13	14	15	16	17	18
49	5	5	5	6	6	7	8	8	9	10	10	11	12	13	14	15	16	17	18	19
50	5	5	6	6	7	8	8	9	10	10	11	12	13	14	15	16	17	18	20	21
51	5	6	6	7	7	8	9	10	11	11	12	13	14	15	16	17	19	20	21	22
52	6	6	7	8	8	9	10	11	11	12	13	14	15	17	18	19	20	21	23	24
53	7	7	8	8	9	10	11	12	13	14	15	16	17	18	19	20	22	23	24	26
54	7	8	8	9	10	11	12	13	14	15	16	17	18	19	21	22	23	25	26	28
55	8	9	9	10	11	12	13	14	15	16	17	18	20	21	22	24	25	27	28	30
56	9	9	10	11	12	13	14	15	16	18	19	20	21	23	24	26	27	29	30	32
57	9	10	11	12	13	14	15	17	18	19	20	22	23	25	26	28	29	31	32	34
58	10	11	12	13	14	16	17	18	19	21	22	24	25	27	28	30	31	33	34	36
59	11	12	13	15	16	17	18	20	21	22	24	25	27	28	30	32	33	35	36	38
60	12	14	15	16	17	19	20	21	23	24	26	27	29	31	32	34	35	37	38	40
61	14	15	16	17	19	20	22	23	25	26	28	29	31	33	34	36	37	39	40	42
62	15	16	18	19	20	22	23	25	27	28	30	32	33	35	36	38	40	41	42	44
63	16	18	19	21	22	24	25	27	29	30	32	34	35	37	39	40	42	43	45	46
64	18	19	21	23	24	26	28	29	31	33	34	36	38	39	41	42	44	45	47	48
65	20	21	23	25	26	28	30	31	33	35	36	38	40	42	43	45	46	47	49	50
66	21	23	25	27	28	30	32	34	35	37	39	41	42	44	45	47	48	50	51	52
67	23	25	27	29	31	32	34	36	38	40	41	43	45	46	48	49	50	52	53	54
68	25	27	29	31	33	35	37	38	40	42	44	45	47	48	50	51	52	54	55	56
69	28	29	31	33	35	37	39	41	43	44	46	48	49	51	52	53	54	56	57	58
70	30	32	34	36	38	40	42	43	45	47	48	50	51	53	54	55	57	58	59	60
71	32	34	36	38	40	42	44	46	47	49	51	52	54	55	56	57	59	60	61	62
72	35	37	39	41	43	45	46	48	50	51	53	54	56	57	59	60	61	62	62	63
73	37	39	41	43	45	47	49	51	52	54	55	57	58	59	60	61	62	63	64	65
74	40	42	44	46	48	50	51	53	54	56	57	59	60	61	62	63	64	65	66	67
75	42	44	46	48	50	52	54	55	57	58	59	61	62	63	64	65	66	67	68	69
76	45	47	49	51	53	54	56	58	59	60	62	63	64	65	66	67	68	69	69	70
77	47	50	51	53	55	57	58	60	61	62	64	65	66	67	68	69	70	70	71	72
78	50	52	54	56	57	59	61	62	63	64	66	67	68	69	70	70	71	72	73	73
79	53	55	56	58	60	61	63	64	65	66	67	68	69	70	71	72	73	73	74	75
80	55	57	59	60	62	63	65	66	67	68	70	71	72	73	74	74	75	75	76	76
81	58	59	61	63	64	66	67	68	69	70	71	72	73	74	75	75	76	76	77	78
82	60	62	63	65	66	68	69	70	71	72	73	74	74	75	76	77	77	78	78	79
83	62	64	66	67	68	70	71	72	73	74	75	75	76	77	77	78	78	79	79	80
84	65	66	68	69	70	71	72	73	74	75	76	77	77	78	79	79	80	80	81	81
85	67	68	70	71	72	73	74	75	76	77	78	78	79	79	80	81	81	82	82	83
86	69	70	72	73	74	75	76	77	77	78	79	80	80	81	81	82	82	83	83	84
87	71	72	73	75	76	77	78	78	79	80	80	81	81	82	83	83	83	84	84	85
88	73	74	75	76	77	78	79	80	80	81	82	82	83	83	84	84	85	85	85	86
89	74	76	77	78	79	79	80	81	81	82	83	83	84	84	85	85	85	86	86	87
90	76	77	78	79	80	81	81	82	83	83	84	84	84	85	85	86	86	86	87	87

Appendix B

Examples of Exclusion Ratio Calculations

Single Life Annuity

Example 1. On October 1, 2012, Mr. Smith purchased an immediate nonrefund annuity which will pay him $125 a month ($1,500 a year) for life, beginning November 1, 2012. He paid $16,000 for the contract. Mr. Smith's age on his birthday nearest the annuity starting date (October 1st) was 68. According to Table V, which he uses because his investment in the contract is post-June 1986, his life expectancy is 17.6 years. Consequently, the expected return under the contract is $26,400 (12 x $125 x 17.6). The exclusion percentage for the annuity payments is 60.6% ($16,000 ÷ $26,400). Since Mr. Smith received 2 monthly payments in 2012 (a total of $250), he will exclude $151.50 (60.6% of $250) from his gross income for 2012, and he must include $98.50 ($250 – $151.50). Mr. Smith will exclude the amounts so determined for 17.6 years. In 2012, he could exclude $151.50; each year thereafter through 2025, he could exclude $909, for a total exclusion of $15,604.50 ($151.50 excluded in 2012 and $15,453 excluded over the next 17 years). In 2026, he could exclude only $395.50 ($16,000 – $15,604.50). In 2026, he would include in his income $1,104.50 ($1,500 – $395.50) and $1,500 in 2027 and in each year thereafter.

Example 2. If Mr. Smith purchased the contract illustrated above on October 1, 1986, so that it had an annuity starting date before January 1, 1987, he would exclude $151.50 (60.6% of $250) from his 1986 gross income and would include $98.50 ($250 – $151.50). For each succeeding tax year in which he receives 12 monthly payments, even if he outlives his life expectancy of 17.6 years, he will exclude $909 (60.6% of $1,500), and he will include $591 ($1,500 – $909).

Refund or Period Certain Guarantee

Example 1. On January 1, 2012 a husband, age 65, purchased for $21,053 an immediate installment refund annuity which pays $100 a month for life. The contract provides that in the event the husband does not live long enough to recover the full purchase price, payments will be made to his wife until the total payments under the contract equal the purchase price. The investment in the contract is adjusted for the purpose of determining the exclusion ratio as follows:

Unadjusted investment in the contract	$ 21,053
Amount to be received annually	$ 1,200
Duration of guaranteed amount ($21,053 ÷ $1,200)	17.5 yrs.
Rounded to nearest whole number of years	18
Percentage value of guaranteed refund	
(Table VII for age 65 and 18 years)	15%
Value of refund feature rounded to nearest dollar (15% of $21,053)	$ 3,158
Adjusted investment in the contract ($21,053 - $3,158)	$ 17,895

Example 2. Assume the contract in Example 1 was purchased as a deferred annuity and the pre-July 1986 investment in the contract is $10,000 and the post-June 1986 investment in the contract is $11,053. If the annuitant elects, as explained earlier, to compute a separate exclusion percentage for the pre-July 1986 and the post-June 1986 amounts, separate computations must be performed to determine the adjusted investment in the contract. The pre-July 1986 investment in the contract and the post-June 1986 investment in the contract are adjusted for the purpose of determining the exclusion ratios in the following manner:

Pre-July 1986 adjustment:	
Unadjusted investment in the contract	$ 10,000
Allocable part of amount to be received annually	
(($10,000 ÷ $21,053) x $1,200)	$ 570
Duration of guaranteed amount ($10,000 ÷ $570)	17.5
Rounded to nearest whole number of years	18
Percentage in Table III for age 65 and 18 years	30%
Present value of refund feature rounded to nearest dollar	
(30% of $10,000)	$ 3,000
Adjusted pre-July 1986 investment in the contract ($10,000 - $3,000)	$ 7,000
Post-June 1986 adjustment:	
Unadjusted investment in the contract	$ 11,053
Allocable part of amount to be received annually	
(($11,053 ÷ $21,053) x $1,200	$ 630
Duration of guaranteed amount ($11,053 ÷ $630)	17.54
Rounded to nearest whole number of years	18
Percentage in Table VII for age 65 and 18 years	15%
Present value of refund feature rounded to nearest dollar	
(15% of $11,054)	$ 1,658
Adjusted post-June 1986 investment in the contract	
($11,053 - $1,658)	$ 9,395

Once the investment in the contract has been adjusted by subtracting the value of the refund or period certain guarantee, an exclusion ratio is determined in the same way as for a straight life annuity. Expected return is computed; then the adjusted investment in the contract is divided by expected return. Taking the two examples above, the exclusion ratio for each contract is determined as follows:

Example (1) above.

Investment in the contract (adjusted for refund guarantee)	17,895
One year's guaranteed annuity payments (12 x $100)	$ 1,200
Life expectancy for Table V, age 65	20 yrs.
Expected return (20 x $1,200)	$ 24,000
Exclusion ratio ($17,895 ÷ $24,000)	74.6%
Amount excludable from gross income each year in which	
12 payments are received (74.6% of $1,200)*	$ 895.20
Amount includable in gross income ($1,200 - $895.20)*	$ 304.80

*Since the annuity starting date is after December 31, 1986, the total amount excludable is limited to the investment in the contract; after that has been recovered, the remaining amounts received are includable in income. However, the Small Business Job Protection Act of 1996 (P.L. 104-188) changed the manner in which the unrecovered investment in the contract is calculated when the annuity has a refund or guarantee feature. Generally, the portion of any amount received as an annuity that can be excluded using the exclusion ratio is not to exceed the unrecovered investment in the contract. In calculating this figure, the value of the refund or guarantee feature was subtracted prior to the 1996 Act. After the 1996 Act, for this purpose, the value of the refund or guarantee feature is not subtracted. Although this change was made in 1996 legislation, it is effective for individuals with annuity starting dates after December 31, 1986 (IRC Sec. 72(b)(4)). Please note, this change does not affect the calculation of the refund or guarantee feature for purposes of calculating the exclusion ratio; it only affects the unrecovered investment in the contract and, thus, the date on which the investment in the contract is recovered.

Example (2) above.

Pre-July 1986 investment in the contract	
(adjusted for period certain guarantee)	$ 7,000
One year's guaranteed annuity payments (12 x $100)	$ 1,200
Life expectancy from Table I, male age 65	15 yrs.
Expected return (15 x $1,200)	$ 18,000
Exclusion ratio ($7,000 ÷ $18,000)	38.9%
Post-June 1986 investment in the contract	
(adjusted for period certain guarantee)	$ 9,395
One year's guaranteed annuity payments (12 x $100)	$ 1,200
Life expectancy from Table V, age 65	20 yrs.
Expected return (20 x $1,200)	$ 24,000
Exclusion ratio ($9,395 ÷ $24,000)	39.1%
Sum of pre-July and post-June 1986 ratios	78%

Amount excludable from gross income each year in which	
twelve payments are received (78% of $1,200)*	$ 936.00
Amount includable in gross income ($1,200 - 936.00)*	$ 264.00

*Since the annuity starting date is after December 31, 1986, the total amount excludable is limited to the investment in the contract; after that has been recovered, the remaining amounts received are includable in income. Note that 1996 legislation changed the manner in which the unrecovered investment in the contract is calculated for this purpose as explained above in Example 1.

Joint and Survivor Annuity
(Same Income to Survivor as to Both Annuitants Before Any Death)

Example 1. After June 30, 1986, Mr. and Mrs. Jones purchase an immediate joint and survivor annuity. The annuity will provide payments of $100 a month while both are alive and until the death of the survivor. Mr. Jones' age on his birthday nearest the annuity starting date is 65; Mrs. Jones', 63. The single premium is $22,000.

Investment in the contract	$ 22,000
One year's annuity payments (12 x $100)	1,200
Joint and survivor multiple from Table VI	
(age 65, 63)	26
Expected return (26 x $1,200)	$ 31,200
Exclusion ratio ($22,000 ÷ $31,200)	70.5%
Amount excludable from gross income each year in which 12	
payments are received (70.5% of $1,200)*	$ 846.00
Amount includable in gross income	
($1,200 - $846.00)*	354.00

*If the annuity starting date is after December 31, 1986, the total amount excludable is limited to the investment in the contract; after that has been recovered, the remaining amounts received are includable in income.

Joint and Survivor Annuity
(Income to Survivor Differs from Income before First Death)

Example 1. After July 30, 1986, Mr. and Mrs. Smith buy an immediate joint and survivor annuity which will provide monthly payments of $117 ($1,404 a year) for as long as both live, and monthly payments of $78 ($936 a year) to the survivor. As of the annuity starting date he is 65 years old; she is 63. The expected return is computed as follows:

Joint and survivor multiple from Table VI (ages 65, 63)	26
Portion of expected return (26 x $936)	$24,366.00
Joint life multiple from Table VIA (ages 65, 63)	15.6
Difference between annual annuity payment before the first death and annual annuity payment to the survivor ($1,404 - $936)	$468
Portion of expected return (15.6 x $468)	<u>$ 7,300.80</u>
Expected return	$31,636.80

Assuming that Mr. Smith paid $22,000 for the contract, the exclusion ratio is 69.5% ($22,000 ÷ $31,636.80). During their joint lives the portion of each monthly payment to be excluded from gross income is $81.31 (69.5% of $117), or $975.72 a year. The portion to be included is $35.69 ($117 – $81.31), or $428.28 a year. After the first death, the portion of each monthly payment to be excluded from gross income will be $54.21 (69.5% of $78), or $650.52 a year. $23.79 of each payment ($78 – $54.21), or $285.48 a year, will be included. If the annuity starting date is after December 31, 1986, the total amount excludable is limited to the investment in the contract. Thus, if Mr. Smith lives for 23 years, he may exclude $81.31 from each payment for 22 years ((12 x 22) x $81.31 = $21,465.84). In the 23rd year he may exclude $534.16 ($22,000 – $21,465.84) or $81.31 from each of the first six payments, but only $46.30 from the seventh. The balance is entirely includable in his income, and on his death, his widow must include the full amount of each payment in income.

Example 2. Assume that in the example above, there is a pre-July 1986 investment in the contract of $12,000 and a post-June 1986 investment in the contract of $10,000. Mr. Smith elects to calculate the exclusion percentage for each portion. The pre-July exclusion ratio would be 44.6% ($12,000 ÷ $26,910—the expected return on the contract determined by using Tables II and IIA and the age and sex of both annuitants). The post-June 1986 exclusion ratio is $10,000 ÷ $31,636.80 or 31.6%. The amount excludable from each monthly payment while both are alive would be $89.15 (44.6% of $117 plus 31.6% of $117) and the remaining $27.85 would be included in gross income. If the annuity starting date is after December 31, 1986, the total amount excludable is limited to the investment in the contract.

Appendix C

Internal Revenue Code Sections

Internal Revenue Code Section 72

26 USC § 72 - Annuities; certain proceeds of endowment and life insurance contracts

(a) General Rules for Annuities

(1) Income inclusion

Except as otherwise provided in this chapter, gross income includes any amount received as an annuity, whether for a period certain or during one or more lives, under an annuity, endowment, or life insurance contract.

(2) Partial annuitization

If any amount is received as an annuity for a period of 10 years or more or during one or more lives under any portion of an annuity, endowment, or life insurance contract:

(A) such portion shall be treated as a separate contract for purposes of this section,

(B) for purposes of applying subsections (b), (c), and (e), the investment in the contract shall be allocated pro rata between each portion of the contract from which amounts are received as an annuity and the portion of the contract from which amounts are not received as an annuity, and

(C) a separate annuity starting date under subsection (c)(4) shall be determined with respect to each portion of the contract from which amounts are received as an annuity.

(b) Exclusion ratio

(1) In general

Gross income does not include that part of any amount received as an annuity under an annuity, endowment, or life insurance contract which bears the same ratio to such amount as the investment in the contract, as of the annuity starting date, bears to the expected return under the contract, as of such date.

(2) Exclusion limited to investment

The portion of any amount received as an annuity which is excluded from gross income under paragraph (1) shall not exceed the unrecovered investment in the contract immediately before the receipt of such amount.

(3) Deduction where annuity payments cease before entire investment recovered

(A) In general

If:

after the annuity starting date, payments as an annuity under the contract cease by reason of the death of an annuitant, and

(ii) as of the date of such cessation, there is unrecovered investment in the contract, the amount of such unrecovered investment, in excess of any amount specified in subsection (e)(5) which was not included in gross income, shall be allowed as a deduction to the annuitant for his last taxable year.

(B) Payments to other persons

In the case of any contract which provides for payments meeting the requirements of subparagraphs (B) and (C) of subsection (c)(2), the deduction under subparagraph (A) shall be allowed to the person entitled to such payments for the taxable year in which such payments are received.

(C) Net operating loss deductions provided

For purposes of section 172, a deduction allowed under this paragraph shall be treated as if it were attributable to a trade or business of the taxpayer.

(4) Unrecovered Investment

For purposes of this subsection, the unrecovered investment in the contract as of any date is:

(A) the investment in the contract, determined without regard to subsection (c)(2), as of the annuity starting date, reduced by

(B) the aggregate amount received under the contract on or after such annuity starting date and before the date as of which the determination is being made, to the extent such amount was excludable from gross income under this subtitle.

(c) Definitions

(1) Investment in the contract

For purposes of subsection (b), the investment in the contract as of the annuity starting date is:

(A) the aggregate amount of premiums or other consideration paid for the contract, minus

(B) the aggregate amount received under the contract before such date, to the extent that such amount was excludable from gross income under this subtitle or prior income tax laws.

(2) Adjustment in investment where there is refund feature

If:

(A) the expected return under the contract depends in whole or in part on the life expectancy of one or more individuals,

(B) the contract provides for payments to be made to a beneficiary, or to the estate of an annuitant, on or after the death of the annuitant or annuitants, and

(C) such payments are in the nature of a refund of the consideration paid, then the value, computed without discount for interest, of such payments on the annuity starting date shall be subtracted from the amount determined under paragraph (1). Such value shall be computed in accordance with actuarial tables prescribed by the Secretary. For purposes of this paragraph and of subsection (e)(2)(A), the term "refund of the consideration paid" includes amounts payable after the death of an annuitant by reason of a provision in the contract for a life annuity with minimum period of payments certain, but, if part of the consideration was contributed by an employer, does not include that part of any payment to a beneficiary (or to the estate of the annuitant) which is not attributable to the consideration paid by the employee for the contract as determined under paragraph (1)(A).

(3) Expected Return

For purposes of subsection (b), the expected return under the contract shall be determined as follows:

(A) Life expectancy

If the expected return under the contract, for the period on and after the annuity starting date, depends in whole or in part on the life expectancy of one or more individuals, the expected return shall be computed with reference to actuarial tables prescribed by the Secretary.

(B) **Installment payments**

If subparagraph (A) does not apply, the expected return is the aggregate of the amounts receivable under the contract as an annuity.

(4) **Annuity starting date**

For purposes of this section, the annuity starting date in the case of any contract is the first day of the first period for which an amount is received as an annuity under the contract; except that if such date was before January 1, 1954, then the annuity starting date is January 1, 1954.

(d) Special Rules for Qualified Employer Retirement Plans

(1) **Simplified method of taxing annuity payments**

(A) **In general**

In the case of any amount received as an annuity under a qualified employer retirement plan:

(i) subsection (b) shall not apply, and

(ii) the investment in the contract shall be recovered as provided in this paragraph.

(B) **Method of recovering investment in contract**

(i) In general Gross income shall not include so much of any monthly annuity payment under a qualified employer retirement plan as does not exceed the amount obtained by dividing:

(I) the investment in the contract, as of the annuity starting date, by

(II) the number of anticipated payments determined under the table contained in clause

(iii) or, in the case of a contract to which subsection (c)(3)(B) applies, the number of monthly annuity payments under such contract.

(ii) Certain rules made applicable Rules similar to the rules of paragraphs (2) and (3) of subsection (b) shall apply for purposes of this paragraph.

(iii) Number of anticipated payments If the annuity is payable over the life of a single individual, the number of anticipated payments shall be determined as follows:

If the age of the annuitant on the annuity starting date is:	The number of anticipated payments is:
Not more than 55	360
More than 55 but not more than 60	310
More than 60 but not more than 65	260
More than 65 but not more than 70	210
More than 70	160

(iv) Number of anticipated payments where more than one life

If the annuity is payable over the lives of more than 1 individual, the number of anticipated payments shall be determined as follows:

If the combined ages of annuitants are:	The number is:
Not more than 110	410
More than 110 but not more than 120	360
More than 120 but not more than 130	310
More than 130 but not more than 140	260
More than 140	210

(C) **Adjustment for refund feature not applicable**

For purposes of this paragraph, investment in the contract shall be determined under subsection (c)(1) without regard to subsection (c)(2).

(D) **Special rule where lump sum paid in connection with commencement of annuity payments**

If, in connection with the commencement of annuity payments under any qualified employer retirement plan, the taxpayer receives a lump-sum payment:

(i) such payment shall be taxable under subsection (e) as if received before the annuity starting date, and

(ii) the investment in the contract for purposes of this paragraph shall be determined as if such payment had been so received.

(E) **Exception**

This paragraph shall not apply in any case where the primary annuitant has attained age 75 on the annuity starting date unless there are fewer than 5 years of guaranteed payments under the annuity.

(F) Adjustment where annuity payments not on monthly basis

In any case where the annuity payments are not made on a monthly basis, appropriate adjustments in the application of this paragraph shall be made to take into account the period on the basis of which such payments are made.

(G) Qualified employer retirement plan

For purposes of this paragraph, the term qualified employer retirement plan means any plan or contract described in paragraph (1), (2), or (3) of section 4974 (c).

(2) Treatment of employee contributions under defined contribution plans

For purposes of this section, employee contributions, and any income allocable thereto, under a defined contribution plan may be treated as a separate contract.

(e) Amounts Not Received as Annuities

(1) Application of subsection

(A) In general

This subsection shall apply to any amount which:

(i) is received under an annuity, endowment, or life insurance contract, and

(ii) is not received as an annuity,

if no provision of this subtitle, other than this subsection, applies with respect to such amount.

(B) Dividends

For purposes of this section, any amount received which is in the nature of a dividend or similar distribution shall be treated as an amount not received as an annuity.

(2) General rule

Any amount to which this subsection applies:

(A) if received on or after the annuity starting date, shall be included in gross income, or

(B) if received before the annuity starting date,

(i) shall be included in gross income to the extent allocable to income on the contract, and

(ii) shall not be included in gross income to the extent allocable to the investment in the contract.

(3) **Allocation of amounts to income and investment**

For purposes of paragraph (2)(B):

(A) **Allocation to income**

Any amount to which this subsection applies shall be treated as allocable to income on the contract to the extent that such amount does not exceed the excess (if any) of

(i) the cash value of the contract, determined without regard to any surrender charge, immediately before the amount is received, over

(ii) the investment in the contract at such time.

(B) **Allocation to investment**

Any amount to which this subsection applies shall be treated as allocable to investment in the contract to the extent that such amount is not allocated to income under subparagraph (A).

(4) **Special rules for application of paragraph (2)(B)**

For purposes of paragraph (2)(B):

(A) **Loans treated as distributions**

If, during any taxable year, an individual:

(i) receives directly or indirectly, any amount as a loan under any contract to which this subsection applies, or

(ii) assigns or pledges or agrees to assign or pledge, any portion of the value of any such contract, such amount or portion shall be treated as received under the contract as an amount not received as an annuity. The preceding sentence shall not apply for purposes of determining investment in the contract, except that the investment in the contract shall be increased by any amount included in gross income by reason of the amount treated as received under the preceding sentence.

(B) **Treatment of policyholder dividends**

Any amount described in paragraph (1)(B) shall not be included in gross income under paragraph (2)(B)(i) to the extent such amount is retained by the insurer as a premium or other consideration paid for the contract.

(C) **Treatment of transfers without adequate consideration**

(i) In general

If an individual who holds an annuity contract transfers it without full and adequate consideration, such individual shall be treated as receiving an amount equal to the excess of:

(I) the cash surrender value of such contract at the time of transfer, over

(II) the investment in such contract at such time,

under the contract as an amount not received as an annuity.

(ii) Exception for certain transfers between spouses or former spouses Clause (i) shall not apply to any transfer to which section 1041 (a) relating to transfers of property between spouses or incident to divorce applies.

(iii) Adjustment to investment in contract of transferee If under clause (i) an amount is included in the gross income of the transferor of an annuity contract, the investment in the contract of the transferee in such contract shall be increased by the amount so included.

(5) **Retention of existing rules in certain cases**

(A) **In general**

In any case to which this paragraph applies:

(i) paragraphs (2)(B) and (4)(A) shall not apply, and

(ii) if paragraph (2)(A) does not apply,

the amount shall be included in gross income, but only to the extent it exceeds the investment in the contract.

(B) **Existing contracts**

This paragraph shall apply to contracts entered into before August 14, 1982. Any amount allocable to investment in the contract after August 13, 1982, shall be treated as from a contract entered into after such date.

(C) **Certain life insurance and endowment contracts**

Except as provided in paragraph (10) and except to the extent prescribed by the Secretary by regulations, this paragraph shall apply to any amount not received as an annuity which is received under a life insurance or endowment contract.

(D) **Contracts under qualified plans**

Except as provided in paragraph (8), this paragraph shall apply to any amount received:

from a trust described in section 401 (a) which is exempt from tax under section 501 (a),

(ii) from a contract

(I) purchased by a trust described in clause (i),

(II) purchased as part of a plan described in section 403 (a),

(III) described in section 403 (b), or

(IV) provided for employees of a life insurance company under a plan described in section 818 (a)(3), or

(iii) from an individual retirement account or an individual retirement annuity.

Any dividend described in section 404 (k) which is received by a participant or beneficiary shall, for purposes of this subparagraph, be treated as paid under a separate contract to which clause (ii)(I) applies.

(E) **Full refunds, surrenders, redemptions, and maturities**

This paragraph shall apply to:

(i) any amount received, whether in a single sum or otherwise, under a contract in full discharge of the obligation under the contract which is in the nature of a refund of the consideration paid for the contract, and

(ii) any amount received under a contract on its complete surrender, redemption, or maturity.

In the case of any amount to which the preceding sentence applies, the rule of paragraph

(2)(A) shall not apply.

(6) **Investment in the contract**

For purposes of this subsection, the investment in the contract as of any date is:

(A) the aggregate amount of premiums or other consideration paid for the contract before such date, minus

(B) the aggregate amount received under the contract before such date, to the extent that such amount was excludable from gross income under this subtitle or prior income tax laws.

[(7) **Repealed. Pub. L. 100–647, title I, § 1011A(b)(9)(A),Nov. 10, 1988, 102 Stat. 3474**]

(8) **Extension of paragraph (2)(b) 1 to qualified plans**

(A) **In general**

Notwithstanding any other provision of this subsection, in the case of any amount received before the annuity starting date from a trust or contract described in paragraph

(5)(D), paragraph (2)(B) shall apply to such amounts.

(B) **Allocation of amount received**

For purposes of paragraph (2)(B), the amount allocated to the investment in the contract shall be the portion of the amount described in subparagraph (A) which bears the same ratio to such amount as the investment in the contract bears to the account balance. The determination under the preceding sentence shall be made as of the time of the distribution or at such other time as the Secretary may prescribe.

(C) **Treatment of forfeitable rights**

If an employee does not have a nonforfeitable right to any amount under any trust or contract to which subparagraph (A) applies, such amount shall not be treated as part of the account balance.

(D) **Investment in the contract before 1987**

In the case of a plan which on May 5, 1986, permitted withdrawal of any employee contributions before separation from service, subparagraph (A) shall apply only to the extent that amounts received before the annuity starting date, when increased by amounts previously received under the contract after December 31, 1986, exceed the investment in the contract as of December 31, 1986.

(9) **Extension of paragraph (2)(B) to qualified tuition programs and Coverdell education savings accounts**

Notwithstanding any other provision of this subsection, paragraph (2)(B) shall apply to amounts received under a qualified tuition program, as defined in section 529 (b), or under a Coverdell education savings account, as defined in section 530 (b). The rule of paragraph (8)(B) shall apply for purposes of this paragraph.

(10) Treatment of modified endowment contracts

(A) In general

Notwithstanding paragraph (5)(C), in the case of any modified endowment contract, as defined in section 7702A

(i) paragraphs (2)(B) and (4)(A) shall apply, and

(ii) in applying paragraph (4)(A), "any person" shall be substituted for "an individual."

(B) Treatment of certain burial contracts

Notwithstanding subparagraph (A), paragraph (4)(A) shall not apply to any assignment, or pledge, of a modified endowment contract if such assignment (or pledge) is solely to cover the payment of expenses referred to in section 7702 (e)(2)(C)(iii) and if the maximum death benefit under such contract does not exceed $25,000.

(11) Special rules for certain combination contracts providing long-term care insurance

Notwithstanding paragraphs (2), (5)(C), and (10), in the case of any charge against the cash value of an annuity contract or the cash surrender value of a life insurance contract made as payment for coverage under a qualified long-term care insurance contract which is part of or a rider on such annuity or life insurance contract:

(A) the investment in the contract shall be reduced (but not below zero) by such charge, and

(B) such charge shall not be includible in gross income.

(12) Anti-abuse rules

(A) In general

For purposes of determining the amount includible in gross income under this subsection:

(i) all modified endowment contracts issued by the same company to the same policyholder during any calendar year shall be treated as 1 modified endowment contract, and

(ii) all annuity contracts issued by the same company to the same policyholder during any calendar year shall be treated as 1 annuity contract.

The preceding sentence shall not apply to any contract described in paragraph (5)(D).

(B) **Regulatory authority**

The Secretary may by regulations prescribe such additional rules as may be necessary or appropriate to prevent avoidance of the purposes of this subsection through serial purchases of contracts or otherwise.

(f) Special Rules for Computing Employees' Contributions

In computing, for purposes of subsection (c)(1)(A), the aggregate amount of premiums or other consideration paid for the contract, and for purposes of subsection (e)(6), the aggregate premiums or other consideration paid, amounts contributed by the employer shall be included, but only to the extent that:

(1) such amounts were includible in the gross income of the employee under this subtitle or prior income tax laws; or

(2) if such amounts had been paid directly to the employee at the time they were contributed, they would not have been includible in the gross income of the employee under the law applicable at the time of such contribution.

Paragraph (2) shall not apply to amounts which were contributed by the employer after December 31, 1962, and which would not have been includible in the gross income of the employee by reason of the application of section 911 if such amounts had been paid directly to the employee at the time of contribution. The preceding sentence shall not apply to amounts which were contributed by the employer, as determined under regulations prescribed by the Secretary, to provide pension or annuity credits, to the extent such credits are attributable to services performed before January 1, 1963, and are provided pursuant to pension or annuity plan provisions in existence on March 12, 1962, and on that date applicable to such services, or to the extent such credits are attributable to services performed as a foreign missionary, within the meaning of section 403 (b)(2)(D)(iii), as in effect before the enactment of the Economic Growth and Tax Relief Reconciliation Act of 2001.

(g) Rules for Transferee Where Transfer Was for Value

Where any contract, or any interest therein, is transferred, by assignment or otherwise, for a valuable consideration, to the extent that the contract, or interest therein, does not, in the hands of the transferee, have a basis which is determined by reference to the basis in the hands of the transferor, then:

(1) for purposes of this section, only the actual value of such consideration, plus the amount of the premiums and other consideration paid by the transferee after the transfer, shall be taken into account in computing the aggregate amount of the premiums or other consideration paid for the contract;

(2) for purposes of subsection (c)(1)(B), there shall be taken into account only the aggregate amount received under the contract by the transferee before the annuity starting date, to the extent that such amount was excludable from gross income under this subtitle or prior income tax laws; and

(3) the annuity starting date is January 1, 1954, or the first day of the first period for which the transferee received an amount under the contract as an annuity, whichever is the later.

For purposes of this subsection, the term "transferee" includes a beneficiary of, or the estate of, the transferee.

(h) Option to Receive Annuity In Lieu of Lump Sum

If:

(1) a contract provides for payment of a lump sum in full discharge of an obligation under the contract, subject to an option to receive an annuity in lieu of such lump sum;

(2) the option is exercised within 60 days after the day on which such lump sum first became payable; and

(3) part or all of such lump sum would, but for this subsection, be includible in gross income by reason of subsection (e)(1),

then, for purposes of this subtitle, no part of such lump sum shall be considered as includible in gross income at the time such lump sum first became payable.

[(i) Repealed. Pub. L. 94–455, title XIX, § 1951(b)(1)(A),Oct. 4, 1976, 90 Stat. 1836]

(j) Interest

Notwithstanding any other provision of this section, if any amount is held under an agreement to pay interest thereon, the interest payments shall be included in gross income.

[(k) Repealed. Pub. L. 98–369, div. A, title IV, § 421(b)(1),July 18, 1984, 98 Stat. 794]

(l) Face-Amount Certificates

For purposes of this section, the term "endowment contract" includes a face-amount certificate, as defined in section 2(a)(15) of the Investment Company Act of 1940 (15 U.S.C., sec. 80a–2), issued after December 31, 1954.

(m) Special rules applicable to employee annuities
and distributions under employee plans

[(1) **Repealed. Pub. L. 93–406, title II, § 2001(h)(2),Sept. 2, 1974, 88 Stat. 957**]

(2) **Computation of consideration paid by the employee**

In computing:

(A) the aggregate amount of premiums or other consideration paid for the contract for purposes of subsection (c)(1)(A) (relating to the investment in the contract), and

(B) the aggregate premiums or other consideration paid for purposes of subsection (e)(6)—relating to certain amounts not received as an annuity, any amount allowed as a deduction with respect to the contract under section 404 which was paid while the employee was an employee within the meaning of section 401 (c)(1) shall be treated as consideration contributed by the employer, and there shall not be taken into account any portion of the premiums or other consideration for the contract paid while the employee was an owner-employee which is properly allocable, as determined under regulations prescribed by the Secretary, to the cost of life, accident, health, or other insurance.

(3) **Life insurance contracts**

(A) This paragraph shall apply to any life insurance contract:

(i) purchased as a part of a plan described in section 403 (a), or

(ii) purchased by a trust described in section 401 (a) which is exempt from tax under section 501 (a) if the proceeds of such contract are payable directly or indirectly to a participant in such trust or to a beneficiary of such participant.

(B) Any contribution to a plan described in subparagraph (A)(i) or a trust described in subparagraph (A)(ii) which is allowed as a deduction under section 404, and any income of a trust described in subparagraph (A)(ii), which is determined in accordance with regulations prescribed by the Secretary to have been applied to purchase the life insurance protection under a contract described in subparagraph (A), is includible in the gross income of the participant for the taxable year when so applied.

(C) In the case of the death of an individual insured under a contract described in subparagraph (A), an amount equal to the cash surrender value of the contract immediately before the death of the insured shall be treated as a payment under such plan or a distribution by such trust, and the excess of the amount payable by reason of the death of the insured over such cash surrender value shall not be includible in gross income under this section and shall be treated as provided in section 101.

[(4) **Repealed. Pub. L. 97–248, title II, § 236(b)(1),Sept. 3, 1982, 96 Stat. 510**]

(5) **Penalties applicable to certain amounts received by 5 percent owners**

(A) This paragraph applies to amounts which are received from a qualified trust described in section 401 (a) or under a plan described in section 403 (a) at any time by an individual who is, or has been, a 5 percent owner, or by a successor of such an individual, but only to the extent such amounts are determined, under regulations prescribed by the Secretary, to exceed the benefits provided for such individual under the plan formula.

(B) If a person receives an amount to which this paragraph applies, his tax under this chapter for the taxable year in which such amount is received shall be increased by an amount equal to 10 percent of the portion of the amount so received which is includible in his gross income for such taxable year.

(C) For purposes of this paragraph, the term "5 percent owner" means any individual who, at any time during the 5 plan years preceding the plan year ending in the taxable year in which the amount is received, is a 5 percent owner, as defined in section 416 (i)(1)(B)).

(6) **Owner-employee defined**

For purposes of this subsection, the term "owner-employee" has the meaning assigned to it by section 401 (c)(3) and includes an individual for whose benefit an individual retirement account or annuity described in section 408 (a) or (b) is maintained. For purposes of the preceding sentence, the term "owner-employee" shall include an employee within the meaning of section 401 (c)(1).

(7) **Meaning of disabled**

For purposes of this section, an individual shall be considered to be disabled if he is unable to engage in any substantial gainful activity by reason of any medically determinable physical or mental impairment which can be expected to result in death or to be of long-continued and indefinite duration. An individual shall not be considered to be disabled unless he furnishes proof of the existence thereof in such form and manner as the Secretary may require.

[(8) **Repealed. Pub. L. 97–248, title II, § 236(b)(1), Sept. 3, 1982, 96 Stat. 510**]

[(9) **Repealed. Pub. L. 98–369, div. A, title VII, § 713(d)(1), July 18, 1984, 98 Stat. 957**]

(10) **Determination of investment in the contract in the case of qualified domestic relations orders**

Under regulations prescribed by the Secretary, in the case of a distribution or payment made to an alternate payee who is the spouse or former spouse of the participant pursuant to a qualified domestic relations order, as defined in section 414 (p), the investment in the contract as of the date prescribed in such regulations shall be allocated on a pro rata basis between the present value of such distribution or payment and the present value of all other benefits payable with respect to the participant to which such order relates.

(n) Annuities Under Retired Serviceman's Family Protection Plan or Survivor Benefit Plan

Subsection (b) shall not apply in the case of amounts received after December 31, 1965, as an annuity under chapter 73 of title 10 of the United States Code, but all such amounts shall be excluded from gross income until there has been so excluded (under section 122 (b)(1) or this section, including amounts excluded before January 1, 1966) an amount equal to the consideration for the contract, as defined by section 122 (b)(2), plus any amount treated pursuant to section 101 (b)(2)(D) (as in effect on the day before the date of the enactment of the Small Business Job Protection Act of 1996) as additional consideration paid by the employee. Thereafter all amounts so received shall be included in gross income.

(o) Special Rules for Distributions from Qualified Plans to Which Employee Made Deductible Contributions

(1) Treatment of contributions

For purposes of this section and sections 402 and 403, notwithstanding section 414 (h), any deductible employee contribution made to a qualified employer plan or government plan shall be treated as an amount contributed by the employer which is not includible in the gross income of the employee.

[(2) **Repealed. Pub. L. 100–647, title I, § 1011A(c)(8), Nov. 10, 1988, 102 Stat. 3476**]

(3) Amounts constructively received

(A) In general

For purposes of this subsection, rules similar to the rules provided by subsection (p)—other than the exception contained in paragraph (2) thereof—shall apply.

(B) Purchase of life insurance

To the extent any amount of accumulated deductible employee contributions of an employee are applied to the purchase of life insurance contracts, such amount shall be treated as distributed to the employee in the year so applied.

(4) **Special rule for treatment of rollover amounts**

For purposes of sections 402 (c), 403 (a)(4), and 403 (b)(8), 408 (d)(3), and 457 (e)(16), the Secretary shall prescribe regulations providing for such allocations of amounts attributable to accumulated deductible employee contributions, and for such other rules, as may be necessary to insure that such accumulated deductible employee contributions do not become eligible for additional tax benefits, or freed from limitations, through the use of rollovers.

(5) **Definitions and special rules**

For purposes of this subsection:

(A) **Deductible employee contributions**

The term "deductible employee contributions" means any qualified voluntary employee contribution, as defined in section 219 (e)(2), made after December 31, 1981, in a taxable year beginning after such date and made for a taxable year beginning before January 1, 1987, and allowable as a deduction under section 219 (a) for such taxable year.

(B) **Accumulated deductible employee contributions**

The term "accumulated deductible employee contributions" means the deductible employee contributions:

(i) increased by the amount of income and gain allocable to such contributions, and

(ii) reduced by the sum of the amount of loss and expense allocable to such contributions and the amounts distributed with respect to the employee which are attributable to such contributions, or income or gain allocable to such contributions.

(C) **Qualified employer plan**

The term "qualified employer plan" has the meaning given to such term by subsection (p)(3) (A)(i).

(D) **Government plan**

The term "government plan" has the meaning given such term by subsection (p)(3)(B).

(6) Ordering rules

Unless the plan specifies otherwise, any distribution from such plan shall not be treated as being made from the accumulated deductible employee contributions, until all other amounts to the credit of the employee have been distributed.

(p) Loans Treated As Distributions

For purposes of this section:

(1) Treatment as distributions

(A) Loans

If during any taxable year a participant or beneficiary receives, directly or indirectly, any amount as a loan from a qualified employer plan, such amount shall be treated as having been received by such individual as a distribution under such plan.

(B) Assignments or pledges

If during any taxable year a participant or beneficiary assigns, or agrees to assign, or pledges, or agrees to pledge, any portion of his interest in a qualified employer plan, such portion shall be treated as having been received by such individual as a loan from such plan.

(2) Exception for certain loans

(A) General rule

Paragraph (1) shall not apply to any loan to the extent that such loan—when added to the outstanding balance of all other loans from such plan whether made on, before, or after August 13, 1982—does not exceed the lesser of:

(i) $50,000, reduced by the excess (if any) of;

(I) the highest outstanding balance of loans from the plan during the 1-year period ending on the day before the date on which such loan was made,;over

(II) the outstanding balance of loans from the plan on the date on which such loan was made; or

(ii) the greater of;

(I) one-half of the present value of the nonforfeitable accrued benefit of the employee under the plan; or

(II) $10,000.

For purposes of clause (ii), the present value of the nonforfeitable accrued benefit shall be determined without regard to any accumulated deductible employee contributions, as defined in subsection (o)(5)(B).

(B) Requirement that loan be repayable within 5 years

(i) In general Subparagraph (A) shall not apply to any loan unless such loan, by its terms, is required to be repaid within 5 years.

(ii) Exception for home loans Clause (i) shall not apply to any loan used to acquire any dwelling unit which within a reasonable time is to be used—determined at the time the loan is made—as the principal residence of the participant.

(C) Requirement of level amortization

Except as provided in regulations, this paragraph shall not apply to any loan unless substantially level amortization of such loan—with payments not less frequently than quarterly—is required over the term of the loan.

(D) Related employers and related plans

For purposes of this paragraph:

(i) the rules of subsections (b), (c), and (m) of section 414 shall apply, and

(ii) all plans of an employer—determined after the application of such subsections—shall be treated as 1 plan.

(3) Denial of interest deductions in certain cases

(A) In general

No deduction otherwise allowable under this chapter shall be allowed under this chapter for any interest paid or accrued on any loan to which paragraph (1) does not apply by reason of paragraph (2) during the period described in subparagraph (B).

(B) Period to which subparagraph (A) applies

For purposes of subparagraph (A), the period described in this subparagraph is the period:

(i) on or after the 1st day on which the individual to whom the loan is made is a key employee, as defined in section 416 (i)); or

(ii) such loan is secured by amounts attributable to elective deferrals described in subparagraph (A) or (C) of section 402 (g)(3).

(4) Qualified employer plan, etc.

For purposes of this subsection:

(A) Qualified employer plan

(i) In general The term "qualified employer plan" means:

(I) a plan described in section 401 (a) which includes a trust exempt from tax under section 501 (a);

(II) an annuity plan described in section 403 (a); and

(III) a plan under which amounts are contributed by an individual's employer for an annuity contract described in section 403 (b).

(ii) Special rule The term "qualified employer plan" shall include any plan which was, or was determined to be, a qualified employer plan or a government plan.

(B) Government plan

The term "government plan" means any plan, whether or not qualified, established and maintained for its employees by the United States, by a State or political subdivision thereof, or by an agency or instrumentality of any of the foregoing.

(5) Special rules for loans, etc., from certain contracts

For purposes of this subsection, any amount received as a loan under a contract purchased under a qualified employer plan, and any assignment or pledge with respect to such a contract, shall be treated as a loan under such employer plan.

(q) 10 Percent Penalty for Premature Distributions from Annuity Contracts

(1) Imposition of penalty

If any taxpayer receives any amount under an annuity contract, the taxpayer's tax under this chapter for the taxable year in which such amount is received shall be increased by an amount equal to 10 percent of the portion of such amount which is includible in gross income.

(2) **Subsection not to apply to certain distributions**

Paragraph 1 shall not apply to any distribution:

(A) made on or after the date on which the taxpayer attains age 59½;

(B) made on or after the death of the holder—or, where the holder is not an individual, the death of the primary annuitant, as defined in subsection (s)(6)(B);

(C) attributable to the taxpayer's becoming disabled within the meaning of subsection (m)(7);

(D) which is a part of a series of substantially equal periodic payments, not less frequently than annually, made for the life, or life expectancy, of the taxpayer or the joint lives, or joint life expectancies, of such taxpayer and his designated beneficiary;

(E) from a plan, contract, account, trust, or annuity described in subsection (e)(5)(D);

(F) allocable to investment in the contract before August 14, 1982; or [2]

(G) under a qualified funding asset, within the meaning of section 130 (d), but without regard to whether there is a qualified assignment;

(H) to which subsection (t) applies, without regard to paragraph (2) thereof;

(I) under an immediate annuity contract (within the meaning of section 72 (u)(4)); or

(J) which is purchased by an employer upon the termination of a plan described in section 401 (a) or 403 (a) and which is held by the employer until such time as the employee separates from service.

(3) **Change in substantially equal payments**

If:

(A) paragraph (1) does not apply to a distribution by reason of paragraph (2)(D), and

(B) the series of payments under such paragraph are subsequently modified (other than by reason of death or disability);

(i) before the close of the 5-year period beginning on the date of the first payment and after the taxpayer attains age 59½; or

(ii) before the taxpayer attains age 59½;

the taxpayer's tax for the 1st taxable year in which such modification occurs shall be increased by an amount, determined under regulations, equal to the tax which—but for paragraph (2) (D)— would have been imposed, plus interest for the deferral period, within the meaning of subsection (t)(4)(B).

(r) Certain Railroad Retirement Benefits Treated as Received under Employer Plans

(1) In general

Notwithstanding any other provision of law, any benefit provided under the Railroad Retirement Act of 1974, other than a tier 1 railroad retirement benefit, shall be treated for purposes of this title as a benefit provided under an employer plan which meets the requirements of section 401 (a).

(2) Tier 2 taxes treated as contributions

(A) In general

For purposes of paragraph (1):

(i) the tier 2 portion of the tax imposed by section 3201—relating to tax on employees—shall be treated as an employee contribution;

(ii) the tier 2 portion of the tax imposed by section 3211—relating to tax on employee representatives—shall be treated as an employee contribution; and

(iii) the tier 2 portion of the tax imposed by section 3221—relating to tax on employers—shall be treated as an employer contribution.

(B) Tier 2 portion

For purposes of subparagraph (A):

(i) After 1984 With respect to compensation paid after 1984, the tier 2 portion shall be the taxes imposed by sections 3201 (b), 3211 (b), and 3221 (b).

(ii) After September 30, 1981, and before 1985 With respect to compensation paid before 1985 for services rendered after September 30, 1981, the tier 2 portion shall be:

(I) so much of the tax imposed by section 3201 as is determined at the 2 percent rate; and

(II) so much of the taxes imposed by sections 3211 and 3221 as is determined at the 11.75 percent rate.

With respect to compensation paid for services rendered after December 31, 1983, and before 1985, subclause (I) shall be applied by substituting 2.75 percent for 2 percent, and subclause (II) shall be applied by substituting "12.75 percent" for "11.75 percent."

(iii) Before October 1, 1981 With respect to compensation paid for services rendered during any period before October 1, 1981, the tier 2 portion shall be the excess, if any, of:

(I) the tax imposed for such period by section 3201, 3211, or 3221, as the case may be—other than any tax imposed with respect to man-hours—over

(II) the tax which would have been imposed by such section for such period had the rates of the comparable taxes imposed by chapter 21 for such period applied under such section.

(C) **Contributions not allocable to supplemental annuity or windfall benefits**

For purposes of paragraph (1), no amount treated as an employee contribution under this paragraph shall be allocated to:

(i) any supplemental annuity paid under section 2(b) of the Railroad Retirement Act of 1974, or

(ii) any benefit paid under section 3(h), 4(e), or 4(h) of such Act.

(3) **Tier 1 railroad retirement benefit**

For purposes of paragraph (1), the term "tier 1 railroad retirement benefit" has the meaning given such term by section 86 (d)(4).

(s) Required Distributions Where Holder Dies
before Entire Interest Is Distributed

(1) **In general**

A contract shall not be treated as an annuity contract for purposes of this title unless it provides that:

(A) if any holder of such contract dies on or after the annuity starting date and before the entire interest in such contract has been distributed, the remaining portion of such interest will be distributed at least as rapidly as under the method of distributions being used as of the date of his death, and

(B) if any holder of such contract dies before the annuity starting date, the entire interest in such contract will be distributed within 5 years after the death of such holder.

(2) Exception for certain amounts payable over life of beneficiary

If:

(A) any portion of the holder's interest is payable to, or for the benefit of, a designated beneficiary,

(B) such portion will be distributed, in accordance with regulations, over the life of such designated beneficiary, or over a period not extending beyond the life expectancy of such beneficiary; and

(C) such distributions begin not later than 1 year after the date of the holder's death or such later date as the Secretary may by regulations prescribe, then for purposes of paragraph (1), the portion referred to in subparagraph (A) shall be treated as distributed on the day on which such distributions begin.

(3) Special rule where surviving spouse beneficiary

If the designated beneficiary referred to in paragraph (2)(A) is the surviving spouse of the holder of the contract, paragraphs (1) and (2) shall be applied by treating such spouse as the holder of such contract.

(4) Designated beneficiary

For purposes of this subsection, the term "designated beneficiary" means any individual designated a beneficiary by the holder of the contract.

(5) Exception for certain annuity contracts

This subsection shall not apply to any annuity contract:

(A) which is provided;

(i) under a plan described in section 401 (a) which includes a trust exempt from tax under section 501, or

(ii) under a plan described in section 403 (a),

(B) which is described in section 403 (b),

(C) which is an individual retirement annuity or provided under an individual retirement account or annuity, or

(D) which is a qualified funding asset (as defined in section 130 (d), but without regard to whether there is a qualified assignment).

(6) Special rule where holder is corporation or other nonindividual

(A) In general

For purposes of this subsection, if the holder of the contract is not an individual, the primary annuitant shall be treated as the holder of the contract.

(B) Primary annuitant

For purposes of subparagraph (A), the term "primary annuitant" means the individual, the events in the life of whom are of primary importance in affecting the timing or amount of the payout under the contract.

(7) Treatment of changes in primary annuitant where holder of contract is not an individual

For purposes of this subsection, in the case of a holder of an annuity contract which is not an individual, if there is a change in a primary annuitant, as defined in paragraph (6)(B), such change shall be treated as the death of the holder.

(t) 10 Percent Additional Tax On Early Distributions from Qualified Retirement Plans

(1) Imposition of additional tax

If any taxpayer receives any amount from a qualified retirement plan, as defined in section 4974 (c), the taxpayer's tax under this chapter for the taxable year in which such amount is received shall be increased by an amount equal to 10 percent of the portion of such amount which is includible in gross income.

(2) Subsection not to apply to certain distributions

Except as provided in paragraphs (3) and (4), paragraph (1) shall not apply to any of the following distributions:

(A) In general

Distributions which are:

(i) made on or after the date on which the employee attains age 59½,

(ii) made to a beneficiary, or to the estate of the employee, on or after the death of the employee,

(iii) attributable to the employee's being disabled within the meaning of subsection (m)(7),

(iv) part of a series of substantially equal periodic payments—not less frequently than annually—made for the life, or life expectancy, of the employee or the joint lives, or joint life expectancies, of such employee and his designated beneficiary,

(v) made to an employee after separation from service after attainment of age 55,

(vi) dividends paid with respect to stock of a corporation which are described in section 404 (k), or

(vii) made on account of a levy under section 6331 on the qualified retirement plan.

(B) **Medical expenses**

Distributions made to the employee, other than distributions described in subparagraph (A), (C), or (D), to the extent such distributions do not exceed the amount allowable as a deduction under section 213 to the employee for amounts paid during the taxable year for medical care—determined without regard to whether the employee itemizes deductions for such taxable year.

(C) **Payments to alternate payees pursuant to qualified domestic relations orders**

Any distribution to an alternate payee pursuant to a qualified domestic relations order, within the meaning of section 414 (p)(1).

(D) **Distributions to unemployed individuals for health insurance premiums**

(i) **In general.** Distributions from an individual retirement plan to an individual after separation from employment:

(I) if such individual has received unemployment compensation for 12 consecutive weeks under any Federal or State unemployment compensation law by reason of such separation,

(II) if such distributions are made during any taxable year during which such unemployment compensation is paid or the succeeding taxable year, and

(III) to the extent such distributions do not exceed the amount paid during the taxable year for insurance described in section 213 (d)(1)(D) with respect to the individual and the individual's spouse and dependents—as defined in section 152, determined without regard to subsections (b)(1), (b)(2), and (d)(1)(B) thereof.

(ii) **Distributions after reemployment.** Clause (i) shall not apply to any distribution made after the individual has been employed for at least 60 days after the separation from employment to which clause (i) applies.

(iii) **Self-employed individuals**. To the extent provided in regulations, a self-employed individual shall be treated as meeting the requirements of clause (i)(I) if, under Federal or State law, the individual would have received unemployment compensation but for the fact the individual was self-employed.

(E) **Distributions from individual retirement plans for higher education expenses**

Distributions to an individual from an individual retirement plan to the extent such distributions do not exceed the qualified higher education expenses, as defined in paragraph (7), of the taxpayer for the taxable year. Distributions shall not be taken into account under the preceding sentence if such distributions are described in subparagraph (A), (C), or (D) or to the extent paragraph (1) does not apply to such distributions by reason of subparagraph (B).

(F) **Distributions from certain plans for first home purchases**

Distributions to an individual from an individual retirement plan which are qualified first-time homebuyer distributions, as defined in paragraph (8). Distributions shall not be taken into account under the preceding sentence if such distributions are described in subparagraph (A), (C), (D), or (E) or to the extent paragraph (1) does not apply to such distributions by reason of subparagraph (B).

(G) **Distributions from retirement plans to individuals called to active duty**

(i) **In general.** Any qualified reservist distribution.

(ii) Amount distributed may be repaid Any individual who receives a qualified reservist distribution may, at any time during the 2 year period beginning on the day after the end of the active duty period, make one or more contributions to an individual retirement plan of such individual in an aggregate amount not to exceed the amount of such distribution. The dollar limitations otherwise applicable to contributions to individual retirement plans shall not apply to any contribution made pursuant to the preceding sentence. No deduction shall be allowed for any contribution pursuant to this clause.

(iii) **Qualified reservist distribution.** For purposes of this subparagraph, the term "qualified reservist distribution" means any distribution to an individual if:

(I) such distribution is from an individual retirement plan, or from amounts attributable to employer contributions made pursuant to elective deferrals described in subparagraph (A) or (C) of section 402 (g)(3) orsection 501 (c)(18)(D)(iii),

(II) such individual was (by reason of being a member of a reserve component (as defined in section 101 of title 37, United States Code)) ordered or called to active duty for a period in excess of 179 days or for an indefinite period, and

(III) such distribution is made during the period beginning on the date of such order or call and ending at the close of the active duty period.

(iv) **Application of subparagraph**. This subparagraph applies to individuals ordered or called to active duty after September 11, 2001. In no event shall the 2 year period referred to in clause (ii) end before the date which is 2 years after the date of the enactment of this subparagraph.

(3) **Limitations**

(A) **Certain exceptions not to apply to individual retirement plans**

Subparagraphs (A)(v) and (C) of paragraph (2) shall not apply to distributions from an individual retirement plan.

(B) **Periodic payments under qualified plans must begin after separation**

Paragraph (2)(A)(iv) shall not apply to any amount paid from a trust described in section 401 (a) which is exempt from tax under section 501 (a) or from a contract described in section 72 (e)(5) (D)(ii) unless the series of payments begins after the employee separates from service.

(4) **Change in substantially equal payments**

(A) **In general**

If:

(i) paragraph (1) does not apply to a distribution by reason of paragraph (2)(A)(iv), and

(ii) the series of payments under such paragraph are subsequently modified, other than by reason of death or disability,

(I) before the close of the 5-year period beginning with the date of the first payment and after the employee attains age 59½, or

(II) before the employee attains age 59½, the taxpayer's tax for the 1st taxable year in which such modification occurs shall be increased by an amount, determined under regulations, equal to the tax which, but for paragraph (2)(A)(iv), would have been imposed, plus interest for the deferral period.

(B) **Deferral period**

For purposes of this paragraph, the term "deferral period" means the period beginning with the taxable year in which, without regard to paragraph (2)(A)(iv), the distribution would have been includible in gross income and ending with the taxable year in which the modification described in subparagraph (A) occurs.

(5) Employee

For purposes of this subsection, the term "employee" includes any participant, and in the case of an individual retirement plan, the individual for whose benefit such plan was established.

(6) Special rules for simple retirement accounts

In the case of any amount received from a simple retirement account, within the meaning of section 408 (p), during the 2-year period beginning on the date such individual first participated in any qualified salary reduction arrangement maintained by the individual's employer under section 408 (p)(2), paragraph (1) shall be applied by substituting 25 percent for 10 percent.

(7) Qualified higher education expenses

For purposes of paragraph (2)(E):

(A) In general

The term "qualified higher education expenses" means qualified higher education expenses, as defined in section 529 (e)(3), for education furnished to;

(i) the taxpayer,

(ii) the taxpayer's spouse, or

(iii) any child, as defined in section 152 (f)(1), or grandchild of the taxpayer or the taxpayer's spouse, at an eligible educational institution, as defined in section 529 (e)(5).

(B) Coordination with other benefits

The amount of qualified higher education expenses for any taxable year shall be reduced as provided in section 25A (g)(2).

(8) Qualified first-time homebuyer distributions

For purposes of paragraph (2)(F)

(A) In general

The term "qualified first-time homebuyer distribution" means any payment or distribution received by an individual to the extent such payment or distribution is used by the individual before the close of the 120th day after the day on which such payment or distribution is received to pay qualified acquisition costs with respect to a principal residence of a first-time homebuyer who is such individual, the spouse of such individual, or any child, grandchild, or ancestor of such individual or the individual's spouse.

(B) Lifetime dollar limitation

The aggregate amount of payments or distributions received by an individual which may be treated as qualified first-time homebuyer distributions for any taxable year shall not exceed the excess (if any) of

(i) $10,000, over

(ii) the aggregate amounts treated as qualified first-time homebuyer distributions with respect to such individual for all prior taxable years.

(C) Qualified acquisition costs

For purposes of this paragraph, the term "qualified acquisition costs" means the costs of acquiring, constructing, or reconstructing a residence. Such term includes any usual or reasonable settlement, financing, or other closing costs.

(D) First-time homebuyer; other definitions

For purposes of this paragraph:

(i) **First-time homebuyer.** The term "first-time homebuyer" means any individual if:

(I) such individual, and if married, such individual's spouse, had no present ownership interest in a principal residence during the 2-year period ending on the date of acquisition of the principal residence to which this paragraph applies, and

(II) subsection (h) or (k) of section 1034, as in effect on the day before the date of the enactment of this paragraph, did not suspend the running of any period of time specified in section 1034 [3] (as so in effect) with respect to such individual on the day before the date the distribution is applied pursuant to subparagraph (A).

(ii) **Principal residence.** The term "principal residence" has the same meaning as when used in section 121.

(iii) **Date of acquisition.** The term "date of acquisition" means the date

(I) on which a binding contract to acquire the principal residence to which subparagraph

(A) applies is entered into, or

(II) on which construction or reconstruction of such a principal residence is commenced.

(E) **Special rule where delay in acquisition**

If any distribution from any individual retirement plan fails to meet the requirements of subparagraph (A) solely by reason of a delay or cancellation of the purchase or construction of the residence, the amount of the distribution may be contributed to an individual retirement plan as provided in section 408 (d)(3)(A)(i), determined by substituting 120th day for 60th day in such section, except that:

(i) section 408 (d)(3)(B) shall not be applied to such contribution, and

(ii) such amount shall not be taken into account in determining whether section 408 (d)(3)(B) applies to any other amount.

(9) **Special rule for rollovers to section 457 plans**

For purposes of this subsection, a distribution from an eligible deferred compensation plan, as defined in section 457(b), of an eligible employer described in section 457 (e)(1)(A) shall be treated as a distribution from a qualified retirement plan described in 4974(c)(1) to the extent that such distribution is attributable to an amount transferred to an eligible deferred compensation plan from a qualified retirement plan, as defined in section 4974 (c).

(10) **Distributions to qualified public safety employees in governmental plans**

(A) **In general**

In the case of a distribution to a qualified public safety employee from a governmental plan, within the meaning of section 414 (d), which is a defined benefit plan, paragraph (2)(A)(v) shall be applied by substituting age 50 for age 55.

(B) **Qualified public safety employee**

For purposes of this paragraph, the term "qualified public safety employee" means any employee of a State or political subdivision of a State who provides police protection, firefighting services, or emergency medical services for any area within the jurisdiction of such State or political subdivision.

(u) Treatment of Annuity Contracts Not Held by Natural Persons

(1) In general

If any annuity contract is held by a person who is not a natural person:

(A) such contract shall not be treated as an annuity contract for purposes of this subtitle, other than subchapter L, and

(B) the income on the contract for any taxable year of the policyholder shall be treated as ordinary income received or accrued by the owner during such taxable year.

For purposes of this paragraph, holding by a trust or other entity as an agent for a natural person shall not be taken into account.

(2) Income on the contract

(A) In general

For purposes of paragraph (1), the term "income on the contract" means, with respect to any taxable year of the policyholder, the excess of:

(i) the sum of the net surrender value of the contract as of the close of the taxable year plus all distributions under the contract received during the taxable year or any prior taxable year, reduced by;

(ii) the sum of the amount of net premiums under the contract for the taxable year and prior taxable years and amounts includible in gross income for prior taxable years with respect to such contract under this subsection.

Where necessary to prevent the avoidance of this subsection, the Secretary may substitute "fair market value of the contract" for "net surrender value of the contract" each place it appears in the preceding sentence.

(B) Net premiums

For purposes of this paragraph, the term "net premiums" means the amount of premiums paid under the contract reduced by any policyholder dividends.

(3) Exceptions

This subsection shall not apply to any annuity contract which:

(A) is acquired by the estate of a decedent by reason of the death of the decedent,

(B) is held under a plan described in section 401 (a) or 403 (a), under a program described in section 403 (b), or under an individual retirement plan,

(C) is a qualified funding asset, as defined in section 130 (d), but without regard to whether there is a qualified assignment,

(D) is purchased by an employer upon the termination of a plan described in section 401 (a) or 403 (a) and is held by the employer until all amounts under such contract are distributed to the employee for whom such contract was purchased or the employee's beneficiary, or

(E) is an immediate annuity.

(4) Immediate annuity

For purposes of this subsection, the term "immediate annuity" means an annuity:

(A) which is purchased with a single premium or annuity consideration,

(B) the annuity starting date (as defined in subsection (c)(4)) of which commences no later than 1 year from the date of the purchase of the annuity, and

(C) which provides for a series of substantially equal periodic payments (to be made not less frequently than annually) during the annuity period.

(v) 10 Percent Additional Tax for Taxable Distributions from Modified Endowment Contracts

(1) Imposition of additional tax

If any taxpayer receives any amount under a modified endowment contract, as defined in section 7702A, the taxpayer's tax under this chapter for the taxable year in which such amount is received shall be increased by an amount equal to 10 percent of the portion of such amount which is includible in gross income.

(2) Subsection not to apply to certain distributions

Paragraph (1) shall not apply to any distribution:

(A) made on or after the date on which the taxpayer attains age 59½,

(B) which is attributable to the taxpayer's becoming disabled, within the meaning of subsection (m)(7), or

(C) which is part of a series of substantially equal periodic payments—not less frequently than annually—made for the life, or life expectancy, of the taxpayer or the joint lives, or joint life expectancies, of such taxpayer and his beneficiary.

(w) Application of Basis Rules to Nonresident Aliens

(1) In general

Notwithstanding any other provision of this section, for purposes of determining the portion of any distribution which is includible in gross income of a distributee who is a citizen or resident of the United States, the investment in the contract shall not include any applicable nontaxable contributions or applicable nontaxable earnings.

(2) Applicable nontaxable contribution

For purposes of this subsection, the term "applicable nontaxable contribution" means any employer or employee contribution:

(A) which was made with respect to compensation:

(i) for labor or personal services performed by an employee who, at the time the labor or services were performed, was a nonresident alien for purposes of the laws of the United States in effect at such time, and

(ii) which is treated as from sources without the United States, and

(B) which was not subject to income tax and would have been subject to income tax if paid as cash compensation when the services were rendered, under the laws of the United States or any foreign country.

(3) Applicable nontaxable earnings

For purposes of this subsection, the term "applicable nontaxable earnings" means earnings:

(A) which are paid or accrued with respect to any employer or employee contribution which was made with respect to compensation for labor or personal services performed by an employee,

(B) with respect to which the employee was at the time the earnings were paid or accrued a nonresident alien for purposes of the laws of the United States, and

(C) which were not subject to income tax under the laws of the United States or any foreign country.

(4) **Regulations**

The Secretary shall prescribe such regulations as may be necessary to carry out the provisions of this subsection, including regulations treating contributions and earnings as not subject to tax under the laws of any foreign country where appropriate to carry out the purposes of this subsection.

(x) **Cross Reference**

For limitation on adjustments to basis of annuity contracts sold, see section 1021.

---

[1] So in original. Probably should be paragraph (2)(B).

[2] So in original. The word "or" probably should not appear.

Internal Revenue Code Section 1035

1035. CERTAIN EXCHANGES OF INSURANCE POLICIES.

Note: Section 1035(a) below applies to exchanges before 2010.

(a) GENERAL RULES

No gain or loss shall be recognized on the exchange of:

(1) a contract of life insurance for another contract of life insurance or for an endowment or annuity contract; or

(2) a contract of endowment insurance (A) for another contract of endowment insurance which provides for regular payments beginning at a date not later than the date payments would have begun under the contract exchanged, or (B) for an annuity contract; or

(3) an annuity contract for an annuity contract.

Note: Section 1035(a) below applies to exchanges after 2009.

(a) GENERAL RULES

No gain or loss shall be recognized on the exchange of

(1) a contract of life insurance for another contract of life insurance or for an endowment or annuity contractor for a qualified long-term care insurance contract; or

(2) a contract of endowment insurance (A) for another contract of endowment insurance which provides for regular payments beginning at a date not later than the date payments would have begun under the contract exchanged, or (B) for an annuity contract, or (C) for a qualified long-term care insurance contract;

(3) an annuity contract for an annuity contract or for a qualified long-term care insurance contract; or

(4) a qualified long-term care insurance contract for a qualified long-term care insurance contract.

Note: Section 1035(b) below applies to exchanges before 2010.

(b) DEFINITIONS

For the purpose of this section:

(1) ENDOWMENT CONTRACT

A contract of endowment insurance is a contract with an insurance company which depends in part on the life expectancy of the insured, but which may be payable in full in a single payment during his life.

(2) ANNUITY CONTRACT

An annuity contract is a contract to which paragraph (1) applies but which may be payable during the life of the annuitant only in installments.

(3) LIFE INSURANCE CONTRACT

A contract of life insurance is a contract to which paragraph (1) applies but which is not ordinarily payable in full during the life of the insured.

Note: Section 1035(b) below applies to exchanges after 2009.

(b) DEFINITIONS

For the purpose of this section:

(1) ENDOWMENT CONTRACT

A contract of endowment insurance is a contract with an insurance company which depends in part on the life expectancy of the insured, but which may be payable in full in a single payment during his life.

(2) ANNUITY CONTRACT

An annuity contract is a contract to which paragraph (1) applies but which may be payable during the life of the annuitant only in installments. For purposes of the preceding sentence, a contract shall not fail to be treated as an annuity contract solely because a qualified long-term care insurance contract is a part of or a rider on such contract.

(3) LIFE INSURANCE CONTRACT

A contract of life insurance is a contract to which paragraph (1) applies but which is not ordinarily payable in full during the life of the insured. For purposes of the preceding sentence, a contract shall not fail to be treated as a life insurance contract solely because a qualified long-term care insurance contract is a part of or a rider on such contract.

(c) EXCHANGES INVOLVING FOREIGN PERSONS

To the extent provided in regulations, subsection (a) shall not apply to any exchange having the effect of transferring property to any person other than a United States person.

(d) CROSS REFERENCES

(1) For rules relating to recognition of gain or loss where an exchange is not solely in kind, see subsections (b) and (c) of section 1031.

(2) For rules relating to the basis of property acquired in an exchange described in subsection (a), see subsection (d) of section 1031.

Internal Revenue Code Section 2033

2033. PROPERTY IN WHICH THE DECEDENT HAD AN INTEREST.

The value of the gross estate shall include the value of all property to the extent of the interest therein of the decedent at the time of his death.

Internal Revenue Code Section 2039

2039. ANNUITIES.

(a) GENERAL

The gross estate shall include the value of an annuity or other payment receivable by any beneficiary by reason of surviving the decedent under any form of contract or agreement entered into after March 3, 1931—other than as insurance under policies on the life of the decedent—if, under such contract or agreement, an annuity or other payment was payable to the decedent, or the decedent possessed the right to receive such annuity or payment, either alone or in conjunction with another for his life or for any period not ascertainable without reference to his death or for any period which does not in fact end before his death.

(b) AMOUNT INCLUDIBLE

Subsection (a) shall apply to only such part of the value of the annuity or other payment receivable under such contract or agreement as is proportionate to that part of the purchase price therefor contributed by the decedent. For purposes of this section, any contribution by the decedent's employer or former employer to the purchase price of such contract or agreement—whether or not to an employee's trust or fund forming part of a pension, annuity, retirement, bonus or profit sharing plan—shall be considered to be contributed by the decedent if made by reason of his employment.

Appendix D

FINRA RULE 2330 for Recommended Purchases of Exchanges of Deferred Variable Annuities

FINRA Regulatory Notice 10 05 Deferred Variable Annuities

FINRA Reminds Firms of Their Responsibilities Under FINRA Rule 2330 for Recommended Purchases or Exchanges of Deferred Variable Annuities

Executive Summary

FINRA reminds firms of their responsibilities under the new consolidated FINRA rule on deferred variable annuities.[1] The implementation date of the FINRA rule—as well as previously approved amendments to parts of the rule covering principal review and supervisory procedures—is February 8, 2010.[2] This *Notice* also addresses issues raised about a firm's ability to hold Checks made payable to entities other than itself (third parties) pursuant to interpretive relief that FINRA previously issued.[3] For easy reference, the text of new FINRA Rule 2330 is set forth in Attachment A.

Questions regarding this *Notice* should be directed to:

James S. Wrona, Associate Vice President and Associate General Counsel, Office of General Counsel, at (202) 728-8270; or Lawrence N. Kosciulek, Director, Investment Companies Regulation, at (240) 386-4535.

---

1. On November 20, 2009, the Financial Industry Regulatory Authority, Inc. (FINRA) filed with the Securities and Exchange Commission (SEC or Commission) a proposed rule change, for immediate effectiveness, to transfer NASD Rule 2821 into the Consolidated FINRA Rulebook, as FINRA Rule 2330, without any substantive changes. See Exchange Act Release No. 61122 (December 7, 2009), 74 FR 65816 (December 11, 2009) (File No. SR-FINRA-2009- 083); Regulatory Notice 09-72 (December 2009) (discussing adoption of consolidated FINRA rules, including FINRA Rule 2330 covering deferred variable annuities). The current FINRA rulebook consists of (1) FINRA Rules; (2) NASD Rules; and (3) rules incorporated from NYSE (Incorporated NYSE Rules) (together, the NASD Rules and Incorporated NYSE Rules are referred to as the Transitional Rulebook). While the NASD Rules generally apply to all FINRA members, the Incorporated NYSE Rules apply only to those members of FINRA that are also members of the NYSE (Dual Members). The FINRA Rules apply to all FINRA members, unless such rules have a more limited application by their terms. For more information about the rulebook consolidation process, see Information Notice, 3/12/08 (Rulebook Consolidation Process).
2. *See Exchange Act Release No. 61122* (December 7, 2009), 74 FR 65816 (December 11, 2009) (File No. SR-FINRA-2009-083); *Regulatory Notice 09-72* (December 2009) (discussing adoption of consolidated FINRA rules and an operative date for FINRA Rule 2330 of February 8, 2010); Exchange Act Release No. 59772 (April 15, 2009), 74 FR 18419 (April 22, 2009) (Order Approving File No. SR-FINRA-2008-019); *Regulatory Notice 09-32* (June 2009) (announcing SEC approval of amendments to NASD Rule 2821 governing purchases and exchanges of deferred variable annuities and an effective date for those amendments of February 8, 2010). FINRA notes that paragraphs (a) (General Considerations), (b) (Recommendation Requirements), and (e) (Training) of NASD Rule 2821 became effective on May 5, 2008.
3. See Regulatory Notice 07-53 (November 2007). 3 See Regulatory Notice 07-53 (November 2007); see also Regulatory Notice 09-32 (June 2009).

Background & Discussion

FINRA Rule 2330 (formerly NASD Rule 2821) establishes sales practice standards regarding recommended purchases and exchanges of deferred variable annuities.[4] The rule has the following six main sections:

General considerations, such as the rule's applicability;

Recommendation requirements, including suitability and disclosure obligations;

Principal review and approval obligations;

Requirements for establishing and maintaining supervisory procedures;

Training obligations; and

Supplementary material that addresses a variety of issues ranging from the handling of customer funds and checks to information gathering and sharing.

As noted above, all of the rule's provisions are applicable as of February 8, 2010.

Recently, questions have been raised regarding FINRA's limited interpretive relief from the requirements of FINRA Rule 2150(a) (formerly NASD Rule 2330(a)) and FINRA Rule 2320(d) (formerly NASD Rule 2820(d)).[5] The former rule generally prohibits firms from making improper use of customer funds, and the latter requires firms to transmit promptly to issuers applications and purchase payments for variable contracts. FINRA provided limited interpretive relief from these rules to allow firms to perform comprehensive and rigorous reviews of recommended transactions in deferred variable annuities under FINRA Rule 2330.[6]

---

4. In general, a variable annuity is a contract between an investor and an insurance company, whereby the insurance company promises to make periodic payments to the contract owner or beneficiary, starting immediately (an immediate variable annuity) or at some future time (a deferred variable annuity). *See* Joint SEC and NASD Staff Report on Broker-Dealer Sales of Variable Insurance Products (June 2004), available at: *www.sec.gov/news/studies/secnasdvip.pdf.*
5. See Regulatory Notice 07-53 (November 2007); see also Regulatory Notice 09-32 (June 2009).
6. *See Regulatory Notice 07-53 (November 2007); see also Regulatory Notice 09-32 (June 2009).* The SEC previously has noted that "many broker-dealers are subject to lower net capital requirements under SEA Rule 15c3-1 and are exempt from the requirement to establish and fund a customer reserve account under SEA Rule 15c3-3 because they do not carry customer funds or securities." *See Exchange Act Release No. 56376 (Sept. 7, 2007),* 72 FR 52400 (Sept. 13, 2007) (Order Granting Exemption to Broker-Dealers from Requirements in SEA Rules 15c3-1 and 15c3-3 to Promptly Transmit Customer Checks). Although some of these firms receive checks from customers made payable to third parties, the SEC does not deem a firm to be carrying customer funds if it "promptly transmits" the checks to third parties. The SEC has interpreted "promptly transmits" to mean that "such transmission or delivery is made no later than noon of the next business day after receipt of such funds or securities." *Id.* at 52400. The SEC provided a conditional exemption for broker-dealers from any additional requirements of Rules 15c3-1 and 15c3-3 due solely to a failure to promptly transmit a check made payable to an insurance company for the purchase of a deferred variable annuity product by noon of the business day following the date the broker-dealer receives the check from the customer, provided (i) the transaction is subject to the principal review requirements of NASD Rule 2821 and a registered principal has reviewed and determined whether he or she approves of the purchase or exchange of the deferred variable annuity within seven business days in accordance with that rule; (ii) the broker-dealer promptly transmits the check no later than noon of the business day following the date a registered principal reviews and determines whether he or she approves of the purchase or exchange

FINRA originally stated that "a firm may hold an application for a deferred variable annuity and a customer's non-negotiated check payable to an insurance company for up to seven business days without violating either NASD Rule 2330 or 2820 if the reason for the hold is to allow completion of principal review of the transaction pursuant to NASD Rule 2821." [7] After the SEC approved amendments that changed the starting point for the review period—from the date when the customer signs the application to the date when a firm's office of supervisory jurisdiction (OSJ) receives a complete and correct application package—FINRA explained that its limited interpretive relief "continues to apply even though the triggering event for the principal review period has changed via the recently approved amendments." [8]

Concerns have been expressed, however, regarding the breadth of the interpretive relief and the conditions that must be present for it to apply. FINRA now clarifies that the interpretive relief applies only if the seven conditions delineated below are present. [9]

1. The reason that the firm is holding the application for a deferred variable annuity and/or a customer's non-negotiated check payable to a third party is to allow completion of principal review of the transaction pursuant to FINRA Rule 2330.

2. The associated person who recommended the purchase or exchange of the deferred variable annuity makes reasonable efforts to safeguard the check and to promptly prepare and forward a complete and correct copy of the application package to an OSJ.

3. The firm has policies and procedures in place that are reasonably designed to ensure that the check is safeguarded and that reasonable efforts are made to promptly prepare and forward a complete and correct copy of the application package to an OSJ.

---

of the deferred variable annuity; and (iii) the broker dealer maintains a copy of each such check and creates a record of the date the check was received from the customer and the date the check was transmitted to the insurance company if approved, or returned to the customer if rejected. *Id.* at 52400. In its order approving recent amendments, the SEC explained that the exemption order continues to apply, notwithstanding the new starting point for the principal review period under NASD Rule 2821. *See* Exchange Act Release No. 59772 (April 15, 2009), 74 FR 18419, at 18422 n.37 (April 22, 2009) (Order Approving File No. SR-FINRA-2008-019).

7. Regulatory Notice 07-53 (November 2007).
8. Regulatory Notice 09-32 (June 2009).
9. FINRA emphasizes that firms are not required to collect and hold checks or funds prior to principal review and approval. A firm may elect to wait until after a principal approves the transaction to collect the check or funds for a deferred variable annuity. Moreover, in accordance with Supplementary Material .03 under FINRA Rule 2330, a firm can forward a check made payable to the insurance company or, if the firm is fully subject to SEA Rule 15c3-3, transfer "funds for the purchase of a deferred variable annuity to the insurance company prior to the member's principal approval of the deferred variable annuity, as long as the member fulfills the following requirements: (a) the member must disclose to the customer the proposed transfer or series of transfers of the funds and (b) the member must enter into a written agreement with the insurance company under which the insurance company agrees that, until such time as it is notified of the member's principal approval and is provided with the application or is notified of the member's principal rejection, it will (1) segregate the member's customers' funds in a 'Special Account for the Exclusive Benefit of Customers' (set up as described in SEA Rules 15c3-3(k)(2)(i) and 15c3-3(f)) to ensure that the customers' funds will not be subject to any right, charge, security interest, lien, or claim of any kind in favor of the member, insurance company, or bank where the insurance company deposits such funds or any creditor thereof or person claiming through the man hold those funds either as cash or any instrument that a broker or dealer may deposit in its Special Reserve Account for the Exclusive Benefit of Customers, (2) not issue the variable annuity contract prior to the member's principal approval, and (3) promptly return the funds to each customer at the customer's request prior to the member's principal approval or upon the member's rejection of the application."

4. A principal reviews and makes a determination of whether to approve or reject the purchase or exchange of the deferred variable annuity in accordance with the provisions of FINRA Rule 2330.

5. The firm holds the application and/or check no longer than seven business days from the date an OSJ receives a complete and correct copy of the application package.

6. The firm maintains a copy of each such check and creates a record of the date the check was received from the customer and the date the check was transmitted to the insurance company or returned to the customer.

7. The firm creates a record of the date when the OSJ receives a complete and correct copy of the application package.

If these seven conditions are not present, FINRA's interpretive relief will not apply and it will enforce FINRA Rules 2150(a) and 2320(d), as appropriate.

Attachment A

Text of FINRA Rule 2330

2000. Duties and Conflicts

2300. Special Products

2330. Members' Responsibilities Regarding Deferred Variable Annuities

(a) General Considerations

(1) **Application.** This Rule applies to recommended purchases and exchanges of deferred variable annuities and recommended initial subaccount allocations. This Rule does not apply to reallocations among subaccounts made or to funds paid after the initial purchase or exchange of a deferred variable annuity. This Rule also does not apply to deferred variable annuity transactions made in connection with any tax-qualified, employer-sponsored retirement or benefit plan that either is defined as a "qualified plan" under Section 3(a)(12)(C) of the Exchange Act or meets the requirements of Internal Revenue Code Sections 403(b), 457(b), or 457(f), unless, in the case of any such plan, a member or person associated with a member makes recommendations to an individual plan participant regarding a deferred variable annuity, in which case the Rule would apply as to the individual plan participant to whom the member or person associated with the member makes such recommendations.

(2) **Creation, Storage, and Transmission of Documents.** For purposes of this Rule, documents may be created, stored, and transmitted in electronic or paper form, and signatures may be evidenced in electronic or other written form.

(3) **Definitions.** For purposes of this Rule, the term "registered principal" shall mean a person registered as a General Securities Sales Supervisor (Series 9/10), a General Securities Principal (Series 24) or an Investment Company Products/Variable Contracts Principal (Series 26), as applicable.

(b) Recommendation Requirements

(1) No member or person associated with a member shall recommend to any customer the purchase or exchange of a deferred variable annuity unless such member or person associated with a member has a reasonable basis to believe

(A) that the transaction is suitable in accordance with NASD Rule 2310 and, in particular, that there is a reasonable basis to believe that

(i) the customer has been informed, in general terms, of various features of deferred variable annuities, such as the potential surrender period and surrender charge; potential tax penalty if customers sell or redeem deferred variable annuities before reaching the age of 59½; mortality and expense fees; investment advisory fees; potential charges for and features of riders; the insurance and investment components of deferred variable annuities; and market risk;

(ii) the customer would benefit from certain features of deferred variable annuities, such as tax-deferred growth, annuitization, or a death or living benefit; and

(iii) the particular deferred variable annuity as a whole, the underlying subaccounts to which funds are allocated at the time of the purchase or exchange of the deferred variable annuity, and riders and similar product enhancements, if any, are suitable (and, in the case of an exchange, the transaction as a whole also is suitable) for the particular customer based on the information required by paragraph (b)(2) of this Rule; and

(B) in the case of an exchange of a deferred variable annuity, the exchange also is consistent with the suitability determination required by paragraph (b)(1)(A) of this Rule, taking into consideration whether

(i) the customer would incur a surrender charge, be subject to the commencement of a new surrender period, lose existing benefits (such as death, living, or other contractual benefits), or be subject to increased fees or charges (such as mortality and expense fees, investment advisory fees, or charges for riders and similar product enhancements);

(ii) the customer would benefit from product enhancements and improvements; and

(iii) the customer has had another deferred variable annuity exchange within the preceding 36 months.

The determinations required by this paragraph shall be documented and signed by the associated person recommending the transaction.

(2) Prior to recommending the purchase or exchange of a deferred variable annuity, a member or person associated with a member shall make reasonable efforts to obtain, at a minimum, information concerning the customer's age, annual income, financial situation and needs, investment experience, investment objectives, intended use of the deferred variable annuity, investment time horizon, existing assets (including investment and life insurance holdings), liquidity needs, liquid net worth, risk tolerance, tax status, and such other information used or considered to be reasonable by the member or person associated with the member in making recommendations to customers.

(3) Promptly after receiving information necessary to prepare a complete and correct application package for a deferred variable annuity, a person associated with a member who recommends the deferred variable annuity shall transmit the complete and correct application package to an office of supervisory jurisdiction of the member.

(c) Principal Review and Approval

Prior to transmitting a customer's application for a deferred variable annuity

To the issuing insurance company for processing, but no later than seven business days after an office of supervisory jurisdiction of the member receives a complete and correct application package, a registered principal shall review and determine whether he or she approves of the recommended purchase or exchange of the deferred variable annuity.

A registered principal shall approve the recommended transaction only if he or she has determined that there is a reasonable basis to believe that the transaction would be suitable based on the factors delineated in paragraph (b) of this Rule.

The determinations required by this paragraph shall be documented and signed by the registered principal who reviewed and then approved or rejected the transaction.

(d) Supervisory Procedures

In addition to the general supervisory and recordkeeping requirements of NASD Rules 3010, 3012, and 3110, and Rule 3130, a member must establish and maintain specific written supervisory procedures reasonably designed to achieve compliance with the standards set forth in this Rule. The member also must (1) implement surveillance procedures to determine if any of the member's associated persons have rates of effecting deferred variable annuity exchanges that raise for review whether such rates of exchanges evidence conduct inconsistent with the applicable provisions of this Rule, other applicable FINRA rules, or the federal securities laws("inappropriate exchanges") and (2) have policies and procedures reasonably designed to implement corrective measures to address inappropriate exchanges and the conduct of associated persons who engage in inappropriate exchanges.

(e) Training

Members shall develop and document specific training policies or programs reasonably designed to ensure that associated persons who effect and registered principals who review transactions in deferred variable annuities comply with the requirements of this Rule and that they understand the material features of deferred variable annuities, including those described in paragraph (b)(1)(A)(i) of this Rule.

Supplementary Material

.01 Depositing of Funds by Members Prior to Principal Approval. Under Rule 2330, a member that is permitted to maintain customer funds under SEA Rules 15c3-1 and 15c3-3may, prior to the member's principal approval of the deferred variable annuity, deposit and maintain customer funds for a deferred variable annuity in an account that meets the requirements of SEA Rule 15c3-3.

.02. Treatment of Lump-Sum Payment for Purchases of Different Products. If a customer provides a member that is permitted to hold customer funds with a lump sum or single check made payable to the member (as opposed to being made payable to the insurance company) and requests that a portion of the funds be applied to the purchase of a deferred variable annuity and the rest of the funds be applied to other types of products, Rule 2330 would not prohibit the member from promptly applying those portions designated for purchasing products other than a deferred variable annuity to such use. A member that is not permitted to hold customer funds can comply with such requests only through its clearing firm that will maintain customer funds for the intended deferred variable annuity purchase in an account that meets the requirements of SEA Rule 15c3-3. In such circumstances, the checks would need to be made payable to the clearing firm.

.03 Forwarding of Checks/Funds to Insurer Prior to Principal Approval. Rule 2330 does not prohibit a member from forwarding a check made payable to the insurance company or, if the member is fully subject to SEA Rule 15c3-3, transferring funds for the purchase of a deferred variable annuity to the insurance company prior to the member's principal approval of the deferred variable annuity, as long as the member fulfills the following requirements: (a) the member must disclose to the customer the proposed transfer or series of transfers of the funds and (b) the member must enter into a written agreement with the insurance company under which the insurance company agrees that, until such time as it is notified of the member's principal approval and is provided with the application or is notified of the member's principal rejection, it will (1) segregate the member's customers' funds in a bank in an account equivalent to the deposit of those funds by a member into a "Special Account for the Exclusive Benefit of Customers" (set up as described in SEA Rules 15c3-3(k)(2)(i) and 15c3-3(f)) to ensure that the customers' funds will not be subject to any right, charge, security interest, lien, or claim of any kind in favor of the member, insurance company, or bank where the insurance company deposits such funds or any creditor thereof or person claiming through them and hold those funds either as cash or any instrument that a broker or dealer may deposit in its Special Reserve Account for the Exclusive Benefit of Customers, (2) not issue the variable annuity contract prior to the member's principal approval, and (3) promptly return the funds to each customer at the customer's request prior to the member's principal approval or upon the member's rejection of the application.

.04 Forwarding of Checks/Funds to IRA Custodian Prior to Principal Approval. A member is not prohibited from forwarding a check provided by the customer for the purpose of purchasing a deferred variable annuity and made payable to an IRA custodian for the benefit of the customer (or, if the member is fully subject to SEA Rule 15c3-3, funds) to the IRA custodian prior to the member's principal approval of the deferred variable annuity transaction, as long as the member enters into a written agreement with the IRA custodian under which the IRA custodian agrees (a) to forward the funds to the insurance company to complete the purchase of the deferred variable annuity contract only after it has been informed that the member's principal has approved the transaction and (b), if the principal rejects the transaction, to inform the customer, seek immediate instructions from the customer regarding alternative disposition of the funds (e.g., asking whether the customer wants to transfer the funds to another IRA custodian, purchase a different investment, or provide other instructions), and promptly implement the customer's instructions.

.05 Gathering of Information Regarding Customer Exchanges. Rule 2330 requires that the member or person associated with a member consider whether the customer has had another deferred variable annuity exchange within the preceding 36 months. Under this provision, a member or person associated with a member must determine whether the customer has had such an exchange at the member and must make reasonable efforts to ascertain whether the customer has had an exchange at any other broker-dealer within the preceding 36months. An inquiry to the customer as to whether the customer has had an exchange at another broker-dealer within 36 months would constitute a "reasonable effort" in this context. Members shall document in writing both the nature of the inquiry and the response from the customer.

.06 Sharing of Office Space and/or Employees. Rule 2330 requires principal review and approval "[p]rior to transmitting a customer's application for a deferred variable annuity to the issuing insurance company for processing…" In circumstances where an insurance company and its affiliated broker-dealer share office space and/or employees who carry out both the principal review and the issuance process, FINRA will consider the application "transmitted" to the insurance company only when the broker-dealer's principal, acting as such, has approved the transaction, provided that the affiliated broker-dealer and the insurance company have agreed that the insurance company will not issue the contract prior to principal approval by the broker-dealer.

.07 Sharing of Information. Rule 2330 does not prohibit using the information required for principal review and approval in the issuance process, provided that the broker dealer and the insurance company have agreed that the insurance company will not issue the contract prior to principal approval by the broker-dealer. For instance, the rule does not prohibit a broker-dealer from inputting information used as part of its suitability review into a shared database (irrespective of the media used for that database, i.e., paper or electronic) that the insurance company uses for the issuance process, provided that the broker-dealer and the insurance company have agreed that the insurance company will not issue the contract prior to principal approval by the broker-dealer.

FINRA Regulatory Notice 11 02

Know Your Customer and Suitability

SEC Approves Consolidated FINRA Rules Governing Know-Your-Customer and Suitability Obligations

Effective Date: October 7, 2011

Executive Summary

The SEC approved FINRA's proposal to adopt rules governing know-your-customer and suitability obligations[10] for the consolidated FINRA rulebook.[11] The new rules are based in part on and replace provisions in the NASD and NYSE rules.

The text of the new rules is set forth in Attachment A. The rules take effect on October 7, 2011.

Questions regarding this *Notice* should be directed to James S. Wrona, Associate Vice President and Associate General Counsel, Office of General Counsel, at (202) 728-8270.

Discussion

The know-your-customer and suitability obligations are critical to ensuring investor protection and promoting fair dealing with customers and ethical sales practices. As part of the process of developing the consolidated FINRA rulebook, FINRA proposed and the SEC approved FINRA Rule 2090 (Know Your Customer) and FINRA Rule 2111 (Suitability). The new rules retain the core features of these important obligations and at the same time strengthen, streamline and clarify them.[12] The new rules are discussed separately below.

Know Your Customer

In general, new FINRA Rule 2090 (Know Your Customer) is modeled after former NYSE Rule 405(1) and requires firms to use "reasonable diligence,"[13] in regard to the opening and

---

10. See *Securities Exchange Act Release No. 63325* (November 17, 2010), *75 FR 71479* (November 23, 2010) (Order Approving Proposed Rule Change; File No. SR-FINRA-2010-039).
11. The current FINRA rulebook consists of (1) FINRA rules; (2) NASD rules; and (3) rules incorporated from NYSE (NYSE rules). While the NASD rules generally apply to all FINRA member firms, the NYSE rules apply only to those members of FINRA that are also members of the NYSE. The FINRA rules apply to all FINRA member firms, unless such rules have a more limited application by their terms. For more information about the rulebook consolidation process, see *Information Notice, 3/12/08* (Rulebook Consolidation Process).
12. To the extent that past *Notices to Members, Regulatory Notices,* case law, etc., do not conflict with new rule requirements or interpretations thereof, they remain potentially applicable, depending on the facts and circumstances of the particular case.
13. FINRA notes that it replaced the term "due diligence" used in former NYSE Rule 405(1) with the term "reasonable diligence" in new FINRA Rule 2090 for consistency with the language used in new FINRA Rule 2111. FINRA did not intend by such action to impair or adversely affect established case law and other interpretations discussing the diligence that is required to comply with know-your-customer or suitability obligations.

maintenance [14] of every account, to know the "essential facts" concerning every customer. [15] The rule explains that "essential facts" are "those required to (a) effectively service the customer's account, (b) act in accordance with any special handling instructions for the account, (c) understand the authority of each person acting on behalf of the customer, and (d) comply with applicable laws, regulations, and rules." [16] The know-your-customer obligation arises at the beginning of the customer-broker relationship and does not depend on whether the broker has made a recommendation. Unlike former NYSE Rule 405, the new rule does not specifically address orders, supervision or account opening—areas that are explicitly covered by other rules.

Suitability

New FINRA Rule 2111 generally is modeled after former NASD Rule 2310 (Suitability) and requires that a firm or associated person "have a reasonable basis to believe that a recommended transaction or investment strategy involving a security or securities is suitable for the customer, based on the information obtained through the reasonable diligence of the member or associated person to ascertain the customer's investment profile." [17] The rule further explains that a "customer's investment profile includes, but is not limited to, the customer's age, other investments, financial situation and needs, tax status, investment objectives, investment experience, investment time horizon, liquidity needs, risk tolerance, and any other information the customer may disclose to the member or associated person in connection with such recommendation."[18]

The new rule continues to use a broker's "recommendation" as the triggering event for application of the rule and continues to apply a flexible "facts and circumstances" approach

---

14. A broker-dealer must know its customers not only at account opening but also throughout the life of its relationship with customers in order to, among other things, effectively service and supervise the customers' accounts. Since a broker-dealer's relationship with its customers is dynamic, FINRA does not believe that it can prescribe a period within which broker-dealers must attempt to update this information. As with a customer's investment profile under the suitability rule, a firm should verify the "essential facts" about a customer under the know-your-customer rule at intervals reasonably calculated to prevent and detect any mishandling of a customer's account that might result from the customer's change in circumstances. The reasonableness of a broker-dealer's efforts in this regard will depend on the facts and circumstances of the particular case. Firms should note, however, that SEA Rule 17a-3 requires broker-dealers to, among other things, attempt to update certain account information every 36 months regarding accounts for which the broker-dealers were required to make suitability determinations.
15. FINRA Rule 2090.
16. FINRA Rule 2090.01.
17. FINRA Rule 2111(a). Former NASD Rule 2310 contained interpretative material (IMs) discussing a variety of types of misconduct. Although FINRA eliminated those IMs, most of the types of misconduct that the IMs discussed were either explicitly covered by other rules or incorporated in some form into the new suitability rule. The exception was unauthorized trading, which had been discussed in IM-2310- 2. However, it is well-settled that unauthorized trading violates just and equitable principles of trade under FINRA Rule 2010 (previously NASD Rule 2110). *See, e.g., Robert L. Gardner*, 52 S.E.C. 343, 344 n.1 (1995), *aff'd*, 89 F.3d 845 (9th Cir. 1996) (table format); *Keith L. DeSanto*, 52 S.E.C. 316, 317 n.1 (1995), *aff'd*, 101 F.3d 108 (2d Cir. 1996) (table format); Jonathan G. Ornstein, 51 S.E.C. 135, 137 (1992); *Dep't of Enforcement v. Griffith*, No. C01040025, 2006 NASD Discip. LEXIS 30, at *11-12 (NAC December 29, 2006); *Dep't of Enforcement v. Puma*, No. C10000122, 2003 NASD Discip. LEXIS 22, at *12 n.6 (NAC August 11, 2003). The new suitability rule does not alter that conclusion. Unauthorized trading continues to be serious misconduct that violates FINRA Rule 2010.
18. FINRA Rule 2111(a).

to determining what communications constitute such a recommendation. The new rule also applies to recommended investment strategies, clarifies the types of information that brokers must attempt to obtain and analyze, and discusses the three main suitability obligations. Finally, the new rule modifies the institutional-investor exemption in a number of important ways.

Recommendations

The determination of the existence of a recommendation has always been based on the facts and circumstances of the particular case. [19] That remains true under the new rule. FINRA reiterates, however, that several guiding principles are relevant to determining whether a particular communication could be viewed as a recommendation for purposes of the suitability rule.

For instance, a communication's content, context and presentation are important aspects of the inquiry. The determination of whether a "recommendation" has been made, moreover, is an objective rather than subjective inquiry. [20] An important factor in this regard is whether— given its content, context and manner of presentation—a particular communication from a firm or associated person to a customer reasonably would be viewed as a suggestion that the customer take action or refrain from taking action regarding a security or investment strategy. In addition, the more individually tailored the communication is to a particular customer or customers about a specific security or investment strategy, the more likely the communication will be viewed as a recommendation. Furthermore, a series of actions that may not constitute recommendations when viewed individually may amount to a recommendation when considered in the aggregate. It also makes no difference whether the communication was initiated by a person or a computer software program. These guiding principles, together with numerous litigated decisions and the facts and circumstances of any particular case, inform the determination of whether the communication is a recommendation for purposes of FINRA's suitability rule.

---

19. See *Michael Frederick Siegel*, Securities Exchange Act Release No. 58737, 2008 SEC LEXIS 2459, at *21 (October 6, 2008) (explaining that whether a communication "constitutes a recommendation is a 'facts and circumstances inquiry to be conducted on a case-by-case basis"), *aff'd in relevant part*, 592 F.3d 147 (D.C. Cir. 2010), *cert. denied*, 2010 U.S. LEXIS 4340 (May 24, 2010). FINRA has stated that "defining the term 'recommendation' is unnecessary and would raise many complex issues in the absence of specific facts of a particular case." Securities Exchange Act Release No. 37588, 1996 SEC LEXIS 2285, at *29 (August 20, 1996), 61 FR 44100, 44107 (August 27, 1996) (Notice of Filing and Order Granting Accelerated Approval of NASD's Interpretation of Its Suitability Rule).

20. FINRA has repeatedly explained that a broker cannot avoid suitability obligations through a disclaimer where—given its content, context and presentation—the particular communication reasonably would be viewed as a recommendation. *See Notice to Members 01-23* (April 2001). FINRA Rule 2111.02, moreover, explicitly states that a firm or associated person "cannot disclaim any responsibilities under the suitability rule." In the same vein, it is well-settled that a "broker's recommendations must be consistent with his customer's best interests" and are "not suitable merely because the customer acquiesces in [them]." *Dane S. Faber*, Securities Exchange Act Release No. 49216, 2004 SEC LEXIS 277, at *23-24 (February 10, 2004); *see also Dep't of Enforcement v. Bendetsen*, No. C01020025, 2004 NASD Discip. LEXIS 13, at *12 (NAC August 9, 2004) ("[A] broker's recommendations must serve his client's best interests and the test for whether a broker's recommendations are suitable is not whether the client acquiesced in them, but whether the broker's recommendations were consistent with the client's financial situation and needs").

Strategies

The new rule explicitly applies to recommended investment strategies involving a security or securities. [21] The rule emphasizes that the term "strategy" should be interpreted broadly. [22] The rule is triggered when a firm or associated person recommends a security or strategy regardless of whether the recommendation results in a transaction. Among other things, the term "strategy" would capture a broker's *explicit* recommendation to hold a security or securities. [23] The rule recognizes that customers may rely on firms' and associated persons' investment expertise and knowledge, and it is thus appropriate to hold firms and associated persons responsible for the recommendations that they make to customers, regardless of whether those recommendations result in transactions or generate transaction-based compensation.

FINRA, however, exempted from the new rule's coverage certain categories of educational material—which the strategy language otherwise would cover—as long as such material does not include (standing alone or in combination with other communications) a recommendation of a particular security or securities. [24] FINRA believes that it is important to encourage firms and associated persons to freely provide educational material and services to customers.

Customer's Investment Profile

The new rule includes an expanded list of explicit types of information that firms and associated persons must attempt to gather and analyze as part of a suitability analysis. The new rule essentially adds age, investment experience, time horizon, liquidity needs and risk tolerance[25] to the existing list (other holdings, financial situation and needs, tax status and investment objectives). [26] Recognizing that not every factor regarding a "customer's investment profile" will be

---

21. See FINRA Rules 2111(a) and 2111.03.
22. Id.
23. *Id.* The new rule does not, however, broaden the scope of implicit recommendations. In limited circumstances, FINRA and the SEC have recognized that implicit recommendations can trigger suitability obligations. For example, FINRA and the SEC have held that associated persons who effect transactions on a customer's behalf without informing the customer have implicitly recommended those transactions, thereby triggering application of the suitability rule. See, e.g., *Rafael Pinchas*, 54 S.E.C. 331, 341 n.22 (1999) ("Transactions that were not specifically authorized by a client but were executed on the client's behalf are considered to have been implicitly recommended within the meaning of the NASD rules."); *Paul C. Kettler*, 51 S.E.C. 30, 32 n.11 (1992) (stating that transactions a broker effects for a discretionary account are recommended). Although such holdings continue to act as precedent regarding those issues, FINRA notes that nothing in the new rule is intended to change the longstanding application of the suitability rule on a recommendation-by-recommendation basis. The new rule would not apply, for instance, to *implicit* recommendations to hold securities that are transferred into an account.
24. See FINRA Rule 2111.03.
25. During the rulemaking process, some commenters argued that factors such as a customer's investment experience, time horizon and risk tolerance are ones to be considered when reviewing a customer's portfolio as a whole, not the individual trades. According to those commenters, requiring consideration of such factors on a trade-by-trade basis would prevent customers from creating a diverse portfolio made up of securities with different levels of liquidity, risk and time horizons. FINRA reiterates that a recommendation-by-recommendation analysis and consideration of a customer's investment portfolio are not mutually exclusive concepts. Although suitability is a recommendation-by-recommendation analysis, FINRA Rule 2111 explicitly permits the suitability analysis to be performed within the context of the customer's other investments. In fact, the rule requires (as did the previous suitability rule) firms and associated persons to make reasonable efforts to gather and analyze information about a customer's other investments as part of the suitability review. Moreover, the new rule explicitly covers recommended investment strategies.
26. See FINRA Rule 2111(a).

relevant to every recommendation, the rule provides flexibility concerning the type of information that firms must seek to obtain and analyze. [27] However, because the listed factors generally are relevant (and often crucial) to a suitability analysis, the rule requires firms and associated persons to document with specificity their reasonable basis for believing that a factor is not relevant in order to be relieved of the obligation to seek to obtain information about that factor. [28]

Main Suitability Obligations

The new suitability rule lists in one place the three main suitability obligations: reasonable-basis, customer-specific and quantitative suitability. [29]

> Reasonable-basis suitability requires a broker to have a reasonable basis to believe, based on reasonable diligence, that the recommendation is suitable for at least some investors. In general, what constitutes reasonable diligence will vary depending on, among other things, the complexity of and risks associated with the security or investment strategy and the firm's or associated person's familiarity with the security or investment strategy. A firm's or associated person's reasonable diligence must provide the firm or associated person with an understanding of the potential risks and rewards associated with the recommended security or strategy.

> Customer-specific suitability requires that a broker have a reasonable basis to believe that the recommendation is suitable for a particular customer based on that customer's investment profile. As noted above, the new rule requires a broker to attempt to obtain and analyze a broad array of customer-specific factors.

> Quantitative suitability requires a broker who has actual or de facto control over a customer account to have a reasonable basis for believing that a series of recommended transactions, even if suitable when viewed in isolation, are not excessive and unsuitable for the customer when taken together in light of the customer's investment profile. Factors such as turnover rate, cost-equity ratio and use of in-and-out trading in a customer's account may provide a basis for finding that the activity at issue was excessive.

The new rule makes clear that a broker must have a firm understanding of both the product and the customer. [30] It also makes clear that the lack of such an understanding itself violates the suitability rule. [31]

Institutional-Investor Exemption

FINRA Rule 2111(b) provides an exemption to customer-specific suitability for recommendations to institutional customers under certain circumstances. The new exemption harmonizes the

27. See FINRA Rule 2111.04.
28. Id.
29. See FINRA Rule 2111.05.
30. See FINRA Rule 2111(a); FINRA Rule 2111.04; FINRA Rule 2111.05(a).
31. See FINRA Rules 2111.04 and 2111.05(a).

definition of institutional customer in the suitability rule with the more common definition of "institutional account" in NASD Rule 3110(c)(4).[32] Beyond the definitional requirements, the exemption's main focus is whether the broker has a reasonable basis to believe the customer is capable of evaluating investment risks independently, both in general and with regard to particular transactions and investment strategies, [33] and whether the institutional customer affirmatively acknowledges that it is exercising independent judgment. [34]

In regard to an institutional investor, a firm that satisfies the conditions of the exemption fulfils its customer-specific obligation, [35] but not its reasonable-basis and quantitative obligations under the suitability rule. FINRA believes that, even when institutional customers are involved, it is crucial that brokers understand the securities they recommend and that those securities are appropriate for at least some investors. FINRA also believes that it is important that a firm not recommend an unsuitable number of transactions in those circumstances where it has control over the account. FINRA emphasizes, however, that quantitative suitability generally would apply only with regard to that portion of an institutional customer's portfolio that the firm controls and only with regard to the firm's recommended transactions. [36]

---

32. See FINRA Rule 2111(b). FINRA is proposing to adopt NASD Rule 3110(c)(4) as FINRA Rule 4512(c), without material change. *See* Securities Exchange Act Release No. 63181 (October 26, 2010), 75 FR 67155 (November 1, 2010) (Notice of Filing Proposed Rule Change; File No. SR-FINRA-2010-052).

33. See FINRA Rule 2111(b). FINRA reiterates that, in some cases, the broker may conclude that the customer is not capable of making independent investment decisions in general. In other cases, the institutional customer may have general capability, but may not be able to understand a particular type of instrument or its risk. If a customer is either generally not capable of evaluating investment risk or lacks sufficient capability to evaluate the particular product, the scope of a broker's customer-specific obligations under the suitability rule would not be diminished by the fact that the broker was dealing with an institutional customer. However, the fact that a customer initially needed help understanding a potential investment need not necessarily imply that the customer did not ultimately develop an understanding and make an independent decision.

34. FINRA Rule 2111(b).

35. FINRA emphasizes that the institutional-customer exemption applies only if all of the conditions in Rule 2111(b) are satisfied. It is not sufficient, for example, that an institutional customer affirmatively indicates that it is exercising independent judgment in evaluating recommendations. The institutional customer also must meet the definitional criteria and the broker must have a reasonable basis to believe that the institutional customer is capable of evaluating investment risks independently, both in general and with regard to particular transactions and investment strategies.

36. It is axiomatic that the suitability rule applies only to recommended transactions. See, *e.g., Dep't of Enforcement v. Medeck*, No. E9B2003033701, 2009 FINRA Discip. LEXIS 7, at *46 (July 30, 2009) (explaining that transactions that were not recommended could not be used to inflate the cost-to-equity ratio and the turnover rate). Case law also has long established that quantitative suitability "occurs when a registered representative has control over trading in an account and the level of activity in that account is inconsistent with the customer's objectives and financial situation." *Harry Gliksman*, 54 S.E.C. 471, 475 (1999), *aff'd*, 24 F. App'x 702 (9th Cir. 2001); *see also Pinchas*, 54 S.E.C. at 337 (same). In general, the control element "is satisfied if the broker has either discretionary authority or de facto control over the account. De facto control is established when the client routinely follows the broker's advice 'because the customer is unable to evaluate the broker's recommendations and to exercise independent judgment.'" *Medeck*, 2009 FINRA Discip. LEXIS 7, at *34 (citations omitted). In *Pryor, McClendon, Counts & Co.*, Securities Exchange Act Release No. 45402, 2002 SEC LEXIS 284 (February 6, 2002), the SEC analyzed allegations of churning by focusing on that portion of the city of Atlanta's portfolio that the broker-dealer respondent controlled and those transactions that the respondent recommended. *Id.* at *4, *15-16, *20-23. The SEC also held that, for purposes of churning, the respondent controlled the portion of Atlanta's portfolio at issue because the respondent engaged in a scheme to defraud Atlanta with the city's investment officer, who had authority to trade Atlanta's securities portfolio. *Id.* at *20-21 & n.10 (citing *Smith v. Petrou*, 705 F. Supp. 183, 187 (S.D.N.Y. 1989)).

Attachment

New FINRA rules.

2000. DUTIES AND CONFLICTS

2090. Know Your Customer

Every member shall use reasonable diligence, in regard to the opening and maintenance of every account, to know (and retain) the essential facts concerning every customer and concerning the authority of each person acting on behalf of such customer.

Supplementary Material

.01 Essential Facts. For purposes of this Rule, facts "essential" to "knowing the customer" are those required to (a) effectively service the customer's account, (b) act in accordance with any special handling instructions for the account, (c) understand the authority of each person acting on behalf of the customer, and (d) comply with applicable laws, regulations, and rules.

2100. TRANSACTIONS WITH CUSTOMERS

2110. Recommendations

2111. Suitability

(a) A member or an associated person must have a reasonable basis to believe that a recommended transaction or investment strategy involving a security or securities is suitable for the customer, based on the information obtained through the reasonable diligence of the member or associated person to ascertain the customer's investment profile. A customer's investment profile includes, but is not limited to, the customer's age, other investments, financial situation and needs, tax status, investment objectives, investment experience, investment time horizon, liquidity needs, risk tolerance, and any other information the customer may disclose to the member or associated person in connection with such recommendation.

(b) A member or associated person fulfills the customer-specific suitability obligation for an institutional account, as defined in NASD Rule 3110(c)(4), if (1) the member or associated person has a reasonable basis to believe that the institutional customer is capable of evaluating investment risks independently, both in general and with regard to particular transactions and investment strategies involving a security or securities and (2) the institutional customer affirmatively indicates that it is exercising independent judgment in evaluating the member's or associated person's recommendations. Where an institutional customer has delegated decision making authority to an agent, such as an investment adviser or a bank trust department, these factors shall be applied to the agent.

Supplementary Material

.01 General Principles. Implicit in all member and associated person relationships with customers and others is the fundamental responsibility for fair dealing. Sales efforts must therefore be undertaken only on a basis that can be judged as being within the ethical standards of FINRA's rules, with particular emphasis on the requirement to deal fairly with the public. The suitability rule is fundamental to fair dealing and is intended to promote ethical sales practices and high standards of professional conduct.

.02 Disclaimers. A member or associated person cannot disclaim any responsibilities under the suitability rule.

.03 Recommended Strategies. The phrase "investment strategy involving a security or securities" used in this Rule is to be interpreted broadly and would include, among other things, an explicit recommendation to hold a security or securities. However, the following communications are excluded from the coverage of Rule 2111 as long as they do not include (standing alone or in combination with other communications) a recommendation of a particular security or securities:

(a) General financial and investment information, including (i) basic investment concepts, such as risk and return, diversification, dollar cost averaging, compounded return, and tax deferred investment, (ii) historic differences in the return of asset classes (e.g., equities, bonds, or cash) based on standard market indices, (iii) effects of inflation, (iv) estimates of future retirement income needs, and (v) assessment of a customer's investment profile;

(b) Descriptive information about an employer-sponsored retirement or benefit plan, participation in the plan, the benefits of plan participation, and the investment options available under the plan;

(c) Asset allocation models that are (i) based on generally accepted investment theory, (ii) accompanied by disclosures of all material facts and assumptions that may affect a reasonable investor's assessment of the asset allocation model or any report generated by such model, and (iii) in compliance with NASD IM-2210-6 (Requirements for the Use of Investment Analysis Tools) if the asset allocation model is an "investment analysis tool" covered by NASD IM-2210-6; and

(d) Interactive investment materials that incorporate the above.

.04 Customer's Investment Profile. A member or associated person shall make a recommendation covered by this Rule only if, among other things, the member or associated person has sufficient information about the customer to have a reasonable basis to believe that the recommendation is suitable for that customer. The factors delineated in Rule 2111(a) regarding a customer's investment profile generally are relevant to a determination regarding whether a recommendation is suitable for a particular customer, although the level of importance of each factor may vary depending on the facts and circumstances of the particular case. A member or associated person shall use reasonable diligence to obtain and analyze all of the factors delineated in Rule 2111(a) unless the member or associated person has a reasonable basis to believe, documented with specificity, that one or more of the factors are not relevant components of a customer's investment profile in light of the facts and circumstances of the particular case.

.05 Components of Suitability Obligations. Rule 2111 is composed of three main obligations: reasonable-basis suitability, customer-specific suitability, and quantitative suitability.

a) The reasonable-basis obligation requires a member or associated person to have a reasonable basis to believe, based on reasonable diligence, that the recommendation is suitable for at least some investors. In general, what constitutes reasonable diligence will vary depending on, among other things, the complexity of and risks associated with the security or investment strategy and the member's or associated person's familiarity with the security or investment strategy. A member's or associated person's reasonable diligence must provide the member or associated person with an understanding of the potential risks and rewards associated with the recommended security or strategy. The lack of such an understanding when recommending a security or strategy violates the suitability rule.

b) (b) The customer-specific obligation requires that a member or associated person have a reasonable basis to believe that the recommendation is suitable for a particular customer based on that customer's investment profile, as delineated in Rule 2111(a).

c) (c) Quantitative suitability requires a member or associated person who has actual or de facto control over a customer account to have a reasonable basis for believing that a series of recommended transactions, even if suitable when viewed in isolation, are not excessive and unsuitable for the customer when taken together in light of the customer's investment profile, as delineated in Rule 2111(a). No single test defines excessive activity, but factors such as the turnover rate, the cost-equity ratio, and the use of in-and-out trading in a customer's account may provide a basis for a finding that a member or associated person has violated the quantitative suitability obligation.

.06 Customer's Financial Ability. Rule 2111 prohibits a member or associated person from recommending a transaction or investment strategy involving a security or securities or the continuing purchase of a security or securities or use of an investment strategy involving a security or securities unless the member or associated person has a reasonable basis to believe that the customer has the financial ability to meet such a commitment.

.07 Institutional Investor Exemption. Rule 2111(b) provides an exemption to customer-specific suitability regarding institutional investors if the conditions delineated in that paragraph are satisfied. With respect to having to indicate affirmatively that it is exercising independent judgment in evaluating the member's or associated person's recommendations, an institutional customer may indicate that it is exercising independent judgment on a trade-by-trade basis, on an asset-class-by-asset-class basis, or in terms of all potential transactions for its account.

Index

Living benefits (cont'd)
guaranteed minimum accumulation benefit.................76, 81-83, 85, 88, 91
guaranteed minimum withdrawal benefit.................83, 84, 90, 96
variable annuities.................101, 103-105, 108
Loan.................3, 19, 23, 29
Longevity annuities.................191-200
death benefit.................192-194, 196-198
Look-through trusts.................47, 131-132
Losses, annuity.................14, 21, 27-28, 105, 108, 110
Lump sum.................44, 48, 49-51, 76, 79-80, 91, 96, 100, 104, 106, 107

M

Marrion, Dr. Jack.................219
Market value adjustment (MVA).................4, 64
interest rate spread.................63, 64, 71
Model Regulations.................203
Morningstar.................70, 71, 73
Mortality and Expense charge (M&E charge).................71, 72, 156
Multiple deferred annuities.................20

N

National Association of Insurance Commissioners (NAIC).................203
NAIC as Suitability in Annuity Transactions Model Regulation #275 (SATMR).................204
NAIC Life Insurance and Annuity Model Regulation of 2002.................207
National Association of Securities Dealers (NASD).................203
Natural person.................23, 24, 25, 27, 34, 47
Negative dollar cost averaging.................146
The Neasham Case.................217
New York Stock Exchange.................203
Non-natural person.................24, 25
Non-qualified annuities.................17, 18, 22, 29, 41, 50, 52
NYSE Regulation, Inc.................203

O

Optional benefits.................71
Optional costs.................75-98
death benefit enhancements.................75, 92
living benefits.................76-92
"enhanced living benefits".................76, 81, 83
guaranteed minimum accumulation benefit.................76, 81-83, 85, 88, 91
guaranteed minimum income benefit.................76, 78, 80
guaranteed minimum withdrawal benefit.................83, 84, 90, 96
Ordinary income.................13, 18, 19, 20, 23, 32, 34, 44, 45, 54, 106
"owner-driven".................45, 51
Owner-driven annuities.................133
Owner-driven annuity contract.................142

P

Partial 1035 exchange.................30
Partial vs. full surrender.................21-22
Payout annuity.................2, 7-9
Payout factor.................60, 61, 73, 107, 108, 110, 111
Payout option.................2, 8, 9, 109-110
"Payout status".................3, 41, 42-43
Penalty for early distribution.................25-27
Period certain.................8, 11, 26, 43, 47
PLR 9009047.................151
PLR 200151038.................147
PLR 200313016.................147
Pocket of money method.................65
Point-of-sale material.................215
Portfolio failure rate.................146
Portfolio insurance.................144-146
Portfolio method.................65, 73
Premium tax.................6
Primary annuitant.................25, 126, 129, 133-134
Principia.................71
Probate.................126
Proportional method.................79, 94
Proportional reduction.................79, 94
Prospectus.................80, 81, 83, 87